London Oriental and African Language Library

The LONDON ORIENTAL AND AFRICAN LANGUAGE LIBRARY aims to make available reliable and up-to-date analyses of the grammatical structure of the major Oriental and African languages, in a form readily accessible to the non-specialist. With this in mind, the language material in each volume is in roman script, and fully glossed and translated. The series is based at the School of Oriental and African Studies of the University of London, Europe's largest institution specializing in the study of the languages and cultures of Africa and Asia. Each volume is written by an acknowledged expert in the field who has carried out original research on the language and has first-hand knowledge of the area in which it is spoken.

Editors

Theodora Bynon
David C. Bennett
School of Oriental and African Studies
University of London

Masayoshi Shibatani
Kobe University, Japan
Rice University, Houston, Texas, USA

Advisory Board

James Bynon
Bernard Comrie
Gilbert Lazard
Christian Lehmann

James A. Matisoff
Christopher Shackle
Andrew Simpson

Volume 15

Sinhala
by Dileep Chandralal

Sinhala

Dileep Chandralal
Okinawa University

John Benjamins Publishing Company
Amsterdam / Philadelphia

The paper used in this publication meets the minimum requirements of American National Standard for Information Sciences – Permanence of Paper for Printed Library Materials, ANSI z39.48-1984.

Library of Congress Cataloging-in-Publication Data

Chandralal, Dileep.
 Sinhala / Dileep Chandralal.
     p.   cm. (London Oriental and African Language Library, ISSN 1382-3485 ; v. 15)
Includes bibliographical references and index.
1. Sinhalese language--Grammar. I. Title.
PK2812.C47   2010
491.4'85--dc22   2009045280
ISBN 978 90 272 3815 3 (Hb ; alk. paper)
ISBN 978 90 272 8853 0 (Eb)

© 2010 – John Benjamins B.V.
No part of this book may be reproduced in any form, by print, photoprint, microfilm, or any other means, without written permission from the publisher.

John Benjamins Publishing Co. · P.O. Box 36224 · 1020 ME Amsterdam · The Netherlands
John Benjamins North America · P.O. Box 27519 · Philadelphia PA 19118-0519 · USA

Table of contents

Foreword   IX

Preface   XI

Romanization and text presentation   XIII

Abbreviations   XV

CHAPTER 1
Introduction   1
1. Genealogy and geography   1
2. Typological character of the language   7
    - 2.1 Structure of simple clauses   7
    - 2.2 Nominal modifiers   10
    - 2.3 Verbal modifiers   10
    - 2.4 Compound and complex sentences   15
    - 2.5 Some additional remarks on the structure of the language   16

CHAPTER 2
Writing system   21

CHAPTER 3
Sounds   28
1. Vowels   28
2. Consonants   30
3. Consonant clusters   32
4. Phonological rules   34
    - 4.1 Vowel length   34
    - 4.2 Nasal assimilation   35
    - 4.3 Other assimilations   35
    - 4.4 Velarizing   35
    - 4.5 Substituting   36
5. Suprasegmental features   36
    - 5.1 Syllables   36
    - 5.2 Stress   37
    - 5.3 Pitch   37
6. Rhyming expressions   38

CHAPTER 4
Words   40
1. Vocabulary strata   40
2. Word classes   43
   - 2.1 Nouns   43
   - 2.2 Adjectives   50
   - 2.3 Verbs   52
3. Minor word classes   54
   - 3.1 Adverbs   54
   - 3.2 Particles   55
   - 3.3 Affixes   56
   - 3.4 Interjections   58
4. Some noteworthy word classes   58
   - 4.1 Numerals   58
   - 4.2 Kinship terms   64

CHAPTER 5
Morphology   66
1. Verb morphology   66
   - 1.1 Inflectional morphology   67
     - 1.1.1 Finite forms   71
     - 1.1.2 Non-finite forms   75
   - 1.2 Derivational morphology   77
2. Noun morphology   78
   - 2.1 Nominal inflections   78
   - 2.2 Nominal derivations and word formation   83
     - 2.2.1 Affixation   83
     - 2.2.2 Compounding   86
     - 2.2.3 Reduplication   89
3. Sandhi   91

CHAPTER 6
Morphology-syntax interface   95

CHAPTER 7
Argument structures   100
1. Argument structure types   100
   - 1.1 Argument structures with inactive predicates   102
   - 1.2 Argument types with active predicates   109

2. Adjunct noun phrases   116
3. Grammatical relations   121

CHAPTER 8
Noun phrase and verb phrase constructions   129
1. Noun phrase   129
   1.1 Simple noun modifiers   129
   1.2 Clausal noun modifiers   130
2. Verb phrase   134
   2.1 Declarative, interrogative, and negative   134
   2.2 Reciprocal verbs and reflexive verbs   136
   2.3 Modality, aspect, and tense   139
      2.3.1 Expressions for modality   139
      2.3.2 Expressions for aspect and tense   143
         2.3.2.1 Tense   143
         2.3.2.2 Aspect   145

CHAPTER 9
Grammatical constructions   152
1. Passive construction   152
2. Causative construction   160
   2.1 Lexical causatives   160
   2.2 Morphological causatives   161
   2.3 Periphrastic causatives   169
      2.3.1 Causative benefactive construction   170
      2.3.2 Simple benefactive construction   173
      2.3.3 Indirect causative construction   176

CHAPTER 10
Extended sentences   181
1. Compound sentences   181
2. Complex sentences   189
   2.1 Nominal clauses   190
   2.2 Adnominal clauses   195
   2.3 Adverbial clauses   197
3. Mixed sentences   204

CHAPTER 11
Sentence and information structure   207
1. The topic-comment organization   207
2. The focus structure   215

CHAPTER 12
Discourse and grammar   227
1. Deictic system of demonstratives   227
2. The deictic parameter   230
3. Functions of deictic expressions   232
   3.1   Identifying function   232
   3.2   Acknowledging function   237
   3.3   Informing function   238
   3.4   Expressive function   239
4. Locative expressions   241
5. Demonstratives as discourse deictic   242
   5.1   Anaphoric use   242
   5.2   Other uses of discourse deixis   245
   5.3   Cataphoric use   247
6. Encoding discourse units   248
7. Tracking the thematic flow of discourse   250

CHAPTER 13
Pragmatics and grammar   254
1. Modality   254
   1.1   Imperative mood   254
   1.2   Permissive mood   258
   1.3   Offer   259
   1.4   Optative mood   260
   1.5   Epistemic modality   261
2. Interrogation   263
3. Negation   265
4. Social deixis and honorifics   267

CHAPTER 14
Sample texts   273

Appendix   283

References   286

Index   292

Foreword

We are very pleased with this publication of a new volume in the London Oriental and African Language Library series. The Indo-Aryan language Sinhala (also known as Singhalese), one of the official languages of Sri Lanka, has a long literary history with the oldest existent literary works dating back to the 8th century and the earlier inscriptions to the 3rd and 2nd century BCE. Besides the recent contacts with European languages, the Vedda language indigenous to Sri Lanka, the continuous influences of various Indo-Aryan languages, the introduction of Buddhism to the island, and the close contacts with the Dravidians, Tamils in particular, have shaped the modern Sinhala language in a unique way, setting it apart from other modern Indo-Aryan languages of the Indian subcontinent.

Sinhala has a rare subtractive system in nominal morphology, where inanimate plural forms are derived by deleting the final vowel of the singular counterparts, at least in their nominative and accusative form. Another unique feature is a four-way deictic system distinguishing reference made to an entity closer to the speaker, the one closer to the hearer, the one closer to the third person visible, and the one closer to the invisible third person. Just as animacy plays an important role in nominal morphology, the Sinhala syntax is highly sensitive to the volitionality feature of the primary event participant, complicating the identification of the grammatical relation Subject. In the realm of discourse, Sinhala allows dropping of "understood" elements rather freely despite there is no verbal agreement.

Dileep Chandralal offers a very accessible, non-technical yet highly informative account of Sinhala grammar in a clear and lucid style. After extensive training in Sanskrit and the classical literature in Sri Lanka, he went to Japan to study Japanese and linguistics. After obtaining a Ph.D. in linguistics at Kobe University in 2000, he has been teaching at Okinawa University, where he is now Professor of Language and Communication. His Ph.D. thesis was revised and published in 2005 as *Language and Space: Cognitive Semantics of Sinhala Grammatical Categories* (Hishva Lekha Publications, Ratmalana, Sri Lanka).

March, 2010
Masayoshi Shibatani

Preface

When I embarked on a research program for a contrastive analysis of the structure of Japanese and Sinhala, the first hurdle I fell at was the inadequacy of my Japanese knowledge to undertake a task of such enormous proportions. However, it soon became apparent that the amount of information and scholarship available on Sinhala was also inadequate to conduct a balanced comparison of the two languages. The comparison had to be terminated until there would be a description on Sinhala. That was the real beginning of my linguistic journey in the world of Sinhala. Today's students of the Sinhala language are very fortunate in that they can absorb the vast body of knowledge accumulated by their predecessors with different approaches. Thanks to this great scholarship, one can know the nature of Sinhala and how vast and complex it is.

The study of the *Sidat Sangarawa* as the earliest extant grammar of Sinhala compiled in the 14th century has been playing a prominent role in the study of the language. However, in the late 19th century western scholars, and native scholars influenced by the western tradition of language study began to analyze Sinhala from a new perspective, integrating the colloquial variety of Sinhala as a living part of the language. This volume adds a very modest contribution to this long tradition of Sinhala linguistics.

In Sri Lanka the spoken and the written language differ from each other in both grammar and usage. The subject matter of this book is the standard variety of spoken Sinhala used in day-to-day life. A major attempt has been made to avoid the common failing of "textbook grammar" which is basically used in Sinhala education in primary and secondary schools. It also excludes some sub-varieties of the spoken language used in highly formal and ritual occasions.

I have endeavored to present the main aspects of Sinhala grammar, exemplifying them on the basis of extensive data. The data for this analysis comes from intuition, elicitation and observation, and were multiply derived from natural conversations, written traditional narratives, traditional oral narratives edited by textbook writers, modern novels, children's books and school textbooks. The emphasis was on presenting natural Sinhala as it really is, and it is hoped that this will be accepted, as such.

A particular concern was to do justice to the semantic and pragmatic aspects of grammar, topics which are generally ignored in more structure-focused approaches to grammar. Hence, even the grammatical constructions were analyzed in a way that the interactions among semantic, pragmatic and grammatical factors become explicit. In the final three chapters, in particular, discourse and textual aspects were brought to the forefront.

This book in general owes a great deal to James W. Gair's pioneering works on Sinhala grammar and the articles by M.W.S De Silva on the phonology and morphology of Sinhala. To anybody who wishes to pursue further exploration into Sinhala grammar, I recommend Gair's volume *Studies in South Asian Linguistics: Sinhala and Other South Asian Languages* (1998) that contains most of his representative papers.

In preparing this volume, I owe a great deal to Professor Masayoshi Shibatani for introducing me to LOALL and providing insightful comments from its earliest stages. In its later stages, Professor Theodora Bynon has been kind enough to read the entire manuscript and offer many invaluable editorial suggestions. I am grateful to Okinawa University for granting a full year sabbatical leave, during which time the manuscript was largely completed, and also to Andrew Pawley (Emeritus Professor, Australian National University) for arranging a one year Visiting Fellowship with a similar period of residence at ANU and giving me warm encouragement throughout this period.

Finally, a note of special thanks to my wife, Yumi Koide, who as always has given unfailing support, encouragement and understanding in all stages of this project and also provided a color picture for the back cover of the book.

Romanization and text presentation

The system of Romanization used in this book mainly consists of seven vowels, two semi-vowels and 21 consonants.

The seven short vowels are represented by *i, e, æ, ə, u, o, a*, and the corresponding long vowels are indicated by doubling the short vowel symbols as *ii, ee, ææ, əə, uu, oo* and *aa*.

Combinations of different vowels are represented by a sequence of two vowels: for instance, the following combinations are common: *ei, æi, ai, oi, ui, iu, eu, æu, au, ou, ae*.

The following symbols are used for consonants:

Voiceless	p	t	ṭ	k	ch
Voiced	b	d	ḍ	g	j
Spirants	f	s	sh	h	
Sonorant	m	n	ŋ	r	l
Semi-vowels	y	w			

There are two sets of capital/simple letters. This distinction is based on the assumption that it needs to differentially represent dental and retroflex sounds. The capital letters represent retroflex consonants. There are two-letter combinations: two alveolar-palatal consonants are represented by two-letter combinations, *ch* and *sh*.

Geminate consonants are represented by a sequence of two identical consonants (e.g. *amma* 'mother', *akka* 'elder sister', *wattə* 'estate', *toppi* 'hats', *ibba* 'tortoise'). When the germination occurs with *ch*, the two-letter combination representing it is doubled. This gives rise to the sequence of four intervocalic consonant symbols (e.g. *achchaaru* 'pickle').

Sinhala doesn't have a convention of capitalization. However, in transliteration the initial letter of a proper noun is capitalized following the Western convention. When examples are introduced in each chapter of this book, personal and place names, whether local or international, are spelt according to this normal convention. That is, both in translation and transliteration the initial letter of a personal or place name is capitalized (e.g. *Ranjit* (personal name), *Anuradhapura* (place name)). However, the initial letter of the first word in a Sinhala example sentence is not capitalized.

Each example sentence is provided with a gloss. In example sentences and glosses a hyphen is used to separate the roots/stems from affixes.

e.g. *Ranjit-ţə   Chitra-ge   wæḍa-t   kəra-nnə   we-nəwa*
     Ranjit-DAT Chitra-GEN   work-too   do-INF   be-IND
     'Ranjit will have to do Chitra's work, too.'

However, a hyphen may not be used when it is not crucial for the discussion. In some cases where it is difficult to separate the root/stem from the affix on the surface form the morphological boundary is indicated by a full stop in the gloss.

Abbreviations

A	active type	IO	indirect object
Abl	ablative	Lit	literal meaning
ABL	ablative case	LOC	locative
ACC	accusative case	mas	masculine
ADJ	adjectival form	NM	nominal marker
AM	assertion marker	NP	noun phrase
anim	animate	NPT	non-past tense non-finite
C	causative type	OCOMP	object of comparison
CAUS	causative	OBJ	object
CONC	concessive form	OBL	oblique case
COND	conditional form	OPT	optative
CONJ	conjunction marker	P	passive type
CONTR	contrastive particle	PASS	passive
CP	causative passive	PAST	past indicative form
DAT	dative case	PERM	permissive form
DO	direct object	PL	plural form
EM	emphatic marker	PP	past participle
FOC	focused form of a verb	PRED	predicate
fem.	feminine	PT	past tense non-finite
FM	focus marker, focus particle	PTAD	past tense adverbial
FN	focus negation	Q	question marker
GEN	genitive case	QM	quotative marker
HON	honorifics	RED	reduplication
HORT	hortative marker	REFL	reflexive form
IMP	imperative	RPP	reduplicated perfect participle base form
inan	inanimate	SG	singular form
IND	present indicative form	SU	subject
INDF	indefinite marker	SUB	subject
INF	infinitive	TAM	temporal and aspectual markers
INFER	inferential form	TEMP	temporal marker
INS	instrumental case	TM	topic marker
INSTR	instrumental	V	verb
INVL	involitive	VA	verbal adjective

CHAPTER 1

Introduction

1. Genealogy and geography

Sinhala is one of the official languages, the other being Tamil, spoken in Sri Lanka, formerly known as Ceylon, an island in the Indian Ocean separated from India by a strip of shallow water, the Palk Strait, which is 29 kilometers at its narrowest. The country, with a total area of 65,610 square kilometers, has an estimated population of 20 million. The population of Sri Lanka is composed of several distinct ethnic groups contributing to the cultural diversity of the country and distributing different linguistic systems within the national boundary. Sinhala is used in all parts of the country except some districts in the north and east.

According to the figures published in the 2001 population Census (Colombo 2001), over 81.09 percent of the population is Sinhala. All persons belonging to the Sinhala ethnic group speak Sinhala as their first language. However, a considerable proportion of Tamils and Moors, especially those who live in the predominantly Sinhala speaking area, also speak it bilingually with Tamil. Sinhala speakers can also be found among immigrant populations in the U.K., North America, Australia and some European and Middle Eastern countries. The co-existence of the two languages in the same area within Sri Lanka and the use of Sinhala bilingually with another language in other countries has inevitably brought some hybrid forms into Sinhala speech though these forms have not made any major inroads into the standard language.

Sinhala has several dialects which are not only geographical but also social, determined by caste, rank and vocation etc. bringing the differences into surface. The Vanni (northern and eastern inland), Highland(central) and southern dialects represent some notable regional varieties. However, all Sinhala dialects are mutually intelligible, as prominent differences remain restricted to the lexicon while phonological and morphological differences are less prominent (De Silva 1979). Moreover, this regional variation is fast disappearing due to the spread of literacy and the influence of mass media, which have reduced communication barriers. The standard variety of Spoken Sinhala, which comprises the subject-matter of this book, comes from the Western Province where the administrative and commercial capital and the mass media of the island are located.

The most noticeable division within the language is between formal and informal or, more precisely, between Literary and Colloquial Sinhala. The existence of these two varieties has continued in a stable manner albeit with hybrid influences, making functional diglossia an established pattern of the Sinhala linguistic community. (De Silva 1967; 1974 and 1976a; Gair 1968 and 1986; Dharmadasa 1967; Paolillo 1997).

Although sociolinguists generally agree that a diglossic situation is one in which two or more varieties of a language, a High variety and a Low variety, are used within a single speech community depending on the relevant communicative purpose, there is little agreement on how to attribute due prestige to a given variety and how to characterize diglossia with respect to the structural properties of the varieties. While this kind of divergence of opinions remains a factor in regarding the Sinhala diglossic situation, too, most people, including ordinary members of the linguistic community as well as scholars and cultural personalities, regard the Literary variety as the prestigious one. However, some prominent linguists (for example, De Silva, 1974) have demonstrated that the superficially literary features of the Literary variety are merely 'added' grammatical markers that have been superimposed by purists.

While the Literary variety, particularly at the grammatical level, has been confined to a centuries-old archaic form which is based on the standard Sinhala prose language, the Colloquial variety has developed freely over the centuries. The language described in this book is the Colloquial variety, the language heard in the street, on the corridors of schools, and which is used for daily communication and understood throughout the country. A child acquires this language before he receives formal education. The language used in the mass communication media, however, is a hybrid variety developed from both the Literary and Colloquial varieties (De Silva 1974).

Sinhala is one of the Modern Indo-Aryan languages along with Hindi, Marathi, Bengali, etc. spoken in India. The origins of the earliest Sinhala people and the continuous history of their language from as early as the third century B.C. has been traced according to the linguistic and other evidences provided by the earliest lithic records and other historical accounts. Despite the large amount of evidence available, there is little agreement among scholars as to the original home of Sinhala and its place among the Indo-Aryan dialects. Most of the early studies of the history of Sinhala reflect a body of desperate attempts by contemporary scholars to find corroborative evidence for their respective theories regarding the original home of the Sinhala people. There are two conflicting theories, one holding that Sinhala originated in the North-Eastern part of India and the other that the original migrants came to Sri Lanka from North-Western India. To understand how the debate centered around two opposing camps, we should go to the root sources.

According to the recorded history, the first king of Sri Lanka is Vijaya. Two early Pali Chronicles named Dipavansa (around 1st century A.D.) and Mahavansa (4th century A.D.), give accounts of the supposed original home of the Sinhala people. According to the story given in the Chronicles, Vijaya's grandmother, Suppadevi, was the daughter of the king of Vanga (Bengal). Running away from home, she lived with a lion (sinha) in the country of Lala or Lada. Her son Sinhabahu left the jungle habitat, at the age of sixteen, with his mother and twin sister to live in the village community. The lion, who was ravaging the country out of the unbearable sorrow and in search of his family, was slain by his own son. After the king died, Sinhabahu was elected as his successor. He built the city of Sinhapura in his native country of Lada. His eldest son, Vijaya, and his companions committed unpardonable crimes in his father's capital. As a punishment, the king banished Vijaya and his companions. After touching at Supparaka, the ship carrying these men ultimately arrived at a place called Tambapanni in (Sri) Lanka.

While some regard this account given in the ancient Chronicles as a legend (Mendis, 1932) some scholars accord it more historical importance and consider that it contains some important clues to the route of the initial Arayan migrations to Sri Lanka (Geiger, 1912; Paranavitana, 1959). Since the historical account mentions several places relatiung to Vijaya's voyage and lineage, such as Vanga, Lala, Sinhapura, Supparaka, etc., the scholars engaged in the debate on the origin of Sinhala people tried to identify these place names, mainly the country of Lala mentioned as Vijaya's homeland, thereby providing non-linguistic evidence for their hypotheses. Proponents of the North-Western hypothesis (Chatterji 1926; Codrignton 1929; Geiger 1935; Paranavitan 1961) identified Lala with Laladesa, present-day Gujarat. The scholars propounding the North-Eastern hypothesis equated Lala with Radha in West Bengal (Shahidullah 1933; Siddhartha 1935; Wijeratne 1945).

Even after extensive research, scholars have acknowledged that there remains much uncertainty as to the exact location of the geographical places relating to the first Aryan settlements in the land. The most puzzling aspect of the Chronicles' version of the origins of the earliest Sinhala people and their language is the possibility of a connection between Bengal and Gujarat on opposite sides of the Indian continent. Paranavitana (1961) expressed this inadmissibility in the following way: "It is very difficult to believe that a migration of people took place in those early days right across the Indian Peninsula from Bengal to Gujarat." After much speculation he concludes that it is likely that Sinhala, as well as the people, was the result of a fusion of elements from the west with those from the east of north India. Codrington, in an earlier stage, had come to a similar conclusion:

> the evidence all points to Vijaya having come from the western coast, and it seems likely that the tale of his mixed ancestry is due to the fact that there were two streams of immigration, one from the western and the other from the eastern side of India. (Codrington 1929)

Discrepancies between the interpretations of the tradition given in the ancient chronicles have compelled scholars to seek supporting evidence in the earliest available linguistic records. First, they established how the North-Eastern and North-

Western dialects differ from each other phonologically and then they demonstrated chronological occurrences of such features in early Sinhala to substantiate their theories. However, there were some points that were neglected, though definitely deserved comment, by these scholars in extracting evidence in support of their theories. What were left unmentioned are some Indo-Aryan elements that did not appear, or non-Aryan elements that did appear in early Sinhala inscriptions. The old Indic aspirated consonants, for example, which are non-existent in the early Sinhala inscriptions, constitute a notable feature which distinguishes Sinhala from other Indo-Aryan vernaculars. Some scholars have pointed out features that their opponents were blind to.

Leaving aside the missing links that are conspicuous in the story of Sinhala, we must now proceed to seek the area of consensus among the scholars involved in the attempt of deciphering the unreadable story. Regardless of their assumed theories, all agreed that Sinhala is a mixed dialect in that it was considered as a fusion of elements not only from the east and west but from the north and south also. Siddhartha (1935), while clinging to his original opinion that Sinhala came from North-Western India, admits that Sinhala is an admixture of both Aryan and Dravidian speech.[1] Intermarriages between Aryan immigrants and indigenous women, Dravidian women from Southern India and Aryan women from Northern India gave ample opportunity for a mixed local language to develop.

At this juncture I think it is advisable to observe some historic and linguistic trends or events that bear direct relevance to the development of Sinhala. As pointed out by Geiger(1937), soon after the first colonization a lively intercourse began between Sri Lanka and the North Eastern provinces of India, Bihar, Bengal and Orissa and this stream of immigrations increased in number. These numerous immigrants brought to the island not only their Aryan dialects but the Buddhist Doctrine also. This special incident, namely the introduction of Buddhism to Sri Lanka gave a strong Aryan character to the language and motivated some scholars (Siddhartha, 1935, for example) to assume that the Prakritic dialect originally brought to Sri Lanka was Magadhi, a highly refined form of which was used to record the Buddhist Canons and a slightly less refined form of which was the language of the Ashoka inscriptions.

Another point to be noted is that soon after their settlement in Sri Lanka, Sinhala people commenced contacts and communication with their immediate neighbors, the Dravidians. As already mentioned, the early settlers got their first batch of wives from South India, which led the way in bringing the first Dravidian Influence on the language of the island. Dravidians were attracted to the island at different times and the island in the course of its history maintained constant communication and contact, peaceful or hostile, with the Dravidian tribes of South India. Despite the genetic relationship of

---

1. The Dravidian family of languages mainly spoken in the southern part of the subcontinent includes four main languages, Tamil, Kannada, Malayalam and Telugu, the first of which is the other national language of Sri Lanka, also accepted as an official language.

Sinhala with North Indian languages, the impact of linguistic contact with Dravidian languages has brought considerable changes to the whole language, making such convergence features explicit in grammar, lexicon and writing system. (De Silva, 1979)

Before observing further contact situations, it is relevant to mention another important turning point in Sri Lanka's linguistic and cultural history which helped to introduce some particular features to Sinhala. As the Indo-Aryan languages of the Indian sub-continent have acquired distinct features by departing from the evolutionary path followed by the languages of the Indo-European family in the west, so Sinhala has distinguished itself from the North-Indian language by acquiring linguistic features resembling South-Indian languages like Tamil. Siddhartha (1935) has grasped the historical factor behind this obvious tendency as relating to Sinhala:

> Up to the end of the Eighth Century the Sinhalese had free communication with the North Indians. Thereafter such communication began to decline gradually..... From the time that the Sinhalese people lost their connection with the Aryans of North India their language which also had already taken another course owing to new influences, began deviating rapidly and in a few centuries it became practically a new language.

'Another course owing to new influences' mentioned by that author includes 'the Dravidian influence over the Sinhalese, along with various and numerous other causes' that widened the gap between Sinhala and the North Indian languages. Paranavitana (1956), who took an independent approach to the analysis of Sinhala phonological processes and their history, has clearly taken this factor into consideration. According to him,

> The Sinhala language had separated itself from the main group of Indo-Aryan languages many centuries before the time when the distinctive features of the Prakrits were evolved, and had led its own life without having any intimate contact with other languages of the family to which it belonged. A solid block of Dravidian-speaking people separated the Sinhalese from the Aryan-speaking races of India. (Paranavitana, 1956)

After sketching out the origin of Sinhala and the foundation of its development, we are now in a better position, I believe, to get a wider picture of the development of the language. Geiger's study (1937) of the evolution of Sinhala based on a careful examination of the inscriptions and literary works available from the 2nd century B.C. will be very useful to trace the path followed by the language. According to him, five periods are distinguishable .

Period 1: Sinhalese Prakrit (2nd c. B.C. to 4th c. A.D. Brahmi inscriptions)
Period 2: Proto-Sinhalese (5th c. to 8th c. Very few inscriptions)
Period 3: Mediaeval Sinhalese (8th c. to 13th c. Inscriptions and from the 9th or 10th c. Literary works)
Period 4: Classical Sinhalese (13th c. to 17th c. Chiefly literary works)
Period 5: Modern Sinhalese (17th c. up to the present time. Literary works, newspapers and modern colloquial language)

It is admitted that the material available for certain periods is as rich as for others. For the period of Proto-Sinhalese, for example, in which Sinhala passed through its greatest changes and some of its features went out of currency or were substituted by others at later periods, the linguistic records available are not abundant. The period of Mediaeval Sinhalese, on the other hand, which formed the transition to the language of modern period, has abundant documents. Among these records, the Sigiri Graffiti – Sinhala verses from the eighth, ninth and tenth centuries written on the Sigiri wall called the Mirror Wall and deciphered and commented on by S. Paranavitana(1956) – provides valuable data enabling us to understand the true character of the contemporary language.

The reason for delineating the period of Classical Sinhalese as starting from the middle of the 13th century, according to Geiger (1937), is that the monumental event in the Sinhala history of compilation of its earliest extant grammar named *Sidat Sangarawa* took place around this particular period. One may wonder how there can be any relationship between the production of a grammar and the beginning of a new historical period in a language. The compilation of Sidat Sangarawa, in fact, became the cardinal event in Sinhala linguistic history by its fixation of an authorized form of the language conforming to a learned treatment. This native grammar laid down, for a large part, the form of the language, not only for composing verse, which was the original purpose of the compiler as argued by some scholars, but also for prose writing, which should thenceforth be used according to the rules based on the proper usages of the educated.

Although the literary language has been preserved in that prescribed form, to a large extent, even up to the present time, the spoken language has undergone many changes acquiring modern forms of speech, following vicissitudes of history, arising from contact situations, etc. During the period of western colonization in Sri Lanka which began in the 16th century, Sinhala received many influences from the languages of colonial rulers such as the Dutch, Portuguese and English. Gunasekara (1891; 1986) has included, apart from the large amount of words naturalized or derived from Tamil, a collection of western lexical items that have had a strong hold on the language. These new vocabularies made their inroads in the language through the dialects of the coastal areas which were occupied by the Dutch and Portuguese rulers before the whole island became a British colony in the 19th century. A native scholar in the first half of the 20th century (Siddhartha 1935) lamented the perceived decline in the standard language:

> One watches with great grief how the Sinhalese dialects spoken by the people in the interior of the Island are fast losing their purity owing to the introduction of words and phrases once peculiar to the language spoken by those who live in the maritime parts.

2. Typological character of the language

Sinhala is a head-final language. In the process of modification, modifiers precede the head.

(1) usə laməya
    tall boy
    'tall boy'

(2) man iiye   gattə potə
    I   yesterday buy-PT book
    'the book which I bought yesterday'

Thus adjectives and relative clauses are placed before the noun.

Sinhala is a highly consistent OV language (Lehmann 1978) in that the subject need not be taken into consideration when verbal modifiers are introduced. The typological characteristics of Sinhala will be sketched below in accordance with the basic patterns and processes.

2.1 Structure of simple clauses

In a Sinhala clause, the predicate constitutes the nuclear constituent. Depending on the nature of the predicate, verbal or non-verbal, there are two main clause-types. Non-verbal clauses include equational sentences and non-equational sentences which appear with non-verbal predicates. The equational sentence consists of a nominal selected as a topic and a nominal or adjectival predicate describing the category, characteristic or the quality of the topic, as in (3) and (4), respectively. The pattern exemplified by (5) has a postpositonal i.e. dative nominal as predicate which combines the topic with a value of dedication.

(3) meewa ambə
    these mangoes
    'These are mangoes.'

(4) meewa rasa-i
    these delicious-AM
    'These are delicious.'

(5) mee paarsəlee oyaa-ţə
    this parcel   you-DAT
    'This parcel is for you.'

With these non-verbal predicates, there is no need to use a copula to combine the subject and predicate. The marker appearing at the end of the adjectival predicate in (4) is recognized as an assertion marker, which is obligatory for vowel-final adjectives when they appear as predicates. When consonant-final adjectives constitute the predicate, the sentence is complete without any morpheme intervening between the predicate and # (sentence boundary).

The other type of clause, namely the verbal clause is identified by a verb occurring as the predicate. Verbal clauses occupy a cardinal position in the language in terms of their distributional potentialities and transformational variations. Clause types can be roughly classified on the basis of verb classes and the permitted number of valency relations. Accordingly, one hierarchy covers the range of transitive, intransitive and ditransitive clauses. Cutting across these classes, there appears the active-inactive dichotomy. In general, transitive and ditransitive clauses are active, with a subject denoting "actor" role whereas intransitive clauses split into active and inactive types depending on whether the subject has the "actor" or "undergoer" role.

(6) laməya duwə-nə-wa   (active intransitive)
    child   run-NPT-IND
    'The child is running.'

(7) gas   perəle-nə-wa   (inactive intransitive)
    trees fall down-NPT-IND
    'The trees are falling down.'

(8) Ranjit pot-ak   gatta   (transitive)
    (name) book-INDF bought
    'Ranjit bought a book.'

(9) Ranjit Chitra-țə   pot-ak   dunna   (ditransitive)
    (name) (name)-DAT book-INDF gave
    'Ranjit gave a book to Chita.'

Thus intransitive, both active and inactive, transitive and ditransitive sentences have their constituents arranged as S-V, S-DO-V and S-IO-DO-V as shown in (6), (7), (8) and (9), respectively. They illustrate the basic SOV order of constituents in the clause; the complement NP precedes the verb; the subject precedes the verb and the complement of the verb as well. In these canonical sentence patterns, although the nominal constituents are governed by the verbal predicate, the governed element does not necessarily undergo a change in form. Both in transitive and intransitive sentences, subject and direct object are realized as direct case nominals, that is, without any change in the form of the substantive. The only changes in form we can see are the indefinite marker -ak added to the direct object in (8) and (9) and the dative marker -țə added to the indirect object in (9). This shows that a case marker or a definite/indefinite marker follows the noun. By the same token, a postposition follows the noun. Look at the example:

(10) man atin liumə iruna
     I   by letter tear(.INVOL).PAST
     'I tore the letter inadvertently.'

This sentence belongs to a subclass of the inactive intransitive clause in Sinhala. Since the verb is in the inactive form, there cannot be a prototypical agent instigating the event. The postposition *atin*, which is added to the first person pronoun, marks the inadvertent actor behind the action. Thus the complement noun precedes the postposition to which it relates.

Another clausal pattern showing the characteristics of an SOV language is seen in constructions involving a standard. In comparative constructions and in names the relationship between a variable and its standard is considered to be comparable to that between a verb and its object (Lehmann 1978). Comparative sentences that express a comparison of inequality are constructed by establishing a variable and comparing this with a proposed object or standard. In an OV language, the accepted order is "Standard – Marker of Comparison – Adjective" (Greenberg, 1963). Sinhala adjectives do not inflect for the comparative or superlative degree but take adverbs like *waḍaa* 'more' and *wæḍimə* 'most' to indicate the variable degree. The degree adverb precedes the adjective. Then this adjectival phrase appears to the right of the standard with which the comparison is intended. However, it is typical of a head-final language that the head, i.e. the adjectival phrase, governs its complement, i.e. the standard. Therefore, the standard is followed by a marker of comparison which must appear to its right. In Sinhala, the dative marker *-ṭə* functions as that comparative marker. Hence the order is standard-marker-adjective. The following examples are illustrative; (a) and (b) represent word-order variants of the same proposition:

(11) a. kaḍuwə-ṭə   waḍaa   pæænə   baləwat
         sword-DAT   more   pen   powerful
         'The pen is mightier than the sword.'

     b. pæænə   kaḍuwə-ṭə   waḍaa   baləwat
         pen   sword-DAT   more   powerful
         'The pen is mightier than the sword.'

Although the position of the variable entity, the subject of comparison, is different in the two variants, the above-mentioned order of comparison remains stable.

This sequence equally applies to patterns like name with title and family name with given name. Thus, in an OV language the standard, namely the family name, precedes the variable element selected from titles or given names. This pattern is also observable in Sinhala:

    Name with title: Liyange mahachaaryətumaa
                  (name) professor
    Family name with given name: Liyanage Gunadasa[2]

---

2. This order has now changed due to the influence of European languages. Thus it is not uncommon to say *mahachaaryə Liyange* or *Gunadasa Liyanage* with the title or given name preceding.

This linear sequence was also followed in the arrangement of the elements in postal addresses in Sinhala before they were influenced by international postal conventions. The name of the largest entity, the postal district was placed first, followed by the place-names and signs for gradually smaller units and finally the name of the addressee.

2.2 Nominal modifiers

Descriptive adjectives, demonstratives, genitive expressions and relative constructions, all of which are considered as characteristic modifiers of nouns, precede the head noun in Sinhala.

(12) hondə rasə tee kooppəy-ak
 good tasty tea cup-INDF
 'a good tasty cup of tea'

(13) arə lassənə katandəree
 that beautiful story
 'that beautiful story'

(14) apee ayya-ge noona-ge malli-ge duwə
 our elder brother-GEN wife-GEN younger brother-GEN daughter
 'Our elder brother's wife's younger brother's daughter'

(15) man iiye gattu potə
 I yesterday bought book
 'the book that I bought yesterday'

In general, a demonstrative precedes a descriptive adjective, as in (13). (14) shows that there is no constraint on the iterative occurrence of genitive modifiers. As the examples show, all the nominal modifiers precede the head noun. The only attested exception to this rule in Sinhala concerns numerals. Observe the two examples in (16):

(16) a. kooppə tunə
 cups three
 'three cups'

 b. pot dekə
 books two
 'two books'

In general, numerals appear to the right of the head noun in Sinhala. This exception also indicates a point in which Sinhala deviates from the Old Indo-Aryan tradition.

2.3 Verbal modifiers

Declarative, interrogative and negative expressions will be shown here as reflecting the typical characteristics of SOV languages. As a prelude to this section, I should add some precursory remarks about the nature of clauses in Sinhala.

In Sinhala, there is a fundamental distinction of clauses as BASIC and EMPHATIC, regardless of whether a verbal or nonverbal sentence is involved (Gair 1970). Each clause has a constituent in focus in it which may be marked by formal means or not be overtly marked in surface structure. In basic clauses, focus and predicate are identical, as in (17a) and (17b).

(17) a. mee tee rasa-i
       this tea tasty-AM
       'this tea is tasty.'
    b. Ranjit kaḍee-ṭə ya-nə-wa
       (name) shop-DAT go-NPT-IND
       'Ranjit is going to the shop.'

The adjectival predicate *rasai* and the verbal predicate *yanəwa* are foci. We can bring into focus a constituent which is not originally in focus position by a "focus shifting" operation by which predicate and focus are separated. The result is an emphatic/focus clause. Thus, the nominal constituent in (17a), i.e. the theme, as well as the nominal constituents in (17b), i.e. the agent and the destination, are brought into focus as follows:

(18) a. rasə mee tee
       tasty this tea
       'It is this tea which is tasty.'
    b. Ranjit ya-nn-e kaḍee-ṭə
       (name) go-NPT-FOC shop-DAT
       'It is to the shop that Ranjit is going.'
    c. kaḍee-ṭə ya-nn-e Ranjit
       shop-DAT go-NPT-FOC (name)
       'It is Ranjit who is going to the shop.'

Now, the theme constituent in (18a), the destination in the dative in (18b) and the agent in the nominative in (18c) are all foci. Accompanying this change, an obvious difference between the basic clause and the emphatic/focus clause has surfaced with respect to word-order. In emphatic/focus clauses, the newly focused constituent has shifted from pre-predicate position to sentence-final position, as in (18). These focused constituents in (18), unlike in (17), have contrastive focus reading, that is, their meanings are interpreted as contrasting with some other possible entities. The nominal complement here follows the predicate whereas its place in the basic clause is to the left of the predicate as shown by the examples in (17). For instance, when one says *rasə mee tee*, the speaker means that it is this particular tea which is tasty, not the other variety.

Next, we will see how interrogative expressions are formed from these declarative sentences. To form a yes-no question, the question particle *də* is added to sentence-final position of the basic declarative sentence, verbal or non-verbal. The assertion-marker *-i*, if present, is deleted from the adjectival predicate. However, it may remain, if it serves some pragmatic purpose like emphasis or doubt. Observe the following examples:

(19) a. mee tee rasə də (cf. 17a)
this tea tasty Q
'Is this tea tasty?'

b. mee tee rasa-i də (cf.17a)
this tea tasty-AM Q
'Is this tea really tasty?'

c. eyaa guruwərəy-ek də
he teacher-INDF Q
'Is he a teacher?'

d. Ranjit kaḍee-ṭə ya-nə-wa də (cf. 17b)
(name) shop-DAT go-NPT-IND Q
'Is Ranjit going to the shop?'

Thus in yes-no questions, the question particle simply stands between the verb and sentence boundary, barring any assertion marker.

The process is not so simple in forming interrogative-word questions. Since an interrogative word is considered to be an inherently focused constituent, question formation by means of it should follow the focused-sentence pattern. To indicate this focus content, the verbal predicate is affixed with the focus marker -e. If the proposition is an event of motion including a destination, two questions can be formed, one regarding the theme/actor and the other concerning the destination. Thus the interrogative-word questions of (17b) are as follows:

(20) a. kaḍee-ṭə ya-nn-e kaudə (about actor, cf.18c)
shop-DAT go-NPT-FOC who
'Who goes to the shop?'
Lit. '(Who/the one who) is going to the shop is who?'

b. Ranjit ya-nn-e kohedə (about destination, cf.18b)
(name) go-NPT-FOC where
'Where does Ranjit go?'
Lit. '(Where/the place where) Ranjit is going to is where?'

Although the interrogative word can be preposed into sentence-initial position, this is not obligatory but can be an optional movement attributable to the relatively free word order in Sinhala. Thus the characteristic SOV order remains unaffected.

Negative sentences are formed by adding the negative particle *næ̃æ* to non-verbal or verbal predicates. In an adjectival clause, the negative particle immediately follows the predicate. The assertion marker *-i* gets obligatorily deleted. In the case of verbal predicates, the negative particle follows the predicate after its change into focus form with the suffix *-e*. Thus, the negative structures formed from (17a) and (17b) are rendered as in (21a) and (21b) respectively.

(21) a. mee   tee   rasə   næǣ
        this   tea   tasty not
        'This tea is not tasty.'

   b. Ranjit   kaḍee-ṭə   ya-nn-e   næǣ
       (name)   shop-DAT   go-NPT-FOC   no
       'Ranjit does not go to the shop.'
       Lit. 'Ranjit is going to shop, not.'

For some verbal or non-verbal sentences there are some other ways to form negative expressions. One such device is adding the negative particle *newei*. In nominal clauses, by simply appearing after the nominal predicate it negates the equation, as in (22a). It can also be added to a verbal predicate. Syntactically, its behavior is different from that of *næǣ* in that the basic declarative form of the verb to which it is added does not change into focus form. Through this behavior it negates the focus of the verbal predicate and implies an alternative possibility. (22b and c) will be illustrative.

(22) a. eyaa   guruwərəy-ek   newei
        he   teacher-INDF   not
        'He is not a teacher.'

   b. Ranjit   kaḍee-ṭə   ya-nə-wa   newei
       (name)   shop-DAT   go-NPT-IND   not
       'Ranjit isn't going to the shop,….'
       Lit. '(That) Ranjit is going to the shop is not.'

   c. miniha   ka-nə-wa   newei,   gili-nəwa
       man   eat-NPT-IND   not   devour-IND
       'The man is not eating; he's devouring.'

The essential point relevant to our discussion is that all negative particles appear to the right of the predicate.

Next, attention is paid to several kinds of elements attached to the predicate, observing their linear order within the clause. First, adverbial expressions appear to the left of the predicate. There are several types of adverbs. Some are particles which occur as attributes to the predicate of a clause, such as *nitərəma* 'always', *aayet* 'again'; some are adjective-based like *lassənə-ṭə* 'beautifully' and *sampuurnə-yen* 'completely'; some others are noun-based like *ætta washəyen* 'as a matter of fact' and *waasaənaawə-ṭə* 'fortunately'. Sentential adverbs are generally used in sentence initial-position. Compare the following two sentences:

(23) a. eyaa   lassənəṭə   chitrə   andi-nə-wa
        She   beautifully   picture   draw-NPT-IND
        'She is very good at drawing pictures.'
        Lit. 'She draws pictures beautifully.'

   b. waasaənaawəṭə   api   edaa   kohewat   giy-e   næǣ
       fortunately   we   that day anywhere   go.PAST-FOC   no
       'Fortunately, we didn't go anywhere that day.'

Second, in expressing modal and aspectual specifications, an auxiliary always follows the main verb. The following examples illustrate some ways in which aspectual and modal meanings are expressed in Sinhala:

(24) oyaa hayə-ṭə issərə gedərə e-nnə oonæ (obligation)
you six-DAT before home come-INF must
'You must come home before six.'

(25) hændææ we-nə koṭə wahi-nnə puluwani (probability)
evening be-NPT when rain-INF may
'It may rain by the evening.'

(26) miniha potə kiyawə-laa tiyenəwa (completive aspect)
man book read-PP has
'He has read the book.'
Lit. 'The man has read the book.'

Apart from modal and aspectual expressions, Sinhala has some compound verbals reflecting the speaker's perspective or attitude or which are reflexive. The following examples are representative.

(27) a. Chitra pantiyə-ṭə duwə genə giyaa (deictic perspective)
(name) class-DAT run take.PP went
'Chitra ran to the class.'
Lit. 'Chitra went running to the classroom.'

b. ahasə kalu kərə genə aawa (deictic path perspective)
sky black do.PP take.PP came
'(I saw) the sky was darkening.'
Lit. 'The sky came darkening.'

(28) Ranjit siiyaa-ṭə dorə ærə-la dunna (benefactive)
(name) grandfather-DAT door open-PP gave
'Ranjit opened the door for his grandfather'
Lit. 'Ranjit gave his grandfather the favor of opening the door.'

(29) Ranji tee ek-ak hadaa gatta (reflexive)
(name) tea one-INDF make.PP took
'Ranjit made himself a cup of tea.'
Lit. Ranjit made and took a cup of tea.'

In all these modal and aspectual expressions and other compounding verbals, the lexical verb precedes the auxiliary verb. There can be multiple auxiliaries in a single clause, as the examples in (27) show. They all stand between the lexical verb and sentence boundary.

2.4 Compound and complex sentences

Clause combination is achieved through participles, suffixed forms of verbals and particles functioning as conjunctions. The dependent clause typically precedes the main clause and a clause is bound to precede the subordinating conjunction. The following examples show some ways in which clauses are combined.

(30) man gedərə **gihilla** kææmə **kaa-la** e-nnam
      I   home go.PP   meals eat-PP come-HORT
      'I'll go home, eat something and come back.'

(31) a. man gedərə ya-nə **kan** amma balaa hiṭiya
        I   home go-NPT till   mother be waiting.PAST
        'My mother was waiting until I went home.'

     b. man gedərə ya-nə **kotə** amma wædə-ṭə gihilla
        I   home go-NPT when   mother work-DAT go.PP
        'When I got home, Mother had gone to work.'

     c. Ranjit e-nə-wa   **nam** kaurut   kæmətii
        (name) come-NPT-IND if   everybody like
        'Everybody will be happy if Ranjit comes.'

     d. ganan   wædi **hinda** baḍu   gatt-e   næ̈æ̈
        expensive much because things buy.PAST-FOC no
        'We didn't buy the things since they were too expensive.'

(32) a. Ranjit aaw-**ahamə**   mee gænə kataa kərə-mu
        (name) come.PAST-TEMP   this about talk talk-HORT
        'Let's talk about this when Ranjit comes.'

     b. Ranjit aaw-**ot**   ræswiimə tiya-nnə puluwan
        (name) come.PAST-COND   meeting have-INF possible
        'If Ranjit comes, we can have the meeting.'

     c. Ranjit aaw-**at**   ræswiimə tiyannə bæ̈æ̈
        (name) come.PAST-CONC   meeting have-INF impossible
        'Even if Ranjit comes, we cannot have the meeting.'

The example in (30) shows how the subordinate clauses are combined by the past participle form to indicate successive events. As (31) shows, particles are used to combine different types of clauses such as temporal clauses (31a and 31b), a conditional clause (31c) and a causal clause (31d). Examples are provided in (32) for suffixed verbals functioning as conjunctions with temporal (a), conditional (b) and concessive (c) clauses. They all follow the dominant order in Sinhala in which main clauses typically follow dependent clauses.

2.5 Some additional remarks on the structure of the language

Given all these facts and patterns, one may think that Sinhala is a rigid SOV language always keeping to the subject-initial and verb-final sentence pattern. This, however, is not the case: its word order is relatively free, especially in colloquial speech. The following word-order variations, for example, can be accepted in Sinhala for the utterance 'Ranjit gave the book to Chitra.'

(33) a. Ranjit Chitraṭə potə dunna
      b. Chitraṭə Ranjit potə dunna
      c. ?Chitraṭə potə Ranjit dunna
      d. Ranjit potə Chitraṭə dunna
      e. Potə Ranjit Chitraṭə dunna
      f. ?Potə Chitraṭə Ranjit dunna
      g. Chitraṭə potə dunna Ranjit
      h. ?Potə dunna Chitraṭə Ranjit
      i. potə Chitraṭə dunna Ranjit
      j. Ranjit potə dunna Chitraṭə
      k. ?Potə Ranjit dunna Chitraṭə
      l. Potə dunna Ranjit Chitraṭə
      m. Chitraṭə dunna Ranjit potə
      n. Ranjit dunna potə Chitraṭə
      o. Ranjit Chitraṭə dunna potə

All these sentences represent the same logical content while each may contain a different discourse presupposition. Even the verbal predicate can be preposed to the sentence-initial position depending on the context and pragmatic force. Compare the following sentences:

(34) a. Chitra   Ranjit-ṭə   hondə sapattu paar-ak   dunna
         (name) (name)-DAT good shoe   blow-INDF gave
         'Chitra gave Ranjit a good blow from her shoe.'
      b. dunna hondə sapattu paar-ak   Chitra Ranjit-ṭə
         gave good shoe   blow-INDF (name) (name)-DAT
      c. dunna hondə sapattu paar-ak   Ranjit-ṭə   Chitra
         gave good shoe   blow-INDF (name)-DAT (name)

(a) and (b) in (34), though identical in logical content, have different word orders. (a) follows the typical word order whereas (b) has its verb preposed along with its direct object. Furthermore, the subject has moved to the sentence-final position in (c). The verbal phrase, to which the speaker attaches a greater pragmatic force, is moved to the sentence-initial position, as in (b) and (c), where the front-most constituent has the greatest pragmatic force marked with a strong intonation. This may indicate that the word order in a language like Sinhala is determined not only by grammatical factors but to some extent by pragmatic considerations also.

Another distracting element that makes it difficult to observe the accepted order in which basic constituents occur in Sinhala is the widespread phenomenon of ellipsis. Noun phrases including subject and object as well are often omitted from utterances. The first and second person pronouns are the most freely deleted subjects. Look at the examples:

(35) a. gatta   də
       bought Q
       'Did you buy it?'

   b. gatta
       bought
       'I bought it.'

   c. aawa, aawa
       came   came
       'It/he/she is coming or they are coming!'
       Lit. 'It came.' or 'The person (expected) came.'

(35a) and (35b) can be taken as a question and a response constituting a part of a conversation. Accordingly, the subject of the former, 'you' and that of the latter, 'I' are omitted. The speaker and listener both seem to have some tacit understanding with respect to what is bought depending on which the referent of the missing object is assumed and interpreted correctly by them. The utterance in (35c) has an intransitive verb in reduplicated form, without a subject. The speaker will be sharing some experience with the listener regarding the appearance or arrival of some object or person. When the expected object or person (it may be a bus or a taxi, a wedding couple or a famous speaker or politician) appears, the speaker expresses his feeling of excitement with reiterations of the word, consciously or unconsciously, and shares the feeling with the others present at the moment. These examples show that discourse-predictable constituents need not appear in surface structures for constructional purposes.

Moreover, the notion "subject" is not such a well-defined one as in English. Consequently, one can observe that Sinhala also allows deletion of non-nominative elements if they are easily recoverable from context. The so-called "experiencer"-subjects, for example, appear in dative form and are better left unmentioned when they bear co-reference with the speaker. They are typically related with experiences of sensation and perception, as follows:

(36) a. badəgini-i
       hungry-AM
       'I'm hungry.'
       Lit. '(To me) hungry.'

   b. siitələ-i
       cold-AM
       'It's cold or I feel cold.'
       Lit. 'Cold.'

In (36a), the first person "experiencer" is deleted since it is recoverable from the non-linguistic context. If the "experiencer" needs to appear in surface structure it should obligatorily take dative form. (36b) shows a different situation where the speaker is not culturally or linguistically bound to specify the subject. Instead, he prefers to leave the subject submerged in the context. These sentences are rather natural without subjects; subjects are included in the sentence only if they need to be emphasized.

There are also some inherently subjectless sentences referring to natural phenomena. Observe the following sentences:

(37) a. wahi-nə-wa
Rain-NPT-IND
'It's raining.'
(Lit. 'Rains.')

b. gorəwə-nə-wa
thunder-NPT-IND
'It's thundering.'
(Lit. 'Thunders.')

Sinhala speakers feel rather comfortable with declarative statements as those above without seeking subjects to allocate natural phenomena to.

While I have mainly drawn attention to noun phrase ellipsis in the preceding discussion, one should not be surprised to see even verbal predicates missing in Sinhala. When the negative marker *nææ* is introduced to negate a stative sentence with existential or possessive verb *innəwa* or *tiyenəwa*, the whole verbal predicate is deleted. For example, see the following question-response utterances:

(38) A: taatta gedəra in-nə-wa də
father home be-NPT-Q
'Is your father home?'

B: a. nææ
no
'No(, he isn't).'

b. nææ, taatta gedəra nææ
no father home no
'No, father isn't home.'

The most natural response utterance to the question asked by A would be (38a) which is logically equivalent to the complete negative sentence in (38b).[3] However, this kind of

---

3. The following sentence, which is formed grammatically according to the ordinary negation rule mentioned in 2.3(cf. (21)), is not acceptable as a response to the question by A. *Be*-verbs are obligatorily deleted from this type of negative sentences.

* næǣ, taata gedərə in-n-e næǣ
no father home be-NPT-FOC no
'No, father isn't home.'

complete negative sentence is usually used only when the listener seems unconvinced by the reply in (38a), that is, it serves to put greater emphasis on the negation. It should be added that this type of verbal ellipsis is extremely common in Sinhala and does not cause any anomaly in production or comprehension.

In the latter part of this chapter, an attempt was made to sketch some linguistic phenomena illustrative of typological patterning, with particular attention to word-order facts. Facts were provided mainly to illustrate Sinhala as a verb-final language. Peripherally, an attempt was made to show how nonverbal elements or nominal complements can appear to the right side of the main-clause verb, bringing to the fore the relatively free order of constituents arising from word-order scrambling and failing to confirm the dominant order. We have also seen some cases of noun phrase ellipsis including that of subject and direct object as well as verbal predicate ellipsis as factors weakening the established pattern.

However, despite these facts advanced in favor of a free word order, it is not difficult, returning to my original argument, to hypothesize the underlying order of constituents as SOV for Sinhala. It will have already been noted that both subject and direct object appear in the unmarked nominative case in Sinhala active transitive clauses.

(39) balla   puusa   dækka
     dog   cat   saw
     'The dog saw the cat.'

The fact that two NPs with opposing grammatical functions appear in identical form next to one another does not cause any difficulty in comprehension. Sentence (39) indicates that Sinhala speakers' intuition informs them that the initial NP denotes the subject while the following NP is the direct object, and not vice versa. There is a natural constraint to the effect that subject and object cannot switch position which works as the "anti-ambiguity" server. To double-check the function, there is an optional accusative marker in colloquial Sinhala. The accusative marker -wə is extremely helpful in disambiguating the roles of some seemingly symmetrical relations when such information is unrecoverable even from the non-linguistic context.

(40) mugaṭiyaa   nayaa-wə   mæru-wa
     mongoose cobra-ACC kill.PAST-IND
     'The mongoose killed the cobra.'

However, one can also argue that the fact that there exists such a secondary disambiguating operator means that there are cases in which the word-order factor does not work as an "anti-ambiguity" server, which in turn suggests that switch of word order for subject and direct object is permitted in Sinhala. Contrary to this argument, I can show again that the norm in Sinhala is SOV. To substantiate my argument, I will use an amusing anecdote in Sinhala told by a famous comedian in Sri Lanka. The joke is based on a parody of the established word order in Sinhala. According to the story, there was a fight between the narrator and another person. They continued to fight each other exchanging good blows. The narrator gives, literally, a blow-by-blow account of the fight, describing it as an apparently symmetrical roughhouse between two formidable protagonists and assuming a boastful tone to persuade listeners of his great fighting spirit. The narrator repeatedly uses the following coordinated clauses to imply the temporal sequence of the blows and their continuance.

(41) eyaa ma-ʈə gæhu-wa, ma-ʈə eyaa gæhu-wa
      he   me-DAT hit.PAST-IND, me-DAT he   hit.PAST-IND
      (Lit. 'He hit me and me he hit.')
      'He hit me repeatedly.'

The narrator implies, with the use of basic Sinhala word order, that the third person hit the first person narrator, the former being the agent and the latter being affected in the first clause and vise versa in the second clause by virtue of their respective positions in two clauses. However, it is merely a parody of the word order SOV, Agent-Patient-Verb. One may understand that the grammatical structure of the clauses, especially the second clause, does not denote this logical structure. The subject of the active transitive verb is the third person pronoun and the first person pronoun marked dative suggests that a narrator is the receiver of the blows in both clauses. No matter how often the narrator repeats the clauses, he remains the sole victim of the fight throughout the narration. The narrator only uses word-order tactics to give the impression that he remained unconquered. The story is amusing as it turns out, at the hands of discriminating listeners, to be an empty boast by a speaker trying to conceal the fact that he is the victim.

CHAPTER 2

Writing system

Sinhala has its own script. Its alphabet is known as *hoodiya*. Only Sinhala is written with the letters of the *Sinhala hoodiya*.

The Sinhala writing system is largely phonetic in that one can understand how words are pronounced simply by looking at their spelling. This said, one may be relieved, thinking that there are no spelling problems in Sinhala. However, as noted before, since there is a disparity between Literary and Colloquial Sinhala, a state of confusion regarding orthography prevails even among the native speakers/writers. One can see that there are more than fifty different letters used for journalistic or academic writing that closely follows the tradition of Literary Sinhala despite the fact that there exist only about thirty five phonetic sounds in Colloquial Sinhala, which includes 21 consonants and 14 vowels (De Silva 1960).[1]

When describing the orthography of the language, all the traditional grammar books introduce two different alphabets, one called 'pure' and the other 'mixed'. The 'pure' alphabet, as accepted by the traditional grammar tradition, contains letters used in writing the so-called 'pure' Sinhala words, by which is meant the variety of the language mainly used for versification by the classical poets. The 'mixed' alphabet, on the other hand, comprises a wider set of letters useful for prose writing accommodating numerous loan wards of Sanskrit and Pali origins.

Either alphabet, taken separately, does not deliver the goods. The 'pure' alphabet is simply inadequate for practical purposes; the 'mixed' one is redundant with obsolete characters never used in modern writing. As a solution, a practical Sinhala alphabet has evolved from the traditional alphabets accommodating symbols that are necessary and adequate for the contemporary writing. This alphabet consists of symbols for all the vowel sounds, except the mid central /ə/, and symbols for all the consonants including conventional symbols for pre-nasalized stops known as "half-nasals" (See Chapter 3). A new symbol that did not prevail in the traditional Sinhala orthography

---

1. There is no consensus among scholars regarding the number of symbols needed to represent the sounds of spoken Sinhala. According to Fairbanks, Gair and De Silva 1968, only 36 symbols are necessary for writing spoken Sinhala. Karunatillake 1992 proposes that only 41 symbols are necessary to represent spoken Sinhala.

also seems to be gaining ground in the modern writing to fulfill the pressing need of representing the bilabial fricative /f/ occurring in borrowed words of English origin.

Our mention at the beginning of this chapter that Sinhala writing is 'largely phonetic' is self-explanatory; it is not fully phonetic. For instance, although the mid central vowel /ə/ has been established as an independent phoneme, there is no separate symbol in the alphabet to represent it. Yet another set of letters prevails there without corresponding phonetic values: Although Sinhala is considered as notable among the major Indo-Aryan languages in having no aspirate stop phonemes (Coates & De Silva 1960), the written variety has preserved the symbols for aspiration in numerous words it has borrowed from Pali and Sanskrit. Such aspirated elements, albeit without distinctly separate phonetic values, are indispensable for the literary variety of Sinhala and therefore represented by separate symbols in the alphabet.

The Sinhala writing system is not primarily alphabetic – that is, not representing the language in terms of regular, one-to-one mapping between letters and phonemes. For instance, separate vowel-letters are used independently only when they occur in initial position. When a vowel appears in union with a consonant, that is, in medial or final positions, this combination is represented by a sign, a stroke or a diacritic mark, added to the consonant-letter. However, there is no distinct sign to represent the short /a/ sound combined with a consonant. A consonant symbol, as it appears in the alphabet, is considered to be containing the vowel sound of /a/ by default which is called *the inherent vowel*. These facts show that the Sinhala writing is rather syllabic.

The traditional Literary Sinhala alphabet consists of 54 symbols plus symbols of the four prenasalized-voiced-stops. The following set of 54 symbols including prenasalized-stop-symbols, having some redundant ones dropped, otherwise closely resembling the traditional list, is considered adequate for the contemporary writing. The linear order of the symbols comes from the traditional 'alphabetical order' as accepted by the authoritative dictionaries:

Literary Sinhala alphabet

a = අ,   aa = ආ,   æ = ඇ,   ææ = ඈ,   i = ඉ,   ii = ඊ,
u = උ,   uu = ඌ,   ṛ = ඍ,   e = එ,   ee = ඒ,   ai = ඓ,
o = ඔ,   oo = ඕ,   au = ඖ,   (a)ń = ං

ka = ක,   kha = ඛ,   ga = ග,   gha = ඝ,   ŋa = ඞ,
cha = ච,   chha = ඡ,   ja = ජ,   jha = ඣ,   ň a = ඤ,
ṭa = ට,   ṭha = ඨ,   ḍa = ඩ,   ḍha = ඪ,   na = ණ,
ta = ත,   tha = ථ,   da = ද,   dha = ධ,   na = න,
pa = ප,   pha = ඵ,   ba = බ,   bha = භ,   ma = ම,
ya = ය,   ra = ර,   la = ල,   wa = ව,

ŝa = ශ,   ṣa = ෂ,   sa = ස,   ha = හ,   ḷ = ළ
nga = ඟ, nḍ = ඬ, nda = ඳ, mba= ඹ

However, after further reducing certain symbols that do not have phonetic values, we get the following 38 letters. These symbols are fully adequate to represent modern Colloquial Sinhala. The final symbol of the list, which is not included in the traditional orthography, represents the bilabial fricative /f/, a recent addition.

Alphabet for Colloquial Sinhala

Vowel-letters: a = අ, aa = ආ, æ = ඇ, ææ = ඈ,
                 i = ඉ, ii = ඊ, u = උ, uu = ඌ,
                 e = එ, ee = ඒ, o = ඔ, oo = ඕ

Consonant-letters: ka = ක,   ga = ග,   ŋ = ඞ,   nga = ඟ,
                    cha = ච, ja = ජ,   ňa = ඤ,
                    ṭa = ට,   ḍa = ඩ,   nḍa = ඬ,
                    ta = ත,   da = ද,   na = න,   nda = ඳ,
                    pa = ප,   ba = බ,   ma = ම,   mba= ඹ,
                    ya = ය,   ra = ර,   la = ල,   wa = ව,
                    ṣa = ෂ,   sa = ස,   ha = හ,   fa = ෆ

The consonants given in the above alphabets appear in the syllabic form that includes the vowel "a", the first letter of the alphabet, following the Sinhala orthographic convention. It seems, at least to the native user, that the unmarked consonant-letter is always the one depending on the vowel /a/.[2] To represent a consonant in its naked form, devoid of a vowel form, an additional mark is to be added to the consonant-letter. Traditionally called the *hal* or *al* ('pure consonant') marker, this symbol appears in two shapes. The flag-shaped mark (්) is appended on the right shoulder of a symbol whereas a curved, horizontal stroke (්) is put on the head of a letter that ends by curving upwards to the left. Examples:

ක = ka ;   ක් = k,   ව = wa ;   ව් = w

There are separate symbols or special diacritics to represent the vowels combined with the consonants, except for the first vowel "a" which is considered inherently included in the consonant-letter. These diacritic symbols, traditionally called *pili* ('limbs'), are given below. The order of letters follows the standard one. Some of the symbols have

---

2. To be precise, the inherent vowel may be /a/ or /ə/ depending upon its position within the word. Fairbanks, Gair and De Silva 1968 has delineated several rules for the inherent vowel (Fairbanks, Gair & De Silva, 1968, p.63).

two forms, one of which is selected depending on the shape of the consonant to be combined with.

Table 1. Diacritic symbols for vowels

Vowel	Symbol	Examples
aa	(ා)	kaa කා , waa වා
æ	(ැ)	kæ කැ , wæ වැ
ææ	(ෑ)	kææ කෑ , wææ වෑ
i	(ි)	ki කි , wi වි
ii	(ී)	kii කී , wii වී
u	(ු) or (ු)	ku කු , wu වු
uu	(ූ) or (ූ)	kuu කූ , wuu වූ
e	(ෙ)	ke කෙ , we වෙ
ee	(ෙ ්) or (ෙ ්)	kee කේ , wee වේ
ko	(ෙ – ා)	ko කො , wo වො
koo	(ෙ – ෝ)	koo කෝ , woo වෝ

The examples in the table show how the consonants "k" and "w" appear in combination with vowels. As apparent from the examples, the vowel "a" originally considered as inherent to the syllabic consonant is automatically dropped when consonants are inflected into other vocalic forms.

Pili or limbs are not considered as independent letters, but only parts of combined symbols. To indicate the long vowel *aa*, the sign ා (called *ælapilla* or side-mark) is placed after the consonantal symbol. To represent the vowels *æ* and *ææ*, the signs ැ and ෑ are placed after the consonantal symbol. The semi-circular strokes ි and ී (called *ispilla*, head-marks), added to the top of the consonantal symbol, represent the vowels *i* and *ii*. The sign *papilla* or foot-mark (ු or ු ; ූ or ූ) is added to the bottom or the side of the consonantal symbol to represent the vowels *u* and *uu*. Depending upon the shape of the consonantal letter, the foot-mark takes a different form. Also note the difference between the marks for the short vowel and the long vowel. The sign (called *kombuwa*, 'cornet' (ෙ) is placed in front of the consonantal symbol to represent the vowel *e*. To represent the long vowel *ee*, the *al-kiriima* sign, the mark otherwise used to indicate that a consonant is not followed by a vowel, is added to the consonantal symbol preceded by the *kombuwa*. A *kombuwa* placed before the consonant symbol and an *ælapilla* or side-mark after it together represent the vowel *o*. Where the vowel is long, the *al-kiriima* sign is put on the *ælapilla* sign.

To indicate a geminate consonant, the consonant symbol is written twice, but the initial consonantal-letter is appended with the *al-kiriima* ('pure consonant'). Examples:

> *attə*   අත්ත   'branch'
> *bassa*   බස්ස   'owl'
> *malli*   මල්ලි   'younger brother'

Consonant clusters are traditionally represented in writing by compound- letters, i.e. by joining the consonantal symbols involved. There are two types of compound letters. In one type, one or more consonantal letters, or their parts are joined with another consonantal letter or with a part of it to form such compounds. This convention, in particular, was used to write borrowed words of Sanskrit and Pali origins. Examples:

wandənaa වඤතා 'worship'
buddhə බුද්ධ³ 'Buddha'
koṭṭaasə කොට්ටාස³ 'division'

However, this convention is considered as outdated; nowadays most of the consonants in such combinations are written separately by representing the initial part of the combination by the *al-kiriima*, the diacritic of the 'pure consonant', as follows:

wandənaa වන්දනා 'worship'
buddhə බුද්ධ 'Buddha'
koṭṭaasə කොට්ටාස 'division'

There is another type of compound-letters representing consonant clusters. In this kind of compounds the initial part comprising a full letter is joined by a second part which is a symbol, or a remnant of the letter it represents. Examples:

krəmə ක්‍රම 'method'
prətəmə ප්‍රථම 'first'
nyaayə න්‍යාය 'theory'
yoogyə යෝග්‍ය 'appropriate'

In the first two examples with the compounds consisting of "k" (ක්) + "r" (ර) and "p" (ප්) + "r" (ර) respectively, the second constitutive consonant is only represented by (‍්‍ර), a small part of "r" (ර) added to the bottom of the first consonant. In the two other examples where the compounds consist of "n" (න්) + "y" (ය) and "g" (ග්) + "y" (ය) the second constituent is a symbol representing "ya" (ය) but resembling a half of it in shape: ‍්‍ය. These orthographical conventions are duly followed even in present-day writing.

There is a subtle phonological and auditory difference between the two types of clusters, or compounds representing them. In the first type of compounds where the initial part of the combination is represented by the diacritic of the 'pure consonant' as in *wandənaa* "වන්දනා" 'worship', this initial consonant of the cluster is always pronounced long. In this case it may be appropriate to transliterate this consonant into Roman characters as *wanndənaa*. This does not apply to the second type of

---

3. The letters are joined together in writing or type-setting, which cannot be shown properly with the available Sinhala word-processing systems.

compounds where the initial part of the combination is written without the diacritic of the 'pure consonant', i.e. appears in full consonant form and the second part is indicated by a symbol, or a remnant of the letter it represents, as in *krəmə* "ක්‍රම" 'method' and *nyaayə* "න්‍යාය" 'theory'. The consonant-compounds of the second type are considered as consisting of two short consonants. That is how they appear in Literary Sinhala, or in the speech of the educated speaker.

Text is written horizontally from left to right. Space is inserted between words, and punctuation marks like full stop and comma are used to indicate sentential and phrasal boundaries following the Western style of arrangement. Thus, elements of print are arranged to represent syllabic units, word boundaries and sentence boundaries. However, Sinhala does not follow the convention of capitalization. Letters are usually written in uniform size, including those at the beginning of sentences and names.[4]

Since the description of the Sinhala writing system in this chapter was meant to give a general picture of it, the particulars regarding the writing of the literary variety of Sinhala were not given here in detail. In fact, there are some additional letters or symbols that occur with less frequency. For example, to represent the vocalic symbol 'ṛ' mainly occurring in borrowed words of Sanskrit origin, the diacritic " ෘ " is added to a consonant. This diacritic is also used to represent clusters with similar pronunciation in non-Indic words.

praakṛtə	ප්‍රාකෘත	'primitive'
pṛtugiisi	පෘතුගීසි	'Portuguese'
koolbṛṛk	කෝල්බෲක්	'Colebrook'

Another symbol, or a diacritic, added to consonants (and the vowel *o* (ඔ) as well) occurring in Indic words represents the vocalic diphthong 'au' as in

auṣada	ඖෂධ	'medicine'
kautukaagaarəyə	කෞතුකාගාරය	'museum'

Our simplified description may also obscure some complications inherent in the writing system. One thorny problem that remains unsolved concerns spelling. For instance, there are some consonant-letters, redundant from the phonological point of view but considered to be necessary from the etymological standpoint, such as 'ṇ' (ණ) and 'ḷ' (ළ). They often get confused with the consonant-letters representing alveolar nasal 'n' (න) and lateral 'l' (ල), respectively. In addition to the letters representing alveolar fricative 's' (ස) and palatal fricative 'ś' (ශ), there is another symbol meant to be retroflex, being loyal to Sanskrit etymology but having no real phonetic value: 'ṣ' (ෂ). Such letters pose problems not only to the novices but also to the professional writers.

---

4. A notable exception is ළ (la). According to the traditional instruction, ළ needs to be bigger than other letters in writing.

Despite the fact that attempts are constantly made through the formal education to train the students in this problematic area encouraging them to follow the correct spelling practices, the evaluations regarding their accuracy, as frequently done by means of scholastic examinations, never show good results.

Another problem concerns setting word boundaries. The use of spacing for word division is a relatively new phenomenon for Sinhala writing. The old practice of running together without leaving space between words prevailed until the advent of printing in Sri Lanka in the 18th century. Although guidelines for word division have been set out with the help of scholars and lexicographers, still these is no consensus even among the experts on some problematic cases such as the use of suffixes, particles and postpositions.

The modern system of writing in Sinhala as described above is a product of a long history of borrowing characters from India, independent developments and adaptations, and relatively recent innovations of extra-alphabetic conventions developed under the influence of Western tradition. The earliest system of writing was introduced to Sri Lanka in the 3rd century B.C. when Buddhism was brought to the island from India. The letters used in earliest extant lithic records accord with the Brahmi script used for inscribing the contemporary Ashoka edicts in India. The shape of the letters and their ways of combination underwent radical changes over time, especially when writing shifted from cave- or rock inscriptions to inscribing on palm-leaves. Later, the letters were greatly influenced by the Southern Indian writing system called the 'Grantha' which is considered a variety of Ashoka characters used for literary purposes. The system of writing developed further as a medium capable of reflecting subtler linguistic and paralinguistic elements after the writings began to appear in print and the language further needed to map into word processing.

CHAPTER 3

Sounds

1. Vowels

Sinhala has seven vowels as shown in the Table 1.

Phonetic Representation:	[i]	[e]	[æ]	[ə]	[u]	[o]	[a]
Phonemic Representation:	/i/	/e/	/æ/	/ə/	/u/	/o/	/a/
Romanization:	i	e	æ	ə	u	o	a

Table 1. Vowels in Sinhala

Phonetic Representation	Phonemic Representation	Romanization
[i]	/i/	i
[e]	/e/	e
[æ]	/æ/	æ
[ə]	/ə/	ə
[a]	/a/	a
[u]	/u/	u
[o]	/o/	o

Phonetic characteristics of the vowels can be given as follows: first, [i], [e],[æ], [u] and [o] are articulated with a slightly lower tongue position compared to their corresponding cardinal vowels. Secondly, the back vowels [u] and [o] are rounded, but the rounding is weak, less than for cardinal vowels. [a] is considered as a little higher, especially when occurring in a closed syllable, and may sound more [æ]-like. The articulatory characterization of the vowels is given in Table 2 below:

Table 2. Tongue positions of vowels

	Front		Central	Back	
	Spread	Round		Spread	Round
High	i				u
High-mid	e				o
Mid			ə		
Low-mid	æ				
Low			a		

Phonemically, all vowels can occur long or short.

/dinə/ 'date'   /diinə/ 'low'
/ekə/ 'one'   /eekə/ 'that one (inanimate)'
/ænum/ 'stab (plural)' /æænum/ 'yawns'
/darə/ 'firewood'   /daarə/ 'edges'
/lunu/ 'salt'   /luunu/ 'onion'
/porə/ 'fights'   /poorə/ 'ferilizer'

The mid central vowel [ə] mostly occurs short; its long occurrence is very infrequent. It can be seen only in loan words from English such as /səər/ 'sir'. In some cases, there are phonetic differences between a short vowel and the corresponding long vowel. For instance, the above-mentioned height fluctuation for the short vowel [a] does not affect the long vowel [aa], which has the lowest tongue position among Sinhala vowels.

Regarding the phonemic status of /ə/, in most cases it occurs in complementary distribution with /a/: for instance, /ə/ occurs preceding a single consonant whereas /a/ precedes a doubled consonant or another vowel. Examples: /warədə/ 'fault'; /waraddə gannəwa/ 'make a mistake'. An exception to this is found in the position after /h/. Only /a/ can occur there; /ə/ is barred. Also note that the occurrence of /ə/ in initial syllables is very rare. A notable exception is its occurrence in the initial syllable of borrowed words. Examples: /prəsiddə/ 'famous', /krəmə/ 'method', /trəstəwaadəyə/ 'terrorism'. /ə/ and /a/ appear in complementary distribution even in final syllables, with /ə/ restricted to absolute final position and /a/ occurring before a final consonant. Examples: /palləmə/ 'slope' vs. /pallam/ 'slopes'. However, the long /aa/, which contrasts with both, remains obscure in absolute final position. In the spoken language unstressed long vowels in final positions are shortened usually. This tendency has caused minimal pairs with /ə/ and /a/: for example, /siiyə/ 'a hundred' and /siiya/ 'grandfather'. Since Sinhala orthography does not provide any special indication for /ə/, this contrast of /ə/ and /a/ does not appear in writing. Thus, identical spelling is used for both the members of the pair in documenting Colloquial Sinhala.

Combinations of different vowels occur: for instance, the following combinations are common: ei, æi, ai, oi, ui, iu, eu, æu, au, ou, ae. These involve varied distances between their respective tongue positions.

There are two semi-vowels: [y] and [w]. They occur only initially and medially. [y] is a weak glide-sound articulated in the position of /i/, while [w] is another weak glide-sound with the mid-central tongue position as for /ə/, not high back as for /u/.

yaturə 'key'
gaayəkəya 'singer'
waturə 'water'
rawənəwa 'stare'

In case of [w], the lips start close together but do not come to a complete contact. Due to this quality, it is considered as bilabial or labiodental. Because of this confusing situation, many writers Romanize it as 'v'. However, we prefer to use 'w' indicating the weak labial contact occurring in its articulation.

2. Consonants

In addition to the seven vowels and the two semi-vowels discussed so far Colloquial Sinhala has nineteen consonants which are, together with the glides (semi-vowels), shown in Table 3. When a slash appears in the table, the symbol to the left of it indicates a voiceless consonant and that to the right a voiced consonant.

Table 3. Inventory of consonants and glides

Consonant	Labial	Dental	Alveol.	Retrofl	Alv.- palatal	Velar	Glottal
Stops	p/b	t/d		ṭ/ḍ		k/g	
Affricates					c/j		
Nasals	m		n			ŋ	
Lateral			l				
Flap			r				
Fricatives	f		s		š		h
Glides	w				y		

A description of the consonant phonemes is provided below. Table 4 shows all the consonant phonemes and their allophonic variants with their phonological environments. Certain details had to be ignored (see Perera & Jones 1919 and Coats & De Silva 1960 for a more detailed description).

The voiceless stops are generally pronounced with slight aspiration, especially in initial position. The aspiration can be strong when the stop is articulated with a clear, distinct voice. The labial stops /p, b/ are bilabial. Examples: /paanə/ 'lamp', /lipə/ 'oven'; /bayə/ 'fear', /abə/ 'mustard'. The dental stops /t, d/ are articulated by raising the tip of the tongue against the upper teeth. Examples: /talə/ 'sesame', /atə/ 'hand'; /dat/ 'teeth', /adə/ 'today'.

The retroflex stops /ṭ, ḍ/ have to be articulated by curling the tip of the tongue further back to make contact with the hard palate. Examples: /ṭikak/ 'a little', /aṭə/ 'eight'; /ḍingə/ 'the little', /baḍə/ 'stomach'.

In pronouncing the velar stops /k, g/, the back of the tongue will touch the soft palate. Examples: /kadə/ 'shouldering pole', /dukə/ 'suffering'; /galə/ 'rock', /agə/ 'end'.

The alveolo-palatal affricates /c, j/ are articulated by the front of the tongue making contact with the hard palate. Examples: /cakkəree/ 'multiplication table', /wacanə/ 'words'; /jayə/ 'victory', /rajə/ 'king'.

Sinhala has three nasals: /m/ is bilabial. Examples: /mal/ 'flowers', /gamə/ 'village'. The alveolar nasal /n/ is articulated by the tip of the tongue against the tooth-ridge. Examples: /nayə/ 'credit', /panə/ 'life'. Its dental allophone occurs before dental stops as in /antəyə/ 'extreme', its retroflex allophone before retroflex stops as in /anḍə/ 'limb'. The velar nasal /ŋ/ is articulated by the back of the tongue against the soft palate. It occurs before velar stops or finally. Examples: /aŋkə/ 'numbers', /naŋgi/ 'younger sister', /walaŋ/ 'pots'. It has a palatal allophone occurring initially as in /ñaane/ 'wisdom', medially as in /pipiñña/ 'cucumber', and before palatal stops as in /wañcaawə/ 'cheating'. The velar nasal /ŋ/ contrasts with the labial nasal /m/ and the alveolar nasal /n/ while the three nasals are in complementary distribution with each other.

The lateral /l/ is formed with the tip of the tongue against the tooth-edge. Examples: /lee/ 'blood', /alə/ 'yam'.

The alveolar flap /r/ is articulated with the tip of the tongue approaching the tooth-ridge and further back. It may consist of one single tap or of several taps formed by flapping the tip of the tongue against the tooth-ridge. Initially and medially it may be pronounced with a strong aspiration, and in final position with repeated tapping. Examples: /rææ/ 'night', /barə/ 'heavy', /kaar/ 'car'.

There are four fricatives. One is bilabial /f/, which only occurs in borrowed words of English origin like /foṭo/ 'photograph'. However, this sound is not so natural in native Sinhala pronunciation. Speakers regularly substitute the bilabial stop /p/ for this borrowed sound. Thus /poṭo/ 'photograph', /soopaa/ 'sofa' and /paiṭ/ 'fight' sound more natural in Sinhala. The alveolo-fricative /s/ is articulated by raising the tip of the tongue towards the tooth-ridge. Examples: /særə/ 'hot', /rasə/ 'tasty'. It allows other variants depending on whether the point of articulation is further forward or further back. The alveolo-palatal fricative /š/ is pronounced by raising the tip of the tongue towards the hard palate. This sound occurs in borrowed foreign words, mainly from Sanskrit. Examples: /šariirəyə/ 'body', /yakšə/ 'devil'. A more natural pronunciation is available by substituting /s/ for it as in /sariire/ and /yaksə/. One non-borrowed term, /šook/ 'great', appears without substituting /s/. The glottal fricative /h/ is partially voiced. Examples: /hæṭə/ 'sixty', /gaha/ 'tree'. It has several allophones as the tongue and lips take up different positions depending on the following vowel.

Table 4. Sinhala Consonants

Phonemic Representation	Phonetic Representation	Romanization	Examples in Romanization
/p/	[p]	p	*papuwə* 'chest'
/b/	[b]	b	*babaa* 'baby'
/t/	[t]	t	*taatta* 'father'
/d/	[d]	d	*dat* 'teeth'
/ṭ/	[ṭ]	T	*ṭikak* 'a little'
/ḍ/	[ḍ]	D	*ḍingə* 'the little'
/k/	[k]	k	*kaakka* 'crow'
/c/	[č]	ch	*chapələ* 'fickle'

(Continued)

Table 4. Sinhala Consonants (Continued)

Phonemic Representation	Phonetic Representation	Romanization	Examples in Romanization
/j/	[j]	j	*jayə* 'victory'
/m/	[m]	m	*mamə* 'I'
/n/	[n]	n	*nææna* 'cousin'
	[n]//_[t, d]	n	*antəyə* 'extreme'
	[n]//_[ṭ, ḍ]	n	*anḍə* 'limb'
/ŋ/	[ŋ]	n	*aŋ* 'horns'
	[ñ]//_[č, ǰ]	n	*ranchu* 'group'
/r/	[r] (word initial)	r	*ratu* 'red'
	[rʰ] (intervocalic)	r	*barə* 'heavy'
/l/	[l]	l	*lee* 'blood'
/f/	[f]	f	*fail* 'file'
/s/	[s]	s	*sawəsə* 'evening'
/š/	[š]	sh	*shakti* 'strength'
/h/	[h]	h	*hayə* 'six'

It was shown above that all vowels occur long or short. Most consonants occur both long and short, too. Long consonants, however, occur only in medial position. The presence of phonetic length, in fact a phonemic distinction between single or doubled consonants, is an important feature that helps distinguish words of subtly similar sounds. This phonetic length is indicated by doubled-consonant symbols in the text. Compare the following minimal pairs:

/atə/ 'hand' /attə/ 'branch'
/katə/ 'mouth' /kaṭṭə/ 'shell'
/malə/ 'flower' /mallə/ 'bag'
/pasə/ 'soil' /passə/ 'back'

Weakened articulation of intervocalic single consonants is very common and is applicable to (a) all stops except retroflex (b) nasals and (c) the semi-vowel /w/. In the following, consonants that are pronounced with weakened articulation are indicated by underlined bold-face.

ni**k**əmətə 'for nothing'
pææ**g**enəwa 'be trampled'
ba**n**inəwa 'scold'
na**m**əyə 'nine'
po**w**ənəwa 'feed'

3. Consonant clusters

Consonants can appear as clusters in initial and medial positions. When two consonants form a cluster in initial position, the first is always pronounced short.

Examples: /wyaakərənə/ 'grammar', /tyaagə/ 'gift', /prəsannə/ 'pleasant', /krəmə/ 'method'. On the other hand, when two consonants form a cluster in medial position, the first is generally pronounced long. However, these long or doubled consonants, which should be represented by a double letter in writing, are actually indicated by single-consonant symbols according to the convention. Examples: /kandə/ 'mountain', /wistəree/ 'detail', /rasne/ 'hot', /kalpanaa/ 'thought'. In fact, they are phonetically and phonologically long as /kanndə/ 'mountain', /wisstəree/ 'detail', /rassne/ 'hot' and /kallpanaa/ 'thought'. Some clusters may consist of more than two consonants. Examples: /saasstriiyə/ 'academic', /nisprabaa/ 'nonsuited', /aassrəyə/ 'associate'. Most of such clusters are from loan words of Sanskrit origin.

One type of double-consonant clusters deserves special attention. This type belongs to the larger category covering the clusters of nasal plus voiced stop. A nasal can cluster with all the four voiced stops. The nasal element of the cluster can occur short or long when the second element is a voiced stop. In each of the four clusters [mb, nd, ɳɖ, ŋg] there is a contrast between the short nasal and long nasal. e.g.:

/tambə/ 'copper' : /tammbə/ 'boil'
/kandə/ 'trunk'   : /kanndə/ 'mountain'
/anɖə/ 'sound'   : /annɖə/ 'limb'
/aŋgə/ 'horn'   : /aŋŋgə/ 'item'.

The right-hand members of these contrasting pairs are similar to normal double-consonant clusters where the first of the two consonants is pronounced long. In contrast, the left-hand members are peculiar with their first element pronounced short.

The short nasal clusters are generally considered as a special class of sounds named "half nasals" by scholars of Sinhala. Scholars prefer to consider the phenomenon of "half nasals" as a specific feature distinguishing Sinhala from other Indo-Aryan languages. The four clusters have special signs in the traditional Sinhala orthography. These characters are different from the regular nasal letters used for "full or doubled nasals" in normal type of clusters. Some scholars have assumed that each of the four "half nasals" represents a separate independent phoneme (Jones 1950). However, some other scholars do not agree with this position and regard them as some peculiar consonant clusters with an extra-short allophone (for example, Coates & De Silva 1960).

In the left-hand member of each of the opposing pair the nasal joins the following consonant and vowel to form a syllable. It represents the only medial/intervocalic cluster whose first element is pronounced short. Because of this prenasalized stop, for example, the word *tambə* 'copper' is divided syllabically as *ta-mbə*. This is in contrast to the right-hand member in which the doubled nasal is considered as syllabically belonging to what precedes, not to what follows. Thus the word *tammbə* 'boil' is divided syllabically as *tamm-bə*. The results of a systematic acoustic examination using the spectrographic evidence show that the "half nasal" clusters are more accurately described as "prenasalized voiced plosives" (Dantsuji 1987). According to this examination, the phonetic properties of the "half nasal" cluster include a nasal murmur portion, a voiced oral murmur portion, a burst and a transition portion to the next vowel.[1]

There is another type of clusters involving nasals in which the second element of the cluster is a voiceless stop, and the preceding nasal element is always pronounced long so that there is no contrast. Examples: /sammpat/ 'resouces', /anntə/ 'extreme', /annkə/ 'number'. This type of cluster is referred to as 'the normal type of cluster with doubled nasal' (Coates & De Silva 1960). The general rule for these clusters is that the first of the two consonants is pronounced long.

Most of the words in which elaborate clusters occur are borrowed terms. To the native tongue, simple alternations with the CVCV type sound to be more palatable. Ordinary speakers tend to simplify initial clusters of such borrowed terms except the ones with nasal plus stop. Initial clusters beginning with complex /ss/ are simplified by inserting a prothetic vowel /i/. Examples: /ssthawərə/ > /isthawərə/ 'stable', /strii/ > /istirii/ 'woman', /snaane/ > isnaane 'bath'. Other initial clusters are simplified by inserting a *svarabhakti* vowel: /klaante/ > /kalante/ 'faintness', /bhrantə/ > biraantə 'dumbfounded', praane > paraane 'life', /prəyoojənə/ > /purəyoojənə/ or /poroojənə/ 'use'. Clusters with semivowels /w/ or /y/ as the second element are simplified by substituting the corresponding full vowel: /swəkiiə/ > /suwəkiiə/ 'one's own', /dhyaanə/ > /diyaanə/ 'transcendental mind'. However, the nasal plus stop (voiced or voiceless) clusters do not appear simplified.

4. Phonological rules

4.1 Vowel length

Vowels in final position tend to be short. This is particularly so when the preceding syllable is a long or heavy one in a disyllabic structure.

/haawa/ 'hare'
/biiwa/ 'drank'
/balla/ 'dog'
/dunna/ 'gave'

When the first syllable is short in a disyllabic structure, the final long vowel remains long.

/meyaa/ 'this person'
/giyaa/ 'went'
/sataa/ 'animal'
/horaa/ 'thief'

---

1. The 'burst' represents the stop articulation.

In a tri-syllabic or polysyllabic structure the final vowel remains short regardless of the
length of the preceding syllable.

/monəra/ 'peacock'
/yaaluwa/ 'friend'
/ælluwa/ 'caught'
/næwətuna/ 'stopped'

4.2 Nasal assimilation

When a nasal-final syllable followed by a pause combines with a consonant- initial syllable, nasal assimilation occurs to complete the combination. The place of articulation of the nasal is assimilated to that of the following consonant.

/koʈin/ + /ʈə/   > [koʈiNʈə]
tigers   DAT
/harəkun/ + /wə/   > [harəkuŋwə]
cattle   ACC
/tun/ + /pat/   > [tumpat]
three leaves

4.3 Other assimilations

To make an acceptable consonant cluster, disparate consonants undergo assimilation, progressive or regressive.

Progressive assimilation:

/ad/ + /wənəwa/   > /addənəwa/ 'cause to pull'
/kap/ + /wənəwa/   > /kappənəwa/ 'cause to cut'
/mahat/ + /wəru/   > /mahatturu/ 'gentlemen'

Regressive assimilation:

/æt/ + /dalə/   > /æddalə/ 'ivory'
/dæn/ + /mə/   > /dæmmə/ 'immediately'
/puwak/ + /gaha/   > /puwaggaha/ 'aricanut tree'

4.4 Velarizing

A nasal before a word boundary is regularly velarized. When medial nasals which are labial or alveolar come to stand in final position for morphological reasons, they are automatically velarized.

/paanə/ 'lamp'   > /paaŋ/
/torana/ 'pandol'   > /toraŋ/
/paalama/ 'bridge' > /paalaŋ/
/pinumə/ 'jump'   > /pinuŋ/

However, these articulations are conditioned by the environment. When the nasal is not in sentence-final position, its articulation is conditioned by the following sound.

4.5 Substituting

In initial or medial position the alveolar fricative /s/ is commonly replaced by the glottal fricative /h/. Then vowel change occurs. Thus the mid-vowel /ə/ following the fricative has to change into the low-mid /æ/ or the low vowel /a/.

/æsə/	> /æhæ/ 'eye'
/wasə/	> /waha/ 'poison'
/kasələ/	> /kahalə/ 'rubbish'
/hawəsə/	> /hawəha/ 'evening'

The variation represents a feature of the colloquialism. The right column has the uses of the colloquial language while the left column carries more formal uses. (See Section 3 in Chapter 5 for a detailed description of the morpho-phonological adjustment rules.)

5. Suprasegmental features

5.1 Syllables

A syllable is characterized by a vocalic nucleus represented by a single vowel (V), which may be long or short. Apart from the obligatory vocalic nucleus, there are optional features. The onset is one such optional feature, which can be either a simple consonant (C), or a palatalized consonant (Cy). Thus, at the phonological level, syllables are CV, V and VC. In prosodic terms, syllables can be open or closed. Open syllables are marked by vocalic finality whereas closed syllables are identified by consonantal finality. The other optional feature, the coda, is either, a nasal (N) or an obstruent (Q), both of which mark closed syllables.

Syllables are of short, medium or long quality according to durational differences of articulation. For instance, /yanəwa/ 'go' consists of three short syllables all of which are open; /paaŋ/ 'bread' is a word of one long, closed syllable; /at/ 'hands' has one medium, closed syllable; /poosat/ 'rich' has two medium syllables, the initial one being open and the second closed; /madyasaarə/ 'spirit' has its initial syllable short, second syllable medium, third syllable long and final syllable short.

/yanəwa/	three syllables: CV, CV, CV
/paaŋ/	one syllable: CVN
/at/	one syllable: VC
/poosat/	two syllables: CV, CVQ
/madyasaarə/	four syllables: CV, CyV, CV, CV

5.2 Stress

Stress is week and therefore its placement is difficult to specify. It is not possible to change the lexical category of a word into another by altering the position of the stress. Since the stressing of accented syllables is much lighter than in languages like English, a phenomenon such as the vowel weakening in unstressed syllables is also not notable. However, long vowels in final position are usually not stressed and consequently are subject to weakening.

If a word of polysyllabic structure needs stressing in the sentence, the speaker can in principle choose any syllable of the word to put the stress on. Although there are no strict rules regulating the placement of the stress, there are certain tendencies. If a word consists of two short syllables, the first syllable will be stressed: /gamə/ ('village'), /matə/ ('view'), /adə/ ('today'). If a word consists of three short syllables, the tendency is to stress the second syllable: /gamətə/ ('to the village'), /matəkə/ ('memory'), /adəmə/ ('today itself'). However, when a word consists of three or more short syllables, the stress may be distributed equally over several syllables: /dawəsəkətə/ ('per day'), /paləwenia/ ('the first'), /hirəgedərə/ ('prison'). Initial syllables get stressed regardless of their length: /adə/ ('today'), /innəwa/ ('be'), naaraŋ ('citron'). The syllables that are medium or long in quantity seem to be stressed in most cases, except in final position: /aassəree/ ('company'), /winaase/ ('destruction'), /apaayə/ ('hell'), /sarampə/ ('measles'), /hæmədaamə/ ('everyday'). In a word mixed with medium and long syllables, position seems to gain priority over quantity: /baŋgəlaawə/ ('bungalow'), /aapassətə/ ('reverse'). Thus, in Sinhala the locus of the stress is determined by the nature of the syllable.

5.3 Pitch

Voice-pitch is not prominent, and tones are not phonemically so distinctive as to distinguish words or different dialects. Although some provincial dialects have distinctive tone patterns, the functional load of the overall accent is insignificant. What is more important is choosing the words one thinks as suitable to receive the high pitch. In a sentence like *Chitrage potə genaawadə?* ('Did you bring Chita's book?'), for instance, one might put the high pitch on *Chitrage* and another might put it on *potə* while yet another might choose *genaawadə?* for it. It is also possible to choose the nominal phrase *Chitrage potə*, or the verbal phrase including the complement *potə* as the pitch unit. Accordingly, the rising pitch is on what is considered the most important part of the sentence; it is never lexically specified.

Nevertheless one has to be attentive to some basic tone patterns to convey the expected force of expression. The sentence-terminal contour, namely rising (↑) and falling (↓), plays an important role distinguishing utterance types. Questions containing a question-word place a high-fall on the question-word.

kohedə yanne? ↑ 'Where do you go?' or 'Where are you going?'

When the listener replies the question, the answer carries a low-falling pitch as follows.

    gaməʈə↓ 'to my village'

The high rising intonation marks an echo question or a similar speech act. Thus, when the interrogator is surprised by the response and repeats it as an interrogative, this surprise is expressed by a high-rising pitch: *gaməʈə?*↑

Yes-no questions take a rise-fall on the verb, mostly on the second syllable of the verb.

    Ranjit gaməʈə yanəwadə/giyaadə? ↓   'Does/did Ranjit go to his village?'

Usually, the level contour marks a non-final clause ending.

6. Rhyming expressions

Rhyming expressions comprise a particular class of reduplications which are highly sound symbolic. The sound symbolism comes from a combination of two phonological units that have the same prosodic structure and the same number of syllables. The two phonological words are the base and the rhyme. A rhyme is added to the base by making a change in its first syllable. There are mainly three types of rhyming expressions.

In one type if the base begins with a consonant, in the rhyme this consonant will be replaced by a different one. Examples:

    wal-pal 'worthless matters'
    paḍi-naḍi 'salary, etc.'
    taṭṭu-maṭṭu 'embarrassed and troubled'
    laṭṭə-paṭṭə 'odds and ends'
    chaṭə-paṭə 'sounds of sudden rupture or crackers'
    jarə-barə 'sound of old machine, or complaining'
    taarə-baarə 'redundant matters'
    taannə-maannə 'gifts and honors'
    saantə-daantə 'calm and quiet'

If the base begins with a vowel, in the rhyme a consonant will appear to precede this vowel. Examples:

    angərə-dangərə 'twists and turns (bodily)'
    andə-mandə 'taken aback'
    æli-mæli 'lazy and not active'

In the other type the whole first syllable changes to form the rhyme. Examples:

    daḍi-biḍi 'sound of continuous falling, or hurry'
    daḍiŋ-biḍiŋ 'sound of something heavy or powerful'

goolə-baalə 'disciples and pupils'
toora-beera 'select and drop'
waṭin-piṭin 'from around or from without'
aturu-mituru 'friendly'
oppu-tirappu 'deeds, etc. (related to land registration)'

In most cases we can see the sound symbolism coming from the choice of reduplicating consonant. However, as shown by some of the examples given above, it is also associated with onomatopoeia. The second unit of the pair can be a meaningful word or a nonsense word.

CHAPTER 4

Words

1. Vocabulary strata

According to traditional grammar, the simplest forms of words called *prakṛti* 'primitive forms', which can be roots of verbs or bases of nouns, can be divided into three categories, namely.

1. *nishpanna:* indigenous forms. These are local words which belong to a substratum.
2. *tatsama:* forms homophonous with their source word, normally in Sanskrit or Prakrit, i.e. unassimilated loan words.
3. *tadbhawa:* words that can be traced to an Indic source, normally Sanskrit, Prakrit, or a Dravidian language, which have become naturalized, that is assimilated to the native phonological pattern.

The division of the Sinhala lexicon into these strata was based mainly on the distinction of native words and words incorporated from foreign languages which included Pali, Sanskrit and other Indic languages. This stratification shows how vocabularies are organized according to their respective source languages, reflecting different phonological characteristics. For instance, indigenous words do not have consonant clusters with the exception of the prenasalized stops. Only the lexical forms of *tatsama* have consonant clusters. The *tadbhawa* forms are distinguished from *tatsama* forms because they are integrated into the native language by necessary alternations of the CVCV type. Almost all Sinhala words which have come down from Old Indo-Aryan and are in day-to-day use belong to the *tadbhawa* category.

Indigenous or native words whose origins cannot be traced to other languages are very few in number. Names of some body parts like *oluwə* 'head' and *kakulə* 'leg' and names of some indigenous flora like *pol* 'coconut' and *kos* 'jack-fruit' are examples. Some words taken from Sanskrit or Pali can be seen in two different forms, both as *tatsama* and *tadbhawa*. However, some words may appear only in one form, *tatsama* or *tadbhawa*. Look at the following examples:

Sanskrit	tatsama	tadbhawa	
raajə	raajə	radə	'king'
putrə	putrə	put	'son'
yakshə	yaksə	yak	'demon'
ganitə	ganitə	ganan	'arithmetic'

aasənə	aasənə	asun	'seats'
karmə	karmə	kam	'action'
wasə	wasə	—	'live'
prətiphala	prətiphala	—	'results'
apaayə	apaayə	—	'hell'
kadali	—	kesel	'banana'
ikshu	—	uk	'sugar-cane'
badhirə	—	bihiri	'deaf'

When there are two different forms for one signification, which form is to be chosen is a matter of context and style. Sinhala traditional poetry only accommodated *tadbhawa* words in its language. The prose language, in contrast, has freely accommodated *tatsama* words for narrative and descriptive exposition. Especially, from the 12th century onwards, while the literary tradition of Sinhala was greatly influenced by the Sanskrit language and literature, Sanskrit *tatsama* words were added to the lexicon rather freely. Even today Sanskrit words are used abundantly to introduce new concepts, to coin technical terms and to provide alternative expressions through word-formation strategies such as compounding. Using Sanskrit words is considered by many scholars as a means of enhancing elegance and dignity of style.

While the language thus underwent great lexical transformations with the impact of North Indian languages, foreign admixture did not end here. As mentioned in the Chapter 1, Sri Lanka continued to be visited by the people of South India and to hold close connection with such people in various ways. The subsequent admixture of South Indian words, the majority of which is from Tamil, brought further change into the lexicon. The following list provides some examples:

<u>Tamil</u>	<u>Sinhala</u>	
akkei	akka	'elder sister'
aanḍu	aanḍu	'government'
iḍam	iḍam	'land'
nangei	nangi	'younger sister'
pudumei	pudumə	'strange'
maṭṭam	maṭṭam	'level'
winaaḍi	winaaḍi	'minute'
siini	siini	'sugar'

Later, from the sixteenth century onwards, the Sinhala lexicon developed with the impact of European languages such as Portuguese, Dutch and English. While a large stock of words borrowed from Portuguese are directly related to the daily life, such as cloths, food and kitchen appliances, items of furniture and things related to architecture, etc., the majority of words borrowed from Dutch represent the level of government and belong to the fields of law and administration. These loan words from Portuguese and Dutch are limited to nouns, mostly representing concrete objects. Borrowed in the sixteenth and seventeenth centuries when Sri Lanka came under direct contact with the Western colonizers, these words have been established in the Sinhala lexicon, but have never increased thereafter.

Most recent addition to the lexicon, the borrowed words from English makes a distinction to the tradition of borrowing: the use of English loan words remains largely restricted to Colloquial Sinhala. Colloquial Sinhala freely accommodates English words, even verbs, related to varied fields including life style, office environment and educational and entertainment fields. There is a very productive lexical process to convert English verbs or adjectives and particles into verbs in Sinhala, namely using verbs *kərənəwa* 'do' or *wenəwa* 'become' as lexical connectors. Examples: *kaṭ kərənəwa* 'cut (a class)', *ṭrai kərənəwa* 'try', *paas wenəwa* 'pass', *auṭ wenəwa* 'be out'. However, the use of these borrowed English words is never considered as part of a valid style in Literary Sinhala, or even in a semi-formal environment. Employment of them is restricted to the conversational language.

Trying to include all these borrowed words into the traditional categories of *tatsama* and *tadbhawa*, separating them from native words is itself a task difficult to achieve without the knowledge of their etymology and likely to pose some problems. For instance, some words aptly matching with the Sinhala phonological system and hence hitherto considered as native words may prove to be borrowed from a foreign language upon closer examination. For example, *manəmaalə* 'bridegroom' in Sinhala, which sounds purely indigenous to native speakers, is in fact adopted from Tamil *manəmaalan*. Another such native-sounding word, *sidaadi* 'city' is traced to Portuguese *cidáde*. In another case, some words that seem to be borrowed from one language, for example, from Portuguese, may actually have been borrowed or adopted from other sources such as Tamil or Hindi. The similarity of certain original words in Portuguese and Dutch may also cause the student of language some difficulty in determining the source language for some words.

The most important thing is that when borrowed words are incorporated into the language, some phonological adjustments are made to suit the native phonological system. Look at the following list to observe how English words have been introduced into Sinhala with such adjustments.

English	Sinhala
English	ingriisi or ingirisi
district	distirikkə
department	departəmeentu
engineer	injineeru
coroner	kornər or korneel
warrant	warentu

When there are no equivalent sounds in Sinhala corresponding to those in English, the nearest equivalents of the native language are employed. Thus English *zoo* has become *soo* in Sinhala, and English *volume* is *wolyum* in Sinhala. However, the traditional tendency to simplify consonant clusters is not the current vogue any more in Colloquial Sinhala, at least, as far as borrowing from English is concerned. Instead, speakers prefer to use borrowed words in forms closer to the pronunciation in the source language. For example, words such as *praiweet* (from 'private'), *ilekshən* (from 'election') and *ilekṭrik* (from 'electric') are used in the colloquial language without much adjustment in the structure of clusters.

2. Word classes

Sinhala words fall into three main classes: nouns, adjectives and verbs. They are all open classes capable of incorporating new words. Nouns and verbs have subclasses determined according to morphological and syntactic criteria. Both nouns and verbs are inflected. In addition to these major word classes, there are some minor classes which include adverbs, particles, affixes and interjections.

2.1 Nouns

As its members are inflected, this class consists of many free morphemes mostly used with bound morphemes. Nouns, in general, inflect for case, definiteness and number. Nouns divide into several classes in terms of usage or composition, such as proper nouns, common nouns, pronouns and verbal nouns.

Proper nouns: Proper nouns denote names of particular individuals, places, objects and events, etc. An individual or personal name consists of a family name and one or several given names. *Rajapaksha Mudiyanselage Siril Ariyaratna* is a traditional personal name, where the first part *Rajapaksha Mudiyanselage* is the family name and the last part includes two given names: *Siril* and *Ariyaratna*. Since Sinhala personal names are relatively long, the family name and, in some cases, even the first given name are written with initials as *R. M. S. Ariyaratna*. The arrangement of personal names has changed with the influence of the Western tradition. The modern tendency is to bring the family name to the end of the name. In that case the given names are written with initials as in *S(iril) A(riyaratna) Rajapaksha* (the latter part of the family name, *Mudiyanselage,* which includes plural marker *-la* and the possessive suffix *-ge* are omitted).

Common nouns: Common nouns refer to a whole class of living beings, objects, places, concepts or events. They are simple or compound nouns.

Living beings: *aliya* 'elephant', *amma* 'mother'
Objects: *potə* 'book', *attə* 'branch'
Places: *gamə* 'village', *iskoole* 'school'
Concepts: *marənəyə* 'death', *ugatkəmə* 'education'
Events: *ussəwəyə* 'festival', *tarəngəyə* 'race'

These are not exclusive categories. A noun may denote an object and a place simultaneously. The common nouns given above are all simple nouns. The following are compound nouns.

Guru deguru samitiyə 'parent-teacher association'
dalə jaatikə nishpaadítəyə 'gross national product'

In writing compound nouns, which are composed of two or more nouns, the constituent nouns are separated by spaces indicating word boundaries. Traditional grammar teaches that in compounding *tatsamə* and *tadbhawə* derivatives should not be mixed, a rule only honored in breach. For example, in the above example *dalə jaatikə nishpaadítəyə*, *dalə* is a *tadbhawə* derivative and *jaatikə nishpaadítəyə* has two *tatsamə* derivatives.

Nouns divide into two main classes in inflectional terms. Traditionally, this division was considered as based on the semantic feature of [+ or – animate].

Animate nouns: *miniha* 'man', *waɖuwa* 'carpenter', *aliya* 'elephant'
Inanimate nouns: *potə* 'book', *puʈuwə* 'chair', *gediyə* 'fruit'

The division is explicit in numeral phrases such as follows:

   Inanimate: *puʈu dekə* 'the two chairs'
   Animate: *waɖuwo denna* 'the two carpenters'

There are rare exceptions in which animate nouns split between the animate and inanimate distinction. For example, *ibba* 'padlock', while inflecting as an animate noun, remains an inanimate noun within a numeral phrase as in *ibbo dekə* 'the two padlocks'. This anomaly comes from metaphorically applying the word for tortoise/turtle to refer to a padlock.

As nouns inflect for case, definiteness and number, the paradigm includes features in the shape of a stem form and suffixes. The citation form of nouns appears in the nominative definite form. Let us compare the paradigms of two nouns from the two classes. The stem form for *waɖuwa* 'carpenter' (animate) is *waɖu* and that for *puʈuwə* 'chair' (inanimate) is *puʈu*.

Paradigm for *waḍuwa* 'carpenter'

Case	Animate		
	Singular	Plural	Indefinite (sg.)
Nominative	waḍuwa	waḍuwo	waḍuwek
Accusative	waḍuwa(wə)	waḍuwanwə	waḍuwekwə
Dative	waḍuwaʈə	waḍuwanʈə	waḍuwekuʈə
Instrumental	waḍuwagen	waḍuwangen	waḍuwekugen
Genitive/Loc.	waḍuwage	waḍuwange	waḍuwekuge

Paradigm for *puʈuwə* 'chair'

Case	Inanimate		
	Singular	Plural	Indefinite (sg.)
Nominative	puʈuwə	puʈu	puʈuwak
Accusative			
Dative	puʈuwəʈə	puʈuwələʈə	puʈuwəkəʈə
Instrumental	puʈuwen	puʈuwəlin	puʈuwəkəʈə
Genitive/Loc.	puʈuwe	puʈuwələ	puʈuwəkə

The optional occurrence of the accusative case is restricted to the animate class. As the above paradigm shows, the inanimate class does not inflect for the accusative case even optionally. The suffix *-n-* occurring in all oblique (non-nominative) plural forms is also restricted to the animate class. While instrumental and genitive/locative suffixes are *-gen* and *-ge* in the animate class they appear as *-en* and *-e* in the inanimate class. Non-nominative plural forms are marked with the *-wəl* or *-wələ* suffix only in the inanimate class.

It appears that there is a difference in indefinite marking for the two classes. However, no clear-cut inflectional difference can be found with respect to the semantic class. Some gender forms, especially feminine nouns, though belonging to the animate class, inflect for definiteness as well as indefiniteness in a manner corresponding to inanimate nouns.

Definite Form   **Indefinite Form**
guruwəriyə 'female teacher'   *guruwəriyak*
bælli 'bitch'   *bælliyak*

The animate/inanimate division seems to be based not only inflectionally but also with respect to some other behavior patterns of nouns. When nouns occur as subjects of existential sentences, their corresponding verb varies according to the animate/inanimate distinction. According to the animacy co-occurrence rule, inanimate subjects take the verb *tienəwa* while animate subjects take the verb *innəwa*. Compare the following examples.

Inanimate: *puṭuwə tienəwa* 'The chair is (there).'
Animate: *waḍuwa innəwa* 'The carpenter is (at home).'

They also take different forms of numerals:

Inanimate: *puṭu dekə* 'the two chairs'
Animate: *waḍuwo denna* 'the two carpenters'

Such numeral phrases also inflect for definiteness. The numeral phrases given above, for example, take indefinite markers as follows:

Inanimate: *puṭu dekak* 'two chairs'
Animate: *waḍuwo dennek* 'two carpenters'

In Sinhala, the sense of definiteness remains unmarked. Not only concrete nouns and numeral forms but even abstract nouns can inflect for definiteness. Look how the following abstract nouns, as inanimate nouns, have taken indefinite marker.

hondə 'wellness' > *hondak* 'a goodness' or 'a good point'
narəkə 'badness' > *narəkak* 'a badness' or 'a bad point'
taniyə 'loneliness' > *taniyak* 'a loneliness'

Some nouns do not inflect for indefiniteness. For example, mass nouns such as *lee* 'blood', *waturə* 'water', *pas* 'soil', *wæli* 'sand', *kiri* 'milk', *wii* 'paddy', *haal* 'rice' and *bat* 'rice' generally appear in the plural form except in cases where a particular kind of the material is implied as in *haalə* 'this particular rice', *batə* 'this rice', *pasə* 'the particular soil' or *wællə* 'the sand'.

Pronouns: There is a large inventory of words standing for other nouns or referring to other noun phrases in which personal pronouns take a prominent place.

Personal pronouns: Personal pronouns are classified by person and number. First person pronouns are *mamə* (sg.) and *api* (pl.). Third person pronouns are *eyaa* (sg.) and *eyaala* (pl.). Second person pronouns, apart from the above-mentioned categories, can be divided into three basic classes referring to differential social status and implying varying degrees of respect or intimacy. Speakers have to choose the appropriate form according to sociolinguistic context. Given below are singular forms; plural forms are made by adding the suffix *-la* to each word unless otherwise indicated.

Respect form: *obəwahanse, tamunnaanse, obətumaa*
Ordinary form: *oyaa, ohee, tamuse*
Vulgar form: *umbə, too*(sg.), *topi*(pl.)

Different noun forms within the same class may imply varying degrees of status. The nouns given as belonging to the ordinary form may have different nuances depending on the speaker's dialect. The word *oyaa* is common among the speakers of the standard dialect used in Colombo and its suburbs. However, the word *ohee* is more accepted in the southern province. While the word *tamuse* is considered as ordinary in some dialects, it may sound derogatory to a speaker of another dialect. The word *umbə* representing the vulgar form is very commonly used to imply intimacy in informal conversation and the use of the word *too* has the tendency of being derogatory. So, one should be extremely careful in handling second person pronouns in Sinhala. Second person pronouns, even of the ordinary form, are avoided in actual conversation, and names and titles or kinship nouns are more readily used.

Demonstrative pronouns: There are four demonstratives showing the type of proximity-anaphora distinction as given below:

Speaker proximal: *mee* 'this/these'
Addressee proximal: *oyə* 'that/those'
Distal from both speaker and addressee: *arə* 'that/those (over there)'
Distal from both speaker and addressee and anaphoric: *ee* 'that/those'

There are two distal demonstratives: one, *arə* 'that/those (over there)', indicates an object visible to both speaker and addressee or makes an anaphoric reference while the other, *ee* 'that/those', indicates an object not in sight or refers to a topic in the discourse.

These four deictic demonstratives are in attributive use, occurring initially in a sequence, without showing inflection for definiteness or number.

> *mee potə* 'this book'
> *oyə meese udə tienə leensuwə* 'that handkerchief over there on the table'
> *arə kalu usə miniha* 'that dark, tall man'
> *ee parənə kataawə* 'that old story'

Now, there are three sets of demonstrative pronouns corresponding to the deictic demonstratives given above. One set refers to inanimate nouns:

Singular	**Plural**
meekə 'this one'	*meewa* 'these ones'
ookə 'that one (by you)'	*oowa* 'those ones (by you)'
arəkə 'that one (distal)'	*arəwa* 'those ones (distal)'
eekə 'that one'	*eewa* 'those ones'

Another set refers to animate nouns standing for animals, and its members are used derogatorily when referring to human beings.

Singular
meka or *muu* 'this one'
ooka 'that one (by you)'
arəka or *aruu* 'that one (distal)'
eeka or *uu* 'that one'

Plural
muŋ 'these ones'
okuŋ 'those ones (by you)'
aruŋ 'those ones (distal)'
euŋ 'those ones'

Yet another set refers to human beings.

Singular
meyaa 'this person'
oyaa 'you'
arəya 'that person (distal)'
eyaa 'that person'

Plural
meyaala 'these persons'
oyaala 'you'
arəyəla 'those persons (distal)'
eyaala 'those persons'

Interrogative pronouns: Interrogative nouns represent a type of noun standing for a noun when its identity is unknown. Most interrogatives closely follow the form of members of deictic sets, showing similarity to them even in distribution.

There is a type of interrogative occurring attributively, resembling deictic demonstratives. *Koi* 'which' and *monə* 'what' are such interrogative demonstratives. They can be used with the interrogative marker *də* as follows:

koi kaamaree də 'which room'
monə paaṭə də 'what color'

Deictic-interrogative pronouns are classified into three categories as Inanimate, Animal and Human, following deictic-demonstrative pronouns.

	Demonstrative pronouns	**Interrogative pronouns**
Inanimate:	meekə 'this one'	mokə 'what one'/kookə 'which one'
	meewa 'these ones'	monəwa 'what ones'/
		koowa 'which ones'
Animal:	meka 'this one'	mokaa 'what one'/kooka 'which one'
	muŋ 'these ones'	monuŋ 'what ones'
Human:	meyaa 'this person'	kauru 'which person'
	meyaala 'these persons'	kauru 'which persons'
		(same as the singular form)

These interrogative pronouns are used with the interrogative marker *də* as follows:

kookə də hondə 'which one is better?'
monəwa də oonæ 'what do you want?'

Some of their singular forms can inflect for definiteness, taking indefinite forms. *Mokə* 'what (inanimate singular)', for example, usually takes the indefinite form in pronominal use as in *mokak də kiiwe* 'what did you say?'. The personal interrogative form *kauru* 'which person', which does not show inflection for number, on the other hand, appears as *kaudə* with the deletion of *ru* as in *kaudə giyee* 'who went?'.

There are some other sets of deictic and demonstrative nouns with varied ranges of distribution. Members of two such sets are introduced below.

Demonstrative pronouns	**Interrogative pronouns**
mehee 'here'	*kohee* 'where'
mehaa 'this way'	*kohaa* 'which way'

The interrogative *kohaa* that refers to direction is always used along with the dative form *-țə* and appears as in *kohaațə də giyee* 'which direction did he go?'.

Verbal nouns: Verbal nouns are nouns derived from verbs, denoting persons, actions or events. They inflect for case, number and definiteness. Verbal nouns denoting persons or agents of actions are formed by adding the ending *-nnaa* to a verbal stem:

liyə 'to write' > *liyannaa* 'person who writes or secretary'
marə 'to kill' > *marannaa* 'person who kills or butcher'
kiyə 'to say' > *kiyannaa* 'a person who says or speaker'
asə 'to listen' > *asannaa* 'a person who listens or listener'

By adding *-iimə* or *-illə* to a verbal stem, verbal nouns denoting actions are formed:

națə 'to dance' > *næțiimə, næțillə* 'dancing'
bani 'to scold' > *bæniimə, bænillə* 'scolding'
duwə 'to run' > *diwiimə, diwillə* 'running'
hoyə 'to look for' > *hewiimə, hewillə* 'looking for'

(First back vowels in the stem change into corresponding front vowels in this lexical process) They inflect for case, number and definiteness.

Another nominal form is derived by adding the ending *-um*.

națə 'to dance' > *næțum* 'dance'
bani 'to scold' > *bænum* 'scolding or criticism'
kadə 'to break' > *kædum* 'break or breakage'
rawə 'to frown' > *ræum* 'frown'

Compared with the former set of words with *-iimə* and *-illə*, the nominal forms with *-um* are more consolidated as nouns as shown by our glosses. *Næțum*, for example, is 'dance', not 'dancing'. In the same way, *kædum* is something that has been broken, not the act of breaking.

Another suffix, *-mənə*, is used in a similar way, though not so productively, to form verbal nouns denoting more concrete senses.

kiyə 'to say' > *kiəmənə* 'saying'
liyə 'to write' > *liəmənə* 'letter'
de 'to give' > *diimənə* 'giving or allowance'
hingə 'to beg' > *hingəmənə* 'begging'

One of the most productive ways of forming verbal nouns is adding the connective *ekə* to a verbal adjective. Verbal adjectives can be of past or non-past forms.

naṭə 'to dance' > *naṭənə ekə* 'dancing', *naṭəpu ekə* 'dancing (in the past)'
bani 'to scold' > *baninə ekə* 'scolding', *bænnə ekə* 'scolding (in the past)'
kaḍə 'to break' > *kaḍənə ekə* 'breaking', *kaḍəpu ekə* 'breaking (in the past) or what has been broken'
liyə 'to write' > *liənə ekə* 'writing', *liəpu ekə* 'writing (in the past) or what has been written'

There are some semantic differences between nominal forms derived from verbal adjectives depending on the transitivity of verbal stems. One such difference is related to non-past verbal adjectives. Verbal nouns derived from non-past transitive verbal adjectives take on another meaning in addition to the meanings given in the above glosses. They may take on instrumental meaning: for example, *kaḍənə ekə* may also denote an object used to break and *liənə ekə* may also mean an instrument for writing. This sense of instrumentality appears only with transitive verbal stems. Another difference can be seen with regard to past verbal adjectives. In this case, verbal nouns derived from intransitive stems only denote acts of V-ing as in *naṭəpu ekə* '(the) dancing (in the past)' and *bænnə ekə* '(the) scolding (in the past)' whereas verbal nouns derived from transitive stems may denote acts of V-ing or objects of V-ing as in *kaḍəpu ekə* and *liəpu ekə* (see the glosses above). (For a sketch of the development of *ekə* as a nominal marker, see Section 4.1 in this chapter).

2.2 Adjectives

Adjectives are classifiable into three classes as descriptive adjectives, nominal adjectives and verbal adjectives.

Descriptive adjectives are words denoting qualities or attributes of the nouns they modify. Examples: *loku* 'big' in *loku geḍiə* 'big fruit, *hondə* 'good' in *hondə lamea* 'good child', *unu* 'hot' in *unu waturə* 'hot water, *alut* 'new' in *alut potə*.

Nominal adjectives are words in nominal forms denoting a certain relationship to the nouns they modify. Examples: *mal* 'flower' in *mal peti* 'flower petals', *paḍi* 'stair' in *paḍi pelə* 'stair case', *mii* 'bee' in *mii pæni* 'bee-honey', *karattə* in *karattə roodə* 'cart wheel'. Unlike descriptive adjectives, these nominal adjectives can function as full-pledged nouns in other contexts. When used as adjectives, these nominal forms do not inflect for case, number or definiteness. They are treated as uninflected stem forms by traditional grammar, though appear identical with nominative plural forms.

Verbal adjectives are words denoting actions, states or experience of the objects modified by them. Examples: *natənə* 'dancing' in *natənə waturə* 'boiling water', *andənə* 'crying' in *andənə lamea* 'crying child', *hædenə* 'growing' in *hædenə gaha* 'growing tree', *uyənə* 'cooking' in *uyənə tel* 'cooking oil'. All the verbal adjectives given above are inflected for non-past tense as indicated by the non-past suffix -*nə*. They can also take past forms. As verbs they can take objects, too, as in *tanəlokə kapənə yantəree* 'grass cutting machine'.

Since nominal adjectives and verbal adjectives appear in identical forms respectively with nouns and verbs and since their respective boundaries remain unclear, only the first class, namely descriptive adjectives are considered as pure adjectives. In our examples given so far, adjectives occur attributively, i.e. preceding nouns. They also occur predicatively in clauses. In occurring predicatively, adjectives are obligatorily marked with the assertion marker -*i*. Thus the descriptive adjectives given above would appear as follows when they function as predicators in equational sentences.

gediə lokui 'The fruit is big.'
lamea hondai 'The child is good.'
waturə unui 'The water is hot.'

However, only vowel-final adjectives undergo this change. It does not apply to consonant-final adjectives even when occurring predicatively.

potə alut 'The book is new.'

Descriptive adjectives can be divided into several subclasses as qualitative adjectives, quantitative adjectives and demonstrative adjectives. The examples given so far represent the class of qualitative adjectives. Quantitative adjectives denote quantity of a noun or a descriptive adjective. They include cardinal numeral adjectives such as *ekə* 'one', *de* 'two', *tun* 'three' and *dolos* 'twelve', indefinite numeral adjectives such as *samaharə* 'some', *noek* 'various', *hungak* 'many' and *okkomə* 'all' and non-numeral adjectives such as *æti* 'enough', *madi* 'not enough' and *wædi* 'too much'.

Cardinal numeral adjectives are used as follows:

ekə gasak 'one tree'
demaupiyo 'parents'
teruwan 'triple gem'
dolosmaha pahanə 'twelve-month-lamp'

However, using cardinal adjectives productively is limited to the first number, *ekə* 'one'. Words with all other cardinal adjectives are idioms or set phrases. The ordinary way for a cardinal number, except for *ekə* 'one', to appear with a noun is to follow it. In Sinhala, numerals are governed by the animacy of nouns as mentioned earlier. With inanimate nouns, numerals appear, following them, just as nouns. Examples: *gas dekə* 'two trees', *gas tunə* 'three trees', *gas doləha* 'twelve trees'. With animate nouns, numerals follow the noun as a combination of numeral plus connective. Examples: *lamai dedena* 'two children', *lamai tundena* 'three children', *lamai dolosdena* 'tweleve children'.

Indefinite numeral or indefinite quantifying adjectives are used as follows:

saməharə guruwəru 'some teachers'
noek ayə 'various persons',
hungak denaa 'many people'
okkomə lamai 'all children'

Non-numeral quantitative adjectives modify a noun as in *madi hariə* 'the part inadequate' and *wædi koṭəsə* 'the portion that is too much'. They also follow descriptive adjectives to form adjectival phrases.

digə æti 'long enough'
usə madi 'not tall enough'
loku wædi 'too big'

Apart from descriptive adjectives, there is a category called demonstrative adjectives. The four deictic demonstratives earlier mentioned by way of introduction to demonstrative pronouns, namely *mee* 'this/these' (speaker proximal), *oyə* 'that/those' (addressee proximal), *arə* 'that/those (over there)' (distal but within sight) and *ee* 'that/those' (distal and anaphoric) are pronominal demonstrative adjectives. Related to them are interrogative adjectives such as *Koi* and *monə* 'which' and 'what'. *Koi* has several variants such as *ko, koo, kawə* and *kii*. They are used as follows:

koi taram 'what extent'
monə widihəṭə 'what way'
kohomə 'how', 'what way'
kookə 'which or what one'
kawədaa 'what day'
kiiak 'how much or how many'
kiiədə 'how much?'

2.3 Verbs

Verbs inflect for tense, i.e. past tense and non-past tense. They are identified morphologically by the final *-nəwa* in the non-past indicative form (e.g. *ka-nəwa* 'eat' and *duwə-nəwa* 'run'). These verbs are composed of a stem such as *ka-* 'eat' or *duwə-* 'run' and a sequence of inflectional suffixes such as *-nə-* (non-past) and *-wa* (indicative form).

On the basis of verbal stem shape, three classes of verbs are identifiable. They are called ə-ending stems, *i*-ending stems and *e*-ending stems. Such stem vowels are also named Thematic Vowels (Gair 1970).

Class 1 [Thematic Vowel -ə-] *balənəwa* 'look', *allənəwa* 'touch', *paraddənəwa* 'defeat'
Class 2 [Thematic Vowel -*i*-] *adinəwa* 'draw', *upədinəwa* 'be born', *æhindinəwa* 'pick'
Class 3 [Thematic Vowel -*e*-] *idenəwa* 'ripen', *igilenəwa* 'fly', *kaləkirenəwa* 'be dissatisfied'

Functionally a more important division is made by assigning verbs into three types as Active, Passive and Causative (De Silva 1960).[1] Every verb is considered to belong to one of these three types. This division should be considered as based on the morphemic composition of verbal stems rather than on semantic concerns (Gair 1970).

Active Type	**Passive Type**	**Causative Type**
andənəwa 'cry'	*ændenəwa* 'get to cry'	*andəwənəwa* 'cause to cry'
kapənəwa 'cut'	*kæpenəwa* 'get cut'	*kappənəwa* 'cause to cut'
hadənəwa 'make'	*hædenəwa* 'be made'	*hadəwənəwa* 'cause to make'

As seen through the foregoing examples, verbs belong to sets containing three types while sharing a common root morpheme. However, every verb does not belong to all three types. There are verbs belonging to one or two types. Accordingly, there can be three-type verbs, two-type verbs and single-type verbs. For example, look at the following set. The Passive type verb *wætenəwa* 'fall' has Causative type: *waṭṭənəwa* 'cause to fall'. Since there is no verbal form representing Active type in this set, it is a two-type verb. Another verb, *ædenəwa* 'creep' (Passive type) is a single-type verb, i.e. it does not have Active and Causative types.

A major semantic division is made between dynamic/active-type verbs and stative/processive verbs. Active- and Causative type verbs belong to the dynamic/active category whereas Passive type verbs, in general, fall into the stative/processive category. With regards to stem vowels or thematic vowels, the dynamic/active category includes ə-ending stems and *i*-ending stems while the stative/processive category incorporates *e*-ending stems. This division is important because it has a direct influence on the event and aspectual interpretation of clauses and makes explicit the role of the agent's control, intentionality and volition in event presentation. Observe this division in the following pair: *lamea naṭənəwa* 'The child is dancing' vs. *lameaṭə næṭenəwa* 'The child gets dancing impulsively'. It is generally accepted that an active-type verb takes a nominative subject to express a volitional meaning while a stative-type verb takes a non-nominative subject (in the above case, the dative -*ṭə*), to give a spontaneous meaning.

---

1. The original term used by De Silva (1960) is 'aspect'. Since the use of the term 'aspect' can be rather confusing as it is reminiscent of the verbal aspect (± perfective, etc.), I have chosen to use the term 'verb type' instead.

Another important division of verbs is based on the morphosyntactic distinction of transitivity. Virtually all verbs in the Passive type are intransitive, whereas verbs in the Active category include both intransitive and transitive verbs. Look at the verbs given under the Active type: *andənəwa* 'cry' (intra.), *kapənəwa* 'cut' (tran.). A transitive verb like *kapənəwa* 'cut' (=Active type) and *kæpenəwa* 'be cut' (=Passive type) makes a transitive-intransitive pair, manifest in *taatta gasə kæpuwa* 'Father cut the tree' vs. *gasə kæpuna* 'The tree got cut'. It is considered that a prototypical transitive verb, like *kapənəwa*, contains two arguments, subject and object, whereas a prototypical intransitive verb contains one argument, a subject as in the case of *andənəwa* 'cry' or an object as in the case of *kæpuna* 'get cut (past)'.

However, there are a considerable number of semi-transitive verbs that satisfy the condition of transitiveness in terms of the number of arguments but do not qualify morphosyntactically to be transitive for the objective argument does not appear as direct object. Verbs like *gahanəwa* 'hit', *baninəwa* 'scold', *salakənəwa* 'treat' and *wandinəwa* 'worship', for example, have their objects appearing in dative form as indirect objects morphosyntactically. On the other hand, many Passive-type verbs take non-nominative, instrumental or dative arguments while allowing them to remain grammatical subjects, thus creating a kind of semi-transitive constructions.

3. Minor word classes

3.1 Adverbs

Adverbs are words that modify verbs, adjectives, other adverbs or sentences. They are placed before the word they modify. This is an open class and includes several subclasses divided according to their functions:

Adverbs of time: *nitərə* 'always', *saməharəwitə* 'sometimes', *langədi* 'lately'
Adverbs of place: *wateetə* 'around', *udin* 'above', *yatin* 'below'
Adverbs of manner: *ibeetə* 'by chance', *nikam* 'without purpose', *poduwe* 'in common'
Adverbs of degree: *tikak* 'a little', *bohomə* 'very much', *wædipurə* 'over and above'
Adverbs of cause: *baen* 'out of fear', *tarəhen* 'out of anger', *aadəreetə* 'because of love'

Adverbs are also classifiable into several morphological subclasses as shown in the following list.

Adverbs formed by adding the instrumental -*in* or -*en* to an adjective. Examples: *tadin* 'strongly', *haien* 'loudly' or 'strongly', *ikmənin* 'quickly', *weegen* 'fast'

Adverbs formed by adding the dative suffix -*tə* to an adjective. Examples: *hondətə* 'well', *lassanətə* 'beautifully', *rasətə* 'tastily'

Adverbs with the stative suffix -*wə*. Examples: *manaawə* 'well', *hudəkalaawə* 'alone', *baləwatwə* 'strongly'

Adverbs with the emphatic suffix *-mə*. Examples: *wahaamə* 'immediately', *taniəmə* 'alone', *wenəmə* 'separately', *bohomə* 'very'

Adverbs not belonging to any of these morphological classes. Examples: *nikan* 'without purpose', *yantam* 'narrowly', *nitərə* 'always'.

This kind of morphological classification shows that there are two broad categories or characteristics of adverbs:

1. Forms derived or inflected from members of other grammatical categories like adjectives
2. Non-derived, primitive forms

Most of adverbs belong to the first category whereas a few adverbs represent the second category.

The boundary between adverbs and nouns is not always clear because there are many adverbs that inflect into case. Observe the following inflected forms related to a corresponding basic form:

Basic Form	Dative	Instrumental	Locative
adə 'today'	*adəṭə*	*adin*	–
ætulə 'inside'	*ætuləṭə*	*ætulen*	*ætule*
digə 'long'	*digəṭə*	*digin*	*digee*

Apart from the adverbs already described, there is another class of adverbs, namely complex adverbial phrases: These phrases are formed by combining an adjective or a noun with another nominal form to render an adverbial form. They function similarly to those simple adverbs mentioned above. Examples: *hondə tatwəen* 'in good condition', *pahat widiəṭə* 'in low standard', *gaambiirə wilaasen* 'in a solemn way', *guruwərəek hæṭiəṭə* 'as a teacher'. They can also be extended to form adverbial clauses like *miniha kataa kərənə widiəṭə* 'in the way he speaks' and *eyaa wædə kərənə hæṭiəṭə* 'according to the fashion he works'.

3.2 Particles

Particles are postpositional words that do not have inflections and are attached mainly to nominal constituents but also can appear with preceding verbal forms.

Case particles: They are used to define the relationship between nominal constituents and predicates. Examples: *atin* 'by' (agentive), *lawa* 'by' (causative), *ekkə* 'with', *indan* 'from', *atee* 'at' (possessive) or 'through'.

Predicative particles: They are mainly used after a noun phrase indicating its relationship to a predicator. Examples: *gænə* 'about', *waage* 'like', *wadaa* 'more', *pataa* 'every' (temporal), *gaane* 'every' (spatial), *tisse* 'throughout'.

Highlighting particles: *tamai* 'indeed', *mai* 'indeed or verily', *naŋ* 'as for', *mə* 'emphatically', *misak* 'except' or 'but', *wat* 'even'.

Conjunctive particles: They are used to conjoin two noun phrases or two clauses. E.g. *hari* 'or', *naŋ* 'if', *hæṭiəṭə* 'as', *turu* 'till', *taak* 'so far as', *hinda* 'because', *koṭə* 'when', *gamaŋ* 'while.

Discourse particles: They denote textual relationships. Mostly appearing at the beginning of a sentence, these particles connect the utterance with something that has been said or has happened previously. Examples: *itin* 'then', *aaet* 'again', *ærat* 'besides', *ehenaŋ* 'if so, then', *eet* 'but', *namut* 'but', *hæbæi* 'but (emphatically)'.

Interrogative particle: The interrogative particle *də* is used at the end of a sentence or phrase to form a question. Examples: *oyaa yanəwa də* 'Do you go?', *hondə də* 'Is that good?'

Quotative particles: The quotative particle *bawə* or *wagə* 'that' is added to the end of the verbal clause to make an indirect statement. The particle *kiəla* is used at the end of the quotation part in reporting direct speech while *lu* 'so they say' is added to the end of an utterance to indicate that the expressed information is hearsay.

Negative particles: *epaa* 'don't' (rejection or prohibition) is added to the end of a verb phrase or used independently to denote rejection or prohibition.

3.3 Affixes

Affixes are bound morphemes that are added to nominal and verbal bases and adjectives to modify these words. Prefixes and suffixes are the two types of affixes used to add lexical or grammatical meanings.

Nouns are modified by prefixes such as *anu-* as in *anukərənəyə* 'imitation', *awə-* as in *awəmaanə* 'contempt', *du-* as in *dusirit* 'bad habits', *apə-* as in *apəkiirtiə* 'disgrace', *awə-* as in *awətæn* 'displace'.

Adjectives are modified by prefixes such as *ati-* as in *atibayaanəkə* 'very scary', *a-* as in *apirisudu* 'unclean', *ni-* as in *nisaru* 'infertile', *nu-* as in *nupurudu* 'unaccustomed', *su-* as in *sumihiri* 'very sweet, *du-* as in *dubələ* 'weak, disabled'.

Verbs are modified by prefixes such as *warə-* as in *warənaganəwa* 'decline, conjugate', *pili-* as in *pilignnəwa* 'accept', *særi-* as in *særisarənəwa* 'go from place to place', *no-* as in *nowenəwa* 'not become' *parə-* as in *parədinəwa* 'be defeated', *hari-* as in *harigassənəwa* 'correct, amend', *piri-* as in *piriwarənəwa* 'surround'.

Some suffixes used to modify nouns are given below. They all denote lexical meanings.

-*məyə*: *pabəluməyə* 'made from beads'
-*wat* : *baləwat* 'having strength, strong'
-*mat*: *asirimat* 'wonderful'

-ikə: jaatikə 'belonging to nation, national'
-tənə: puraatənə 'related to the past, ancient'
-karu: lipikaru 'dealing with letters and documents, clerk'
-aanu: indiyaanu 'related to India, Indian'
-niə: diəniə 'beloved daughter'

By contrast, the following suffixes added to adjectives denote more grammatical meanings like comparative degree, superlative degree, nominal sense and diminutive sense.

-tərə: garutərə 'more respectable'
-təmə: priyətəmə 'most favorite'
-kəmə: duppatkəmə 'poverty'
-ə: burulə 'lightness'
-aa: hækiaa 'ability'
-taa: dubələtaa 'weakness'
-iti: singiti 'very small'
-iri: ændiri 'less dark or dim'

Some suffixes used to modify verbs were introduced before when illustrating verbal nouns in this chapter. For example, -nna (to denote agent or doer), -iimə, -illə, -um, and -mənə (to denote verbal actions or verbal objects) were mentioned. Some other suffixes used to modify verbal stems are: -nə (adjectival and instrumental senses), -pu and -unu (perfect adjectival sense).

Adjectival -nə: kaḍənə 'breaking'
                  puchchənə 'burning(trans.)'
Instrumental -nə: dawəṭənə 'wrapping'
                  (yaturu)liənə '(type)writer'
Active perfect adjectival -pu: kaḍəpu '(one) who broke' or '(thing) broken'
                                 puchchəpu '(one) who burnt' or '(thing) burnt'
Passive perfect adjectival -unu: kædunu 'broken'
                                 pichchunu 'burnt'

Some suffixes are redundant, i.e. do not effect any semantic or grammatical modification. However, they may denote rather formalized senses than base forms. The following examples are of this type:

-tu: dorəṭu 'door'
-at: sawənat 'ear'
-as: senehas 'affection'

Only examples illustrating derivational suffixes were given here. Inflectional suffixes will be described later in chapters concerning nouns and verbs.

3.4 Interjections

Interjections are words used to show a short sudden expression of emotion or some kind of mental attitude or response.

Expressing delight or triumph: *ohoo, hooia*
Expressing grief and sorrow: *ahoo, apoo, appoo, anee, appee, ammee*
Expressing surprise and wonder: *ahaa, aai, aau*
Expressing pain: *uui*
Expressing disappointment or rebuke: *ah, chah*
Expressing dislike and disgust: *chii, chih, chikee*
Expressing contempt or curse: *tuu, tuh, nodəkin*
Expressing helplessness or sympathy: *anee anichchan, ane aparaade*
Vocative expressions: *eei, ooi, aɖoo, bolə, bolaŋ*
Expressing appreciation: *shah, shook*
Expressing surprise, disbelief or direction: *annə, onnə, mennə*
Expressing agreement and affirmation: *saadu saadu*
Expressing assent: *hm, ou, ehemai*
Expressing the sign of stop: *hoow*
Expressing prohibition or warning: *haa haa*
Expressing deliberation: *əə…*

Some of them such as *chii chii, saadu saadu, hoow hoow, haa haa* are used in reduplication to make their effects emphatic.

4. Some noteworthy word classes

4.1 Numerals

The numeral system in Sinhala was naturalized from Old and Middle Indo-Aryan languages and gained its modern shape after independently developing on the island. Numerals inflect for case, number and definiteness. Some numerals have identical free and bound forms and some forms show several variants. All numerals have citation forms, but the actual use of numerals is found in combinations of base forms and various functional particles, suffixes, or measure words. The following list shows the citation forms and the corresponding base forms of numerals.

Number	Citation Form	Base form
1	*ekə*	*ekə*
2	*dekə*	*de*
3	*tunə*	*tun*

4	satərə or hatərə	hatərə
5	paha	pas
6	hayə	hayə
7	hatə	hat
8	aṭə	aṭə
9	nawəyə, naməyə	nawə, namə
10	dahayə	daha
11	ekolaha	ekolos
12	dolaha	dolos
13	daha tunə	daha tun
14	daha hatərə, daa hatərə	daa hatərə
15	pahalohə	pahalos
16	daasəyə	daasəyə
17	daahatə	daahat
18	daha aṭə	daha aṭə
19	daha nawəyə or naməyə	daha nawə or namə
20	wissə	wisi
30	tihə	tis
40	hatəlihə	hatəlis
50	panahə	panas
60	hæṭə	hæṭə
70	hættææwə	hættææ
80	asuuwə	asuu
90	anuuwə	anuu
100	siiyə	siyə
1,000	daaha	daas
10,000	daha daaha	daha daas
100,000	lakshəyə	lakshə
1,000,000	dasə lakshəyə or miliənəyə	dasə lakshə or miliənə
10,000,000	kooṭiə	kooṭi

The numeral compounds are formed by giving lower digits with reference to a specific standard, in that lower numerals follow decimal multiples or higher numerals, reflecting SOV characteristics (Lehmann 1978). According to this typological universal, the arrangement of numerals will be 10 + 1 = 11; 10 + 2 = 12; 10 + 3 = 13 and so on for a SOV language like Sinhala. However, a glance through the numerals in Sinhala will reveal that the order is not observed consistently in the "additive" pattern for "teen" numerals:

11 ekolaha '1 + 10'
12 dolaha '2 + 10'
15 pahalohə '5 + 10'

Laha or *loha* in these numerals denotes the decimal number. The formation of these numerals by having lower numerals immediately preceding the decimal number is quite contrary to the SOV pattern. Other numbers, 13; *daha tunə*, 14; *daha hatərə*, 16; *daasəyə*, 17; *daahatə*, 18; *daha aṱə* and 19; *daha nawəyə* have the SOV arrangement, lower numerals following the decimal number.

These aberrant patterns can be explained by having a look at their historical development. Sinhala, before changing to its consistent SOV patterning of today evidently shared some SVO characteristics with Classical Sanskrit. The construction of numeral compounds in Old Sinhala (and Classical Sanskrit), in contrast to the accepted SOV pattern, followed the order of placing the lower digit before the decimal number.

	Sanskrit	Old Sinhala	
11	ekaadasa	ekolos	'1+10'
12	dwaadasa	dolos	'1+10'
13	trayodasa	teles	'1+10'

This old tradition remains preserved in some numerals of modern Sinhala without undergoing much modification as seen above in case of words for 11, 12 and 15, and it changed to the normal SOV patterning in other numerals like 13, 14, 16, 17, 18 and 19. Thus, the inconsistency of the "additive" patterns of numerals in modern Sinhala is a remnant of the old system which showed a mixture with some SVO characteristics. (See Hundirapola 1975 for a detailed study of earlier and modern patterning in Sinhala)

What is more important in terms of linguistic practice is how numerals are combined with other elements to form numeral phrases. Ordinal numbers are formed by attaching the suffix -*wæni* to the base form of the numeral, except in the case of *ekə* (1). Examples: *dewæni* 'second', *tunwæni* 'third', *hatərəwæni* 'fourth'. The first number, *ekə*, takes the special form *paləmu*, a free form, or *palə-*, a bound form, when combining with the base form, making its ordinal number as *paləmuwæni* or *paləwæni*. By inflecting for case and number, an ordinal number can indicate a person: *paləmuwænia* or *paləwænia* 'first person', *dewænia* 'second person'.

When counting animals or humans, numeral-classifiers are added to numerals. The system of classifiers in Sinhala is neither complex nor elaborate. Nouns denoting things or creatures are classified according to the animate -inanimate dichotomy. Inanimate things do not take any classifier; numerals are directly placed after the noun as in *gas dekə* '(the) two trees', *kaar tunə* '(the) three cars' and *rupial paha* '(the) five rupees'. By contrast, the animate numeral classifier *denaa* is added to the base of the numeral before placing it after the noun. Examples: *yaaluo dedenaa* or *dennaa* '(the) two friends', *wanduro tundenaa* '(the) three monkeys' and *kurullo pasdenaa* '(the) five birds'. However, as the glosses indicate, all the forms given here have a definite sense.

This calls for a comment. In Sinhala, unmarked numeral forms are definite. To render them indefinite they should be followed by the indefinite marker *-ak* or *-ek*. Therefore, the English sentence 'There are five birds', for example, should be rendered in Sinhala as *kurullo pasdenek innəwa*. One can say *kurullo pasdenaa innəwa* only to mean 'The five birds are there'.

It is also interesting to note that humans and non-humans are categorized together by using the same classifier for counting, although they are distinguished in referring, as seen with regard to demonstrative adjectives. The only exception is the classifier *kenaa* attached to the numeral 'one' referring to humans. This is usually not used when the referent is an animal. Another noteworthy feature is that while numeral-classifiers or quantifiers appear in singular form, the common nouns immediately preceding these classifiers and quantifiers for that matter appear in plural form as in *gas dekə* '(the) two trees'(inanimate) and *kurullo pasdenek* 'five birds' (animate). Thus classifiers and quantifiers form a part of complex noun phrases.

Another complex numeral phrase consists of a common noun + "measure word" + classifier (inanimate). "Measure words" describe an object's weight, length, the area of land, the duration of time, etc., such as *raattal* 'pounds', *kilo* 'kilograms', *miitərə* 'meters', *akkərə* 'acres', *aurudu* 'years', *maasə* 'months' and *dawas* 'days'. They make quantifier phrases as follows:

paan raatal dekak 'two pounds of bread'
idam akkərə dahayak 'two acres of land'
aurudu pahak 'five years'

Instead of "measure words", some common nouns can be used as quantifiers. They make quantifier phrases as follows:

arakku bootal dekkak 'two bottles of Arrack'
baisikal kənteenərə dekak 'two containers of bicycles'
tee petti pahak 'five boxes of tea'

There are several quantifiers used to count the frequency of events, such as *warak*, *wataawak*, *særəyak* and *paarak*. They are used interchangeably as in *dewarak* 'two times', *tunwataawak* 'three times' or *passærəyak* 'five times'.

Another type of quantifier includes *keepəyak* 'several or a few', *saməharak* 'some' and *wagəyak* 'some'. These words are used to denote an amount or quantity that is indefinite or incomplete. Especially, *wagəyak* 'some' is used when not only the quantity but also the nature of the object is not clearly known. Usually they follow common nouns appearing in plural forms. However, *saməharak* 'some' can also precede a noun. *Keepəyak* 'several or a few' goes with inanimate nouns; when used with animate nouns it has to be combined with the animate classifier *denaa* or *denek*.

pot keepəyak 'several books'
guruwəru keepə denek 'a few teachers'
lamai saməharak 'some children'
saməharak gæænu 'some women'
minissu wagəyak 'some men'
lium wagəyak 'some letters'

These are non-enumerated quantifiers.

Coming back to numerals, when two consecutive numerals are used in indefinite form this expression denotes alternation between the two. Examples: *dekə tunak* 'two or three', *tunə hatərak* 'three or four'. The quantity denoted by such expressions may include a number close to the given numerals. Thus *dekə tunak* may, in fact, mean two, three or five.

Finally, the numeral *ekə* 'one' deserves special attention. While demonstrative expressions like *meekə* 'this one' (from *mee ekə*) obviously are related to the numeral *ekə*, it is not clear whether *ekə* itself in Modern Sinhala is a noun like 'one' in English.

Ekə can be modified by an adjective like *sudu ekə* 'white one' and *alut ekə* 'new one'. However, it cannot be modified by a demonstrative because it is lexically blocked by demonstrative nouns like *meekə* 'this one' and *arakə* 'that one'. It does not inflect for plural. That is, it still retains its singular sense. It cannot occur after a noun; so *puṭuwa ekə* 'the one chair' or *puṭuwak ekə* '(a) one chair' is unacceptable. To mean 'the one chair', the noun *puṭuwa* is adequate; to mean '(a) one chair', the numeral precedes the noun as *ekə puṭuwak*. However, the numeral can follow the noun when it is needed to indicate emphasis as in *puṭu ekak* '(a) one chair' or to indicate alternate senses as in *puṭu ekak hari dekak* '(a) one or two chairs'.

When an English singular noun is adopted in Sinhala, it is followed by *ekə* which functions as a nominal marker. E.g. *bas ekə* 'the bus', *ṭooch ekə* 'the electric torch'. This suggests that the noun *ekə* has developed as a nominalization expression in modern Sinhala. Another restriction for the use of *ekə* as a nominalization expression is that it can only be used with inanimate nouns: The expression *arə kalu usə ekə* 'that dark tall one' cannot be used in referring to a human being or an animal. This means that the noun *ekə* involves animacy. To say 'that dark tall one (is my friend)', *ekaa*, the animate form of *ekə*, should be used as in *arə kalu usə ekaa*. It can be used in definite or indefinite sense as in the following examples:

a. usə   ekaa   aawa
   tall one(anim.)   came
   'The tall one came.'

b. usə   ek-ek   aawa
   tall one-anim.INDF   came
   'A tall one came.'

Strictly speaking, *ekaa* is the masculine form. The feminine form is *ekii*. The acceptable way to indicate a female person is shown in (c).

    c.   usə ek-ii   aawa
        tall one-anim.female came
        'The tall one(female) came.'

Both the masculine and feminine forms are not polite expressions. They can only be used in informal/casual situations. The polite expression *kenaa* (definite), *kenek* or *ekkenek* (indefinite) doesn't have male/female distinction.

Ekə and its variants function as nominalization markers when they occur in the head position of the structures resembling relative clauses.

    d.   Ranjit gattə   ekə   ganan
        Ranjit buy.PT one expensive
        'The one Ranjit bought was expensive.'

    e.   Ranjit gattə   eewa ganan
        Ranjit buy.PT ones expensive
        'The ones that Ranjit bought were expensive.'

A relative clause occurs with a head noun without the involvement of *wh*-word or any other syntactic form. A concrete noun or a formal noun directly interferes in the formation of the relative clause.

    f.   mamə [Ranjit dunnə] potə kiəwə-nəwa
        I   Ranjit give.PT book read-IND
        'I am reading the book which Ranjit gave me.'

    g.   mamə [Ranjit dunnə] dee   kiəwə-nəwa
        I   Ranjit give.PT thing read-IND
        'I am reading what Ranjit gave me.'

    h.   mamə [Ranjit dunnə] ekə   kiəwə-nəwa
        I   Ranjit give.PT one read-IND
        'I am reading the one that Ranjit gave me'

As (g) and (h) show, we can replace *dee* with *ekə* conveying the same meaning. However, the two sentences are somewhat different in nuances to the native speaker. With *ekə* the content of the object clause becomes specific whereas *dee* does not specify the content.

It is clear that the noun *ekə*, which originated as a numeral doesn't remain simply numeral but has given rise to a nominal marker for the constructions resembling relative clauses. (For further illustrations see examples (38) and (39) in Chapter 10.)

4.2 Kinship terms

Sinhala kinship terms deserve special treatment because the family structures and the set of nouns and significations underlying them can be extended to the whole society. Kinship nouns are used widely and applied not only within the immediate family but also, in referring to or addressing, to the local community and to the whole linguistic community, perhaps even to the 'out-group' members of their community. First, look at the following representative list of terms (Most of them have alternative forms):

siiya, aata, atta, kiri-atta 'grandfather'
aachchi, attamma, kiri-amma 'grandmother'
tatta, appachchi, appa 'father'
amma 'mother'
lokutaatta, lokuappachhi, mahappa 'father's elder brother'
punchitaatta, baappa, kuḍappa 'father's younger brother'
loku nænda 'father's elder sister'
punchi nænda 'father's younger sister'
loku maama 'mother's elder brother'
punchi maama 'monther's younger brother'
loku amma, mahamma 'mother's elder sister'
punchi amma, kuḍamma 'mother's younger sister'
ayya 'elder brother'
malli 'younger brother'
akka 'elder sister'
nangi 'younger sister'
putaa 'son'
duwə 'daughter'
munuburaa 'grandson'
minibirii 'granddaughter'

Now observe commonalities among some terms and dissimilarities among some other terms. There are close affinities between father and his brothers in terms of nominal forms and their underlying obligations as seen below. On the other hand, there are obvious similarities between mother and her sisters.

tatta, appachchi, appa 'father'
loku taata, loku appachhi, mahappa 'father's elder brother'
punchi taata, baappa, kuḍappa 'father's younger brother'
≠ *loku nænda* 'father's elder sister'
≠ *pinchi nænda* 'father's younger sister'

amma 'mother'
loku amma, mahamma 'mother's elder sister'
punchi amma, kuḍamma 'mother's younger sister'
≠ *loku maama* 'mother's elder brother'
≠ *punchi maama* 'mother's younger brother'

Terms with similarities have their literal meanings in Sinhala: father's elder brother and younger brother are 'big father' and 'little father' respectively whereas mother's elder sister and younger sister are encoded as 'big mother' and 'little mother' respectively. The kinship system is based on the principle of equivalence of same-sex siblings. According to this principle, family members who are of the same sex and belong to the same sibling line are treated as the same. Two brothers are considered to be equivalent to the extent that if one has a child, that child treats not only his biological father but also his father's brother as father and applies the same term to them both, making the difference only as 'big' or 'little'. However, the father's sister, though on the same sibling line but because of the different sex, is identified not as mother but as aunt (*nænda*), the same term used to identify 'mother-in-law'.

The same principle applies to two sisters, where if either one bears a child both will be mothers, *loku amma/ mahamma* 'big mother' or *punchi amma/kuḍamma* 'little mother'. A mother's brother is different because of the difference in sex and will be an uncle (*maama*), which is identical with 'father-in-law'. Under this classificatory system, there is no need to expand the range of relationship terms. Instead, the scope of actual relationships to be identified by a term is wide. Several people are identified by one and the same classificatory term. Even people who do not belong to the immediate family are addressed and referred to by kinship terms like *ayya* 'elder brother', *akka* 'elder sister', *nangi* 'younger sister', *malli* 'younger brother', *nænda* 'aunt/mother-in-law' and *maama* 'uncle/father-in-law'. These terms reflect an attitude and a world view that enables speakers to apply a limited system to a wider world.

CHAPTER 5

Morphology

A clear understanding of the verbal system and of the nominal system of Sinhala is essential for gauging their place within the lexicon and the related morpholexical processes of the language. The long process of simplification of the verbal system has undergone from the Old Indian period to the present day is considered to be a major source of the gap between the colloquial language of Sinhala and its literary idiom. In fact, continuous transformations that have taken place within the verbal system have failed to make significant inroads into the literary or written language because they are not socially sanctioned among scholars in particular and within the writing tradition in general.

1. Verb morphology

Verbs are divided into three groups on morphological grounds. The three groups are identified as ə-ending stems, i-ending stems and e-ending stems. Mainly, the termination of the verb root is considered to be responsible for this classification. (In a strict sense, "root" is a term used to distinguish the underlying stem from its derived variants.) A root consists of non-past stem used for present and future senses and a past stem used for past tenses. The non-past indicative form is considered as the citation form. Based on the citation form, three types of conjugations are identified alongside with their three different stem-vowels.

Class 1, Stem-vowel - ə-: *balənəwa* 'look', *allənəwa* 'touch', *piinə-nəwa* 'swim'
Class 2, Stem-vowel - i-: *adinəwa* 'draw', *maninəwa* 'measure', *æhindinəwa* 'pick'
Class 3, Stem-vowel - e-: *idenəwa* 'ripen', *igilenəwa* 'fly', *kaləkirenəwa* 'be dissatisfied'

There are three lexical items in each verb form given above. Each verb ends in -*wa* (or -*a*) which is the suffix for indicative mood. This bound morpheme is one lexical item, and preceding it there is another bound morpheme, namely -*nə* which is the suffix for the present tense. What remains after separating these endings is the verb stem. A suffix or an ending is a morpheme whose lexical entry specifies a grammatical meaning. Hence they are limited in number. A stem is different from a suffix in that it contains a lexical meaning, and also different from a full verb in that it does not subcategorize another morpheme. Since both stems and suffixes are grammatical abstractions, they cannot exist independently as pronounceable units. Therefore, verb stems must be accompanied by suffixes to form useable verbal forms. This combination of stem plus suffix is called Inflection.

1.1 Inflectional morphology

Verbs inflect for tense. There are two tenses, non-past and past. In inflecting for past tense, just adding the past tense suffix -*u*- is not adequate. Some other changes occur in the formation of the past tense form from the citation form. These changes vary according to the verb class or conjugation type. Below I will describe the inflectional characteristics of verbs of each conjugation class.

Class 1, stem-vowel - *ə*-:
This verb class includes the widest range of verbs in the lexicon, both transitive and intransitive. Before adding the past tense suffix -*u*, the stem-vowel -*ə* is removed. The main inflectional characteristic of the past verb is vowel fronting. If the first vowel of the stem is a back vowel, i.e. *a*, *u* or *o*, it changes into the corresponding front vowel, i.e. *æ*, *i* or *e*. These changes are exemplified below. In the examples the present tense stem is separated from the suffixes by putting a hyphen (-) between them.

Stems of two syllables:

Citation	**Past tense**
andə-nəwa 'cry'	*ænduwa*
balə-nəwa 'look'	*bæluwa*
urə-nəwa 'suck'	*iruwa*
duwə-nəwa 'run'	*diuwa*
otə-nəwa 'wrap'	*etuwa*
gotə-nəwa 'weave'	*getuwa*
hoodə-nəwa 'wash'	*heeduwa*

If the first vowel is a front vowel, i.e. *æ*, *i* or *e*, only the final vowel of the stem will change.

æædə-nəwa 'connect'	*ææduwa*
dinə-nəwa 'win'	*dinuwa*
piinə-nəwa 'swim'	*piinuwa*
temə-nəwa 'wet'	*temuwa*

Stems of three syllables:

akulə-nəwa 'fold'	*ækiluwa*
sarəsə-nəwa 'decorate'	*særəsuwa*
udurə-nəwa 'uproot'	*idiruwa*
pupurə-nəwa 'split'	*pipiruwa*
osəwə-nəwa 'hoist'	*eseuwa*
gorəwə-nawa 'thunder'	*gereuwa*

Stems of four syllables:

ambərəwə-nəwa 'twist'   *æmbareuwa*
uturawə-nəwa 'boil'   *itireuwa*
poləmbəwə-nəwa 'tempt'   *peləmbuwa*

Class 2, stem-vowel - *i*-:
Verbs in this class can be either transitive or intransitive. There are several subclasses, each of them accommodating different changes.

One subclass has the following changes. First, the stem-vowel -*i* is removed before adding the indicative suffix -*aa*. This long vowel in final position is usually shortened in the colloquial language. Then, vowel fronting occurs. Finally, gemination of the final consonant takes place. This subclass, for example, includes the following verbs.

Citation	Past tense
adi-nəwa 'draw'	*ædda*
padi-nəwa 'paddle'	*pædda*
nægiṭi-nəwa 'get up'	*nægiṭṭa*
pirimadi-nəwa 'stroke'	*pirimædda*
lowi-nəwa 'lick'	*lewwa*

There is another subclass where the stem-vowel -*i* remains intact when the indicative suffix -*aa* (though it appears in shortened form) is added. As usual, vowel fronting occurs. However, gemination is optional. As the following examples show, gemination occurs only when the final consonant is an alveolar nasal. Otherwise, it is not called for.

ani-nəwa 'stick'   *ænna*
bani-nəwa 'scold'   *bænna*
ari-nəwa 'open or send'   *æria*
hiṭi-nəwa 'stop or stay'   *hiṭia*

Another subclass consists of verbs whose final consonant includes a pre-nasal. The stem-vowel is removed and the indicative suffix -*aa* (it appears shortened) is added. The pre-nasal component of the final consonant (cluster) is replaced with the corresponding full nasal consonant. Vowel fronting occurs.

andi-nəwa 'draw (pictures)'   *ænda*
bandi-nəwa 'tie or marry'   *bænda*
æhindi-nəwa 'pick'   *æhinda*
imbi-nəwa 'kiss'   *imba*
windi-nəwa 'feel or suffer'   *winda*

For another subclass, the stem-vowel is removed and the past tense prefix -*un* is added before the indicative mood termination -*aa*. Vowel fronting occurs.

nahi-nəwa 'perish'   næhuna
nawəti-nəwa 'stop'   næwətuna
warədi-nəwa 'mistake'   wærəduna
parədi-nəwa 'be lost'   pærəduna
puudi-nəwa 'bear fruit or flowers'   piiduna

Class 3, stem-vowel - *e*-:
There are several special features characteristic to conjugation class 3. One outstanding feature of this class is that all verbs belonging to it are intransitive. In terms of inflection, the past tense suffix -*un* is added to the verb stem, after the stem-vowel -*e* is removed.

Citation	Past tense
pæhe-nəwa 'ripen'	pæhuna
wæṯe-nəwa 'fall'	wæṯuna
ide-nəwa 'ripen'	iduna
gile-nəwa 'drown'	giluna
pipe-nəwa 'bloom'	pipuna
ere-nəwa 'sink in'	eruna
kærəke-nəwa 'spin'	kærəkuna
igile-nəwa 'fly'	igiluna
dilihe-nəwa 'shine'	diluhuna

As seen in the above examples, the vowel in the first syllable is *æ, i* or *e* and appears immutable, that is, there is no need for vowel fronting. However, there are a few exceptions like *kaləkirenəwa* 'be dissatisfied' where the past tense form remains with the back vowel as *kaləkiruna*.

Another peculiar feature of this class is that a large number of verbs belonging to it are derived forms from other verbs. In fact, nearly all the transitive verbs belonging to the other two main classes, Class 1 and 2, can be changed into intransitive verbs following the morphophonemic shape of the verbs of Class 3. What needs to be done is changing the stem-vowel -*a*- or -*i*- into -*e*- after this stem-shape and vowel fronting within the first syllable of the stem. The left column of the following list consists of verbs belonging to Class 1 and 2, which have been extracted from the examples already given therein whereas the right column shows their corresponding intransitive forms.

Transitive	Intransitive
sarəsa-nəwa 'decorate'	særəse-nəwa 'be decorated'
urə-nəwa 'suck'	ire-nəwa 'be sucked'
gotə-nəwa 'weave'	gete-nəwa 'be woven'
adi-nəwa 'draw'	æde-nəwa 'be drawn'
ari-nəwa 'open or send'	ære-nəwa 'open'
bandi-nəwa 'tie or marry'	bænde-nəwa 'be tied'

Evidently, this process turns the verb class into a derivational type. Some indigenous scholars, mainly for this reason, have argued that this verb class is not a conjugation class (Paranavitana 1956). However, we have to admit that there is a considerable number of independent verbs in this class. For example, verbs like *pipenəwa* 'bloom' and *ridenəwa* 'be painful' do not have corresponding transitive verbs in class 1 or 2.

Apart from working as an independent conjugation type, the scope of this verb class has expanded to embrace larger derivational and semantic functions. For instance, verbs derived from transitive verbs, after this type, are used as passive forms. Some verbs, including those derived from intransitive verbs of Class 1 and 2, assume reflexive or spontaneous meanings (See Chapter 9, Section 1). Examples:

Derived from transitives:

kapənəwa 'cut'	*kæpenəwa* 'cut' as in 'X cuts well'
arinəwa 'open'	*ærenəwa* 'open' as in 'The door opened when pushed'
ahanəwa 'listen'	*æhenəwa* 'hear' as in 'We can hear gun sounds from here'
hitənəwa 'think'	*hitenəwa* '(it) occurs (to me)'
toorənəwa 'select'	*teerenəwa* 'understand' as in 'X can understand one's feelings'

Derived from intransitives:

naṭənəwa 'dance'	*næṭenəwa* 'dance (impulsively)'
anḍə-nəwa 'cry'	*ænḍenəwa* 'be in tears'
nahi-nəwa 'perish'	*næhe-nəwa* 'perish by one's own fault'

Irregular verbs:
There are some verbs that do not follow the morphophonemic rules given above and hence do not fall into any of the verb classes described above. Almost all verbs of such peculiar inflectional character consist of one syllable, except a rare case with two syllables.

Citation	Past tense
ka-nəwa 'eat'	*kææwa*
ya-nəwa 'go'	*giaa*
naa-nəwa 'bath'	*nææwa*
gaa-nəwa 'smear'	*gææwa*
e-nəwa 'come'	*aawa*
de-nəwa 'give'	*dunna*
bo-nəwa 'drink'	*biiwa*
in-nəwa 'be'	*hiṭia*
gan-nəwa 'take'	*gatta*
kərə-nəwa 'do'	*kəlaa*

1.1.1 *Finite forms*

We have already considered the basic forms of the verb and how their inflections for present tense (or non-past tense) and past tense occur. It will be useful here to notice some difference between the indicative forms and another category of inflected forms that commonly occur in sentence final position. The examples we have described so far are those generally occurring at the sentence final position in Sinhala as a SOV language. More importantly, they have a specific location in time with respect to the time of 'speaking'. They are called Finite forms.

Apart from the past and non-past forms expressing the Indicative Mood, there are some other finite forms. The Imperative Mood, which expresses a command or a request, is one such form. Formally, the imperative form is made by adding the suffix *-nnə* to the end of the verb stem.

balə 'see' > *balannə*
adi 'draw or pull' > *adinnə*
hinæhe 'laugh or smile' > *hinæhennə*

However, since the Imperative Mood directly involves the second person or addressee, there are various forms employed to suit the context including the social status of participants and appropriate level of politeness. By adding *-pan* and *-piə*, two non-polite forms are made. While the former is frequently used in expressing intimacy in informal situations the latter form is generally used in a derogatory sense. Note that the stem-vowel *i* changes to *ə* in Class 2 verbs and that these imperative forms are not accepted for Class 3 verbs. For Class 3 verbs, there is a separate ending, *-an*, to render the imperative sense, whose adding to the stem changes the stem-vowel *-e* to *-i*.

-pan, -piə:	*baləpan, baləpiə* 'see'	(Class 1)
-pan, -piə:	*ædəpan, ædəpiə* 'draw or pull'	(Class 2)
-an:	*wæṭian* 'fall', *næmian* 'bend'	(Class 3)

The organization of imperative forms can be viewed more comprehensively in the light of some uncommon characteristics inherent in them. For instance, there are special imperative forms for some verbs, though such occurrences are very rare. Examples:

Citation	verb stem	Imperative form
enəwa 'come'	*e-*	*wareŋ*
yanəwa 'go'	*ya-*	*pələyan*

Another characteristic which is widely observable with regard to imperative forms is that they have plural forms. This phenomenon is conspicuous because number remains an inflectional category attached to the noun phrase in Sinhala, and verbs usually do not inflect for it. *-lla* and *-w* are imperative plural forms.

Singular	Plural	
balǝpan	balǝpalla	'see'
ædǝpan	ædǝpalla	'draw or pull'
balǝpiǝ	balǝpiaw	'see'
ædǝpiǝ	ædǝpiaw	'draw or pull'
wæṭian	wæṭialla	'fall'
næmian	næmialla	'bend'

Another uncommon feature of the Imperative Mood verbs is related to iconicity, i.e. their correspondence between phonological appearance and semantic implications. For instance, the verbal stem alone is used as the most non-polite form of demand. This clearly breaks a rule we mentioned earlier, that is, a verbal stem, being a bound morpheme, cannot stand independently. However, this breach goes to illustrate another rule, i.e. symbolism. The stem of a verb is its crude form that remains to be fleshed out with the help of endings. Using a stem without any ending implies the directness of a demand and derogatoriness of expression. The following stems from Class 1 and the irregular group are good examples: *balǝ* 'look', *gaha* 'hit', *kapǝ* 'cut', *gan* 'take'. That verbs of Class 2 and 3 do not admit of this use seems to be a phonological restriction. Class 2 verbs can be converted into this particular imperative use by a slight change in the stem, as in *hiṭu* and *anu* from the stems *hiṭi-* and *ani-* respectively. Periphrastic imperatives, on the other hand, make the exact opposite of the crude form. Periphrastic expressions formed by combining verbal infinitives and an appropriate adjective such as *hondǝ* 'good' serve as honorifics of the highest level. Example: *yannǝ hondai* 'Be pleased to go.'

Another uncommon aspect can be observed in relation to the usage of imperatives. The present tense Indicative Mood or citation form is used as a direct or non-polite imperative. It also has a plural form. Thus *kanǝwa* 'eat', *enǝwa* 'come' and *innǝwa* 'be' appear in imperative contexts in the following examples.

Citation	Imperative (sg.)	Imperative (pl.)
kanǝwa 'eat'	ookǝ kanǝwa 'Eat that'	ookǝ kanǝwǝlaa 'Eat that'
enǝwa 'come'	mehe enǝwa 'Come here'	mehe enǝwǝla 'Come here'
innǝwa 'be'	ohomǝ innǝwa 'Be there'	ohomǝ innǝwǝla 'Be there'

The other peculiar feature that can be stated for imperatives is that not only second persons but third persons and, depending on the interpretation, even first persons become the affectees of the Imperative Mood. Permissive forms, for instance, which are considered as an indirect form of imperative, take third person nouns, animate or inanimate, as their subjects. There are three permissive form suffixes: *-dden*, *-we* and *-den*. The first one, *-dden*, is directly added to the verb stem; *-we* is added to the past tense of verbs; *-den* is suffixed to the past participial adjective. All three forms with the following verbs, for example, can be used to mean 'Let him look', 'Let him pull' and 'Let it fall'.

Citation	*-dden*	*-we*	*-den*
balənəwa 'look'	*baladden*	*bæluwaawe*	*bæluwəden*
adinəwa 'pull'	*adidden*	*æddaawe*	*æddəden*
wæṭenəwa 'fall'	*wæṭedden*	*wæṭunaawe*	*wæṭunəden* or *wæṭichchəden*

Hortative forms are considered to be associated with the Imperative Mood as they may express a request or an intention (Abhayasinghe 1973). However, they are different from the Indicative Mood in that they take the first person plural noun as their grammatical subject. Hortative forms are obtained by affixing *-mu* to the verb stem as in the following examples.

Citation	Hortative form
balənəwa 'look'	*baləmu* 'Let's look'
adinəwa 'pull'	*adimu* 'Let's pull'
wæṭenəwa 'fall'	*wæṭemu* 'Let's fall'

The first person plural is always used with hearer inclusive reference in the Hortative Mood. It might be because of this inclusive sense, which adds an overtone of request, advice or recommendation to the overall expression extending to the addressee that hortative forms are regarded as a subclass of the Imperative Mood.

Taking all these instances into consideration one can say that the Imperative mood including permissive forms and hortative forms affects participants of all three persons.

The Optative Mood is yet another structure considered to be related to the Imperative Mood and realized in finite forms. Verbs expressing a wish (or a curse), a will or a desire with the implication of futurity are regarded to be in the Optative Mood. The optative suffix *-waa* is added to the verb stem and the stem-vowel is doubled to express a wish.

Citation	Optative (-waa)
balənəwa 'look'	*balaawaa*
dakinəwa 'see'	*dakiiwaa*
penenəwa 'be seen'	*peneewaa*

There is an additional suffix *-iə* to denote a curse. In this case, however, since a curse generally occurs against the wish of a participant, the verb form (citation form) should be changed into intransitive/involitive form before adding the suffixes. (cf. examples for the optative *-waa* above)

Citation	Optative (-waa)	Optative (-ia)
kaḍənəwa 'break'	kæḍeewaa	kæḍiə
hæppenəwa 'strike against'	hæppeewaa	hæppiə
wæṭenəwa 'fall'	wæṭeewaa	wæṭiə

According to these examples, vowel fronting in the first syllable and vowel doubling in the second syllable (stem-vowel) occur when -waa is added; when -iə is added, the stem-vowel is removed in addition to the vowel fronting.

Optative forms frequently used for greetings in letter-writing, public broadcasts and addresses such as *sæpə weewaa* 'May you be healthy', *jayə weewaa* 'Be victory with you' and *subə udææsənak weewaa* 'Good morning' have compelled some scholars to identify *weewaa* as a separate optative affix. However, a close examination will reveal that the first part of these expressions comprises a noun or an adjective, and the final part is obtained by adding the affix *-waa* to the verb stem *we* 'be or become'. Accordingly, there is no need to establish a separate morpheme.

The expression of will or desire is realized with another form of the Optative Mood for which the ordering of subject and finite verb is different. As this form always appears with first person pronouns it may be regarded as a Volitional Optative. Volitional optative forms are obtained by affixing *-nnaŋ* to the verb stem, as in the following examples.

Citation	Volitional Optative
balənəwa 'look'	balannaŋ 'I'll see' or 'We'll see'
adinəwa 'pull'	adinnaŋ 'I'll pull' or 'We'll pull'
wæṭenəwa 'fall'	wæṭennaŋ 'I'll fall' or 'We'll fall'(pretend to fall)

A noteworthy feature of this form is that its subject may be first person singular or plural. Either way, it will have hearer exclusive reference, in contrast to the Hortative Mood. This exclusiveness is responsible for the volition on the part of the subject. By using this form, even an intransitive/involitive verb (Class 3) can be converted into the volitional sense as in *wæṭennaŋ* 'I'll/we'll fall (pretend to fall)' above.

Another finite form, the Inferential Mood, always expresses futurity, giving a sense of tentativeness to the action. The grammatical subject, in general, is a second person or third person pronoun or a noun, that is, the speaker is exempted from the responsibility over the action. The two inferential suffixes are *-i* and *-wi*. The former can be directly attached to the verb stem whereas the latter joins the stem with the stem-vowel doubling.

Citation	-i	-wi
balənəwa 'look'	balai	balaawi 'may/might look'
adinəwa 'pull'	adii	adiiwi 'may/might pull'
wæṭenəwa 'fall'	wæṭei	wæṭeewi 'may/might fall'

Note that the same verb *wæṭenəwa* 'fall' remains in the involitive form here due to the non-involvement of the speaker (cf. the Volitional Optative form above).

For expressing surprise and unexpectedness towards the action, the usual selection is the Exclamatory Mood. The suffix -*pi* is used for verbs in Class 1 and 2, and -*chchi* for verbs in Class 3.

Citation	-*pi*	-*chchi*
balənəwa 'look'	*baləpi*	---
adinəwa 'pull'	*ædəpi*	---
wæṭenəwa 'fall'	---	*wæṭichchi*

The vowel fronting in the first syllable is obligatory for Class 2 and 3 verbs.

So far we have examined inflected forms of verbs realized through the suffixes of termination. They can be considered as finite forms of verbs with some independent status. We have also seen that except the basic forms of past tense and non-past tense, all finite forms have to do with the categories of person and/or number. Some of them may even represent a speech level such as politeness.

Naturally verbal forms need not occur in sentence final position. They can occur sentence-initially or in the middle of a sentence. For instance, participial, conditional and infinitive forms fall into this category. They are non-finite not only lineally but even as regards time and consequently have to depend on the finite verb for location in time. In the next section, inflection suffixes for non-finite forms are briefly considered.

1.1.2 *Non-finite forms*

Verbs are inflected into non-finite forms through non-finite or connective suffixes. They include the adjectival forms -*nə* and -*ə*, the focus form -*nne* and -*e*, the conditional forms -*tot* and -*ot*, the concessive forms -*tat* and -*at*, the temporal forms -*ddi*, -*hamə*, the perfect participial form -*la*, the perfect adjectival -*pu* and -*chchə*, the reduplicated form and the infinitive form -*nnə*. The following list shows how the stems of the three main verb classes attach those non-finite inflectional suffixes with an inherent tense distinction.

	Non-finite inflectional forms		
	Class 1	**Class 2**	**Class 3**
Stem:	*kapə-*	*adi-*	*wæṭe-*
Adjectival forms:			
Non-past -*nə*	*kapənə*	*adinə*	*wæṭenə*
Past -*ə*	*kæpuə*	*æddə*	*wæṭunə*
Focus forms:			
Non-past -*nne*	*kapanne*	*adinne*	*wæṭenne*
Past -*e*	*kæpue*	*ædde*	*wæṭune*
Conditional forms:			
Non-past -*tot*	*kapətot*	*aditot*	*wæṭetot*
Past -*ot*	*kæpuot*	*æddot*	*wæṭunot*

Concessive forms:

Non-past -tat	kapətat	aditat	wæṭetat
Past -at	kæpuat	æddat	wæṭunat

Temporal forms:

Non-past -ddi	kapaddi	adiddi	wæṭeddi
Past -hamə	kæpunəhamə	æddəhamə	wæṭunəhamə

Perfect participial forms:

Base form:	kapə	ædə	wæṭi
-la	kapəla	ædəla	wæṭila

Perfect adjectival forms:

-pu, -chchə	kapəpu	ædəpu	wæṭichchə
Reduplicated form:	kapə kapaa	ædə ædaa	wæṭi wæṭii

Infinitive form:

-nnə	kapannə	adinnə	wæṭennə

For adding non-finite suffixes, first we have to identify the verb stem form of verbs. The stems may be easily determined from the basic, inflected forms of the non-past tense and past tense that we are already familiar with. The present tense indicative form or citation form without the finite termination -nəwa is identical with the stem, as in kapə 'cut' (Class 1), adi 'pull' (Class 2), wæṭe 'fall' (Class 3). For the past tense, however, it will be useful to identify the past tense base leaving out the past indicative terminations. Thus we get the corresponding past tense bases as kæpu, æddu and wæṭu. By affixing different affixes to these bases, non-finite inflectional forms are obtained. When verbs of Class 3 inflect for past tense, some changes occur, like geminating of the consonant of the final syllable.

Though there is a morphological distinction of non-past and past tenses, as already mentioned, non-finite forms do not bear non-past and past meanings independently. In actual use, they have to depend on finite clauses to get such temporal senses. Conditional and concessive non-past tense forms are rather restricted to Literary Sinhala, and when used in Colloquial Sinhala they generally become part of idiomatic expressions. Temporal forms of the non-past tense are used to denote events of simultaneous occurrence while those of the past tense may be associated with non-simultaneous or temporally prior occurrences.

Some forms, though given here as non-finite, evidently have properties sharing with finite forms. For example, focus forms and perfect participial forms occur in finite clauses as well as in non-finite clauses in Sinhala.

There are some phonological combinatory rules, called sandhi, for euphoniously admitting suffixes, a description of which is provided later (See Section 3).

Inflection of some irregular verbs into perfect participial form, past adjectival form and perfect adjectival form occurs as follows.

Citation	Perfect participle	Past adjective	Perfect adjective
ka-nəwa 'eat'	kaala	kææwə	kaapu
ya-nəwa 'go'	gihin	giə	giəpu
naa-nəwa 'bath'	naala	nææwə	naapu
gaa-nəwa 'smear'	gaala	gææwə	gaapu
e-nəwa 'come'	æwit	aawə	aapu
de-nəwa 'give'	diila	dunnə	diipu
bo-nəwa 'drink'	biila	biiwə	biipu
in-nəwa 'be'	indəla	hiţiə	hiţəpu
gan-nəwa 'take'	aran	gattə	gattə

Although the past adjective and the perfect adjective are used interchangeably, the latter sounds more colloquial.

1.2 Derivational morphology

There are two derivational suffixes whose presence is very important for the verbal system. The passive/intransitive -e and causative -wə are these suffixes. Adding each to a verbal root makes a different verb stem. In the case of the former, the new verb form is born after the composite structure undergoes a morphological process while admitting the suffix. The derivation of the passive from the active is similar to the formation of -e- ending stems (Class 3) from the stems of Class 1 and 2 with the stem-vowel -a- or -i-, as described before. In adding the causative suffix -wə, the elision of the final vowel and consonant assimilation occur for some verb roots.

Now we have three verbal forms with three separate verb stems sharing a common root morpheme. While one of them (active from) is identical with the original verbal root, the two others (passive and causative) are derived forms. However, there is another independent form which is obtained by passivizing the causative form, in addition to the passive form directly derived from the active form. Functionally, the causative-passive form behaves in a similar way to the passive. Therefore some scholars prefer to define the Sinhala verbal system as a three-way distinction (De Silva 1960; Gair 1970). However, morphologically, the causative-passive needs to be distinguished. According to some scholars, the causative passive needs to be properly treated even in a syntactical observation (De Abrew 1963). All available forms for the selected verbs are given below:

Active form	Passive form	Causative form	Causative-passive form
balənəwa 'look'	bælenəwa	baləwənəwa	bæləwenəwa
kapənəwa 'cut'	kæpenəwa	kappənəwa	kæppenəwa
adinəwa 'pull'	ædenəwa	addənəwa	æddenəwa
--- 'fall'	wæţenəwa	waţţənəwa	wæţţenəwa
naţənəwa 'dance'	næţenəwa	naţəwənəwa	næţəwenəwa

There may be verbs lacking some forms. For instance, some active forms do not have passive forms. Irregular verbs like *kanəwa* 'eat', *bonəwa* 'drink' and *yanəwa* 'go' are such verbs without passive forms. In such cases, the usual selection is causative-passive. There are some cases that even if corresponding forms exist, they are not in actual use. The passive of 'dance', for example, is in less use. Instead, the causative-passive is preferred.

When a concatenation of suffixes occurs, the order is: first [causative], and then [passive]. The result is [causative-passive]. The opposite is not allowed. Some verbs have double suffixation. What is meant by 'double suffixation' is the occurrence of the same suffix for the second time. This is not uncommon for causative verbs when the causative morpheme becomes obscured after consonant assimilation. Observe the verbs *kappənawa* 'cause to cut', *addənawa* 'cause to pull' and *waṭṭənawa* 'cause to fall' in the list given above. When the suffix -*wə*- is not overtly seen or heard, speakers are tempted to add the suffix again. Subsequently the new forms *kappəwənəwa*, *addəwənəwa* and *waṭṭəwənəwa* have appeared. Verbs born from this kind of double suffixation are not considered as a separate derivation.

The active-passive morphological distinction can be introduced as an important characteristic of verb morphology in Sinhala. Verbs are divided into volitive, i.e. verbs expressing actions that are performed intentionally by an animate agent, and involitive verbs, i.e. verbs denoting events occurring without active participation of an agent. While active or causative verbs are used to express volitional actions, passive forms and causative-passive forms become instrumental in expressing involitive events. The latter type of forms is widely used in a range of construction types called 'impersonal', 'inactive' or 'processive'.

2. Noun morphology

Nouns divide into two main classes, as animate and inanimate. This dichotomy is pervasive in noun morphology, bringing out two types of affixes for all categories. Affixes are added to the base form of a noun, which may be simple or derived. A simple base may easily be identified by looking at a nominal compound which includes that noun. The first member of a compound is always identical with the base of the noun. Take the nominal *koṭia* 'tiger', for example, and look at a compound made from it like *koṭi waligəyə* 'tiger's tail'. The first member of it, *koṭi*, is the noun stem.

2.1 Nominal inflections

Nouns inflect for case, number and definiteness. Their inflection is governed by the animate/inanimate distinction. Depending on which class a member belongs to, the number of cases it is allowed to take is different. Further, when the base is animate, the feminine/masculine distinction has to be taken into consideration in some cases.

The range of inflectional cases include the nominative, accusative, dative, instrumental, ablative, genitive, locative and vocative. These case distinctions are expressed by suffixes. For the inanimate class, there are only four cases: nominative, dative, instrumental and locative. Animate nouns, on the other hand, inflect for six cases: nominative, accusative, dative, ablative, genitive and vocative. Members of the inanimate class do not inflect for the accusative. The instrumental is generally selected for inanimate nouns. The genitive is exclusive to animate nouns whereas the locative is exclusive to inanimate nouns. The vocative is generally taken by animate nouns, though it is not relevant syntactically.

The category of number appears as singular and plural. When expressing plurality referring to an entity or when used as part of a numeral phrase, a noun takes the plural form. The gender distinction of feminine/masculine affects only singular suffixes. Nominal forms may not contain a discrete morpheme indicating number. In such cases number information appears fused with case information. However, there is no concord between subject NP and verb in terms of number.

The category of definiteness appears as definite and indefinite. As for the definiteness, there is no separate suffix. When nominals appear unmarked they denote definiteness. There are two suffixes to mark indefiniteness: -ak and -ek. Animate nouns take -ak and -ek while inanimate nouns only take -ak. Most animate nouns denoting male members take -ek, and most animate nouns denoting females take -ak. When a nominal inflects for both categories, [definiteness], i.e. [–definite], and [case], the acceptable order is [definiteness]-[case].

The following list shows suffixes for the nominative, which is also called direct case as it denotes both grammatical subject and object relations. The suffixes differ not only according to the animate/inanimate distinction of the base but also along the gender line.

	Singular	**Plural**
Animate (mas.):	a, aa	o, u, laa
Animate (fem.):	ə	o, u, laa
Inanimate:	ə, ee	wal, n, ɸ

Examples:
Animate (mas.):

gowi 'farmer'	gowia	gowio
nari 'fox'	naria	nario, nari
daru 'child'	daruwa	daruo
wasu 'calf'	wassa	wasso
horə 'thief'	horaa	horu
æt 'elephant'	ætaa	ættu
raaləhaami 'constable'	raaləhaami	raaləhaamilaa 'constables'

Animate (fem.):
nili 'actress'   nilia   nilio
gaaikaa 'singer'   gaaikaawə   gaaikaao
keli 'lass'   kellə   kello
den 'cow'   denə   dennu
duu 'daughter'   duwə   duula (laa)
guruwərə 'teacher'   guruwəriə   guruwərio

Inanimate:
gas 'tree'   gasə   gas
paarə 'road'   paarə   paarəwal
puṯu 'chair'   puṯuə   puṯu
kalə 'pot'   kalee   kalə
koḍi 'flag'   koḍiə   koḍi
dorə 'door'   dorə   dorəwal
kandə 'trunk'   kandə   kandaŋ

There are a considerable number of nouns that appear in singular or plural form without any suffixes added. Most of them expressing the nominative with a zero morpheme (ɸ) belong to the inanimate category. However, they can be found in the animate category, too. For example, the following singular forms of kinship nouns are identical in form with their stems: *amma* 'mother', *taatta* 'father', *maama* 'uncle', *nænda* 'aunt'. The following plural forms of animate (non-human) nouns are identical with their stems: *nari* 'foxes', *koṯi* 'tigers', *harak* 'oxen'. The following inanimate nouns have identical forms for the singular and the stem: *raṯə* 'country', *baḍə* 'stomach', *ændə* 'bed', *paarə* 'road' whereas the following inanimate nouns are identical with the stem in the plural: *gas* 'trees', *puṯu* 'chairs', *ænə* 'nails', *kaḍu* 'swords', *ganaŋ* 'numbers'.

Another fact to be noted is that the plural suffix -*laa* mostly appears with kinship nouns, status nouns, pronouns, and proper nouns.[1] The plural forms given in the following examples may mean genuine plurality, as in 'more than one mother', or inclusive plurality, as in 'mother and others'.

Kinship nouns:
ammalaa 'mothers', *taattəlaa* 'fathers', *nangilaa* 'younger sisters', *mallilaa* 'younger brothers', *putaalaa* 'sons' and *duwəla* or *duula* 'daughters'

Status nouns:
mahattealaa 'gentlemen', *noonalaa* 'madams', *səərlaa* (an honorific for males), *æmətitumaalaa* 'honorable ministers'

---

1. The long vowel in the termination will often appear short in accordance with the phonological rule given in Chapter 3.

Pronouns:
oyaalaa, tamuselaa, umbəlaa, oheelaa, obətumaalaa, tamunnaanselaa, all of which are second person pronouns with varied degrees of respect or politeness.
Proper nouns:
Sarathlaa, Cyrillaa, Sunilla, Silvalaa   (in each case '... and others')

In Sinhala the nominative or direct case serves as the citation form. After the direct case, several oblique cases are identified for both animate and inanimate bases. The number of oblique cases can be reduced to five for the animate class whereas it remains three for the inanimate class since inanimate nouns do not inflect for the accusative and the vocative cases.[2] The accusative, unlike other cases, is an optional category.

The simplest way to identify a case suffix in synchronic terms: take a case form, i.e. an inflected form, and remove the citation form, i.e. the nominative singular, from it. What remains is the case suffix. Under this system, there is no need to establish a separate base form as introduced earlier.[3] Even the nominative singular may be considered as a form with a zero morpheme. Following this method, we may recognize six case categories with separate case suffixes including their variants. The set of suffixes thus recognized are given below.

Case suffixes

Case	Animate		Inanimate	
	Singular	Plural	Singular	Plural
Nominative	ɸ	-o/-u	ɸ	ɸ/-wal
Accusative	-wə	-nwə/-unwə	---	---
Dative	-ʈə	-nʈə	-ʈə	-wələʈə/ -walwələʈə
Instr/Abl	-geŋ	-ngeŋ	-en/-in	-wəlin/ -walwəlin
Gen/Loc	-ge	- nge	-ee	-wələ/ -walwələ
Vocative	-ee/-oo	- ne/-nee	---	---

---

2. Though there are eight cases, counting all together. Some of them are specific either to the animate bases or the inanimate bases. Since the members of the two pairs, ablative-cum-instrumental and genitive-cum-locative, are in complementary distribution for animate and inanimate bases, we can treat each pair as one case.

3. This method contrasts with the conventional thinking of extracting the base form. According to the conventional way, there is a separate base form identical with the first lexical member of a compound, as exemplified at the beginning of this section.

It must be noted that some of the oblique case suffixes have free variants. It must also be admitted that the case description given above is a somewhat oversimplified version of facts. Especially it would seem so as long as we rely upon the traditional concept of the noun as consisting of a base form and a suffix. If we accept the traditional way of establishing a base form corresponding to each inflected form, we need to establish a larger number of case affixes. The following table provides a guide to the case suffixes as admitted by base forms.

Case suffixes admitted by base forms

Case	Animate		Inanimate	
	Singular	Plural	Singular	Plural
Nominative	-aa/-a	-o/-u/-laa/ɸ	-ə/ɸ/-ee	-ɸ/-wal
Accusative	-aawə/-awə/ -wə	-anwə/-unwə	---	---
Dative	-aaʈə/-aʈə/ -ʈə	-anʈə/-unʈə	-ʈə/-əʈə/eeʈə	-wəlaʈə/ -walwəlaʈə
Instr/Abl	-aageŋ/-ageŋ/ -gen	-angeŋ/-ungen	-en/-in/-eken	-wəlin/ -walwəlin
Gen/Loc	- aage/-age/ -ge	- ange/-unge	-ee,-ə	-wəla/ -walwəla
Vocative	-ee/-oo	- ane/-unee	---	---

There arises another complexity from this system since sometimes there are different bases derived according to gender. Feminine nominal bases derived from simple bases take different forms, and they have to admit different suffixes for some cases. If we consider the gender difference in terms of allomorphy, we may recognize the following gender allomorphs: the nominative singular -ə, accusative -əwə, dative -əʈə, ablative -əgen and genitive -əge.

We have seen before that nouns inflect for definiteness. Animate masculine singular nouns may be marked with -ek and inanimate singular nouns with -ak, though there are some exceptions. Animate feminine bases will have either -ak or -ek. These indefinite markers will be added to bases before the accusative -wə, dative -ʈə, ablative/ instrumental -gen/-in or genitive/locative -ge/-e. The different allomorphs in each case feature are determined by the properties of animacy, gender, number and definiteness. Mainly, the animate/inanimate distinction of nouns can be seen to be made on the base of these allomorphs.

Finally, it must be noted that we have described case suffixes only to the extent that they will explain the facts related to inflectional morphology. In Sinhala there are some other means of expressing case, such as postpositions and particles to which no attention was paid here. Instead, it will be clear from the foregoing account that cases express various properties such as animacy, gender and number, apart from their primary function of denoting syntactic and semantic relations such as the nominative and the accusative.

2.2 Nominal derivations and word formation

Apart from the inflectional suffixes described so far, there are other suffixes in the language that are added to nominal bases and verbal stems to form some other words. This section deals with morphological processes involved in nominal and adjectival derivations and word-formation processes engaged in combining lexical bases.

2.2.1 *Affixation*

Affixation is extensively used to create new words. In this process a bound morpheme, a prefix or a suffix, is added to a lexical base to form a word. Some of these derivational suffixes will be described here.

Deriving Feminine nouns:
In the foregoing discussion, reference was made to derived bases. For instance, some feminine bases are simple bases, such as *kaantaa* 'woman', *bisəwə* 'queen', *duwə* 'daughter' and *sebəɖə* 'peahen', while some other feminine bases are derived from masculine animate bases. Examples of such feminizing suffixes and the resultant bases are given below.

Suffix -*i*:
    kukulu 'cock' > *kikili* 'hen'
    kolu 'lad' > *keli* 'lass'
    balu 'dog' > *bælli* 'bitch'
    wanduru 'monkey' > *wændiri* 'female monkey'
    wasu 'calf' > *wæsi* 'female calf'
    nalu 'actor' > *nili* 'actress'

Suffix -*ii*:
    mituru 'friend' > *miturii* 'female friend'
    munupuru 'grandchild' > *minipirii* 'granddaughter'
    kimbulu 'crocodile' > *kimbulii* 'female crocodile'
    pissu 'mad' > *pissii* 'mad-woman'

Suffix -*ini*:
    rajə 'king' > *ræjini* 'queen'
    kok 'crane' > *kekini* 'female crane'
    æt 'elephant' > *ætini* 'female elephant'
    widuhalpəti 'principal' > *widuhalpətini* 'female principal'

Suffixes -*inni*,-*nii*, -*ichchii*, -*issii*:
- *walas* 'bear' > *wælǝhinni* 'she-bear'
- *liǝnǝ* 'writing' > *liyanni* 'female writer or clerk'
- *yak* 'devil' > *yakinnii* 'female devil'
- *yassǝ* 'devil' > *yassǝnii* 'female devil'
- *raassǝ* 'devil' > *rassǝnii* 'female devil'
- *elu* 'goat' > *elichchii* 'she-goat'
- *gæṭǝ* 'adolescent' > *gæṭissii* 'female adolescent'

Nouns derived from adjectives or nouns:
Words may be formed from different sources. Words are formed by adding suffixes to nominal or adjectival bases or verb roots. Words derived by adding suffixes to nominal or adjectival bases are exemplified below. The nouns derived from adjectives inflect for case, number and definiteness like ordinary nouns.

Suffix	Base	Derivative
ǝ	*hingǝ* 'deficient'	*hingǝyǝ* 'deficiency'
	mahat 'large'	*mahatǝ* 'largeness or size'
aa	*nihanḍǝ* 'silent'	*nihænḍiaa* 'silence'
	lædi 'loyal'	*lædiaa* 'loyalty'
aa	*baḍǝ* 'belly'	*baḍaa* 'a person who has a big belly'
	ræulǝ 'beard'	*ræulaa* 'a person who has a beard'
	sudu 'white'	*suddaa* 'a white fellow'
kǝmǝ	*ugat* 'educated'	*ugatkǝmǝ* 'education'
	duppat 'poor'	*duppatkǝmǝ* 'poverty'
	bæri 'unable'	*bærikǝmǝ* 'inability'
taa	*dubǝlǝ* 'weak'	*dubǝlǝtaa* 'weakness'
	dakshǝ 'clever'	*dakshǝtaa* 'cleverness, skill'
twǝ	*garu* 'respectful'	*garutwǝ* 'respect'
	wishaalǝ 'large'	*wishaalatwǝ* 'largeness, size'
karu	*kam* 'work'	*kamkaru* 'labourer'
	lipi 'letters'	*lipikaru* 'clerk'
	waartaa 'report'	*waartaakaru* 'reporter'
kaarǝ	*naḍu* 'legal case'	*naḍukaarǝ* 'judge'
	shaakshi 'evidence'	*shaakshikaarǝ* 'witness'
	kiri 'milk'	*kirikaarǝ* 'one who delivers milk'

Forming adjectives:
By adding the following suffixes to nouns or adjectives, new adjectives are derived.

Suffix	Base	Derivative
muwaa 'made from'	dæwə 'wood'	dæwəmuwaa 'wooden'
	ridii 'silver'	ridiimuwaa 'made from silver'
məyə 'made from'	loohə 'metal'	loohəməyə 'made from metal'
	kaawyə 'poetry'	kaawyəməyə 'poetic'
ikə 'related to'	arthə 'economy'	aarthika 'economic'
	shariirə 'body'	shaariiirika 'physical'
wat 'possessing'	danə 'wealth'	danəwat 'wealthy'
	balə 'power'	baləwat 'powerful'
mat 'possessing'	asiri 'wonder'	asirimat 'wonderful'
	diri 'courage'	dirimat 'courageous'
tərə 'comparative'	bahu 'many'	bahutərə 'many more' or 'majority'
	kruurə 'cruel'	kruurətərə 'crueler'
təmə 'superlative'	priə 'favorite'	priətəmə 'most favorite'
	dakshə 'clever'	dakshətəmə 'most clever'

Suffixes for deriving nouns from verbs:
There is another set of suffixes which are added to the roots of verbs to derive nouns.

Suffix	verb root	Derivative
nnaa 'agent'	liə 'write'	liannaa 'the person who writes or clerk'
	asə 'listen'	asannaa 'listener'
um 'objective'	kərə 'do'	kerum 'doing'
	balə 'look'	bælum 'looking'
iim '-ing'	kapə 'cut'	kæpiim 'cutting'
	uganwə 'teach'	igænwiim 'teaching'
ili '-ing'	natə 'dance'	nætili 'dancing'
	widi 'shoot'	widili 'shooting'
mənə '-ing'	kiə 'say'	kiəmənə 'saying'
	wiə 'weave'	wiəmənə 'weaving'
nə 'instrumental'	dawətə 'wrap'	dawətənə 'something used for wrapping'
	daki 'see'	daknəyə 'something used for seeing (for example, durədaknəyə 'telescope')

Although the process of word formation is very productive in Sinhala, there are some suffixes which are not so productive. The last two suffixes given above, -mənə and -nə, for example, are not very productive and are found only in fixed expressions.

Prefixes:
Prefixes are added to nouns, adjectives and verbs to modify the concepts, qualities or events denoted by these words.

Prefix	Prefixed word
ati 'very or excessively'	*atibhayaanəkə* 'very dangerous',
	atidhaawənə 'running excessively, i.e. extreme'
adhi 'over, on'	*adhipati* 'chief', *adhitakseeru* 'overestimate'
anu 'according to, after'	*anukərənə* 'imitation', *anubalə* 'support'
apə 'from, away, off'	*apəkiirti* 'disgrace', *apəhaasə* 'contempt'
upə 'sub-, deputy'	*upəsabhaapati* 'vice president',
	upəmaatrukaa 'subtitle'
du 'bad'	*dugandə* 'bad smell', *dusirit* 'bad conduct'
ni 'down, in'	*nigraha* 'abuse' *niwaasə* 'residence'
piri 'round, about'	*piriwərə* 'retinue', *pirisudu* 'very clean or pure'
pili 'back, towards'	*pilituru* 'reply', *piliwelə* 'order'
wi 'apart, away'	*wikalpə* 'exception, alternative', *wiyoogə* 'depart'
su 'good'	*suwəndə* 'good smell', *sucharitə* 'good conduct'
su 'very'	*sumihiri* 'very sweet', *supprəkətə* 'very famous'

ni-, no-, nuu- and *a-* are used as negative prefixes:

ni	*nikarunee* 'without purpose', *niwærədi* 'faultless'
no	*nobəlaa* 'without looking', *nopamaawə* 'without delay'
nu	*nupurudu* 'unaccustomed', *nuugat* 'uneducated'
a	*apirisidu* 'unclean', *akəmæti* 'unwilling'

As these examples show, prefixes do not change the lexical category of the base.

2.2.2 Compounding

Compound noun formation is a very productive process. It must be noted, however, that all compounds do not necessarily exhibit productivity. For example, compound verbs like *digaarinəwa* 'unfold' (= *digə* 'long' + *arinəwa* 'open'), *ataarinəwa* 'release' (= *atə* 'hand' + *arinəwa* 'send'), *sinaasenəwa* 'laugh, smile' (= *sinaa* 'laugh(N)' + *senəwa* 'smile (V)') and compound adjectives like *usə-mahatə* 'well-built' (= *usə* 'tall' + *mahatə* 'fat, large'), *suurə-wiirə* 'bold and fearless' (= *suurə* 'competent' + *wiirə* 'brave'), *daksə-paksə* 'clever and smart' (= *daksə* 'clever' + *paksə* 'loyal') only serve as idiomatic expressions.

Compound nouns are made up of two or more lexical bases. The bases may belong to different lexical categories or to different grammatical categories within the same lexical category. The lexical category of the compound word is determined by the head which appears as its right-most element.

Adjectival compounds:
alutbat 'rice cooked from the new harvest' (= *alut* 'new' + *bat* 'rice')
ratmal 'a kind of flowers, called 'red flower'' (= *rat* 'red' + *mal* 'flowers')

sudəduwə 'fair daughter or loving daughter' (= *sudu* 'white' + *duwə* 'daughter')
lokumahattea 'head, boss' (= *loku* 'big' + *mahattea* 'master')

Numeral compounds:
dewaruwə 'morning and evening' (= *de* 'two' + *waru* 'period in the day')
tunmaase 'three months' (= *tun* 'three' + *maase* 'month')
hatərəpooyə 'all four full moon days' (= *hatərə* 'four' + *pooyə* 'full moon day')

Let it be noted that the order of components in these numeral compounds is the reverse of the complex numeral phrases discussed earlier (see 4.1.) where the numeral word follows the common noun.

Collective compounds:
kæmæbiimə 'food and beverages' (= *kæmə* 'food' + *biimə* 'drinks')
mæsimaduruwo 'bugs' (= *mæsi* 'fly' + *maduru* 'mosquito'
maupiyoo 'parents' (= *mau* 'mother' + *piyaa* 'father')

As evident from the examples above, only the last component of the compound undergoes case inflection, in this case nominative plural. Even when the individual noun is singular, the collective noun takes plural ending as in *maupiyoo* 'parents'.

A subclass of this group has compounds whose individual members, particularly the second members, if taken separately, do not make much sense; only when taken together, they make a real sense, contributing to the collective sense.

atə-miṭə 'wealth, means' (= *atə* 'hand' + *miṭə* 'fist')
ahalə-pahalə 'neighborhood' (= *ahalə* 'near' + *pahalə* 'down')
gewal-dorəwal 'dwellings' (= *gewal* 'houses' + *dorəwal* 'doors')

There is another subclass in which compounds are composed of words having the same or similar meaning, amplifying each other.

kataa-bas 'talks' (= *kataa* 'talk' + *bas* 'word')
yaanə-waahanə 'transport' (= *yaanə* 'vehicle' + *waahanə* 'vehicle')
sanḍu-dabərə 'cat-and-dog life' (= *sanḍu* 'quarrel' + *dabərə* 'wrangle')

Some compounds of this subclass are composed of cognate words; while the second component remains homophonous with an Old- or Middle Indian word (*tatsama*), the first component is an assimilated form of it (*tadbhava*). Both have the same or similar meaning.

awi-aayudha 'weapons'
pudə-puujaa 'offerings'
rækii-rakshaa 'employment, livelihood'

Another subclass consists of compounds whose components are the opposites of one another.

udə-yatə 'facts' (= *udə* 'up' + *yatə* 'down')
gunaagunə 'pros and cons' (= *gunə* 'advantage' + *agunə* 'disadvantage')
ganu-denu 'transactions' (= *ganu* 'take' + *denu* 'give')

Yet another subclass has compounds whose second component is a nonsense word added to form a rhyme and reinforce the meaning.

oppu-tirappu 'deeds' (= *oppu* 'deeds' + *tirappu* '***')
kaar-baar 'vehicles' (= *kaar* 'car' + *baar* '***')
paḍi-naḍi 'salary' (= *paḍi* 'salary + *naḍi* '***')

Case compounds:
This group was named after case in traditional grammar studies because of the fact that the first component of the compound is always considered to have had an obscured case relation implied by the second component. The inflected case form of the compound becomes explicit only when it is analyzed.

kiribath 'milk-rice' (= *kiri* 'milk + *bat* 'rice', i.e. 'rice cooked with milk')
waskawi 'cursing poem' (= *was* 'curse' + *kawi* 'poem', i.e. 'poems read for cursing somebody')
wæhiwaturə 'rain-water' (= *wæhi* 'rain' + *waturə* 'water', i.e. 'water coming from rain')

Epithetic compounds:
Compounds of this group do not signify the referents of the individual nouns they are composed of; they mean something other than the lexical meaning of the components. In some cases their meanings are unpredictable.

tunə-paha 'blended spice' (= *tunə* 'three' + *paha* 'five')
wangu-hatə 'a road with seven bends' (= *wangu* 'bend' + *hatə* 'seven')
siuru-horaa 'name of a bird' (= *siuru* 'yellow robe' + *horaa* 'thief')

Hybrid compounds:

baicikal roode 'bicycle wheel'
potoo saappuwə 'photo shop'
telinaatya 'television drama'

Examples for each class of nominal compounds are abundant, out of which only a few were introduced here. The situation proves the productivity of nominal compounding in Sinhala doubtlessly.

While most of the compounds given here comprise two components, there are compounds made up of a number of words and which have a more complex structure. They may represent collective compounds formed by simply joining together a string of words such as *næṭum-gæyum-wæyum* 'dancing-singing-playing'. They may be complex compounds formed by embedding one kind of compound in another kind of compound. Look at the following examples:

kukul-mas-kariə 'chicken curry' (= [[*kukul* 'chicken' + *mas* 'meat'] + *kariə* 'curry'])
ayə-wæyə-wiwaadəyə 'budget debate' (= [[*ayə* 'revenue' + *wæyə* 'expenditure', i.e. 'budget'] + *wiwaadəyə* 'debate']], i.e. 'debate on budget proposals')
gihi-pæwidi-depakshəyə 'two parties of laymen and priests' (= [[*gihi* 'layman' + *pæwidi* 'priest'] + [*de* 'two' + *pakshəyə* 'party']]

Such complex compounds are often used in naming new concepts, vocations, object or products, and institutes or public bodies.

sanwatsərə sabaa waartaawə 'Minutes of the annual meeting': Lit. 'anniversary + meeting + minutes'
ruupəwaahinii niweedəkəyaa 'television announcer': Lit. 'picture + broadcasting + announcer'
apənayənə sanwardhənə manḍələyə 'Exports Development Board': Lit. 'exports + development + board'
banḍaarənaaayəkə anusmarənə jaatyantərə sammantrənə saalaawə 'Bandaranaike Memorial International Conference Hall': Lit. 'Bandaranaike + memorial + international + conference + hall'

However, such long compounds are mostly limited to the formal use. What can be found in daily use are acronyms like *EDB* (Exports Development Board) and *BMICH* (Bandaranaike Memorial International Conference Hall).

A problem associated with the word formation process of compounding in Sinhala is the lack of consensus among grammarians as well as language-users regarding the maintenance of internal boundaries within a compound in writing. While a compound is considered grammatically as one word, this stance conflicts with the idea of clarity expected in writing. It is often found in writing that even short compounds are marked with a space boundary between the two components. Longer compounds are usually written with spaces indicating boundaries between the components.

2.2.3 Reduplication

Reduplication can be considered a special kind of compounding by which two identical lexical bases are combined. Verbs are reduplicated to perform different syntactic or semantic functions.

Infinitive forms are reduplicated to denote iterativity or continuity.

kannə-kannə 'the more eaten, (the better it tastes)'
kiannə kiannə 'the more you say, (the more he becomes stubborn)'
ahannə ahannə 'as listening goes on'
balannə balannə 'as looking goes on'

The reduplication of a verb's past participle base form denotes iterativity or durativity. In the process of reduplication, if the participle base form has a long vowel at its end, in the first component this changes to the corresponding short vowel.

ka-kaa 'eating or while eating'
bi-bii 'drinking or while drinking'
kapə-kapaa 'cutting or while cutting'
aṇḍə-aṇḍaa 'crying or while crying'
kærəki-kærəki 'rotating'

When the inflected past participial form with *-laa* is reduplicated, only the sense of iterativity is obtained.

kaala-kaala 'having eaten (heartily)'
biila-biila 'after drinking (heavily)'
kapəla-kapəla 'having cut (repeatedly)'
aṇḍəla-aṇḍəla 'having cried (incessantly)'
kærəkila-kærəkila 'after rotating (continuously)'

Verbal adjectives are reduplicated to express individuality and emphasis.

kapənə kapənə (gaha) 'every tree that is cut'
wæṭenə wæṭenə (geḍi) 'every fruit that falls'
hiṭəpu hiṭəpu (tænə) 'every place (they) were standing or living'
hitichchə hitichchə (deewal) 'every thing that occurred to (my) mind'

The reduplication functions as an intensifier for adjectives and adverbs.

loku loku (minissu) 'big or high-class (people)'
hondə hondə (baḍu) 'good (commodities)'
paaṭə paaṭə 'of different colors'
hemin hemin 'slowly'
balen balen 'by force, involuntarily'
ræætə ræætə 'for the night'
krəma-krəməen 'gradually'

Note the idiosyncrasy of the last example given above: its first part has the base form and the second part has the case form while in other examples the same form of the adjective or adverb appears doubled.

Nouns are reduplicated to denote gradualness, separateness or plurality.

ekə ekə 'one by one' or 'one for each'
ʈikə ʈikə 'little by little'
kææli kææli 'by or in pieces'
mulu mulu(wələ) 'in various corners'
panuwo panuwo 'numerous worms'

3. Sandhi

The process of Sandhi or sound euphony is widespread in both inflectional and derivational processes in Sinhala (Chapter 3: 3, 4). Some sandhi rules are obligatory. The phonological combinatory rules applied for euphoniously admitting suffixes into lexical bases, which are regarded to occur word-internally, are of this type. Some sandhi rules, on the other hand, may be optional. For instance, if any adjustment is made in phonological structures when two lexical bases are combined, the rules applied may be optional.

Final vowel deletion:
When a vowel final lexical base is followed by a vowel initial morpheme, the final vowel of the preceding component is deleted so that the two components coalesce together easily.

horə + aa → horaa 'thief'
wanduru + ek → wandurek 'a monkey'
biiwə + e → biiwe 'drink (past tense focus form)'
kæpuwə + ot → kæpuwot 'cut (conditional form)'

Semivowel insertion:
In some cases, two components are combined together by inserting a new element, rather than deleting the final vowel. When a vowel final lexical base is followed by a vowel initial morpheme, the insertion of a semivowel, *-y-* or *-w-*, makes the coalescence easier. Which semivowel is to be added is determined by the phonological character of the final vowel of the first component. According to the general rule, if the final vowel is a front vowel (*i, e, æ*), the semivowel will be *-y-*, and if it is a back vowel (*u, o, a*), then the semivowel is *-w-*.

   ræki + aa → ækiyaa 'employment'
   gææni + ek → gææniyek 'a woman'
   haa + aa → haawaa 'hare'

However, the rule is not obligatory in the colloquial language, except in the cases in which the speaker intends to put more stress on an element or wants to speak in a more formal style. In ordinary speech, vowel clustering occurs without an intervening semivowel:

baaldi + ə → baaldiə 'bucket'
koṭi + a → koṭia 'tiger'
olu + ə → oluə 'head'
maduru + o → maduruo 'mosquitoes'

Gemination:
When a vowel final lexical base is followed by a vowel initial morpheme, the final vowel of the preceding component is deleted and the immediately preceding consonant undergoes gemination before combination occurs.

atu + ə → attə 'branch'
kolu + a → kolla 'lad'
adi + a → ædda 'pull(past tense)'
raki + a → rækka 'protect (past tense)'

Assimilation:
When a consonant final lexical base is followed by a consonant initial morpheme, the new combination must achieve a form to accord with the consonant cluster pattern of the language. Assimilation is one device used to bring such phonological adjustment. Assimilation may be progressive, as in the first three examples, or regressive, as in the last three examples below.

kap + wə-nəwa → kappənəwa 'cause to cut'
dan + wə-nəwa → dannənəwa 'inform'
warad + wə-nəwa → waraddənəwa 'make a mistake'
æwit + la → æwilla 'having come'
putek + gen → puteggen 'from a son'
gan + mu → gammu 'let's take'

Epenthetic vowel:
In some cases, an unwelcome consonant cluster is split by an epenthetic vowel like *-u-* or *-e-*.

gææniyek + ṭə → gææniyekuṭə 'to a woman'
potak + ṭə → potakəṭə 'to or for a book'

Nasalization:
If the final consonant of the lexical base is a prenasalized stop, it will change to a full nasal stop, creating an ordinary consonant cluster.

aɳɖu + ə → aɳɖə 'limb'
kaɳɖu + ə → kaɳɖə 'mountain'
bæɳɖi + a → bæɳɖi + a → bæɳɖa 'tie or marry (past tense)'

Glottalization:
The fricative alveolar phoneme (s) and the fricative glottal (h) are often interchangeable in Sinhala. The fricative alveolar -s occurring as the final consonant of a lexical base often changes to the fricative glottal -h when it admits a vowel initial suffix. Simultaneously, ə following h changes to a or æ, as in the first examples below. However, this substitution is optional, as the two other examples show.

gas + ə → gaha 'tree'
æs + ə → æhæ 'eye'
wayas + ə → wayəsə 'age'
dawas + ə → dawəsə 'day'

External sandhi:
Next, some external sandhi rules, i.e. those used for combining two lexical bases are briefly introduced. Some of the internal sandhi rules described above are also applied in combining independent lexical items when similar phonological environments are present.

When the two components of a compound comprise a vowel final word and a vowel initial word in that order, the two vowels at the place of combination are replaced by their corresponding long vowel.

gunə + agunə → gunaagunə 'merits and demerits'
hatə + aṭak → hataaṭak 'approximately seven or eight'
hondə + aakaarə → hondaakaarə 'of a good extent'

If the first component is a consonant final word while the second component is a vowel initial word, the final consonant of the former is doubled before joining the two words together.

mal + aasənee → mall + aasənee → mallasəne 'flower altar'
pas + aurudda → pass + aurudda → passauruddə 'the five years'
kat + ædiimə → katt + ædiimə → kattædiimə 'shouldering the burden'

When a consonant final word and a consonant initial word constitute a compound in that order, assimilation occurs in some particular environments.

æt + dalə → æddalə 'elephant tusk'
puluk + gobee → puluggobee 'shoot of young coconut leaves'
harak + paṭṭiə → harappaṭṭiə 'herd of cattle'

Consonant assimilation does not occur in some environments.

pot kaḍee 'bookshop'
bat waṭṭiə 'rice basket'
mas kariə 'meat (beef) curry'

Though they are not completely arbitrary, sandhi rules are difficult to establish as regular grammatical rules.

CHAPTER 6

Morphology-syntax interface

The previous chapter described some morphological patterns considered to be well developed and established in Sinhala. However, their interaction with syntactic (and semantic) structures is in some instances complex and inconsistent with what one would expect. Before proceeding to syntax, therefore, a brief consideration of some facts regarding the interface between morphology and syntax will be appropriate.

First, the morphological description of the verb provided so far needs some review. The verbal derivation given earlier was four-fold as follows:

Active form	**Passive form**	**Causative form**	**Causative-passive form**
balənawa 'look'	bælənawa	baləwənawa	bæləwenawa
kapənawa 'cut'	kæpənawa	kappənawa	kæppenawa
adinawa 'pull'	ædənawa	addənawa	æddənawa
——— 'fall'	wæṭənawa	waṭṭənawa	wæṭṭenawa
naṭənawa 'dance'	næṭenawa	naṭəwənawa	næṭəwenawa

We used the term 'Passive form' following earliest descriptions such as Geiger 1938 and De Silva 1960. As emphasized by later research (Gair 1970 and Inman 1993), 'Involitive form' might be a better choice in light of its use in actual discourse.

However, a certain conflict between a morphological form and its practical use can be seen as regards all morphological patterns, not just in the 'passive form'. The given designations should be taken as a nomenclature used to mark in a structured way the workings of morphemes and their boundaries relevant to the respective morphological processes. A closer examination will reveal that their boundaries are not so clear-cut, in particular, with respect to syntax and semantics. The mapping of the verb morphology with syntactic structures is never one to one. The verbal forms occur with different nominal constituents appearing in different case forms including postpositional phrases. While occurring in successive and recursive patterns, they interact with semantic categories such as animacy, volitionality, control and causativity to construct different clause-types.

Part of the solution for these problems would be to assume that morphological forms do not correspond to their syntactic distribution in a straightforward way. Further they should not be assumed to work in isolation but to enter relations with different types of participants with the involvement of important semantic and pragmatic considerations. Some diachronic dimensions also seem to be responsible for inequalities in distribution. Some idiosyncrasies and dialectic variations cannot be refuted, either.

To begin with, we have identified two separate forms as Passive (P) form and Causative Passive (CP) form. However, their distribution is not always identical with the semantic references of the particular form. There are instances where either of the verbal forms is used in the same sentence type. For example, the following two sentences, each with distinct P and CP forms represent the same context.

(1) a. Ranjit-ṭə næte-nəwa
Ranjit-DAT get dance(P)-IND
'Ranjit impulsively dances (hearing the music).'

b. Ranjit-ṭə nætəwe-nəwa
Ranjit-DAT get dance(CP)-IND
'Ranjit impulsively dances (hearing the music).'

Sinhala speakers thus, in some instances, alternate P forms with CP forms, and in some other instances, they prefer to use the CP form to relate to different contexts. Look at the following example.

(2) a. ma-ṭə eekə kiəuna (= kiyəwuna)
I-DAT it get-said(CP).PAST.IND
'I said it unintentionally.'

b. ?ma-ṭə eekə kiuna
I-DAT it get-said(P).PAST.IND
'I said it unintentionally.'

Although (2b) is grammatically correct, as far as our data is concerned its P form would not seem to occur in a sentence frame. To a native speaker, this form of the verb may seem inadequate to express the spontaneous event in question; the speaker admits here that she/he has said something without intending it.

Considering the alternate use of P and CP forms for denoting an identical context as well as the tendency to use the very same forms, be it P or CP, for denoting two different contexts such as spontaneity and causation, we may treat P and CP verbs together rather than as separate. Indeed, some scholars have done so relegating the difference to a case of mere morphological variation (De Silva 1960 and Gair 1970).

Next, we need to deal with the formal differences within the Active (A)-Causative (C) distinction. Before dealing with the distinction, a clarification is due regarding a problem internal to the C form. There may be several C forms for the same verb. For example, the C form for the A verb *kapənəwa* 'cut' has three variants: *kapəwənəwa* ; *kappənəwa* ; *kappəwənəwa*. *kapəwənəwa* is the straightforward C form with a transparent C morpheme (*kapə* + *wə* +*nəwa* (= Root + C + Indicative form). Then, *kappənəwa* is obtained after applying the phonological rule of gemination. Since the C morpheme becomes obscured with this form, a secondary C morpheme is inserted for the sake of explicitness. The resultant form is *kappəwənəwa*. As alternate variants they can occur in the same context with no difference in meaning or distribution. Indeed, scholars have treated them accordingly (De Silva 1960 and Gair 1970). However, this is not always the case as there are instances where a clear distinction is made in meaning as well as distribution. For example, *addənəwa* or *addəwənəwa*, the C form of the A verb *adinəwa* 'pull, draw' may appear in a sentence type as follows:

(3) a. ænjimə addənəwa horai
   engine cause-to-draw (c).IND unsatisfactory
   Lit. 'The engine is not pulling well.'
   'The engine is not running well.'

   b. kauruhari lauwa baɖu ʈikə addala daamu
   somebody by goods amount cause-to-draw(c).PP put-HORT
   Lit. 'Let's make somebody draw the goods.'
   'Let's get somebody to carry the goods.'

This is a further example of active C forms sometimes having causative meanings and sometimes not. As these sentences show, a causative verb can be used in a non-causative context (3a) as well as in a causative context (3b). The example poses the question of A/C distinction.

A verb may be transitive or intransitive. Intransitive stems are transitivized by adding the C morpheme. These causatives of intransitives may behave as usual causatives, i.e. with the involvement of a causee, or as base transitives, i.e. without the involvement of a causee. Thus, *yawənəwa*, the causative of *yanəwa* may mean 'cause to go' or 'send', and *kiyawənəwa*, the causative of *kiyənəwa* may mean 'cause to say' or 'read'. However, some C forms seem to have the division of labor between transitive and causative meaning separated among their variants. Observe how C forms of *gahanəwa* 'hit, beat' behave.

(4) a. rediwælə ʈikak gassənəwa naŋ kuumbi wætei
   clothes-line a little cause-to-hit (c).IND if ants fall-INFER
   'The ants will fall if you shake the clothes-line a bit.'

   b. *rediwælə ʈikak gassəwənəwa naŋ kuumbi wætei
   clothes-line a little cause-to-hit (c).IND if ants fall-INFER
   'The ants will fall if you shake the clothes-line a bit.'

   c. waɖuwa lameya laua ænə gassəwənəwa
   carpenter child by nails cause-to-hit (c).IND
   'The carpenter makes the child hit the nails.'

To denote the transitive sense, only the *gassənəwa* variant is used as in (4a); the explicit causative or double causative variant *gassəwənəwa* does not deliver the goods, as (4b) shows for it has assumed the strict causative sense, which is separate from the transitive sense, as in (4c). These facts also show that causative formation is a lexical process, not a syntactic process. Interestingly, P forms can be obtained from most C forms and can be equated with detransitivization (*gæssenəwa* 'jolt, quake, be startled') or involitivization (*liyəwenəwa* 'write spontaneously').

In general, C verbs occur in causative, transitive, and, though rarely, even in intransitive clauses. They have some commonality with A verbs with respect to morphology, i.e. by having verb stems ending in *-(w)ə* as well as with respect to syntax, i.e. having direct-case subjects, by virtue of which they can be contrasted with P verbs. P verbs, on the other hand, occurring mainly in intransitive clauses with various types of oblique case subjects, as will be described in detail later, render involitive, inactive, impersonal readings.

An important caveat that needs to be made at this point is that morphological shape alone cannot provide a proper guide to a verb's syntactic distribution. While there is a general pattern of verbs identified by the morphological shape of the stem, nevertheless, their correlation with clause types is not absolute. A verb of a given morphological shape, in particular with a stem of *-e*, may occur either in an active, volitive type construction or in an inactive, involitive construction depending on various other factors. The following directional verbs are of this type: *ædenəwa* 'be drawn or drag oneself', *perəlenəwa* 'roll down', *kærəkenəwa* 'turn, rotate', *hærenəwa* 'turn sideways)', *wæṭenəwa* 'fall'.

Some of these verbs, while apparently representing the P form morphologically, occur in active-type constructions. The following are of this type: *igilenəwa* 'fly out', *gæwəsenəwa* 'loiter', *pækilenəwa* 'hesitate', *sætəpenəwa* 'sleep (honorific)', *wætirenəwa* 'lie down'. However, these verbs, though void of corresponding A forms, are considered as active, volitive verbs accidentally being in the *-e* form. There are also some P verbs that do not have corresponding A forms. These belong to the inactive-, involitive-type, like *idimenəwa* 'swell', *pipenəwa* 'blossom', *ridenəwa* 'be painful' and *idenawa* 'ripen, be cooked'. Conversely some verbs, while retaining the A form, occur in inactive-type constructions: *warədinəwa* 'fail, make a mistake', *parədinəwa* 'be lost, defeated', *lissənəwa* 'slip', *aarənəwa* 'become fat', *russənəwa* 'endure'. This latter type of verbs well illustrates the mismatch between morphological forms and syntactic behavior. Two other verbs, *kahinəwa* 'cough' and *gorəwənəwa* 'snore', despite lexically denoting involitive events highly marked with lack of control and volition on the part of the participant, remain active in form and distribution, for which it is hard to find a valid explanation. However, 'cough' can also form an involitive-type construction by means of a non-verbal structure, i.e. as a noun with a dative participant.

Although an A verb can be considered to achieve detransitivization or involitivization by transforming into a P form, as in *ussənəwa* 'lift' > *issenəwa* 'be lifted', this kind of relationship does not remain consistent as verbs undergo recurring semantic change. As historical semanticists have demonstrated, semantic or grammatical change involves not only "A > B", i.e. the simple replacement of one item by another, but also "A > A ~ B" and sometimes "> B" alone (Traugott and Dasher 2001:11). This is exactly what can be observed in Sinhala with respect to verbal derivation. While the derived form (P from) shares lexical meaning with the original stem (A form) in the lexical process, an accretion of new meanings occurs, at another layer, with respect to the newly derived verb. The new meaning with the same phonological form will develop as a homonymic lexeme and will coexist with the lexical meaning of the shared stem. Observe the following examples: (To make the semantic disparity explicit, only the meanings acquired later are given for the derived forms.)

obənəwa 'press' > *ebenəwa* 'peep'
koṭənəwa 'pound' > *keṭenəwa* 'strain (a muscle)'
gahanəwa 'hit' > *gæhenəwa* 'shiver, tremble'
gewənəwa 'pay' > *gewenəwa* 'pass or wear away'
tawənəwa 'warm' > *tæwenəwa* 'be distressed (in mind)'
toorənəwa 'choose, select' > *teerenəwa* 'understand'
pahadənəwa 'explain' > *pæhædenəwa* 'be pleased with (somebody)'

Here the derived verbs have split from the regular derived forms to emerge semantically distinct and no longer remain predictable in terms of patterned relationship. On a close examination, however, it will not be difficult to establish historical relationships between the related forms. For example, *ebenəwa* derives its 'peep' sense through the derived meaning of 'getting pressed down, pressing oneself down or lowering one's own position'; it is not unnatural for *teerenəwa* ' get chosen' to obtain its 'understand' sense if we think that understanding is derived from clear thinking or discrimination, i.e. ability to know and act on the difference between various things. There is cross-linguistic evidence supporting this analysis. For example, the same pairing can be found in Japanese: *wakeru* 'part, divide'> *wakaru* 'understand'. However, from a synchronic point of view, these particular P verbs can no longer be linked with the corresponding A forms or active-type sentences.

The Sinhala verb has a basic pattern which is a set of forms in derivational relationships. Forms identified by their morphological structure show differences in meaning and, to a great extent, in distribution as well. The basic differentiation is between A and P forms. Each set of forms is characterized by a distinct inflectional pattern.

On close inspection, however, this finely woven pattern seems to be an idealized one, particularly when it comes to syntax. The relationship of a single morphological form with a single semantic reading with a single underlying syntactic function would be ideal for a user-friendly grammar of a language. However, the everyday use of a living language goes far beyond this ideal. Rigidly patterned derivational relationships and their one-to-one correspondence with syntactic patterns are no longer available for a language with a long historical development and recurrent contacts with other languages.

CHAPTER 7

Argument structures

The term "argument structure" is used to refer to the organization of the sentence in terms of the relationship between the predicate and its argument. The sentence is considered to be built around the predicate, and its argument structure is considered to consist of the predicate together with the minimal number of noun phrases taken by it to convey the information which is intended to be expressed in the sentence. The argument structure provides information about the number of arguments that a particular predicate has and about their syntactic types. In Sinhala the predicate occupies the final position in the sentence and can be a verb, an adjective, a noun phrase or a postpositional phrase. A predicate may have a single argument or multiple arguments, or no argument at all, each argument being identified by its position in the linear organization. Arguments are also identified by the case suffixes or postpositional case particles attached to them.

Argument structures are understood as abstractions, kind of patterns abstracted from concrete examples of discourse. They are essentially symbolic and hence representative. Accordingly, some clear-cut rules are followed for presenting data in this chapter. First, predicates are cited in the non-past, finite form ending in -*nəwa*, often referred to in the literature as the basic form. Indeed, verbs are cited as entries in dictionaries in this form. This will help understand a predicate in terms of atemporality, i.e. without reference to a specific time frame. This has caused problems for English translations. Let it be noted that the English glosses provided here are formulae to help the reader identify the elements of the Sinhala structures. Second, basic patterns are presented as full structures, that is, with all the arguments necessary to complete the information intended to convey. In actual discourse it is often found that one or more constituents are omitted when the referent is understood by the context. Such deleted constituents are retained in the structures presented here. Third, structures are presented in the standard linear order. It is admitted that the linear order of constituents is variable in Colloquial Sinhala. Notwithstanding this flexibility in word order, a predicate is identified by its unmarked focal position, i.e. sentence-final position.

1. Argument structure types

Argument structure types are classified on the basis of (a) the class of the predicate, (2) the lexical semantic character of the predicate, including the dynamicity and volitionality of the verb and the thematic roles associated with the verb, (3) the lexical-semantic characteristics of the nominal arguments, (4) their grammatical marking by means of case inflection and particles, and (5) the relative prominence of the participants. For example, depending on whether the predicate is verbal or nonverbal, two large classes are distinguished. The volitionality of the verb divides argument structures into an active (volitive) and an inactive (involitive) type. The transitive-intransitive distinction, another division of two large classes depends on whether the verb permits selecting the most prominent participant (= agent) as subject and another participant at a relatively low level of prominence as object, or whether a single participant is selected as subject by virtue of its relative prominence in the absence of a more prominent participant. Naturally, the valency of the verbs allows argument structures to be classified by the number of arguments.

The following table provides a list of possible argument structure types in Sinhala. The widest classification is the division of argument structures as active and inactive structures. While each group may contain several subtypes, the main distinction can be stated in terms of some highly generalized properties which are identified with the lexical semantic characteristics of the individual participants in a predicate. Active sentences, whether transitive or intransitive, take animate nominals as subjects and generally express the voluntary participation on the part of the subject NP in the action expressed in the sentence. Therefore, the major semantic role of the first constituent is Agent or Actor. Sentences of the inactive types, on the other hand, express processes or states in which the major participant, whether nominative or non-nominative, is marked by lack of volition and control with respect to the event. Therefore, the major semantic role of the first constituent is Undergoer, Experiencer, Involitive Agent or Theme. The *atin* constituent in Sinhala denotes an involitive agent whereas the *laua* constituent indicates the causee of a causative action. Not only the nominative but also the dative, accusative or *atin* marked constituent may appear as subject. Depending on the number of arguments, there can be zero-place, one-place, two-place, or three place predicates. The optional marking of constituents is indicated by parentheses in the schematic formulae for argument structure types. PP is a postpositional phrase.

Table 1. Argument Structure Types

Arg.	Inactive		Active	
0	(a) Pred.$_{VP}$ (b) Pred.$_{ADJ}$			
1	(c) $NP_{1\ NOM(ACC)}$ (d) $NP_{1\ DAT}$	Pred.$_{VP/NP/ADJ/PP}$ Pred.$_{VP/NP/ADJ}$	(l) $NP_{1\ NOM}$	Pred.$_{VP/NP}$
2	(e) $NP_{1\ NOM}\ NP_{2\ DAT}$ (f) $NP_{1\ DAT}\ NP_{2\ NOM(ACC)}$ (g) $NP_{1\ LOC/PP}\ NP_{2\ NOM}$ (h) $NP_{1\ NOM}\ NP_{2\ LOC/PP}$ (i) $NP_{1\ atin}\ NP_{2\ NOM(ACC)}$	Pred.$_{ADJ}$ Pred.$_{VP}$ Pred.$_{VP}$ Pred.$_{VP}$ Pred.$_{VP}$	(m) $NP_{1\ NOM}\ NP_{2\ NOM(ACC)}$ (n) $NP_{1\ NOM}\ NP_{2\ DAT}$ (o) $NP_{1\ NOM}\ NP_{2\ INS}$ (p) $NP_{1\ NOM}\ NP_{2\ ekkə}$	Pred.$_{VP}$ Pred.$_{VP}$ Pred.$_{VP}$ Pred.$_{VP}$

(Continued)

Table 1. Argument Structure Types (Continued)

Arg.	Inactive		Active	
	(j) $NP_{1DAT} NP_{2NOM}$	$Pred._{ADJ}$		
	(k) $NP_{1NOM} NP_{2ekkə}$	$Pred._{ADJ}$		
3			(q) $NP_{1NOM} NP_{2DAT} NP_{3NOM(ACC)}$	$Pred._{vp}$
			(r) $NP_{1NOM} NP_{2NOM(ACC)} NP_{3DAT}$	$Pred._{vp}$
			(s) $NP_{1NOM} NP_{2NOM} NP_{3LOC/PP}$	$Pred._{vp}$
			(t) $NP_{1NOM} NP_{2NOM} NP_{3ABL}$	$Pred._{vp}$
			(u) $NP_{1NOM} NP_{2ABL} NP_{3NOM}$	$Pred._{vp}$
			(v) $NP_{1NOM} NP_{2ekkə} NP_{3NOM}$	$Pred._{vp}$

Note that an assertion marker (AM) is added to vowel-ending adjectival predicates. Consonant-ending adjectival predicates appear in bare form.

1.1 Argument structures with inactive predicates

(a) [Pred.$_{VP}$] and (b) [Pred.$_{ADJ}$]

Examples for this sentence type are limited. They can be found in some expressions regarding the weather.

> wahinəwa 'It's raining'
> paayənəwa 'No rain'; 'The sun shines'; 'It will clear up'
> rasnei 'It's hot'
> siitəlai 'It's cold'

(c) [$NP_{1 NOM(ACC)}$ PRED.$_{VP/NP/ADJ/PP}$]

(1) With verbal predicates the subject constituent may optionally be marked by the accusative case when it is an animate nominal.

> gas   wæṭe-nəwa
> trees   fall-IND
> 'The trees are falling'

> lamea   wæṭe-nəwa
> child   fall-IND
> 'The child is falling' (intentionally, in play)

> lamea-wə wæṭe-nəwa
> child-ACC fall-IND
> '(Look out!)The child is falling'

(2) Equational sentences: Nominal and adjectival predicates appear with a single argument.

Ranjit guruwərə-ek
Ranjit teacher-INDF
'Ranjit is a teacher'

Ranjit dæn widuhalpati
Ranjit now principal
'Ranjit has become principal'

Chitra daksha-i
Chitra clever-AM
'Chitra is clever'

(3) Non-equational sentences: Non-equational sentences are realized with NPs of several oblique case forms as predicates. Predicates may be nouns marked with dative, genitive, ablative or locative case.

mee tæægga oyaa-ṭə
This present you-DAT
'This present is for you'

mee baisikəlee ma-ge
this bicycle I-GEN
'This bicycle is mine'

meekə ma-gen
this I-ABL
'This is from me'

meyaa indiyaawe
this person India.LOC
'He is from India'

kannaḍiə naləl-e
glasses forehead-LOC
'The glasses are on (your) forehead'

(4) A locative NP in predicate position may denote a less concrete situation or a cognitive activity.

Ranjit amaaru-e
Ranjit difficulty-LOC
'Ranjit is in difficulties'

warədə ma-ge at-ee
fault I-GEN hand-LOC
'The fault lies with me'

mahattea barə kalpənaawəkə
gentleman heavy thought.INDF.LOC
'The gentleman is engaged in a deep thought'

(5) The predicate may comprise a postpositional phrase.

> puusa gahə udə
> cat tree on
> 'The cat is in the tree'

> amma lində langə
> mother well near
> 'Mother is at the well'

> babaa Chitra ekkə
> baby Chitra with
> 'The baby is with Chitra'

(d) [NP$_{1\text{ DAT}}$ Pred.$_{\text{VP/NP/ADJ}}$]

The dative constituent denotes an involuntary participant or an experiencer.

(1) With verbal predicates

> Ranjit-ţə æṇḍe-nəwa
> Ranjit-DAT cry.INVL-IND
> 'Ranjit breaks out crying (suddenly)'

> lamea-ţə diwe-nəwa
> child-DAT run.INVL-IND
> 'The child gets to running (involuntarily)'

> Chitra-ţə kæægæhe-nəwa
> Chitra-DAT scream.INVL-IND
> 'Chitra screams (involuntarily)'

(2) With nominal predicates

> ma-ţə unə
> I-DAT fever
> 'I have a fever'

> apə-ţə niwaaḍu
> we-DAT vacation
> 'We are on vacation'

> eyaa-ţə karədərəy-ak
> she/he-DAT trouble-INDF
> 'She/he is in trouble'

(3) With adjectival predicates

> ma-ţə kanəgaatu-i
> I-DAT sad-AM
> 'I feel sorry'

apə-ṭə   mahansi-i
we-DAT   tired-AM
'We are tired'

eyaa-ṭə   dæn   honda-i
she/he-DAT   now   good-AM
'Now she is well/in a good condition'

(e) [NP$_{1\,\text{NOM}}$ NP$_{2\,\text{DAT}}$ Pred.$_{\text{ADJ}}$]

Predicates of this type express an attitude or a mental state of the referent of the first constituent towards the referent of the second constituent marked by the dative -ṭə.

amma   putaa-ṭə   aadəre-i
mother   son-DAT   loving-AM
'Mother loves her son'

mamə   kalu   kuḍee-ṭə   kæməti-i
I   black   umbrella-DAT fond-AM
'I prefer the black umbrella'

miniha   gææni-ṭə   baya-i
man   woman-DAT   scared-AM
'He is scared of his wife'

(f) [NP$_{1\,\text{DAT}}$ NP$_{2\,\text{NOM(ACC)}}$ Pred.$_{\text{VP}}$]

With this structure, voluntary participation is eliminated even from a transitive event. The dative constituent denotes an external cause (1), an involuntary participant of the event (2), an involuntary participant of a perceptive, sensory or mental experience (3), or an inalienable possessor (4). The construction is also used to express ability, needs and emotion (5).

(1) External cause

huləngə-ṭə   gas   perəle-nəwa
wind-DAT   trees   fall down-IND
'The trees are falling from the wind'

kaḍuə-ṭə   atə   kæpe-nəwa
sword-DAT   hand   cut.INVL-IND
'The sword is cutting his hand'

katurə-ṭə   miiyo   ahuwe-nəwa
trap-DAT   rats   get caught-IND
'Rats get caught to the trap'

(2) Involuntary participant of the event

    lamea-ṭə waturə pewe-nəwa
    child-DAT water drink.INVL-IND
    'The child unintentionally swallows water'

    Chitra-ṭə nitərə asəniipə we-nəwa
    Chitra-ṭə often ill become-IND
    'Chitra often falls ill'

    Ranjit-ṭə puusa(-wə) pæge-nəwa
    Ranjit-DAT cat(-ACC) step on.INVL-IND
    'Ranjit is accidentally stepping on the cat'

Consider that the second constituent is optionally marked by the accusative -wə to indicate its Undergoer status as in the last example.

(3) Involuntary participant of a perceptive, sensory and mental experience

    ma-ṭə pintuurə-ak pee-nəwa
    I-DAT picture-INDF see.INVL-IND
    'I can see a picture'

    balla-ṭə keek suwəndə hondəṭə dæne-nəwa
    dog-DAT cake smell well feel.INVL-IND
    'The dog senses the smell of the cake'

    taatta-ṭə kuḍee amətəkə we-nəwa
    father-DAT umbrella forget.INVL-IND
    'Father (often) forgets his umbrella'

(4) Possessor

    ma-ṭə put-ek in-nəwa
    I-DAT son-INDF be-IND
    'I have a son'

    Chitra-ṭə kaarek-ak tie-nəwa
    Chitra-DAT car-INDF be-IND
    'Chitra has a car'

    Ranjit-ṭə salli hambə we-nəwa
    Ranjit-DAT money get.INVL-IND
    'Ranjit is getting money'

(5) In expressing ability, need and emotion, the dative constituent represents the person implicated in such states.

    Ranjit-ṭə waḍu wædə puluwan
    Ranjit-DAT carpentry can
    'Ranjit can do carpentry work'

ma-tə   salli   oonæ
I-DAT   money   need
'I need money'

taata-tə   taraha   ya-nəwa
father-DAT anger   go-IND-
'Father gets angry'

Note that *puluwan* and *oonæ* are two quasi-verbs in Sinhala which do not have verbal inflection (Gair 1970).

(g)   [NP$_{1\ LOC/PP}$ NP$_{2\ NOM}$ Pred.$_{VP}$]

Existential construction: Existential predicates express the existence of entities. The existential verb *innəwa* is used for animate referents and *tienəwa* for inanimates. The first constituent with a locative suffix or with a postpositional phrase indicates the location. The second constituent denotes the located entity.

att-e   kurull-ek   in-nəwa
branch-LOC   bird-INDF   be-IND
'There is a bird on the branch'

at-ee   booləy-ak   tie-nəwa
hand-LOC   ball-INDF   be-IND
'There is a ball in (her) hand'

puṭuwə   yaṭə   kuumbi   in-nəwa
chair   under   ants   be-IND
'There are ants under the chair'

(h)   [NP$_{1\ NOM}$ NP$_{2\ LOC/PP}$ Pred.$_{VP}$]

This argument type is used to assert the existence of a known entity with respect to a new location. The first constituent expresses the located entity as shared information; the second constituent presents a location as new information; the verb asserts the existence.

kurulla   kuudu-e   in-nəwa
bird   cage-LOC   be-IND
'The bird is in the cage'

yaturə   laachchu-e   tie-nəwa
key   drawer-LOC   be-IND
'The key is in the drawer'

boole   puṭuwə   yaṭə   tie-nəwa
ball   chair   under   be-IND
'The ball is under the chair'

(i) [NP$_{1\,\text{atin}}$ NP$_{2\,\text{NOM(ACC)}}$ Pred.$_{\text{VP}}$]

The main characteristic of this structure is the involitive verb. The first constituent marked by the *atin* particle denotes the unintentionally acting or accidental agent (1). However, the *atin* constituent may also denote a 'potential' agent in sentences with the nuances of potentiality or possibility (2).

(1) unintentional actions

    Ranjit atin gaha kæpe-nəwa
    Ranjit atin tree cut.INVL-IND
    'Ranjit unintentionally cuts the tree'

    Chitra atin baisikəle hæppe-nəwa
    Chitra atin bicycle strike.INVL-IND
    'Chitra accidentally strikes her bicycle against (the fence)'

    tawapoddən man atin babaa-wə ætæære-nəwa
    nearly I atin baby-ACC drop.INVL-IND
    'I nearly dropped the baby (accidentally)'

(2) Potentiality expression

The *atin* constituent expresses the 'potential' actor.

    kellə atin maalu ageetə pihe-nəwa
    girl atin fish well cook.INVL-IND
    'The girl can cook fish very well' (De Silva 1960: 101)

    Banda atin pol siiyak witərə kæde-nəwa
    Banda atin coconut hundred about pick.INVL-IND
    'Banda can pick about a hundred coconuts (in an hour)' (Gair 1970: 40)

    miniha atin lassənətə pælə hæde-nəwa
    he atin very well plants make.INVL-IND
    'He can do tree planting in a systematic way'

(j) [NP$_{1\,\text{DAT}}$ NP$_{2\,\text{NOM}}$ Pred.$_{\text{ADJ}}$]

This structure expresses a potential match between two entities conceptualized as a situation in which a variable represented by the second constituent is located against a fixed object or standard indicated by the first, dative marked constituent.

    ma-tə mee kaaməree honda-i
    I-DAT this room good-AM
    'This room is good for me'

    eyaa-tə siini kææmə aguna-i
    she/he-DAT sugary food unwholesome-AM
    'Sugary food is not good for him'

apə-ṭə barə wæḍə purudu-i
we-DAT heavy work accustomed-AM
'We are used to heavy work'

(k) [NP$_{1\text{NOM}}$ NP$_{2\,\text{ekkə}}$ Pred.$_{\text{ADJ}}$]

Ekkə is a comitative particle in Sinhala. The *ekkə* marked phrase indicates a relationship the referent of the first constituent has with the referent of the second constituent.

Ranjit Sunil ekkə honda-i
Ranjit Sunil ekkə good-AM
'Ranjit is on good terms with Sunil'

eyaa api ekkə taraha-i
she/he we ekkə angry-AM
'She is angry with us (on bad terms)'

Ranjit Chitra ekkə yaalu-i
Ranjit Chitra ekkə friendly-AM
'Ranjit is friendly with Chitra/is having a love affair with Chitra'

1.2 Argument types with active predicates

(l) [NP$_{1\text{ NOM}}$ Pred.$_{\text{VP/NP}}$]

This structure represents the typical intransitive pattern. The nominal constituent denotes an Actor role appearing in the nominative. The typical subject takes an animate noun which generally appears with a verbal predicate (1). However, there is a group of predicates referred to in the literature as Action Nominals (Gair & Paolillo 1988) which contain as predicates nouns in the nominative (2). These nominal predicates are of limited distribution.

(1) With verbal predicates

Ranjit duwə-nəwa
Ranjit run-IND
'Ranjit is running'

lamea naṭə-nəwa
child dance-IND
'The child is dancing'

balla burə-nəwa
dog bark-IND
'The dog is barking'

(2) With Action-Nominal predicates

taatta wæḍə
father work
'Father is at work'

minissu digəṭəmə kataawə
people continuously talk
'The people are continuously talking'

lamai hiki-hiki ga-gaa hinaawə
children giggling   laugh
'The children were giggling'

(m) [NP$_{1\text{ NOM}}$ NP$_{2\text{ NOM(ACC)}}$ Pred.$_{\text{VP}}$]

This structure is realized in three sub-types.

(1) Transitive construction: The construction encodes a typical transitive event. The second constituent may denote different kinds of objects, such as a physically affected patient, a physically non-affected patient, and an object created in the action. When the second NP is an animate noun, it may be marked by the accusative.

amma keek kapə-nəwa
mother cake cut-IND
'Mother is cutting cakes'

Chitra puusa(-wə) hoyə-nəwa
Chitra cat(-ACC) find-IND
'Chitra is looking for the cat'

Ranjit tee hadə-nəwa
Ranjit tea make-IND
'Ranjit is making tea'

(2) Habitual motion event: This is an intransitive structure in spite of consisting of two nominal constituents. The predicate comprises a volitional intransitive motion verb. The first nominative NP denotes an Actor while the second nominative NP indicates the goal of a habitual motion. This pattern is not used for non-habitual motion with an emphasis on the goal.

Chitra iskoole ya-nəwa
Chitra school go-IND
'Chitra goes to school'

Ranjit hæmə pooyəkə ṭəmə pansal ya-nəwa
Ranjit every full moon day temple go-IND
'Ranjit goes to temple every full moon day'

hæmə sikuraadamə taatta koləmbə ya-nəwa
every Friday father Colombo go-IND
'Father goes to Colombo every Friday'

(3) Perceptive, sensory and mental actions: This is a transitive event. The first constituent denotes the volitive actor or initiator of the perceptive, sensory and mental event, and the second constituent specifies the object of the experience.

Ranjit pintuurəy-ak balə-nəwa
Ranjit picture-INDF look-IND
'Ranjit is viewing a picture'

Chitra sindu aha-nəwa
Chitra songs listen-IND
'Chitra is listening to songs'

mamə eekə matak kərə-nəwa
I that remember-IND
'I am trying to remember it'

(n) [NP$_{1\ NOM}$ NP$_{2\ DAT}$ Pred.$_{VP}$]

Predicates of motion, evoking a sense of directionality from one participant to another, code the two constituents with the nominative and the dative. The second constituent marked by the dative morpheme indicates a goal of a real or perceived motion. The goal may include a place arrived at (1), a target of a physical or mental action (2), or the addressee of a communication event (3).

(1) Motion towards a place

Ranjit pansələ-ṭə ya-nəwa
Ranjit temple-DAT go-IND
'Ranjit is going to the temple'

puusa gaha-ṭə nagi-nəwa
cat tree-DAT climb-ING
'The cat is climbing the tree'

lamai gangə-ṭə pani-nəwa
children river-DAT jump-IND
'The children jump into the river'

(2) Target of a physical or mental action

    Ranjit balla-ṭə gaha-nəwa
    Ranjit dog-DAT hit-IND
    'Ranjit is hitting the dog'

    Chitra hæmədaamə amma-ṭə wandi-nəwa
    Chitra everyday mother-DAT worship-IND
    'Chitra worships her mother everyday'

    mahattea minisun-ṭə hondəṭə saləkə-nəwa
    master people-DAT well treat-IND
    'The master treats people well'

(3) Addressee of communication activities

    taatta Ranjit-ṭə kataa kərə-nəwa
    father Ranjit-DAT call-IND
    'Father is calling Ranjit'

    Mendis səər apə-ṭə ugannə-nəwa
    Mendis Sir we-DAT teach-IND
    'Mr Mendis teaches us'

    guruwərəya laməin-ṭə prəsansa kərə-nəwa
    teacher children-DAT praise-IND
    'The teacher praises the children'

(o) [NP$_{1\ NOM}$ NP$_{2\ INS}$ Pred.$_{VP}$]

Inclusive construction: The second constituent marked by the instrumental morpheme indicates an object or a quality the referent of the first constituent is endowed with.

    gaha mal-wəlin pire-nawa
    tree flower-PL.INS be full-IND
    'The tree will be full of flowers'

    miniha saniip-en in-nəwa
    man health-INS be-IND
    'The man is well'

    lamea weedanaw-en kææ gaha-nəwa
    child pain-INS cry-IND
    'The child is crying with pain'

(p) [NP$_{1\ NOM}$ NP$_{2\ ekkə}$ Pred.$_{VP}$]

Active comitative construction: Reciprocal verbs are used with the first constituent indicating an active agent and the second constituent marked by *ekkə* indicating a partner.

Ranjit Chitra ekkə wiwaahə we-nəwa
Ranjit Chitra ekkə marry-IND
'Ranjit is getting married to Chitra'

Sunil Nimal ekkə raṇḍu we-nəwa
Sunil Nimal ekkə quarrel-IND
'Sunil is quarreling with Nimal'

eyaa man ekkə amənaapə we-nəwa
she/he me ekkə be displeased-IND
'She will be displeased with me'

(q) [NP$_{1\ NOM}$ NP$_{2\ DAT}$ NP$_{3\ NOM(ACC)}$ Pred.$_{vp}$]

This is the typical ditransitive structure. Verbs of giving or transferring are subcategorized for an agent, a transferred object and a recipient. In terms of constituent order, the recipient indicated by the dative appears before the transferred object marked by the nominative or optionally by the accusative. In some cases transferred objects will be abstract entities.

Ranjit Chitra-ṭə leensu-ak de-nəwa
Ranjit Chitra-DAT handkerchief-INDF give-IND
'Ranjit gives Chitra a handkerchief'

taatta lemea-ṭə salli yawə-nəwa
father child-DAT money send-IND
'Father sends his child money'

nangi mal gaha-ṭə waturə daa-nəwa
yanger sister flower tree-DAT water put-IND
'Younger sister is watering the flower plants'

Mendis səər apə-ṭə ingriisi uganwə-nəwa
Mendis Sir we-IND English teach-IND
'Mr Mendis teaches us English'

minissu maləgiyə ayə-ṭə pin de-nəwa
people dead persons-DAT meritorious feelings give-IND
'People transfer to dead persons their meritorious feelings (according to the Buddhist tradition)'

Transferred objects may precede recipients in the argument structure according to the structure of information intended to be expressed, as in the following.

Ranjit leensuə Chitra-ṭə de-nəwa
Ranjit handkerchief Chitra-DAT give-IND
'Ranjit gives the handkerchief to Chitra'

Such sentences are rather based on the following structure.

(r)   [NP$_{1\text{ NOM}}$ NP$_{2\text{ NOM(ACC)}}$ NP$_{3\text{ DAT}}$ Pred.$_{vp}$]

This ditransitive structure seems to be appropriate for more concrete transfer actions, compared with the sentences in (q). Verbs of placement are employed with an agent, a transferred object and a destination. Thus the constituent order is nominative + nominative (accusative) + dative.

taatta   salli   laachchuə-ṭə   daa-nəwa
father   money   drawer-DAT   put-IND
'Father puts money into the drawer'

babaa   hændə   boonikka-ge   kaṭə-ṭə   obə-nəwa
baby   spoon   doll-GEN   mouth-DAT   push-IND
'The baby is pushing the spoon into the doll's mouth'

lamea   puusa(-wə)   midulə-ṭə   wiisi kəlaa
child   cat(-ACC)   yard-DAT   throw.PAST
'The child threw the cat into the yard'

Destination may be indicated by a postpositional phrase instead of a dative constituent. Thus the last sentence given above can be rendered with a postposition as follows.

lamea   puusa(-wə)   ændə   uḍəṭə   wiisi kəlaa
child   cat(-ACC)   bed   onto   throw.PAST
'The child threw the cat onto the bed'

(s)   [NP$_{1\text{ NOM}}$ NP$_{2\text{ NOM}}$ NP$_{3\text{ LOC/PP}}$ Pred.$_{vp}$]

This structure is obtained when the third constituent of placement verbs is conceptualized as a location rather than a destination. Thus the third constituent is added with a locative suffix or a locative postposition. Compare with the pattern (r).

taatta   salli   laachchu-e   daa-nəwa
father   money   drawer-LOC   put-IND
Lit. 'Father puts money in the drawer'
'Father leaves money in the drawer'

amma   haal   watur-e   daa-nəwa
mother   money   water-LOC   put-IND
'Mother soaks rice in water/'Mother leaves rice to soak in the water'

Chitra   pot   meese   uḍə   tiə-nəwa
Chitra   books   table   on   put-IND
'Chitra keeps books on the table'

(t) [NP$_{1\,\text{NOM}}$ NP$_{2\,\text{NOM}}$ NP$_{3\,\text{ABL}}$ Pred.$_{vp}$]

When the destination of an object needs to get expressed, in particular, when a sense of movement is included in the semantic scope, the resultant structure has the third constituent marked by the ablative *-en/-in*.[1] Compare with the patterns (r) and (s).

    Ranjit puṭuə midul-en tiə-nəwa
    Ranjit chair yard-ABL put-IND
    'Ranjit is moving the chair and putting it in the yard'

    mamə babaa(-wə) kaamər-en tiə-nəwa
    I   baby(-ACC) room-ABL put-IND
    'I'll carry the baby and put him in the room'

    Chitra leensuə   meese uḍ-in tiə-nəwa
    Chitra handkerchief table on-ABL put-IND
    'Chitra is leaving the handkerchief on the table'

(u) [NP$_{1\,\text{NOM}}$ NP$_{2\,\text{ABL}}$ NP$_{3\,\text{NOM}}$ Pred.$_{vp}$]

Verbs of receiving are used with the first constituent representing the receiver, the second constituent marked by the ablative marker *-en/-in* or *-gen* indicating the source and the third constituent denoting the transferred object. The ablative marker *-en/-in* is added to an inanimate participant while *-gen* is attached to an animate participant. An act of receiving denoted by this type of sentence may also contain a transfer of some abstract entity.

    api mee kaḍ-en   baḍu   gan-nəwa
    we this shop-ABL commodities buy-IND
    'We buy things from this shop'

    mamə Ranjit-gen yaturə illa gan-nəwa
    I   Ranjit-ABL key   ask and get-IND
    'I will borrow the key from Ranjit'

    lamai   Mendis səər-gen ingriisi igenə gan-nəwa
    children Mendis sir-ABL English learn-IND
    'The children learn English from Mr Mendis'

This structure is also used to express a "fictive transfer" when a transfer is anticipated to occur from an animate participant, as in the following sentences.

---

[1] One may find it odd that the destination should be in the ablative. However, to native speakers of Sinhala, these are very natural sentences. At least when a motion is involved, the dative is overrun by the ablative.

mamə Ranjit-gen prasnə-ak aha-nəwa
I Ranjit-ABL question-INDF ask-IND
'I will ask a question of Ranjit'

eyaa Chitra-gen pilutura dænəgan-nəwa
she/he Chitra-ABL answer know-IND
'She will know the answer from Chitra'

api oyaa-gen meekə balaaporottu we-nəwa
we you-ABL this expect-IND
'We expect this from you'

(v) [NP$_{1\,\text{NOM}}$ NP$_{2\,\text{ekkə}}$ NP$_{3\,\text{NOM}}$ Pred.$_{\text{vp}}$]

One comitative construction occurring with two-place reciprocal verbs was already given as (p). The present comitative construction occurs with three-pace predicates formed with reciprocal verbs, creating a transitive event. While the second constituent marked by *ekkə* denotes the partner of the reciprocal event, the third constituent indicates the shared object.

Ranjit Chitra ekkə jil boolə bedaa gan-nəwa
Ranjit Chitra ekkə marbles divide-IND
'Ranjit shares the marbles with Chitra'

Chitra Sumana ekkə saariə maaru kərə gan-nəwa
Chitra Sumana ekkə sari exchange-IND
'Chitra exchanges the sari with Sumana'

mamə mudəlaali ekkə prasne kataa kərə gan-naŋ
I trader ekkə problem discus-OPT
'I'll discuss the problem with the trader'

2. Adjunct noun phrases

To understand a wider range of sentences used in the language, we need to pay attention to NPs beyond the scope of arguments. While most argument structure types are realized in the form of case relations, not all case relations represent argument structures. Many noun phrases that do not qualify as arguments are used optionally to modify predicates. Such adjunct phrases are discussed in this section. Both case inflections and postpositional particles are used as adjunct markers. Some case suffixes used to encode arguments given above are also used to combine adjunct phrases with predicates.

(a) Dative -*tə*: Dative -*tə* is used to express purpose, source, time, standard or similar domains of application.

mamə winoode-ṭə   mal   wawənəwa (purpose)
I   pleasure-DAT flowers   grow
'I grow flowers for pleasure'

eyaa stuṭə-ṭə anḍə-nəwa (source)
she/he joy-DAT cry-IND
'She's crying out of joy'

amma   maalu kirə-ṭə   uyə-nəwa (manner)
mother fish   milk-DAT   cook-IND
'Mother cooks fish in 'milk style''

lamai   tarənge-ṭə   oru   padinəwa (manner)
children competition-DAT rafts paddle
'Children are racing their rafts against each other'

kamkaruwo akurə-ṭə   wæḍə kərə-nəwa (standard)
laborers   letter-DAT work-IND
'The laborers work to rule'

paha-ṭə   saappu waha-nəwa (temporal)
five-DAT   shops   close-IND
'Shops close at five'

(b) Instrumental/ablative *-in/-en/-gen*: Instrumental/ablative *-in/-en/-gen* is used to express instrument, duration of time, and various sources.

miniha taraadi-en baḍu   kirə-nəwa   (instrument)
man   scale-INS   commodities measure-IND
'He measures commodities with scales'

minissu tawəmə harəkun-gen kumburu haa-nəwa   (instrument)
people   still   cattle-INS   fields   plough-IND
'people still plough their fields with cattle'

Ranjit pæy-en   wæḍee iwərə kərə-nəwa (duration of time)
Ranjit hour-INS   work   finish-IND
'Ranjit will finish his job in an hour'

miniha gææni-ge   konḍ-en   alla gan-nəwa (measure for grasping)
man   woman-GEN   hair-INS grasp-IND
'The man grasps the woman by her hair'

gah-en   geḍiə wæṭe-nəwa (source)
tree-ABL fruit fall-IND
'The fruit falls from the tree'

tuwaal-en   lee   galə-nəwa (source)
wound-ABL   blood flow-IND
'Blood is flowing from the wound'

maduruwan-gen ledə boowe-nəwa (source)
mosquitoes-ABL diseases spread-IND
'Diseases are spread through mosquitoes'

kussiə pætten suwənd-ak e-nəwa (source)
kitchen side-ABL good smell-INDF come-IND
'There is a good smell coming in the direction of the kitchen'

(c) Locative marker: Locative *-e* marks the location of an activity, in addition to the location of states given earlier.

maaluwo ṭænki-e piinə-nəwa
fishes tank-LOC swim-IND
'The fishes are swimming in the tank'

Ranjit bænku-e wædə kərə-nəwa
Ranjit bank-LOC work-IND
'Ranjit works for a bank'

amma midul-e wii wanə-nəwa
mother yard-LOC paddy spread (for drying)-IND
'Mother is spreading paddy on the yard'

(d) Genitive marker: Genitive *-ge/-gee* indicates a possessive relationship between one noun phrase and another noun phrase. The constituent that takes the suffix *-ge/-gee* must be an animate noun. The possessor role in an inanimate noun is marked by the locative suffix.

aliya-ge hondəwælə
elephant-GEN trunk
'the trunk of the elephant'

Ranjit-ge karunaawə
Ranjit-GEN kindness
'Ranjit's kindness'

pot-ee pitu
book-LOC pages
'the pages of the book'

winaasy-ee mulə
destruction-LOC beginning
'the beginning of destruction'

(e) Vocative marker: The vocative marker does not indicate an argument relation at the sentential level; it occurs outside the sentence, pragmatically relating a noun to a sentence. It is added to a noun when its reference is addressed by the speaker. The vocative marking suffixes include *-e, -ee, -oo, -ni* and *-ənee*.

nangi-e 'younger sister,'
amm-ee 'Mother,'
laməy-oo 'child,'
noonaawəru-ni mahatwəru-ni 'ladies and gentlemen,'
dewi-ənee 'God,'

Note that common names, kinship terms, status names or titles may be used in the address form in Sinhala.

(f) Postpositional phrases are often used to convey various spatial meanings. The postpositions in the following group of examples indicate the location of stationary objects or animate referents with regard to the major constituent used with the existential verb.

iskoole langə kaḍə-ak tie-nəwa
school near shop-INDF be-IND
'There is a shop near the school'

ṭoiləṭ ekə ætule gemb-ek in-nəwa
toilet one inside frog-INDF be-IND
'There is a frog inside the toilet'

gee piṭipasse lind-ak tie-nəwa
house behind well-INDF be-IND
'There is a well behind the house'

gee issəraha ambə gah-ak tie-nəwa
house in front of mango tree-INDF be-IND
'There is a mango tree in front of the house'

gaha yaṭə ball-ek in-nəwa
tree under dog-INDF be-IND
'There is a dog under the tree'

wæṭə digəṭə mal
fence along flowers
'There are flowers along the fence'

Most of the postpositions of location are relational nouns appearing in bare form, while some of them take case suffixes as in *ætule* (locative), *piṭipasse* (locative) and *digəṭə* (dative).

(g) The following group of sentences has postpositions of movement. Most of them have the ablative *-in* to indicate movement.

Ranjit paarə digee duwə-nəwa
Ranjit road along run-IND
'Ranjit is running along the road'

lamai   paarə   harəha   pani-nəwa
children road   across   leap-IND
'Children suddenly run across the road'

booṭṭuwa paaləmə yaṭin   ya-nəwa
boat   bridge   under   go-IND
'The boat is sailing under the bridge'

walaakulu atərin   handə   matuwe-nəwa
clouds   through moon   appear-IND
'The moon appears through the clouds'

gamə   mædin   paar-ak   ya-nəwa
village through road-INDF go-IND
'There is a road running through the village'

balla boole uḍin   pani-nəwa
dog   ball   over   jump-IND
'The dog jumps over the ball'

(h) Possessive *langə* and *atee*: Some postpositional phrases, occurring in limited distribution, indicate a type of possessive relation. The locative postposition *langə* whose literal meaning is 'near' and *atee* whose lexical source is 'hand' plus locative suffix are used to denote such possessive relations.

man langə salli   tie-nəwa
I   langə money   be-IND
'I have money'

man atee yaturə tie-nəwa
I   atee key   be-IND
'I have the key'

(i) Ablative *indan/indəla* and allative *turu/kan*: Ablative *indan/indəla* specifies both the spatial and temporal inceptive points of an activity, while allative *turu* and *kan* are only used to denote the temporal terminal point of an activity.

api aṭ-ee   indan paha wenə   kan wædə kərə-nəwa
we   eight-LOC   from   five become to   work do-IND
'We work from eight o'clock to five o'clock'

Ranjit pansəl-ee   indan isṭeesəmə-ṭə   duwə-nəwa
Ranjit temple-LOC   from   station-DAT   run-IND
'Ranjit runs from the temple to the station'

Notice that the spatial terminal point is indicated by the allative/dative suffix *-ṭə*, not the postposition. Also notice that the postpositional phrase for the inceptive point consists of the locative case nominal plus the postposition *indan* whereas the postpositional phrase for the temporal terminal point is of complex type. It is of the "cased head" type, similar to the relative clause construction: the direct case nominal is followed by the verbal form *wenə* before it joins the postposition.

3. Grammatical relations

The first noun phrase of a clause that serves as an argument of the verb is referred to as the "subject", which is defined within the grammar by some specific characteristics, surface or covert. Some have argued, especially in the context of the South Asian linguistic area (Bhat 1988, for example), that there is no need to postulate a subject relation in the case of languages that make use of distinct grammatical devices for representing the semantic and pragmatic relations, and use some of these very same semantic relations as the "pivots" of their grammatical processes (Foley & Van Valin 1984).

The situation in Sinhala with regard to subject remains controversial. Arguments both in favor of and refuting the existence of a subject role are found in the literature. Gair 1976 demonstrates that there are neither surface nor covert characteristics to prove that the subject relation occupies a central and fundamental position in Sinhala syntax. As the result of an analysis of covert characteristics such as control of null arguments, Henadeerage (2002) has established that control and syntactic pivots in participle adjunct phrases provide reliable evidence for syntactic subjecthood in Colloquial Sinhala and that non-nominative subjects share the same subjecthood properties displayed by nominative subjects.

While carrying opposing arguments and conclusions, these studies are agreed on one important fact: surface characteristics such as morphological marking on NPs, namely case marking, do not provide evidence to postulate grammatical relations like subject and object in Sinhala. This fact is highly relevant to the description of functional categories of sentence constituents. The illustration of simple sentence types given in Section 1 of this chapter indicates that constituents with subject-like features appear in intransitive, transitive and ditransitive sentences in Sinhala. The relevant sentences are repeated here.

(1) a. balla burə-nəwa
dog bark-IND
'The dog is barking.'

b. lamea-wə wæṭenəwa
child-ACC fall
'The child is falling.'

c. Ranjit-ṭə æṇḍe-nəwa
Ranjit-DAT cry.INVL-IND
'Ranjit breaks out crying (suddenly).'

(2) a. Chitra puusa(-wə) hoyə-nəwa
       Chitra cat(-ACC) find-IND
       'Chitra is looking for the cat.'

   b. Ranjit-ṭə puusa(-wə) pæægē-nəwa
      Ranjit-DAT cat(-ACC) step on.INVL-IND
      'Ranjit is accidentally stepping on the cat.'

   c. miniha atin lassənəṭə pælə hæde-nəwa
      he atin very well plants make.INVL-IND
      'He can do tree planting in a systematic way.'

(3) taatta lemea-ṭə salli yawə-nəwa
    father child-DAT money send-IND
    'Father sends his child money.'

Observe that nominative, accusative and dative subjects occur with intransitive verbs, as shown in (1a–c) while nominative, dative and instrumental subjects occur with transitive verbs, as shown in (2a–c). The example in (3) shows a nominative subject appearing in a ditransitive construction. Also note that direct objects marked by the accusative appear with transitive verbs regardless of the case marking on the subject NP, as shown by (2 a and b). Further, the accusative marker appears not only on direct objects but also on subject NPs, as in (1b). Based on the facts relating to the appearance of accusative marking on both objects and intransitive subjects, some scholars, like Gunasinghe (1985), assumed that Sinhala, at least with respect to its colloquial variety, is an ergative language. Some others (Chandralal 1993 and Kishomoto 1996) have attempted to solve this problem of grammatical relations in terms of the notions of Actor and Undergoer based on the Role and Reference Grammar theory of verbal semantics (Foley & Van Valin 1984).

Now recall the aspects of Sinhala verb morphology (Chapters 5 and 6). There are two forms of the verbs distinguished on morphological grounds as A and P, whose derivational relationship is established through a productive lexical process. It is true to say, to a large extent, that non-nominative subjects appear with P (inactive) verbs whereas nominative subjects appear with A (active) verbs. It is not difficult to see that with this lexical process the subjects of derived structures (1b, c and 2b, c) are changed to non-nominative subjects bearing the semantic roles of Undergoer, Experiencer and Accidental agent. Interestingly, the internal arguments of these verbs remain unaffected by the lexical process. Thus, two-place predicates may take their subjects in the dative while allowing their objects to appear in the accusative, as in (2b). This shows why morphological case marking on NPs cannot be taken as reliable proof of syntactic subjecthood in Sinhala, as mentioned before. To sum up, Sinhala case marking and underlying thematic roles are lexically determined.

These facts and, further, the resistance of Sinhala case to change under syntactic processes have led Gair (1996) to form the view called the STRONG LEXICAL CASE-ASSIGNMENT HYPOTHESIS.

The strong lexical case-assignment hypothesis claims that Sinhala is a "strong case marking" language, in which case the case marking of arguments is intimately linked to theta-roles. Since verbs are associated in the lexicon with a theta-grid, the links between the corresponding A and P verbs would be shown either by incorporating lexical rules or by consolidating lexical entries. Under this proposal, the order of arguments in lexical entries gives the unmarked surface order of Sinhala verbal sentences, though the case is not so clear for nonverbal sentences. In Sinhala, volitive agents are not only unmarked subjects but also nominative marked because the nominative remains specified for the first constituent for both transitive and intransitive verbs. Subjects marked for dative, accusative and instrumental are never active agents. Their thematic role is experiencer, patient/theme, or "accidental agent".

This state of affairs explains why transitive constructions require animate subjects whereas most intransitive constructions are odd with animate subjects in Sinhala. For example, the sentence in (4) will sound unnatural to Sinhala speakers, while a construction of the intransitive inchoative type, as in (5), will be normal in colloquial speech.

(4) gaŋ waturə mulu gamə mə winaasə kəlaa
     flood   whole village EM destroy.PAST
     'The flood destroyed the whole village.'

(5) a. gaŋ watur-en mulu gamə mə winaasə unaa
       Flood-INST   whole village EM be destroyed.PAST
       'The whole village was destroyed by the flood.'

    b. gaŋ waturə-ţə mulu gamə mə winaasə unaa
       flood-DAT   whole village EM be destroyed.PAST
       'The whole village was destroyed because of the flood'

This contrasts with English, which has argument types such as the instrument, location, cause, etc. which can be brought to the position of the topic (Fillmore 1968). Examples:

(6) a. The key opened the door.
    b. The wind toppled the tree.
    c. The caravan sleeps four comfortably.

These examples show cases of grammatical cases changing under syntactic processes. Non-agents like instrument (a), cause (b) and location (c) are brought to the pre-verbal position as topics by not specifying the agent (Batt 1988). What happens in

Sinhala is that nominative remains the default unmarked case with underlying volitive agent, while the remaining arguments may appear in subject position without any change in their case marking. An array of intransitive, impersonal constructions allows these non-agentive arguments to appear in the accusative, dative or instrumental cases as specified by the relevant intransitive or detransitivized verbs. Thus, the animacy factor closely works with case marking to bring out the volitional/involitional distinction in Sinhala.

This can also explain apparent anomalies of some verbal structures. In general, verbs in Sinhala do not show number, person, and gender agreements. However, there are a few exceptions in which subject-verb agreement seems to work to some extent, particularly with respect to person, which were described in Chapter 5.

Verbs in the imperative mood, since they are intrinsically involved with second person subjects, need to be selected according to a grading system in which second person pronouns are allocated. The grades of second person pronouns represent levels of respect and intimacy between the speaker and the addressee. For instance, a pronoun of a lower grade in terms of the speaker-addressee relationship, such as *umbə*, is not used with a polite imperative form like *yannə*, the imperative form of the intransitive verb *yanəwa* 'go'. Thus *umbə yannə* is an extremely unnatural expression. Instead, *oyaa/ohee/obətumaa yannə* (respect/polite form) or *umbə paləyaŋ* (impolite/informal form) is acceptable as they show agreement between the second person subject and the verb.

Permissive forms, which are considered as indirect imperatives, take common nouns or third person pronouns as their subjects.

(7) a. lamea ṭiiwii baladden
       child TV   see.PERM
       'Let the child watch TV'

   b. potə wæṭunaawe
       book fall.PERM
       'Let the book fall'

   c. eekə ohe tibunəden
       it   just be.PERM
       'Let it just be there'

Another type of verb that has restrictions on the subject is the inferential mood. Verbs in the inferential mood, in general, have common nouns and second person or third person pronouns as their subject.

(8) a. miniha pol   adiiwi
       man   coconut pull.INFR
       'The man might pull the (load of) coconuts.'

b. lamea-wə wæʈeewi
child-ACC fall.INFR
'The child may fall.'

c. oyaa hondəʈə nidaaganiiwi
you well sleep.INFR
'You might sleep well!' (sarcastically)

The reason why both permissive verbs and inferential verbs take non-first person subjects can be attributed to the verbal suffixes. Permissive and inferential suffixes are basically involitive. As involitive suffixes, they cannot support agentive role for their initial argument. The absence of a specific agent is supported by the optional accusative marking on animate nouns as in (8b). Third persons or common nouns are free to appear in these structures as speakers show a general reluctance to accord volition to third persons.

Let us turn to another two verb forms that require some semblance of agreement. Hortative verbs and volitional optative verbs, conversely, only take first person subjects. Observe the examples for hortative verbs in (9) and those for optative verbs in (10).

(9) a. api karatte adi-mu
we cart draw-HORT
'Let's pull the cart.'

b. api piʈʈəni-e perəle-mu
we ground-LOC roll-HORT
Let's roll on the ground.'

c. api soopaaw-en wæʈe-mu
we sofa-ABL fall-HORT
'Let's fall down from the sofa.'

(10) a. mamə gaha kapa-nnaŋ
I tree cut-OPT
'I'll cut the tree'

b. mamə wæʈe-nnaŋ
I fall-OPT
'I'll fall (pretend to fall).'

Hortative verbs and optative verbs both have volitive suffixes, which means that they are specified for volitive agents. Their first person subjects are compatible with this agent specification. The lexical specification of the agent in the suffix leads to all subjects being agentive even when they appear with intransitive, involitive lexical verbs. The verb *perəlenəwa*, which has both volitive and involitive interpretations, gets the volitive meaning solidified by the hortative suffix as in (9b). The verb *wæʈenəwa*, which lexically has only involitive meaning, is converted into the volitional sense, as in (10b), by virtue of the volitional suffix.

The Sinhala subject-verb correlation pattern is given below.

Verb	Suffix	Subject	Theta role
Inferential verb	involitive suffix	non-first person subject	non-agentive
Hortative verb	volitive suffix	first person subject	agentive
Optative verb	volitive suffix	first person subject	agentive

How this kind of correlation obtains may be explained by referring to the animacy hierarchy of NPs pointed out by Silverstien (1976) and Dixon (1979). The animacy hierarchy works along the NP types as follows:

> first/second person pronoun < third person pronoun < proper noun < human common noun < animate common noun < inanimate common noun.

An NP from the leftmost end is more likely to occur in agent position, and the degree of agentivity decreases along the rightward line. Accordingly, an NP from the rightmost end is more likely to occur in patient position. Thus inferential verbs, being inherently marked for a lesser degree of volition, appear with non-first person or common nouns whereas hortative and optative verbs with a higher degree of volition take first person subjects. This correlation pattern shows how the verbal suffixes associated with animacy and volition impose restrictions on thematic roles and that case roles are assigned to NPs under appropriate environments including the influence of animacy.

Although all these verbs including the verbs in the imperative mood accommodate the occurrence of agreement in a restricted sense, i.e. with respect to the category of person, this does not affect the notion that Sinhala does not have subject-verb agreement. Moreover, since the category of person thoroughly interacts with contextual and pragmatic factors, the restrictions imposed by these verbs can easily be considered to be of a pragmatic rather than of a grammatical nature.

This brings us to another aspect of subject NPs in Sinhala. Although most examples provided for the example sentences are given in their full form, in actual discourse one or more constituents are omitted when they are readily recoverable from the linguistic or nonlinguistic context. For instance, the first person and second person pronouns are such constituents that often go missing from sentences. Instead of second person pronouns, kinship terms, status names and titles are more likely to appear. Observe the following examples.

(11) tawə keek kæǣll-ak de-nnə də
more cake piece-INDEF give-INF Q
'Can I give you another piece of cake?'

(12) poḍi kæællæ-ak de-nnə
    small piece-INDF give-IMP
    'Give me a small piece.'

(13) amma ya-nnə
    mother go-IMP
    'You may go, Mother.'

(14) a. Ranjit koo?
       Ranjit where
       'Where is Ranjit?'

   b. bat ka-nəwa
      rice eat-IND
      'He's eating rice/is having a meal.'

In (11) the first person subject and second person indirect object and in (12) the second person subject are deleted. In (13) the kinship name *amma* 'mother' is used instead of the second person subject. In (14b), which is given in response to the question in (14a), the third person subject, if inserted, would be redundant; the sentence sounds natural without it.

While the status of the grammatical subject has been treated in some detail, the syntactic role of the object is given residual attention in this discussion. In Sinhala the same nominative or direct case provides the surface form to both subject and direct object. However, when an animate/human noun takes on an unaccustomed role, i.e. as Undergoer, instead of its customary agentive role, it is marked by the accusative. This is, again, compatible with the animacy hierarchy since an inanimate common noun as the most qualified candidate for object/patient relation appears unmarked. The direct object in Sinhala is identified by its preverbal, post-subject, mid-sentence position. When there is any ambiguity, for instance, when both subject and direct object are animate nouns or when the object is preposed the ambiguity may be dispelled by marking for the accusative, as in the following examples.

(15) a. balla nayaa hæpuwa
       dog cobra bite.PAST
       'The dog bit the cobra.'

   b. balla nayaa-wə hæpuwa
      dog cobra-ACC bite.PAST
      'The dog bit the cobra.'

   c. nayaa-wə balla hæpuwa
      cobra-ACC dog bite.PAST
      'The dog bit the cobra.'

All the three sentences, though a little different in surface form, have the same semantic interpretation. There is a disambiguated sentence in (b), and the object has come to the topic position in (c).

The direct object may appear not only in the nominative and accusative but also in dative form, as shown in the previous chapter. Direct objects governed by the following types of verbs take the dative marker: *wandinəwa* 'worship', *saləkənəwa* 'treat', *kataa kərənəwa* 'call', *baninəwa* 'scold, blame', *prəsansaa kərənəwa* 'praise', *yadinəwa* 'pray, beseech', *gahanəwa* 'hit, beat', *talənəwa* 'beat, strike', *widinəwa* 'shoot', *aninəwa* 'stab, poke', etc. The dative marking may here indicate the sense of directionality commonly associated with these verbs.

CHAPTER 8

Noun phrase and verb phrase constructions

1. Noun phrase

Sinhala nominal phrases observe the canonical order of SOV languages; the modifier, whether a relative clause, an adjective or a genitive phrase, precedes the modified noun.

1.1 Simple noun modifiers

Genitives appear with the genitive suffix -*ge* before the head noun as in [[NP -*ge*] NP]. Genitive phrases generally indicate the possessor of the head noun, as in the following examples.

(1) ma-ge   atə
    I-GEN   hand
    'my hand'

(2) Ranjit-ge   warədə
    Ranjit-GEN fault
    'Ranjit's fault'

(3) Chitra-ge   maama
    Chitra-GEN uncle
    'Chitra's uncle'

In a similar way, two NPs are connected through case markers like the locative and the dative to indicate different semantic relations:

Locative marker:

(4) pot-ee   piṭu
    book-LOC   pages
    'the pages of the book'

(5) hit-ee   dukə
    mind-LOC   pain
    'the pain of the mind'

(6) awaasənaa-we   mahatə
    ill fortune-LOC largeness
    'the immensity of the ill fortune'

The dative is used to indicate the cause related to the referent of the head noun:

(7) marənəyə-ṭə heetuwə
death-DAT reason
'the reason for the death'

(8) prasne-ṭə mulə
problem-DAT origin
'the origin of the problem'

(9) leḍee-ṭə beetə
illness-DAT medicine
'the medicine for the disease'

All the major word categories of noun, adjective, and verb can serve as modifiers of a head noun. Their placement before the head noun fulfills that function.

(10) dat kækkumə (noun)
tooth ache
'tooth-ache'

(11) badee kækkumə (noun)
stomach-LOC ache
'stomach-ache'

(12) usə miniha (adjective)
tall man
'the tall man'

(13) kalu galə (adjective)
black stone
'the black stone'

(14) duə-nə kochchiə (verb)
run-NPT train
'the running train'

(15) allə-pu gedərə (verb)
join-PTAD house
'the house next door'

When serving as a modifier, a noun may take the base form, as in (10) or a case form, as in (11). In case of verbs, the adjectival form is applied, as in (14) and (15).

1.2 Clausal noun modifiers

In clausal noun modification, modifying clauses regularly precede head nouns in the following form: [modifying clause] [head noun]. The most widely used clausal noun modification is realized in the relative construction.

Relative clauses in Sinhala do not use relative pronouns. Relative clauses are verb final and, therefore, having a verb phrase to mark the clause boundary, they do not need particular means such as relative pronouns. The case of the head noun that is coreferential with the constituents specified by the predicate of the relative clause indicates various semantic relations. In the following examples, where the relative clause is given in brackets, the head nouns *amma* 'mother' (16), *darua* 'child' (17), *lamea* 'child' (18), *pihiə* 'knife' (19), *kaḍee* 'shop' (20) and *garaajəyə* 'garage' (21) have nominative, accusative, dative, instrumental, ablative and locative relation, respectively, with reference to the predicate of the relative clause. The original location of the head noun within the relative clause is indicated by the symbol ø. As (16) below shows, the Sinhala relative construction does not make a distinction between restrictive and descriptive relative clauses.

(16) [ø darua-wə hoyə-nə] amma
child-ACC search-NPT mother
'the mother who searches for her child'
or 'the mother, who searches for her child'

(17) [amma ø hoyə-nə] darua
mother search-NPT child
'the child that the mother is searching for'

(18) [Ranjit potə ø dunnə] lamea
Ranjit book give.PTAD child
'the child to whom Ranjit gave the book'

(19) [Ranjit ø paan kapə-pu] pihiə
Ranjit bread cut-PT knife
'the knife with which Ranjit cut bread'

(20) [Ranjit ø baḍu gan-nə] kaḍee
Ranjit commodities buy-NPT shop
'the shop that Ranjit buys his commodities'

(21) [Ranjit ø wædə kərə-nə] garaajəyə
Ranjit work-NPT garage
'the garage where Ranjit works'

The case marking that indicates the relation between the noun phrase and the predicate of the relative clause is not present in the surface construction. This shows that relative clause formation in Sinhala is achieved through the "gapping" strategy and that there is no need for dangling case markers. The first three examples, (16), (17) and (18), respectively showing subject, direct object and indirect object and the remaining examples with oblique relations all demonstrate how the first four positions of the "Noun Phrase Accessibility Hierarchy" postulated by Keenan and Comrie 1977 are relativized.

Noun Phrase Accessibility Hierarchy
SU > DO > IO > OBL > GEN > OCOMP (object of comparison)

The relativized dative constituents include not only the indirect object but also some other oblique relations:

(22) [nayaa ø ringuə] gulə
cobra creep. PT hole
'the hole that the cobra crept into'

(23) [alia ø wæṭunə] wæwə
elephant fall. PT tank
'the tank that the elephant fell into'

Further, one may observe that a genitive constituent can be relativized, too, as the following examples show.

(24) [Ranjit ø oluwə atəgaa-pu] lamea
Ranjit head stroke-PTAD child
'the child whose head Ranjit stroked'

(25) [Ranjit ø leensuwə hangə-pu] lamea
Ranjit handkerchief hide-PTAD child
'the child whose handkerchief Ranjit hid'

(26) [Ranjit ø baisikəlee ussə-pu] lamea
Ranjit bicycle steal-PTAD child
'the child whose bicycle Ranjit stole'

Since the case relation of the head noun is identified by pragmatic factors as well as syntactic processing rather than by overt case marking the gapping strategy may not always bring satisfactory results. Look at the following sentence.

(27) ??[Ranjit ø baisikəlee happə-pu] lamea
Ranjit bicycle strike-PTAD child
'the child whose bicycle Ranjit struck (against something)'

Sentence (27) is unintelligible for the intended interpretation. It will be felicitous if the intended interpretation is 'the child against whom Ranjit struck the bicycle'. Let us get the problem straightened out this way. While the relative clause is expected to be a statement about the head noun, the lexical predicate of the relative clause and some other factors are relevant for judging the nature of this relationship. In the sentence above, on the one hand, there is an intended genitive relation that does not represent an inalienable relationship between the head noun and the complement of the clausal predicate, and, on the other hand, the verbal predicate has the potential of bearing an adjunct relation in addition to the direct object relation. In fact, this adjunct relation is more aptly assumed, perhaps due to pragmatic reasons, as qualified to modify the head noun, thereby rendering the sentence in the unintended interpretation.

There are cases where even major constituents may confront problems in gapping:

(28) alia   marə-pu   miniha
elephant kill-PTAD man
a. 'the man who killed the elephant'
b. 'the man whom the elephant killed'

(28) is ambiguous between two structures: the first takes the head noun *miniha* 'man' as coreferential with the subject of the clausal predicate *marə* 'kill' whereas the other takes the head noun as coreferential with the direct object of the predicate. In (29) below, either the subject or the indirect object of the relative clause can be understood as deleted under coreferentiality with the head noun. Thus two interpretations obtain.

(29) potə   dunnə   lamea
book give-PT child
a. 'the child who gave the book (to someone)'
b. 'the child to whom (someone) gave the book'

The case interpretation of a head noun becomes more difficult when the predicate is inextricably involved with pragmatic factors. The deleted constituent is the object in (30) and the subject in (31) of the respective transitive verb. The gapping brings confusion to the structure because the subject can be freely deleted from a sentence like (30), and some transitive verbs like *wandinəwa* 'worship' can be used in an intransitive context, i.e. without a direct object, as in (31).

(30) [ø bala-nnə ya-nnə hiṭiə] leḍaa
see-INF   go-INF be-PT patient
'the patient whom (we) were going to see'

(31) [ø wandi-nnə ya-nnə hiṭiə] miniha
worship-INF go-INF be-PT man
'the man who was going to worship (some place/object/person)'

Another type of clausal noun modification is represented by "appositive construction" in which the head noun is modified by a clause providing an explicit statement about it. To introduce this clause and link it to the head noun, the hearsay expression *kiənə* 'say' is used which is equivalent to the English *that*.

(32) Ranjit bænda   kiənə aaranchiə
Ranjit got married say   news
'the news that Ranjit got married'

(33) Martin hitəla gaha kæpuwa kiənə kataawə
Martin intentionally tree cut.PAST say story
'the story that Martin cut the tree intentionally'

(34) kawədahari gey-ak hada-nnə oonæ kiənə kalpənaawə
someday house-INDF make-INF want say thought
'the thought that (I) want to build a house someday'

Finally, Sinhala allows double relativization. Observe the examples:

(35) [[anun pattu kərə-pu] paan-en eliə balə-nə] minissu
others light-PTAD lamp-INS light see-NPT people
'people who see by the light of a lamp lit by someone else'

(36) [[iie igenə gattə] paaḍəmə amətəkə we-chchə] lamai
yesterday learn.PT lesson forget-PT children
'children who have forgotten the lesson that was learned yesterday'

In (35) and (36) above the relative clause modifying the head noun has another clause embedded in it.

2. Verb phrase

In Sinhala, expressions modifying a verb can appear before or after it.

2.1 Declarative, interrogative, and negative

The formation of declarative expressions simply observes the normal word order.

(37) Ranjit bat ka-nəwa
Ranjit rice eat-IND
'Ranjit is eating.'

The same utterance can be used as a question albeit with a final rise in pitch.

(38) Ranjit bat ka-nəwa?
Ranjit rice eat-IND
'Ranjit is eating?'

"Interrogation" sounds legal and brutal after the verb when a yes-no question is involved.

(39) Ranjit bat ka-nəwa də?
Ranjit rice eat-IND Q
'Is Ranjit eating?'

If the question involves an interrogative word, the question particle *də* is added but there is no invariant rule regarding its position. The interrogative word accompanied by the particle *də* may appear either sentence-initially, as in (40a) and (41a), or sentence-finally, as in (40b) and (41b).

(40) a. kaudə   bat   ka-nn-e?
        who.Q   rice   eat-NPT-FOC
        'Who eats rice?'

   b. bat   ka-nn-e   kaudə?
      rice   eat-NPT-FOC   who.Q
      'Who eats rice?'

(41) a. monəwa-də   ka-nn-e?
        what-Q   eat-NPT-FOC
        'what do you eat?'

   b. ka-nn-e   monəwa-də?
      eat-NPT-FOC   what-Q
      'what do you eat?'

Note that with the interrogative word the verb should be changed to the focus form.

Negative expressions are formed by adding the negative particle *næœ* to the focus form of the verbal predicate.

(42) Ranjit   bat   ka-nn-e   næœ
     Ranjit   rice   eat-NPT-FOC   no
     'Ranjit does not eat rice.'

For a non-verbal predicate, the negative particle is *newei*.

(43) eyaa   guruwərə-ek   newei
     She/he   teacher-INDF   no
     'She is not a teacher.'

A negative question, that is, a negated yes-no question, is formed by simply adding the question particle *də* to the negative formation. (The question particle *də* coalesces with the negative particle *næœ* to form the negative question particle *næddə*.)

(44) Ranjit   bat   ka-nn-e   næddə?
     Ranjit   rice   eat-NPT-FOC   no.Q
     'Doesn't Ranjit eat rice?'

(45) eyaa   guruwərə-ek   newei   də?
     She/he   teacher-INDF   no   Q
     'Isn't she a teacher?'

The same negative question particle *næddə* is used to express a presupposition in a yes-no question. It has the function of the tag question found in English. However, there is another device to register a presupposition. That is, the particle *needə* is placed close to the final sentence boundary.

(46) Ranjit bat kanəwa needə?
Ranjit rice eat-IND needə
'Ranjit is eating, isn't he?'

(47) Ranjit bat ka-nn-e næĕ needə?
Ranjit rice eat-NPT-FOC no needə
'Ranjit isn't eating, is he?'

Consider that there is a notable difference between these sentences and English tag questions. Unlike in English, the same particle, *needə,* is added to the declarative sentence regardless of whether the latter is affirmative or negative. Further, the morpheme, being a particle, does not correspond in form to that of the lexical verb.

All the cases described above, except the interrogative word question, show that expressions for verbal modification follow the verbs. This is especially so for the negative particle. However, this does not represent an absolute universal. There are opposite cases. For instance, when an individual segment of a sentence is negated, the negative marker is placed before the negated constituent. In the following sentences the noun modifier, more specifically, the predicate of the relative clause is negated.

(48) no-kere-nə deewal
not-do.INVL-NPT things
'things that would not get done'

(49) no-kiə-pu kataa
not-say-PTAD talk
'words that were not uttered'

In these sentences only the relativized element is negated, and the negative marker is a prefix added to the verb.

2.2 Reciprocal verbs and reflexive verbs

Some expressions for verbal modification appear in the form of auxiliary verbs and are placed after the principal verb. Such verbal phrases are involved in the form of [Perfect Participle Form + Auxiliary Verb]. Reciprocal verbs and reflexive verbs, for instance, are formed thus by adding auxiliary verbs to the perfect participle form of the principal verb. The auxiliary verb *gannəwa* for both reciprocal and reflexive verbs has been grammaticalized from the lexical verb 'take'.

Reciprocal verbs:

(50) amma-i taatta-i bænə gan-nəwa
mother-and father-and scold-PP take-IND
'Father and mother are scolding each other.'

(51) Ranjit-ui Chitra-i badaa gatta
Ranjit-and Chitra-and embrace-PP take.PAST
'Ranjit and Chitra embraced each other.'

(52) Sunil-u-i Nimal-u-i gaha gan-nəwa
Sunil-and Nimal-and hit-PP take-IND
'Sunil and Nimal are hitting each other.'

The two arguments have been conjoined by the noun-coordinating particle -i, which is added to every item that enters into coordination. A consonant-ending noun and the particle -i are mediated by junction vowel -u-.

Reflexive verbs:

(53) lamea temaa gatta
child wet-PP take-PAST
'The child wet himself.'

(54) Ranjit hapaa gatta
Ranjit bite-PP take-PAST
'Ranjit bit himself.'

(55) lamea suura gatta
child scratch-PP take-PAST
'The child scratched himself.'

These sentences are considered as reflexive in the true sense of the word since the subject of the verb is simultaneously understood as the object of it as well. Therefore, they do not contain an object phrase or a lexical item expressing 'self'. The facts become explicit when the principal verb is placed in a sentence without the reflexive auxiliary. Compare the following sentences with (53), (54) and (55) above:

(56) lamea ø temuwa
child wet-PAST
'The child wet (something)'

(57) Ranjit ø hæpuwa
Ranjit bite-PAST
'Ranjit bit (something).'

(58) lamea ø siiruwa
child scratch-PAST
'The child scratched (something).'

The lexical verb alone cannot render the reflexive sense; it requires a separate argument in its second argument position.

Some reflexive sentences still retain the transitive sense in that they have as their object a body part or some other item in their surface construction.

(59) Chitra koṇḍe piira gatta
 Chitra hair comb-PP take-PAST
 'Chitra combed her hair.'

(60) oyaa atə hoodə gatta də?
 you hand wash-PP take.PAST Q
 'Did you wash your hands.'

(61) mamə bat bedaa gannəwa
 I rice serve-PP take-IND
 'I serve myself with rice.'

These sentences may appear without the reflexive form when the reflexive meaning is not intended. In that case, in (59) for instance, the object NP can be modified by a genitive phrase involving a third person.

Some lexical verbs have their meanings strengthened by the reflexive construction in which case the non-reflexive form does not necessarily convey the corresponding contrast. The following sentences represent this sub-type.

(62) mamə naa gatta
 I bathe-PP take.PAST
 'I bathed/had a shower.'

(63) api duk wində gan-nəwa
 we pain suffer-PP take-IND
 'We endure suffering.'

(64) eekə kiə-pu-hamə Ranjit bumma gan-nəwa
 that say-PTAD-TEMP Ranjit pout-PP take-IND
 'When it gets mentioned, Ranjit just pouts.'

There is another group of reflexive verbs in which the verb has developed into a separate transitive verb with a sense lexically shared with the original verb.

balənəwa 'look' > *balaa gannəwa* 'look after'
hadənəwa 'grow' > *hadaa gannəwa* 'bring up or adopt'
tiənəwa 'place' > *tiaa gannəwa* 'keep for good'
hitənəwa 'think' > *hitaa gannəwa* 'keep in mind or determine'

Another group of reflexive verbs have frozen into 'body-posture-change' verbs. They virtually do not have an independent existence without the surface reflexive form. The original non-reflexive verb denotes a state, and the corresponding reflexive form expresses a change of state, i.e. change in body posture.

Examples: *hiṭə gannəwa* 'stand up'; *ində gannəwa* 'sit down'

However, at least, one member of this group, *nidaa gannəwa* 'go to sleep', retains the non-reflexive verb as an independent form, i.e. *nidənəwa* 'sleep'.

There are also some reflexive verbs that have developed into separate idiomatic expressions scantily associated with the original lexical meaning: *kanəwa* 'eat' > *kaa gannəwa* 'spoil'; *anənəwa* 'mix' > *anaa gannəwa* 'mess up'. However, the glosses do not provide the exact equivalents of the verbs: the Sinhala reflexives have a strong non-volitional, reflexive sense which is absent from the English glosses given above. For example, these Sinhala reflexives cannot be used in the following contexts:

(65) "Mom's getting home early spoiled everything", the child said.
(66) "You'll mess up my hair", the father said.

Our discussion shows that a large number of reflexive verbs in Sinhala may be lexical rather than grammatical expressions or the result of syntactic processes. The exact conditions for the use of reflexive verbs are poorly understood, and await future study.

2.3 Modality, aspect, and tense

2.3.1 *Expressions for modality*

There are various ways in which modality is expressed in Sinhala. Specific verbs or adjectives are used as modal auxiliaries to achieve the purpose.

Necessitiative modals:
The necessitiative modality is expressed through the construction [Verbal Infinitive Form + Auxiliary Verb]. The infinitive form consists of the verbal root plus the suffix -*nnə*.[1] The verbs *tienəwa* 'be' and *wenəwa* 'be, become' serve as modal auxiliary verbs. The subject of the verbal phrase thus formed takes the dative form.

(67) ma-ṭa   heṭə   Kolamba   ya-nnə   tie-nəwa
     me-DAT   tomorrow   Colombo   go-INF   have-IND
     'I have to go to Colombo tomorrow.'

(68) api-ṭa   wædæ   goḍak   kara-nnə   tie-nəwa
     we-DAT   work   a lot   do-INF   be-IND
     'We have to do a lot of work.'

---

1. The suffix -*nnə* has several dialectal variations, such as -*nnəṭə/-nṭə/-nḍə*.

(69) Ranjit-tə   Chitra-ge   wæɖa-t   kara-nnə   we-nəwa
Ranjit-DAT   Chitra-GEN   work-too   do-INF   be-IND
'Ranjit will have to do Chitra's work, too.'

The subject's appearing in the dative with this type of verbal phrase has a semantic impact on the overall construction. It is particularly interesting that the [dative subject-involitive verb] pattern is typical to the Sinhala involitive construction. With the dative marking, the animate participant is no more considered as a volitive agent. This has led the construction to acquire the meanings of obligation and necessity. If an action is undertaken to be completed by a participant, not out of will and volition, but for some internally felt conditions or for some external conditions such as law, moral pressure, promise, etc., it should be a sense of necessity or a sense of obligation. Such contextual information will facilitate the interpretation of the sentences (67)–(69).

Deontic and epistemic modals:[2]
Both necessitiative and voluntative meanings are expressed through the constructions of [Verbal Infinitive Form + Adjective]. The constructions based on *oonæ*, originally an adjective meaning 'need' or 'want', have developed to cover both deontic and epistemic meanings. That is, the verbal phrase may appear morphosyntactically in two different constructions. In one construction it appears with a dative subject expressing the desiderative modality.

(70) ma-ṭa   ya-nnə   oonæ
I-DAT   go-INF   want
'I want to go.'

When the designated verbal phrase appears with a nominative subject, on the other hand, as in (71) below, it usually indicates the modality of obligation in a deontic context. The meaning of the auxiliary turns out to be 'should, must'.

(71) mamə   ya-nnə   oonæ
I   go-INF   should
'I should go.'

In this case *oonæ* should be considered as a grammatical particle indicating obligation, not as a lexical adjective.[3] The grammatical case of the subject is specified by the modal

---

2. We follow the characterizations of the two terms provided by Traugott (1989) based on Palmer (1986): "deontics have to do with will, obligation and permission, while epistemics have to do with knowledge and belief about possibilities, probabilities, and so forth" (Traugott 1989: 32).

3. From a synchronic lexical point of view, it may be appropriate to consider the auxiliary as a separate item without associating it with the desiderative adjective.

construction, not by the original lexical adjective. The lexical desiderative construction can exist without a verb because the speaker assumes that the nominal entity denoting the desideratum is deleted from the surface construction whereas the modal construction cannot prevail without a verb. Compare the following minimal pair.

(72) a. ma-ṭa ø oonæ
I-DAT want
'I want it.'

b. *mama ø oonæ
I should

As a further development, we can see that the modal *oonæ* used in the sense of obligation in the deontic context, i.e. [[Nominative subject] [Verbal Infinitive Form + Auxiliary]] has later taken on the epistemic sense of probability. Consider the following sentences:

(73) kaurut ræswiimə-ṭa e-nnə oonæ
everybody meeting-DAT come-INF should
'Everybody should come to the meeting.'

(74) paha wenə koṭa miniha e-nnə oonæ
five become when man come-INF should
'He should come by five o'clock.'

(75) adə heṭa wahi-nnə oonæ
today tomorrow rain-INF should
'It should rain today or tomorrow.'

(76) eyaa-ṭa eekə teere-nnə oonæ
he-DAT it understand-INF should
'He should understand it.'

(77) paha wenə koṭa miniha-ṭa e-nnə oonæ (cf. (74))
five become when man-DAT come-INF want
'He wants to come by five o'clock.'

Sentence (73), containing necessitiative force, is an example for the modal of obligation. The example in (74), with a supposition, is an expression for epistemic modality. Sentence (75) gives probability (epistemic) reading. Some facts require explanation in connection with (76). Though there is an animate participant coded in the dative, this is not due to the auxiliary and hence cannot be taken to express desiderative modality. It belongs to the same epistemic domain as (74), which does not require a volitive agent. The grammatical case is assigned by the lexical verb; the subject takes the nominative or dative form depending on the verb class, volitive vs. involitive. Sentence (76) has an involitive verb, *teerenəwa* 'understand', and accordingly takes a dative subject. The example in (77) shows that the epistemic interpretation is out when the sentential subject is coded in the dative while the complement verb remains volitive. The sentence is only acceptable in the desiderative sense.

Another instance of modality constructed with the infinitive form plus auxiliary concerns the expression of ability/possibility. The verbal phrase takes the form [Verbal Infinitive Form + Adjective] and appears with a dative subject. The adjectives *puluwaŋ* 'able' and *bææ* 'unable' serve as the auxiliary. Ability as a state or an attribute internally situated in an animate participant is expressed by the auxiliary, and the nature of ability is expressed by the lexical verb surfacing in the infinitive form.

(78) eyaa-ṭə   hondəṭə   naṭa-nnə   puluwaŋ
     she/he-DAT well   dance-INF   can
     'She can dance well.'

(79) mee   bas ek-en   ya-nnə   puluwaŋ
     this   bus-INST   go-INF   can
     'You can go by this bus.'

(80) ma-ṭə   piina-nnə   bææ
     I-DAT   swim-INF   cannot
     'I can't swim.'

Puluwaŋ, as in (78) and (79), is the adjectival auxiliary commonly used for the ability sense. *Bææ*, as in (80), is the particle expressing negation of ability.[4] The modal predicate requires an animate participant in the subject position which is to be marked for dative. By this case relation, the quality of ability is attributed to the animate participant.

A later development has led the modality of ability into a shift towards the modality of possibility. The *puluwaŋ* construction loses the agent-attributed, internal quality in its semantics as well as the morphosyntactic means of expressing it when it comes to express the sense of possibility. The new construction does not require an animate participant marked by dative and allows the subject to appear in unmarked nominative case. With this shift, the construction no longer involves an internal condition of an animate participant, but rather presents a general occurrence or a prophetic future.

(81) hawas   we-nə   koṭə   wahi-nnə   puluwaŋ
     evening   be-NPT   when   rain-INF   may
     'It might rain by the evening.'

(82) minissu   wædə   natərə kəra-nnə   puluwaŋ
     people   work   stop-INF   may
     'People might stop work.'

---

4. *Bææ* is rather considered as a particle since it is limited to predicative use and there is a different form, *bæri*, for attributive use.

(83) miniha aayet teere-nnə puluwaŋ
    man again elect.INVL-INF may
    'He might be elected again.'

(84) Chitra-ṭə æhe-nnə puluwaŋ
    Chitra-DAT hear-INF may
    'Chitra might hear (it).'

The propositions contained in the utterances above do not represent agent-oriented actions; instead they express the speaker's evaluation or belief regarding a situation. One can say that they evoke the feeling that the general situation is such that the proposition is true, thus leading to an epistemic interpretation. (81) includes a prediction about a weather situation and (82) the possibility of an action. The expression of possibility is related to an involuntary event in (83) and to an "impersonal" perceptiion verb in (84).[5]

2.3.2 Expressions for tense and aspect

2.3.2.1 Tense

In Sinhala, tense is two-fold, non-past and past, and is expressed in two inflectional forms. The non-past form is simple, being identical with the citation form, while the past tense inflection is more complex involving different forms according to the conjugation class. The non-past form refers to the present and/or future and the past form denotes the past tense. However, this is a simplified statement. In fact, tense forms express more nuanced senses depending on the nature of the verbal predicate. For instance, the non-past tense of an active-type verb may represent a generic or a habitual action, a continual action, a future action or a command.

(85) Ranjit bat ka-nə-wa
    Ranjit rice eat-NPT-IND
    'Ranjit eats rice.' or 'Ranjit is eating just now.'

(86) Ranjit labənə maase Japan ya-nə-wa
    Ranjit next month Japan go-NPT-IND
    'Ranjit will go to Japan next month.'

(87) Ranjit, ya-nə-wa
    Ranjit, go-NPT-IND
    'Ranjit, go out!'

---

5. In this case *teerenəwa* in Sinhala denotes an event without an agent and beyond control of the subject and *æhenəwa* literally means 'to be audible to somebody' and therefore is impersonal.

The past tense form expresses an event that occured in the past time:

(88) Ranjit   uḍə   pænna
      Ranjit   up   jump. PAST
      'Ranjit jumped up.'

(89) issərə   minissu   ausədə   paanə   biiwa
      before   people   medicine drinks drink. PAST
      'People in the past drank medicinal drinks.'

(90) irə   giluna
      sun   sink. PAST
      'The sun went down.'

Since adjectives do not inflect for tense in Sinhala, some periphrastic ways have to be used to express past states. Compare the (a) and (b) pairs in (91) and (92) below:

(91) a. gee   lassəna-i
          house   beautiful-AM
          'The house is beautiful.'

      b. issərə   gee   lassəna-ṭə   tibuna
          before   house   beautiful-DAT be(inan.).PAST
          'The house was beautiful before.'

(92) a. Ranjit-ṭə   asəniipa-i
          Ranjit-DAT   ill-AM
          'Ranjit is ill.'

      b. Ranjit   asəniip-en   hiṭiya
          Ranjit   ill-INS   be(anim). PAST
          'Ranjit was ill.'

A fact needs to be mentioned regarding the tense forms of subordinate clauses or non-finite forms. Non-finite forms depend on the finite clause for location in time. Even though the verb form appears morphologically in the past tense this need not indicate an event in the past. For instance, the conditional, concessive and temporal forms, which appear in past form, do not denote absolute past tense. The conditional, concessive and temporal subordinate verbs respectively in (93), (94) and (95) below, all have past tense form but denote non-past events of the tense of the main clause.

(93) Kolamba   giyot   maama   bala-nna-t   ya-mu
      Colombo   go. COND uncle   see-INF-too   go-HORT
      'Let's go to see uncle if we go to Colombo.'

(94) kauru   biiwat   mamə   bo-nn-e   næǣ
    anybody drink.CONC   I   drink-NPT-FOC   no
    'Whoever drinks (Let anybody drink), I will not drink.'

(95) taatta   Kolamba   giyaamə   boonikk-ek   araŋ   ee-wi
    Father   Colombo   go.TEMP   doll-INDF   buy.PP   come.INFER
    'Father will buy a doll when he goes to Colombo.'

The actual location in time of the subordinate event is determined by its temporal relation to the main clause event. Look at the use of the perfect participle form in the following sentences.

(96) alə   kæǣli-wələ-ʈə   kapə-la   haʈʈiə-ʈə   daa-nnə
    potato   piece-PL.DAT   cut-PP   pot-DAT   put-IMP
    'Cut the potatoes into pieces and put them into the pot.'

(97) Ranjit   alə   kæǣli-wələ-ʈə   kapə-la   haʈʈiə-ʈə   dæmma
    Ranjit   potato   piece-PL.DAT   cut-PP   pot-DAT   put.PAST
    'Ranjit cut the potatoes into pieces and put them into the pot.'

The perfect participle form in (96) denotes an action due to occur in the future by virtue of the finite, imperative verb whereas in (97) it indicates an event that occurred in the past in relation to the finite, past tense verb.

2.3.2.2 *Aspect*

The most common type of aspectual expression in Sinhala is the construction consisting of the perfect participle form plus an aspectual auxiliary ([Perfect Participle Form + Auxiliary Verb]). Most aspectual auxiliaries are grammaticalized forms of lexical verbs, such as *innəwa* 'be (animate)', *tienəwa* 'be (inanimate)' and *yanəwa* 'go', *enəwa* 'come' and *daanəwa* 'put'. The need to express situations occurring prior to the reference time but still relevant at the speech time has given rise to the Perfective, Resultative, and Completive aspects (See Bybee et al. 1994).

Perfective aspect: Perfective aspect is often indicated by means of the perfect participle accompanied by the auxiliary *tienəwa* 'be'.

(98) kauruhari   ma-ge   laachchuwə   ærəla   tie-nəwa
    somebody   I-GEN   drawer   open.PP   be-IND
    'Somebody has opened my drawer.'

(99) lamai   hondəʈə   duwəla   tie-nəwa
    children   well   run-PP   be-IND
    'The children have had a good run.'

(100) miniha-ṭə dæn eekə teerila tie-nəwa
man-DAT now that understand.PP be-IND
'Now he has understood it.'

The Perfective aspect is used generally in contexts when the speaker finds something in the physical environment signaling the event's occurrence prior to the reference time. However, simple verb forms, such as past tense, are often used to express perfective actions in day-to-day language, as in *bat kǽæwa də?* 'did you eat? (= eat.PAST Q)' to mean 'Have you eaten?'.

Resultative aspect: In expressing the Resultative aspect, the perfect participle may be accompanied either by the auxiliary *tienəwa* (inanimate) or the auxiliary *innəwa* (animate). In this construction the event mentioned is conceived of as the result of another event that occurred prior to it. Predicates intersect with animate/inanimate auxiliaries syntactically to form resultative constructions. It is true that the inanimate auxiliary *tienəwa* is invariably associated with inanimate participants, as in (101). However, in addition to this, transitivity has a greater influence on selecting the type of auxiliary: transitive structures take the auxiliary *tienəwa,* as in (102) and intransitive structures *innəwa*, as in (103), regardless of the participants' animacy.

(101) man yanə koṭə baisikəlee perəlila tibuna
I go when bicycle topple.PP be.PAST
'When I got there the bicycle had fallen over.'

(102) taatta adə kuuḍa dek-ak wiə-la tie-nəwa
father today basket two-INDF weave-PP be-IND
'Father has woven two baskets today.'

(103) paarə ain-e menih-ek wæṭila in-nəwa
road side-LOC man-INDF fall.PP be-IND
'There is a man fallen down by the side of the road.'

Resultative states seem to have greater relevance for the time of speech and frequently appear with the auxiliary verb deleted, as in (104–106), or with the auxiliary in the focus form, as in (107), making the verbal predicate a focused element within the sentence.

(104) səər æwilla
teacher come.PP
'The teacher has come.'

(105) bittəree narak we-laa
egg be rotten-PP
'The egg is spoiled.'

(106) ambə geḍiə idila næ̃æ
mango fruit ripen.PP no
'The mango is not ripe.'

(107) lamai kaala in-n-e
children eat.PP be-NPT-FOCUS
'The children have eaten.'

Completive aspect: Completive aspect is indicated by means of the perfect participle accompanied by the auxiliary *daanəwa*. The auxiliary *daanəwa* has developed from the homophonous lexical verb which means 'put, put away'. Unlike the perfect and resultative aspects which indicate the completion of an event prior to the reference time, the completive aspect indicates an action that extends beyond the reference time. This means that the completive aspect in Sinhala denotes a perceived completion, expressing a speaker's attitude towards the occurrence of an unavoidable or unpleasant event. Consider also that inactive, involitive verbs do not occur in the completive aspect; the completive interpretation is obtained with active verbs ("activity" and "accomplishment" verbs in terms of Vendler (1957)).

(108) monəwa hæduwat wal ali kaala daa-nəwa
what grow-CONC wild elephants eat.PP daa-IND
'Whatever we grow, wild elephants will eat it completely.'

(109) oyə balla bændəla daa-nnə
that dog tie-PP daa-IMP
'Tie up the dog.'

(110) lamea liyum okkomə ædəla dæmma
child letters all draw.PP daa.PAST
'The child scattered all the letters.'

The examples above, (109) appearing in the imperative mood in particular, show that the completive aspect may include, but goes beyond, the reference time.

The completive aspect may change an action to a sudden, instantaneous event. It takes on connotations of abrupt termination of events.

(111) miniha arakku wiiduruwə ekə husmə-ṭə biila dæmma
man arrack glass one breath-DAT drink.PP daa.PAST
'He drank off the glass of arrack in one gulp.'

(112) Chitra laampuwə nimə-la dæmma
Chitra lamp put out-PP daa.PAST
'Chitra put out the lamp immediately/on the spot.'

It is also used for expressing regret or the feeling of refreshment after an action:

(113) apəraade man idəmə wikunə-la dæmma
      in shame I   land   sell-PP   daa.PAST
      'What a shame I sold the land.'

(114) mamə kiya-nnə tie-nə eewa   okkomə   kiə-la dæmma
      I   say-INF   be-NPT things everything say-PP daa.PAST
      'I have said all I have to say.'

Inchoative aspect: The device of expressing the Inchoative aspect is the perfect participle accompanied by the auxiliaries *yanəwa* and *enəwa*, which lexically mean 'go' and 'come' respectively. Since in its original sense *yanəwa* indicates movement away from the speaker and *enəwa* movement towards the speaker, they have turned out to be convenient tools to indicate a change of state associated with a sense of directionality.

(115) mee   gadol   nikammə   kædila   ya-nəwa
      these bricks automatically break.PP ya-IND
      'These bricks break easily.'

(116) oowa   tikə   kaalekin   amətəkə we-laa   ya-nəwa
      those short time-INS   forget-PP   ya-IND
      'Those things will be forgotten shortly.'

(117) yudde hinda   tarunə kollo apəraade   mærila ya-nəwa
      war   because young   lads   wastefully die-PP ya-IND
      'Because of the war, young people die without any purpose.'

(118) pælə   ikmənətə hædila   e-nəwa
      plants soon   grow.PP   e-IND
      'The plants will grow soon.'

(119) æŋgillə balaaiddi idimila   aawa
      finger   soon   swell.PP   e.PAST
      '(My) finger has swollen up in a twinkle.'

The *yanəwa* 'go' auxiliary and the *enəwa* 'come' auxiliary seem to indicate different nuances, though they are yet to be delineated. *Yanəwa* indicates that the participant of an event is regarded as moving away from the speaker. This movement towards distance may subtly convey that some unfolding events are beyond the cognizant's grasp. The auxiliary *enəwa*, on the other hand, which indicates the participant of an event moving towards the speaker, may depict events in terms of proximity and visibility. However, these are tentative observations that need to be examined further. Particularly deserving to be investigated are the conditions under which the mapping of aspectual structures with particular event-types occurs.

Processive aspect: Processive aspect is a category for depicting an event as a gradual process. To mark the "gradual process" of an event, a complex structure is used, which is [Perfect Participle Base Form + Auxiliary Verb + Auxiliary Verb]. The perfect participle base form is accompanied by two auxiliary verbs: The first auxiliary is *genə*, which is the perfect participle form of *gannəwa* 'take', and the second auxiliary the *yanəwa/enəwa* 'go/come' form. The first three examples below appear with *enəwa* and the last three examples with *yanəwa*.

(120) waturə rat wii genə e-nəwa
 water boil.PP genə e-IND
 'The water is coming to the boil.'

(121) mage æs piə wii genə aawa
 my eyes close.INVL.PP genə e.PAST
 'My eyes were closing themselves (from sleepiness).'

(122) dæn mee nagəre hondəṭə diunu wii genə e-nəwa
 now this town well develop.PP genə e-IND
 'This town is developing well now.'

(123) gaŋ waturə-ṭə iurə kaḍaa genə giyaa
 flood-DAT bank break.PP genə ya.PAST
 'The bank (of the river) broke through in the flood.'

(124) dæn ṭikə ṭikə rasne aḍu wii genə ya-nəwa
 now little by little heat decrease.PP genə ya-IND
 'The heat is little by little decreasing now.'

(125) apee situm pætum wenas wee genə ya-nəwa
 our thinking wishes change.PP genə ya-IND
 'Our thinking and values are changing little by little.'

Whether it is realized with or without an adverb of graduality, this construction signals that the encoded event occurs as a gradual process. An overwhelming majority of verbs involved in this category denote inactive or uncontrollable events. This aspectual sense should be distinguished from the progressive aspect, although they seem somewhat similar to each other.

Progressive aspect: The progressive aspect expresses iterative and durative meanings of verbs. In terms of lexical engagement, both active, volitive verbs and inactive, involitive verbs are involved in this aspect. The grammatical device is the repetition of the perfect participle base form accompanied by the 'be' verb *innəwa/tienəwa*. The first three examples below have active verbs and the last two examples inactive verbs, appearing in the progressive aspect.

(126) miniha   atu   kapə kapə   innəwa
      man   branches   cut-PP.RED   be-IND
      'The man is cutting off the branches.'

(127) lamea   puusa   atə ga-gaa   otənə hiţia
      child   cat   touch-PP.RED   there be. PAST
      'The child was there caressing the cat.'

(128) maŋ   ya-nə   koţə   Ranjit   ka-kaa   hiţia
      I   go-NPT   when   Ranjit   eat-PP.RED   be-PAST
      'When I got there, Ranjit was eating.'

(129) paipp-en   waturə   wækkeri wækkeri   tie-nəwa
      pipe-ABL   water   flow out-PP.RED   be-IND
      'The water is flowing out from the pipe.'

(130) Tin   ek-ak   perəli perəli   tibuna
      tin   one-INDEF   roll.PP.RED   be. PAST
      'A tin was rolling down there.'

However, simple verb forms too are often used to indicate the progressive aspect. For example, the following two sentences, respectively, can be used in the same context as (126) and (129) to indicate the progressive aspect.

(131) miniha   atu   kapə-nəwa
      man   branches   cut-IND
      'The man is cutting off the branches.'

(132) paipp-en   waturə   wækkere-nəwa
      pipe-ABL   water   flow-IND
      'The water is flowing from the pipe.'

Speakers generally use the progressive aspectual form rather than the simple verb form when they need to emphasize the iterative and continuous aspect of an event.

Inceptive aspect: The inceptive aspect is different from the inchoative aspect in that it allows users to focus on the inception or starting point, not the change of state or intermediary stage of an event. The inception indicated by this particular construction is a situation prior to the starting point of the event, including mental or physical steps preparatory to the actual occurrence of the event denoted by the lexical verb. One of its main characteristics, distinguishing it from other aspectual expressions described above, is using the infinitive form of the verb, instead of relying on the perfect participle form or perfect participle base form. The resultant verbal construction is [Infinitive Form + Auxiliary Verb]. The auxiliary verbs accompanying the infinitive verb have developed from lexical verbs such as *balənəwa* 'see', *hadənəwa* 'make', *gannəwa* 'take' and *yanəwa* 'go'.

(133) ehenaŋ   mamə   ræswiimə-țə   ya-nnə   balə-nnam
      then   I   meeting-DAT   go-INF   balə- OPT
      'Then I will try to go to the meeting.'

(134) Ranjit   poosțerəyə   bitte-e   aləwa-nnə   hadə-nəwa
      Ranjit   poster   wall-LOC   paste-INF   hadə- IND
      'Ranjit is trying to paste the poster on the wall.'

(135) Chitra   hondə   salaadəy-ak   hada-nnə   ya-nəwa
      Chitra   good   salad-INDF   make-INF   ya-IND
      'Chitra is going to make a good salad.'

(136) leḍaa   weedənaaw-en   kendirigaa-nnə   gatta
      patient pain-INS   groan-INF   gan.PAST
      'The patient got down to groan with pain.'

The differences in the extent of the participant's involvement in the event as indicated by each auxiliary are not clear. One thing that can be said with certainty is that the distance between the preparatory step signaled by the auxiliary and the actual occurrence of the event denoted by the lexical verb is minimal in the case of the *gannəwa* auxiliary. Thus the sentence (136) may be the closest in meaning to (137) below, which expresses the inchoative sense more explicitly.

(137) leḍaa   weedənaaw-en   kendirigaa-nnə   pațan gatta
      patient pain-INS   groan-INF   begin.PAST
      'The patient began to groan with pain.'

However, in this case the verbal phrase *kendirigaannə pațan gatta* 'began to groan' is considered to be a compound verb composed of two lexical verbs.

While tense is largely expressed through affixes and vowel change, modality and aspect are expressed through auxiliary-based constructions. With the development of auxiliaries, Sinhala has acquired a complex verb phrase consisting of a principle verb and one or several auxiliary verbs. Though we have, for descriptive purposes, used as data simpler sentences with fewer grammatical categories, in actual discourse, expressions for aspect and modality are often used in conjunction with each other and in combinatory forms with tense and mood. In all cases, however, auxiliaries as modifiers are added after the lexical verb.

CHAPTER 9

Grammatical constructions

In the three previous chapters (Chapter 6, 7 and 8) the morphological and syntactic expression of valency or argument structure of verbs and related facts were described. This chapter deals with the phenomenon of voice, namely valency changing devices in Sinhala. Mainly, valency reducing constructions, often related to the passive, and valency increasing constructions, centered round the causative, are observed as a means of altering the argument structure of verbs.

1. Passive construction

The canonical passive construction is universally regarded as a syntactic process for voice alteration, triggered by the morphological process of turning the transitive verb into a passive form. In this process a major alteration occurs in grammatical relations: the active subject is demoted to become an optional oblique phrase or adjunct phrase; the object is promoted to become a full-fledged subject. In this sense, Colloquial Sinhala can be considered to be void of a passive construction. According to some observations, passive sentences, even as stylistic variations of active sentences, may not exist in Colloquial Sinhala (Abhayasinghe 1973).

There are some constructions superficially resembling the passive structure. One such construction is the involitive construction described before. The following (a) examples represent involitive structures (some of them repeated from Chapter 7) while the (b) examples are added as their volitive counterparts.

(1) a. kellə atin maalu ageeṭə pihe-nəwa
girl atin fish well cook.INVa. IC Y
'The girl can cook fish very well' (De Silva 1960: 101)

b. kellə maalu ageeṭə pihi-nəwa
girl fish well cook-IND
'The girl cooks fish very well'

(2) a. miniha atin pingaanə binduna
he atin plate break.INVL.PAST
'He unintentionally broke the plate.'

  b. miniha pingaanə binda
    he   plate   break.PAST
    'He broke the plate.'

(3) a. Ranjit-ţə puusa(-wə) pææge-nəwa
    Ranjit-DAT cat(-ACC) step on.INVL-IND
    'Ranjit accidentally steps on the cat.'

  b. Ranjit puusa(-wə) paagə-nəwa
    Ranjit cat(-ACC) step on-IND
    'Ranjit steps on the cat.'

Compared with their active counterparts which highlight agency, the involitive constructions denote the participant's non-agentive involvement in the event. However, the first constituent of these constructions retain the status of grammatical subject (Henadeerage 2002). The objects of volitive sentences have not become subjects in involitive sentences. This becomes explicit from the pair in (3) which has an animate participant marked in the accusative in the object position. Observe also that there is no change in the linear position of constituents between the volitive and involitive counterparts. Thus, the canonical requirements for passivization are not fulfilled.

  Although the verb appears in the P-form, this does not represent a special passive morpheme. Rather than passivization, what occurs is involitivization of the transitive by defocusing the highest argument of the verb. The fact that these structures do not harmonize with purposive adverbials proves their involitive state.

(4) *kellə atin maalu oonækəmin pihe-nəwa
   girl atin fish willfully   cook.ʌVL.ʌED
   'Fish gets cooked by the girl willfully'

(5) *miniha atin hitəla   pingaanə binduna
   he   atin intentionally plate   break.INVL.PAST
   'The plate was broken by him intentionally.'

(6) *Ranjit-ţə hitaa-mataa puusa(-wə) pææge-nəwa
   Ranjit-DAT purposely cat(-ACC) step on.INVL-IND
   'Ranjit purposely steps on the cat.'

Both the *atin* construction and the dative subject construction are marked by the non-agentive features as shown here.

  The *atin* construction can occur with dative object clauses and indirect object clauses as well.

(7) Ranjit atin miniha-ţə ægill-en ænuna
   Ranjit atin man-DAT finger-INS poke.PAST
   'Ranjit spontaneously poked the man with his finger.'

(8) man atin lamea-ṭə salli yæwe-nəwa
    I   atin child-DAT money send.INVL.-IND
    'I find myself sending the child money.'

In (7) the dative constituent is the direct object of (the P-form of) the verb *aninəwa* 'poke' and in (8) the indirect object of (the P-form of) the verb *yawənəwa* 'send'. The crucial point is that there appears no change in object case assignment under this construction. That is, there is no syntactic process affecting the complements of VP with regard to case or thematic role as generally assumed for the passive.

Another type of construction similar to the passive construction is what referred to in the literature as the "inactive construction" or "agentless construction".

(9) gas   wæṭe-nəwa
    trees fall-IND
    'The trees fall'

(10) pingaanə binduna
     plate   break.INVL.PAST
     'The plate broke.'

(11) lamea-wə wæṭe-nəwa
     child-ACC fall-IND
     'The child is falling'

(12) lamea-wə perəle-nəwa
     child-ACC roll-IND
     'The child is rolling down'

The single participant can be an inanimate object, as in (9) and (10) or have an animate referent, as in (11) and (12). This construction-type has connotations of accidental occurrence suggesting that no one is responsible for the action, as (9) and (10) show, when put into a proper context. Events with animate participants denoted by non-past tense verbs, as in (11) and (12) may add particular overtones of warning that something might happen if the situation is left unattended. The non-involvement of an agent is their main semantic characterization. Suppression of agent is achieved through the verbs characterized as detransitivized (Gair 1991) or decausative (Henadeerage 2002). The examples in (11) and (12) clearly show that the semantic roles remain constant, without the semantic objects getting promoted through case marking. These facts in combination with some other factors like morphosyntactic irregularities show that it is difficult to establish a straightforward syntactic derivation for these sentences, and therefore they do not receive passive characterization.

While suppression of agent is achieved through involitive and intransitive constructions with the P-form of the verb, there might be some other constructions strongly related to functional motivations of passive voice. The following sentence might be important from the functional sentence perspective of topic-comment articulation.

(13)   sapattuwə   balla   kæəwa
        shoe   dog   eat-PAST
        'The shoe was eaten by dogs.'

This sentence is different from the clause-types discussed above in that the object has been preposed to the subject position, and the verb is not a P-verb but a typical transitive verb. This sentence, appearing without any change in verbal morphology, cannot be considered as a passive. What has happened is movement of the object from its verb-phrase internal or comment internal position to the position of topic, i.e. subject position. As this example shows, Sinhala may exhibit a great flexibility with its free word order and permits an object's movement to topic position without using any syntactic ordering device like passive.

Sinhala also permits objectless transitive sentences.

(14)   maduruwo   ka-nəwa
        mosquitoes   eat-IND
        'We are/I am bitten by mosquitoes.'

(15)   at-ee   maduruw-ek   kaala
        hand-LOC   mosquito-INDF eat.PP
        'A mosquito has bitten me on the hand.'

When referring to a situation where persons are troubled by mosquitoes, the usual choice would be sentence (14) whose verb is transitive and the object constituent is deleted since its referent is clear through the situational context. When referring to an individuated situation, on the other hand, the first constituent's place is taken by the affected body part, and the subject, which may appear in indefinite form, moves to the position immediately before the verb, as in (15). This sentence-type, usually referred to as 'antipassive' construction, is certainly not passive.

A more widespread construction that substitutes for a passive is a subjectless transitive clause.

(16)   saapuwə   paha-ṭə   waha-nəwa
        shop   five-DAT   close-IND
        'The shop closes at five.'

(17)   ee   kaḍ-ee   horə-ṭə   baḍu   kirə-nəwa
        that   shop-LOC thieving-DAT commodities measure-IND
        'Commodities are weighed fraudulently in that shop.'

(18)   heṭə   alut   niladaarin-wə   toorə-nəwa
        tomorrow new   officers-ACC   choose-IND
        'Tomorrow new office-bearers are chosen.'

These sentences cannot be considered as the result of a subject-deletion device. Since they contain general statements or are assumed as involving indefinite subjects, speakers may conceptualize such a situation without subject/agent constituents. They all use active transitive verbs, without any special morpheme for valence reduction. The important point is there is no case changing or other device for object promotion, either. As (18) shows, the object phrase retains the accusative marker -*wə*. This type of subjectless sentences can be freely used in Sinhala in place of the passive construction appearing in a language like English. Thus the existence of this type of clauses may have prevented the need for a passive construction in Sinhala.

Another fact emerging from this discussion, as shown elsewhere, is that a nominative subject is not an obligatory category in Sinhala, whether for transitive or intransitive/involitive structures. While many intransitive/involitive sentences have oblique constituents in their subject position, as further evidence shows, even transitive verbs may appear with oblique subjects. Observe the following examples:

(19) polisi-en pænəla baḍu ælluwa
 police-ABL jump-PP commodities confiscate.PAST
 'The police suddenly appeared and confiscated the commodities.'

(20) adə aadaayam baḍu ek-en aawa
 today income tax one-ABL come.PAST
 'Today income tax officers came here.'

For this clause-type, as the case is, the ablative constituent always represents a public body or an institution. This structure emerges when somebody representing that body is involved as the referent of the first constituent. Thus the subject constituent may be considered as developed from the source concept, and hence ablative. Owing to such devices that are equivalent to agent defocusing or subject demotion, there might be no need for the syntactic process of passivization.

Sinhala also has a particular kind of notional passives realized in the form of active structures which denotes a situation of someone undergoing a negative action. This clause-type is used to encode a situation in which an animate subject suffers or undergoes an offensive action or humiliating treatment initiated by somebody. The Undergoer appears as the subject and the initiator of the action is marked by the ablative as the source.

(21) Ranjit adə hondətə bænuŋ aha-nəwa
 Ranjit today well blame hear-IND
 'Ranjit will receive good blaming today.'

(22) Ranjit taatta-gen guṭi kaa-wi
 Ranjit father-ABL beating eat.INFER
 'Ranjit might get beaten by his father.'

(23) Ranjit   Chitra-gen   hondə   kammul   paarak   kææwa
    Ranjit   Chitra-ABL   good   cheek   slap   eat.PAST
    'Ranjit got a good slap on his face from Chitra.'

(24) Ranjit   gææni-gen   sapattu   paar-ak   kææwa
    Ranjit   woman-ABL   shoe   beating-INDF   eat.PAST
    'Ranjit got a shoe-beating from the woman.'

It is true that sentences of this type put the affected participant or patient into the topic position while taking the agent out of the subject position into an adjunct position. However, this cannot be equated with the "is blamed/is beaten/was slapped/was hit" passive commonly occurring in languages like English. Lexically and syntactically, the Sinhala sentences represent an active construction.

So far we have delineated some particular conditions under which passives are not required in Sinhala. However, one can argue that most of the impersonal, involitive constructions in Sinhala can be identified as non-basic passives, also referred to as 'complex passives' by some linguists (Keenan 1981).

Particular attention is drawn here to the type of sentences given in (11) and (12) and repeated as (25) and (26).

(25) lamea-wə   wæṭe-nəwa
    child-ACC   fall-IND
    'The child is falling'

(26) lamea-wə   perəle-nəwa
    child-ACC   roll-IND
    'The child is rolling down'

Verbs like *wæṭenəwa* 'fall' and *perəlenəwa* 'roll' have in the past been treated as passive or spontaneous as well as intransitive since the same suffixation has multiple morphological function of deriving intransitive verbs, passive forms and spontaneous forms also. The semantic functions of each of these verbs are sensitive to the volitive/involitive distinction. That is to say, these verbs may occur both in volitive clauses as well as involitive clauses. One may argue that there are two different semantic forms under the same phonological shape of each sentence as long as the single participant appears in the nominative. The special device to rule out the ambiguity and possibility for alternative analysis would be forming impersonal passives. By marking the participant for the accusative, as in (25) and (26), the impersonal passive construction is formed; no other alteration is needed as the verb has already gained passive morphology and there is no other NP available for attendant promotion. The impersonal nature of the construction is evident with the P-verb and demoted actor. The patient/undergoer relation is marked by the accusative regardless of their subject or object position. The identification of thematic relations by their corresponding case markers as shown here and some other related facts have propelled some scholars towards the view that Colloquial Sinhala is fundamentally an ergative language (Gunasinghe 1985).

The next candidate for passive analysis, the *atin* construction, has been characterized as a 'semantic passive' in the literature (See Gunasinghe 1985) as against its identification as a basic passive construction (Gair 1970). The fact that its verb bears the elements of passive morphology is generally held supportive of the "passive" argument. However, this matter is not an unambiguous indication of this passive analysis, as we have already shown. Another piece of evidence is the appearance of the demoted agentive constituent in the *atin* form. However, there is an important point that weakens the overall weight of the *atin* constituent which has emerged from the passive characterization of Wickramasinghe (1973). The subject element of the active sentence must be a [+ animate], in the strict sense, [+ human] nominal to qualify as the *atin* constituent. The following three examples were given by Wickramasinghe 1973) for comparison.

(27) kolla   atin   wæṭa   hæde-nəwa
     boy   atin   fence make.INVL-IND
     'The fence is made by the boy.'

(28) eladenə atin   wæṭa   kæde-nəwa
     cow   atin   fence break.INVL-IND
     'The fence is broken by the cow.'

(29) balla   atin   pingaanə binde-nəwa
     dog   atin   plate   break.INVL-IND
     'The plate is broken by the dog.'

Wickramasinghe has pointed out that despite being grammatical, (28) and (29) do not please the speaker-hearer as accepted usages in the language. The reason given for this awkwardness is the fact that despite being a grammaticalized form developed from *atə* 'hand', the *atin* form has, with its literal meaning, a bearing with regard to the nominal it is attached to. An important fact not mentioned there is that the *atin* form has greater association with volitionality, to be specific, in ruling out a participant's volition. The awkwardness arises here by attaching the "volitionality" distinction to a non-human participant. Viewed in this way, the *atin* construction has limitations to a great extent in terms of semantic and syntactic distribution.

There are two other restrictions on passivization of this type (Gair 1979). One is that most passive sentences are not natural with the subject constituent of the base clause being overtly present. According to native intuition, the active clause in (30a) is best expressed in the form of (30c) rather than as (30b), which retains the demoted agent.

(30) a. hungak denaa   bohoo welaawə-ṭə oyə   gænə   kataa karə-nəwa
        many   people many   time-DAT   that about speak-IND
        'Many people generally talk about it.'

b. hungak denaa atin boohoo welaawa-ṭa oyə gænə
   many people atin many time-DAT that about
   kataa kere-nəwa
   speak.INVL-IND
   'Many people generally talk about it these days.'

c. boohoo welaawa-ṭa oyə gænə kataa kere-nəwa
   many time-DAT that about speak. INVL- IND
   'They generally talk about it these days.'

The other restriction is that some passive clauses are unacceptable unless they are accompanied by certain adverbials; *ageeṭa* 'very well', *hondəṭa* 'well' and *lassənəṭa* 'beautifully' are such adverbials that often appear with these expressions. Both the restrictions show that a straightforward transformation from active to passive, as in English, does not work in Sinhala.

We can also consider some potentials of the *atin* construction. The *atin* construction exhibits some modal-specific characteristics.[1] While the involitive interpretation of the *atin* construction is widely known, all the expressions with *atin* do not denote non-volitional, unintentional events. Some of them indicate volitional, intentional actions, as some examples cited before show; they can be taken as modal expressions indicating potentiality.

(31) kellə atin maalu ageeṭa pihe-nəwa
     girl INS fish well cook. INVL- IND
     'The girl can cook fish very well.' (De Silva, 1960:101)

(32) æə atin ageeṭa goyam kæpe-nə-wa
     she INS well paddy cut. INVL- IND
     'She can reap paddy very well' (De Silva, 1960:101)

(33) Banda atin pol siiyak witərə kæde-nə-wa
     Banda INS coconut hundred about pick. INVL- IND
     'Banda can pick about a hundred coconuts.' (Gair, 1970:40)

(34) miniha atin lassənəṭa sarungal hæde-nə-wa
     man INS beautifully kites make. INVL- IND
     'The man can make kites in a beautiful fashion.'

These sentences, as De Silva's (1960) glosses show and as Gair (1970) has correctly pointed out, have some special meanings such as potentiality or possibility. According to the viewpoint presented by Shibatani (1985), passive constructions are often associated

---

1. See Inman 1992 for a modal analysis of Sinhala involitive sentences.

with a range of meanings including 'potential' meaning and 'spontaneous' interpretation. Evidence from Sinhala supports this view (Wijayawardhana et al. (1995).

The *atin* construction is also used for humble expressions.

(35) man atin dawasə-kə-ṭə piṭu   dahay-ak   witərə liyəwe-nəwa
      I   atin day-INDF-DAT pages ten-INDF   about   write.INVL-IND
      'I might write about ten pages a day.'

However, again, these meanings cannot be separated from the involitive interpretation as proven by the fact that similar meanings are expressed through the dative subject construction, too. For example, a speaker may attach involuntariness to his own action by using the dative subject construction, as follows.

(36) maṭə dawasə-kə-ṭə sigəræṭ   wiss-ak   witərə pewe-nəwa
      I   day-INDF-DAT cigarettes twenty-INDF   about   drink. INVL- IND
      'I might smoke about twenty cigarettes a day.'

According to one scholar, if there are passive constructions in Sinhala, their existence can be attributed to "the influence of the written variety, or an attempt to use the written variety for speech as well" (Abhayasinghe 1973). Then this may be taken as a case of linguistic development achieved by sharing different varieties or modes within the language, which is a case of diglossia.

2. Causative construction

Causative sentences are meant to contain a proposition where an agent or causer does something causing a second participant or causee to undergo a change of state, to engage in another action or to bring out an event or state. Causative sentences may appear in the form of lexical, morphological, or periphrastic causatives.

2.1 Lexical causatives

Lexical causatives are based on simple transitive verbs distinguished as A verbs. Most of these lexical transitive verbs have their corresponding intransitive counterparts, i.e. P verbs. The following list shows such pairs of lexical causative (transitive) and intransitive pairs.

Lexical Causative	Intransitive
bandinəwa 'tie'	bændenəwa 'get tied'
kapənəwa 'cut'	kæpenəwa 'get cut'
kaḍənəwa 'break'	kæḍenəwa 'get broken'
temənəwa 'wet'	temenəwa 'get wet'
toorənəwa 'select'	teerenəwa 'get selected, understand'

marənəwa 'kill'	*mærenəwa* 'die'
pudənəwa 'offer'	*pidenəwa* 'be offered'
lihənəwa 'untie'	*lihenəwa* 'get untied'
arinəwa 'open'	*ærenəwa* 'open'
adinəwa 'pull'	*ædenəwa* 'get pulled'

These lexical causatives occur in sentences in the following way (a) and can be semantically and syntactically contrasted with the (b) sentences, which are non-causative.

(37) a. Ranjit   balla(-wə)   bandi-nəwa
       Ranjit   dog-ACC   tie-IND
       'Ranjit is tethering the dog.'

   b. balla   bænde-ewi
      dog   get tied-INFER
      'The dog will be tethered.'

(38) a. Chitra   gæʈee   lihə-nəwa
       Chitra   knot   untie-IND
       'Chitra is untying the knot.'

   b. gæʈee   lihe-nəwa
      knot   get untied-IND
      'The knot is getting untied.'

The nominal constituents which are not present in the (b) sentences but appear in the (a) sentences as subjects have acquired the role of agent/causer while the constituents appearing as subjects in the (b) sentences are relegated to the direct object position in the (a) sentences. The object position represents the causee/object role in lexical causatives and may be optionally marked by the accusative if it has an animate referent. Lexical causatives are inherently two-place predicates as opposed to intransitive verbs, which are one-place verbs.

2.2 Morphological causatives

Morphological causatives have causative verbs derived from transitive or active intransitive (unergative) verbs. A causative verb, i.e. the C-form of a verb is ideally obtained by adding the causative morpheme *-wə-* to an A verb. This lexical process allows the new verb to be a two-place verb, and the subsequent syntactic process may increase the valency of the base verb. If the base verb is intransitive, the resultant causative verb will have two arguments, the underlying subject becoming the direct object and a new argument coming to the subject position:

NP_1 V → NP_0 NP_1 V
Sub.   Sub.   Obj.

When the base verb is transitive, the original subject becomes an optional adjunct and the original object remains the object:

NP$_1$ NP$_2$ V → NP$_0$ (NP$_1$)   NP$_2$ V
Sub.   Obj.   Sub.   Obl.   Obj.

The following list contains some examples of intransitive-based morphological causatives with their corresponding intransitive verbs.

Intransitive	Causative
anḍənəwa 'cry'	ænḍə-wə-nəwa
yanəwa 'go'	ya-wə-nəwa
enəwa 'come'	e-wə-nəwa
naginəwa 'climb'	nangənəwa (< nang-wə-nəwa)
bahinəwa 'get off'	bassənəwa (< bas-wə-nəwa)
nægiṭinəwa 'get up'	nægiṭṭənəwa (< nægiṭ-wə-nəwa)
duwənəwa 'run'	duwə-wə-nəwa
pupurənəwa 'crack'	pupurə-wə-nəwa
parədinəwa 'lose'	paraddənəwa (< parad-wə-nəwa)
sinaasenəwa 'laugh'	sinassənəwa (sinas-wə-nəwa)

For some verbs, the causative morpheme may be disguised in some other phonetic form. For such verbs as *bassənəwa* 'cause to get off, or drop', *nægiṭṭənəwa* 'cause to get up' in the list, the morphologically explicit form is given in parentheses. When the causative morpheme is obscured due to progressive assimilation in this way, the -wə- morpheme may be added again to make the causativizer explicit. This morphological form called "double causatives" by traditional grammarians does not indicate a double causation in the syntactic sense. The reverse also does not occur: for syntactic double causation there is no need to causativize the verb twice. This note applies to transitive-based causatives, too.

The morphosyntactic manifestation of an intransitive-based causative, [NP$_1$ V] → [NP$_0$ NP$_1$ V], may have different interpretations depending on the situational context. Observe the following example (The verb has double causative marking but one marker is obscured).

(39) guruwərəya   lamea(-wə)   nægiṭ-ṭəwə-nəwa
      teacher   child(-ACC)   stand up-CAUS- IND
      'The teacher makes the child stand up.'

This sentence may describe different situations. It may indicate situations with physical involvement where the teacher physically helps the child to stand up, or the teacher's physical manipulation towards the child is so strong that he cannot resist and has to stand up. It may also indicate situations where the teacher's instruction, verbal or otherwise, rather than physical involvement, makes the child act accordingly. This difference in interpretation broadly agrees with the two kinds of morphological causatives delineated by Shibatani (1976) in terms of the means of causation, namely "manipulative" and "directive".

Semantic interpretations of the morphological causative may also be divided between "coercive" and "permissive" according to the degree of forcefulness (Shibatani 1976). When the force on the part of the causer is relatively strong, the sentence denoting the causative event is interpreted as "coercive". On the other hand, when willingness on the part of the causee is admitted into the situation, it represents an instance of "permissive" causation. Although the coercive/permissive distinction is largely attributed to the lexical semantics of the verbs, some verbs are open for both interpretations. The following example is ambiguous between the two interpretations.

(40) Ranjit   lamea(-wə)   naʈə-wə-nəwa
      Ranjit   child(-ACC)   dance-CAUS- IND
      'Ranjit makes/lets the child dance.'

If, in the depicted situation, the child shows willingness to perform the action, that is, he enjoys dancing, the sentence is interpreted as permissive. Conversely, if it depicts a situation where the child does not want to dance but was compelled to do so by the causer, it is interpreted as coercive.

According to the characterization given so far, lexical causative verbs have their corresponding intransitive counterparts, i.e. P verbs, and morphological causative verbs have their corresponding intransitive counterparts, albeit A verbs. However, causativization does not always follow this pattern of correlation. Even P verbs can have morphological causatives through the -wə- morpheme provided they don't have corresponding lexical causatives.

Intransitive	**Causative**
ængenəwa 'feel'	angəwənəwa 'cause to feel'
ælenəwa 'stick'	aləwənəwa 'paste'
æhærenəwa 'wake up'	æhærəwənəwa 'cause to wake up'
idenəwa 'ripen'	idəwənəwa 'cause to ripen'
gilenəwa 'drown'	gillənəwa (< gilwənəwa) 'cause to drown'
pæhenəwa 'ripen or boil'	passənəwa 'cause to boil'
pipenəwa 'bloom'	puppənəwa (< pupwənəwa) 'cause to bloom'
penenəwa ' be seen'	pennənəwa (< penwənəwa) 'show'
ridenəwa 'be painful'	ridəwənəwa 'cause to feel pain'
wæʈenəwa 'fall'	waʈʈənəwa 'cause to fall'
hærenəwa 'turn'	harəwənəwa 'cause to turn'
kærəkenəwa 'turn'	karəkəwənəwa 'cause to turn'

These intransitive verbs do not have corresponding A forms. Causative verbs are formed from these verbs by analogy with the lexical component. Therefore the verbal component preceding the causative morpheme -wə- in the resultant causative verbs should not be taken as the genuine verbal root as is the case in other causative verbs.

On the other hand, some intransitive verbs, even when a corresponding lexical causative is not available, do not undergo morphological causativization. At least, two such rare cases are found (cited in Abhayasinghe 1973):

galənawa 'flow'   *gala-wə-nəwa
wæḍenəwa 'grow'   *waḍə-wə-nəwa

For these verbs, causativization is achieved through periphrastic means. Intransitive-based morphological causatives are generally blocked when a corresponding lexical causative is available.

Next, the nature of transitive-based morphological causatives is described. In this structure, as already mentioned, with a new subject added, the old subject becomes an optional adjunct while the old object remains the object:

$NP_1 \quad NP_2 \: V \rightarrow NP_0 \quad (NP_1) \quad NP_2 \quad V$
Sub.   Obj.   Sub.   Obl.   Obj.

What mainly distinguishes the transitive-based morphological construction from other causative constructions is the causee's appearance as an adjunct constituent. This adjunct constituent is marked by the dative suffix -*ṭə* plus post-position *kiəla* 'by (telling)', or direct case plus *lauwa* 'by (deploying)'. The former has the following lexico-grammatical structure as its origin, which has the composite meaning of 'tell somebody (to do)': a dative case nominal plus the perfect participle form of the verb *kiənawa* 'say, tell'. The latter has developed from the perfect participle form of the causative verb *la-wə-nəwa*, from the verb *lanəwa* 'put, place' and has the sense of 'after deploying'. The transitive-based causatives with this causee constituent are exemplified by the following sentences.

(41) taatta   Ranjit   lauwa   gas   kappə-nəwa
     father   Ranjit   by   trees   cut. CAUS- IND
     'Father makes Ranjit cut the trees.'

(42) miniha   alia   lauwa   koṭə   addə-nəwa
     man   elephant   by   timber   pull. CAUS- IND
     'The man makes the elephant pull the timber.'

(43) amma   Chitra-ṭə kiəla   ændum   massə-nəwa
     mother   Chitra-by   garments   sew. CAUS- IND
     'Mother is getting Chitra to make garments.'

(44) Ranjit   Chitra-ṭə kiəla   lamea-wə   unandu kərə-wə-nəwa
     Ranjit   Chitra-by   child-ACC   encourage-CAUS- IND
     'Ranjit is getting Chitra to encourage the child.'

Though the two forms -*ṭə kiəla* and *lauwa* are considered to be in free variation by many linguists (for example, Gair 1970 and Wickramasinghe 1973), this is not necessarily true. Their grammatical development from lexical meanings, as elucidated above, is a testimony to, and their morphosyntactic features are iconic of, the fact that the two forms exhibit differential degrees of coercion. A causee marked by -*ṭə kiəla* enjoys a high degree of permissiveness shown by the agent to the extent that the referent of the former may have the right to refuse the task expected. The form *lauwa*, on the other hand, shows a high degree of forcefulness exerted by the agent. The choice of the causee marker, to a great extent, depends on the relative social standing between the causer and the causee. Compare the following sentences:

(45) Ranjit   amma-ṭə kiəla   seewikaawə lauwa   ændum   massə-nəwa
      Ranjit   mother-by   maid-by   garments make-CAUS- IND
      'Ranjit is getting his mother to have the maid make garments.'

(46) ??Ranjit amma lauwa   seewikaawə-ṭə kiəla   ændum   massə-nəwa
      Ranjit   mother-by   maid-by   garments make-CAUS-IND
      'Ranjit is getting his mother to have the maid make garments.'

The awkwardness of (46) comes from the pragmatic facts mentioned above, namely using the marker *lauwa* to indicate a causee who is in relatively higher position than the causer and the use of the marker -*ṭə kiəla* to indicate a participant of lower ranks in terms of power in relation to the causer. Also observe the following Sinhala proverb.

(47) balallu   lauwa   kossæṭə   baa-wə-nəwa
      cats   by   jack-fruit nuts pull-CAUS- IND
      (Lit.) 'Getting cats to pull jack-fruit nuts (from the fire-place where the nuts are being fried.)'

Since the causee is an animal, the marker -*ṭə kiəla* is considered inappropriate. The same applies not only to a proverb, as in (47), but also to an ordinary sentence, as in (42).

The transitive verbs that form the base for morphological causatives considered so far include lexical causative verbs. The following list has these transitive (lexical causative)-based morphological verbs extracted from the above sentences with the sentence number given within parentheses.

Lexical Causative	Morphological Causative	
kapə-nəwa (cut)	kappə-nəwa	(41)
adi-nəwa (pull)	addə-nəwa	(42)
maha-nəwa (sew)	massə-nəwa (< mas-wə-nəwa)	(43, 45 and 46)
unandu kərənawa(encourage)	unandu kərə-wə-nəwa	(44)
baa-nəwa (pull)	baa-wə-nəwa	(47)

However, some transitive-based causatives have verbs as their base, which are themselves derived causatives. Some examples are shown below:

bassə-nəwa > (*bassə-wə-nəwa*) 'cause to get down'
paddə-nəwa > (*paddə-wə-nəwa*) 'cause to rock, sway'
waṭṭə-nəwa > (*waṭṭə-wə-nəwa*) 'cause to fall'
nawattə-nəwa > (*nawattə-wə-nəwa*) 'cause to stop'
nægiṭṭə-nəwa > (*nægiṭṭə-wə-nəwa*) 'cause to get up'[2]

How they can be considered as transitive-based causatives is described below with individual examples.

(48) a. Ranjit draiwər-ṭə kiəla lamea-wə gedərə lang-in
     Ranjit driver   by   child-ACC house near-ABL
     bassə-nəwa
     get down-CAUS-IND
     'Ranjit gets the driver to make the child get down near his house.'

   b. draiwər lamea-wə gedərə lang-in bassə-nəwa
      driver child-ACC house near-ABL get down-CAUS-IND
      'The driver makes the child get down near his house.'

Although the sentence in (48a) is considered as a morphological causative, that is, with the agent in the nominative, the causee marked by *lauwa* and the object marked in the accusative, the immediate base of it can be traced to (48b) where the present causee, the driver, remains the agent in the nominative. Thus the morphological causative in (48a) is considered as derived from that of (48b).

(49) a. amma   lamea-ṭə kiəla toṭillə paddə-nəwa
        mother child-by   cradle rock.CAUS-IND
        'Mother gets the child to rock the cradle.'

   b. lamea toṭillə paddə-nəwa
      child cradle rock.CAUS-IND
      'The child is rocking the cradle.'

The verb in (49b) is a morphological causative derived from *padinəwa* 'swing, sway'. Its agent becomes the causee, with a new agent added to the subject position in (49a). However, it must be noted that this type of base verbs have been established in the language as lexical causatives (Gair 1970: 66–67). At least to do justice to them, they might be considered as a separate subtype of morphological causatives. The verbs like

---

2. See the description given for the Intransitive-Causative pairs at the beginning of this section.

yawənəwa 'cause to go' or 'send', *ewənəwa* 'cause to come' or 'send', and *kiəwənəwa* 'cause to say' or 'read' also can be added to this group.

Causative constructions may contain dative objects and indirect objects. What we call "dative objects" are complements of 'treat'-type verbs appearing in the dative form, as in (50). Di-transitive verbs of the 'give'-type have their indirect objects marked by the dative, as in (51).

(50) miniha lamea lauwa gonaa-ṭə talə-wə-nəwa
 man child by bull-DAT hit-CAUS-IND
 'The man makes the child hit the bull.'

(51) rajəyə graaməseewəkə lauwa minissun-ṭə
 Government village officer by people-DAT
 shanadaarə bedə-wə-nəwa
 relief supplies distribute-CAUS-IND
 'The government makes the village officer distribute relief supplies to people.'

The presence of dative objects and indirect objects in the causative constructions should be considered not as the result of any case changing device but, conversely, as the natural result of the case retaining principle attested in Sinhala. This is another example of the phenomenon of case persistence.

There is a subtype of morphological causative constructions which consists of 'ingestive' verbs such as *kawənəwa* 'cause to eat or feed' (derived from *kanəwa* 'eat') and *powənəwa* 'cause to drink or feed liquids' (derived from *bonəwa* 'drink'). In the causativization of this type of verbs, the old subject changes to a dative constituent, as in (52a). However, the new subject may change into an intermediate agent or causee marked by *-ṭə kiəla* or *lauwa*, if yet another new subject is incorporated to form a secondary causative construction, as in (52b).

(52) a. Chitra lamea-ṭə kiri powə-nəwa
 Chitra child-DAT milk drink.CAUS-IND
 'Chitra is feeding the child milk.'

 b. amma Chitra lauwa lameya-ṭə kiri powə-nəwa
 mother Chitra by child-DAT milk drink.CAUS-IND
 'Mother is getting Chitra to feed the child milk.'

In (52b) the new subject has taken the position of subject, pushing the former subject in (52a) into the place of causee constituent. In both sentences the person who is allowed to eat or drink is encoded in the dative which indicates that the experiencer of the ingestive process is considered as a target rather than an intermediate agent. There is one non-ingestive verb belonging to this causative group, which is *danwənəwa* 'cause to know or inform' derived from the cognitive stative verb *dannəwa* 'know'. This verb is morphosyntactically treated in the same way as those of the ingestive group in that the participant who is allowed to know or be informed is invariably in the dative.

Causative verbs may appear in P form in which the suffixes are concatenated in the order of CAUSATIVE-PASSIVE. However, their independent presence is not noticeable. Once the causative morpheme is added to a verb root, it is assumed as a new verb root undergoing passivization. There are morphophonemic processes which may obscure these markers.

Intransitive	Causative	Causative-passive
kiənəwa 'say'	kiə-wə-nəwa	kiəwe-nəwa
yanəwa 'go'	ya-wə-nəwa	yæwe-nəwa
enəwa 'come'	e-wə-nəwa	ewe-nəwa
balənəwa 'look'	balə-wə-nəwa	bælǝwe-nəwa
naṭǝnǝwa 'dance'	naṭǝ-wǝ-nǝwa	næṭǝwe-nǝwa
hærenǝwa 'turn'	harǝ-wǝ-nǝwa	hærǝwe-nǝwa
anḍǝnǝwa 'cry'	anḍǝ-wǝ-nǝwa	ænḍǝwe-nǝwa

Most of these causative-passive verbs are used to denote involuntary activities. For some verbs, the involitive form and the causative-passive form are in free variation. For example, both næṭǝnǝwa and næṭǝwǝ-nǝwa mean 'dancing impulsively'. For some verbs, which do not have an independent morphological P-form, the causative-passive simply serves as the involitive form. Of this type are kiǝwe-nǝwa 'say unintentionally', yæwe-nǝwa 'go impulsively' and ewe-nǝwa 'come impulsively'. For some other verbs, the simple P-form and the causative-passive form bear the intransitive-transitive distinction, as in (53).

(53)   a.   maa-wǝ   nikammǝ   ee   pættǝ-ṭǝ   hæruna
            I-ACC   just   that   direction-DAT   turn. INVL. PAST
            'I spontaneously turned in that direction.'

       b.   man   atin   baisikǝlee   dakunǝ-ṭǝ   hærǝuna
            I   atin   bicycle   right-DAT   turn. CAUS- PASS. PAST
            'I impulsively turned the bicycle to the right.'

(53a) denotes an intransitive event whereas (52b) contains a transitive event. The two verb forms cannot be used alternately in this situation.

There is another use of the causative-passive form, which has an independent semantic content. As seen in (54), the causative-passive form is used to indicate a warning.

(54)   ṭiiwii   bælǝwe-i,   taatta   aapuhamǝ!
       TV   look. CAUS- PASS- INFER   farther   come-TEMP
       'You'll never watch TV when Father comes home!'
       Lit. 'You would be allowed to watch TV when Father comes home.'

This sentence consists of two clauses: the preceding clause has the causative-passive form in the inferential mood and the one which follows is an adverbial clause of time. Consider that the finite clause has been preposed for emphasis; its subject, the second person pronoun, is elliptical. This type of utterance with a causative-passive verb in the inferential mood says 'You'd be allowed' and has an overtone of warning towards the listener with the sense 'You will not be allowed to carry out the action'.

Most of the examples given here for transitive-based morphological causative constructions include the causee constituent. This was arranged deliberately since it helps to identify the key characteristics of the construction. In actual discourse, however, there appear causative sentences without causee constituents.

(55) Ranjit alut kamisəy-ak massə-wə-nəwa
Ranjit new shirt-INDF sew-CAUS- IND
'Ranjit is going to get a tailor-made shirt.'
Lit. 'Ranjit is getting a new shirt made.'

(56) taatta raa maddə-nəwa
father toddy tap.CAUS- IND
'Father has somebody tap toddy.'

(57) taatta wæʈə bandəwənəwa
father fence tie. CAUS- IND
'Father is getting somebody to mend the fence.'

In (55) the causee is understood from the context as a tailor and hence need not overtly appear in the sentence. In (56) and (57) the causee is unclear or indefinite; it might be not important to mention who actually does the tapping or the mending job. What seems to be important is the topic of the sentence, i.e. the father, and the comment that he is getting somebody to tap toddy or to build the fence. These sentences seem rather natural without causee constituents.

2.3 Periphrastic causatives

Two constructions are discussed here as periphrastic causatives: the benefactive construction and the indirect causative construction. A benefactive construction consists of a verbal complex formed from a main verb plus benefactive auxiliary and several nominal constituents. The two obligatory constituents represent a benefactor (someone who acts for other participant's sake) and a beneficiary (someone at the receiving end). There is a subdivision of benefactive constructions into simple and causative benefactives. The causative benefactives, which are closely associated with the morphological causatives just discussed will be considered first, and then the simple benefactive construction will be described. Finally, the indirect causative construction will be introduced.

2.3.1 *Causative benefactive construction*

The causative benefactive construction is formed with the perfect participle base of the morphological causative verb and the benefative auxiliary *gannəwa* 'take, receive'. The auxiliary *gannəwa* is a grammaticalized form of the homophonous lexical verb meaning 'take or receive'. Since the causative verb and the auxiliary together make a composite structure, inflectional suffixes of tense, etc. are added to the end of the whole structure. As for case marking and grammatical relations, the beneficiary is coded as the subject in the nominative case while the benefactor is marked by *-ṭə kiəla* or *lauwa*.

(58) Ranjit   ayya   lauwa   baisikəlee   hadə-wa   gatta³
      Ranjit   elder brother by   bicycle   make-CAUS.PP   gan.PAST
      'Ranjit got his elder brother to fix his bicycle.'

(59) Ranjit   səər-ṭə kiəla   sahatikəy-ak   liə-wa   gatta
      Ranjit   teacher-by   certificate-INDF write-CAUS.PP   gan.PAST
      'Ranjit had his teacher write a certificate (for him).'

Thus the morphosyntactic manifestation of the construction resembles that of the causative construction, in particular, the transitive-based morphological causative. The causer has become a beneficiary while the causee has changed to a benefactor. This change achieved through the benefactive auxiliary has an overall effect on the conceptual structure of the construction. While a prototypical causative situation is conceived of as including a causer showing a greater degree of coercion towards a causee, the causative benefactive construction is supposed to impose a structure under which a causer makes a request for an action to a causee who is capable of carrying out the task required. The request in this case does not come with force or out of any authority; even a person with authority or of considerable standing may turn into a humble beneficiary under this construction.

(60) a. mæneejər   Chitra-ṭə kiəla   liumə   ṭaip kərə-wa   gan-nəwa
         manager   Chitra-by   letter   type-CAUS. PP   gan- IND
         'The manager is getting Chitra to type the letter.'

     b. mæneejər   Chitra-ṭə kiəla   liumə   ṭaip kərə-wə-nəwa
         manager   Chitra-by   letter   type-CAUS- IND
         'The manager is making Chitra type the letter.'

(61) a. siiya   lamea-ṭə kiəla   kaamə ree   atugaa-wa   gan-nəwa
         grandfather   child-by   room   sweep-CAUS. PP   gan- IND
         'Grandpa is getting the child to sweep the room.'

---

3. ə in the causative morpheme *wə* changes to *a* in the formation of the perfect participle base.

b. siiya   lamea-ṭə kiəla kaaməree atugaa-wə-nəwa
    grandfather child-by   room   sweep-CAUS-IND
    'Grandpa is making the child sweep the room.'

Suppose that Chitra is a typist working under the manager mentioned in (60), who has official authority over her. Still, under the benefactive construction in (60a), the manager is posited as beneficiary who does not exert pressure or power on the secondary participant to carry out the action required. By contrast, the example in (60b) encodes a prototypical causative situation with a stronger sense of coercion. In the same way, the grandfather and the child are in a beneficiary-benefactor relationship in (61a), and causer-causee relationship in (61b). The causative benefactive construction structurally assigns a greater freedom or capacity to the secondary participant to comply with, or reject, the request made by the primary participant. The scope of freedom accorded to the secondary participant may be larger than that of the causee of a permissive causative.

There are, however, also some similarities between morphological causatives and causative benefactives: both constructions impose an animacy restriction on the selection of the subject and the adjunct constituent. That is to say, both have an active participant or an agent for their first constituent, and an animate participant for their second constituent. Some causative benefactives do contain inanimate nouns, but they duly represent animate participants.

(62) a. mamə saappuwə-ṭə kiəla kamisəy-ak massəwa   gatta
         I   shop-by   shirt-INDF sew.CAUS.PP gan-PAST
         'I had the shop tailor a shirt (for me).'

     b. *mamə saappuwə lauwa kamisəy-ak massəwa   gatta
         I   shop   by   shirt-INDF sew.CAUS.PP gan-PAST
         'I had the shop tailor a shirt (for me).'

In (62a) the inanimate nominal used in the place of the second constituent represents people working in the shop, and therefore the sentence is grammatical. Yet, (62b) with the same nominal constituent is unacceptable due to a different semantic constraint. The difference between the two sentences can be attributed to the lexical and semantic properties of the two causative/benefactive postpositions. Although both these postpositions are only attached to animate nouns (or to inanimate nouns with connotations of animacy), -ṭə kiəla, to some extent, retains its lexical sense, namely the "verbal transmission" sense, while *lauwa*, as a grammatical morpheme, represents a higher level of abstraction with the causative sense. As mentioned before, the conceptual structure underlying the causative benefactive construction demands that a request or message is communicated to the benefactor by the beneficiary in order to get something done. The compatibility of the verbal transmission sense of the -*tə kiəla* postposition with the "animacy" connotation of the inanimate noun creates a natural sentence like (62a). The inanimate noun followed by the postposition *lauwa*, which does not overtly possess the verbal transmission sense does not contribute to the production of the animacy connotation, leading (62b) to end up as an ungrammatical sentence.

Another related fact is that causative benefactives in Sinhala cannot be based on intransitive verbs. As it becomes explicit from the foregoing account, both the beneficiary and the benefactor are active participants in causative benefactives. Thus there are no passive benefactives in Sinhala. If intransitive verbs are used for benefactives, they will be accompanied by direct causation with a strong sense of coercion on the part of the primary agent. As we have seen before, intransitive-based causatives appear with the original subject changed to the direct object, taking the form of direct case or optionally marked by the accusative case. This kind of causation does not lead to the causative benefactive construction, as (63) shows.

(63) *Ranjit wandurawə natə-wa gannəwa
Ranjit monkey-ACC dance-CAUS.PP gan-IND
'Ranjit is getting the monkey to dance.'

In such situations, the causation is so direct and straightforward that there is no space for benefactive conceptualization. Even the addition of a benefactor constituent, or the addition of a separate subject constituent turning the present subject to the benefactor, does not yield a grammatical sentence.

(64) *taatta Ranjit lauwa wandurawə natə-wa gannəwa
father Ranjit by monkey-ACC dance-CAUS.PP gan-IND
'Father is getting Ranjit to make the monkey dance.'

The transitivity of the lexical verb seems to be crucial to the causative benefactive construction. However, no detailed examination has been carried out regarding this aspect of the grammar. Since the *gannəwa* auxiliary is also used for reflexive constructions as described before (Chapter 8:2.2), the problem of benefactives involving intransitives appears more complex. For example, the following sentence with an intransitive base is acceptable to some speakers.

(65) taatta Ranjit lauwa lamea-wə naa-wa gannəwa
father Ranjit by child-ACC bathe-CAUS.PP gan-IND
'Father is getting Ranjit to bathe the child.'

Thus a finer-grained analysis regarding the involvement of verbs in the causative benefactive construction is yet to be done.

It should be added finally that some examples of the morphological causative which may sound awkward from the viewpoint of native speakers will be fully natural if they are combined with the causative benefactive construction. In fact, Sinhala speakers often use the two constructions in combination. This kind of co-existence of two constructions known as layering can be seen in some other languages, too. The principle of layering, for example, has been observed with regard to the Japanese causative benefactives: the outer layer being periphrastic and the internal layer working with morphological or lexical forms (Iwasaki 2002).

2.3.2 Simple benefactive construction

Conceptually, the simple benefactive construction also contains a benefactor and a beneficiary. The benefactor constituent appears in the nominative while the beneficiary noun takes the dative form. This distinguishes the simple benefactive construction from the causative benefactive construction whose beneficiary constituent always occupies the subject position. The verbal compound consists of the perfect participle form of the principal verb and the auxiliary derived from *denəwa* 'give'[4]. The auxiliary is always *denəwa* regardless of the direction of giving. The trajectory of giving may take an outward orientation, i.e. from the speaker to a listener or a third person, as in (66), or an inward orientation, i.e. towards the speaker, as in (67).

(66) mamə   Chitra-ţə   illum   pattəree   purəwə-la   dunna
     I   Chitra-DAT   application   form   fill-PP   *de*. PAST
     'I filled the application form for Chitra.'

(67) Chitra   ma-ţə   chittrəy-ak   ændə-la   dunna
     Chitra   I-DAT   picture-INDF   draw-PP   *de*. PAST
     'Chitra drew a picture for me.'

This shows that the basic benefactive auxiliary does not code a particular viewpoint to depict the act of giving, as to whether it is benefactor's viewpoint or beneficiary's viewpoint. Evidently, it is the lexical semantics of the principal verb that imposes restrictions on the simple benefactive construction. "Activity" and "accomplishment" verbs are easily admitted to the construction, as in (68) and (69). However, intransitive verbs are excluded, as in (70) and (71), though some cognitive verbs are acceptable, if they are active-type verbs, as in (72).

(68) Ranjit   taatta-ţə   baisikəlee   tallu kərə-la   dunna
     Ranjit   father-DAT   bicycle   push-PP   *de*.PAST
     'Ranjit pushed the bicycle for his father.'

(69) Chita   Ranjit-ţə   næw-ak   hadə-la   dunna
     Chitra   Ranjit-DAT   ship-INDF   make-PP   *de*.PAST
     'Chitra made a ship (from paper) for Ranjit.'

---

4. To get the perfect participle form of a verb, the perfect participle suffix *laa* is added in the colloquial language.

(70) *Ranjit   amma-ṭə   polə-ṭə   gihin   dunna
     Ranjit   mother-DAT   market-DAT   go-PP   de.PAST
     'Ranjit went to the market for his mother.'

(71) *Ranjit   Chitra-ṭə   taniyə-ṭə   ində-la   dunna
     Ranjit   Chitra-DAT   loneliness-DAT   be-PP   de.PAST
     'Ranjit stayed for Chitra to dispel her loneliness.'

(72) Chitra   Ranjit-ṭə   ræswiimə   matak kərə-la   dunna
     Chitra   Ranjit-DAT   meeting   remind-PP   de.PAST
     'Chitra reminded Ranjit about the meeting.'

The above shows that the simple benefactive construction represents a series of actions in which the benefactor appearing as the subject produces something or brings something into effect, as denoted by the principal verb, and the result is transferred, as denoted by the *denəwa* auxiliary, to the other animate participant marked by the dative. The selection of nominal constituents and case marking is determined by the lexical properties of the principal verb plus the *denəwa* auxiliary. It may also be induced from the given state of affairs that the *denəwa* auxiliary, which retains its transitive identity has not undergone the process of grammaticalization to the extent of being syntactically de-categorized. This is amply demonstrated by the fact that there are no intransitive-based *denəwa* constructions in the simple benefactive.

The act of producing denoted by the verb, however, need not contain concrete things as their objects:

(73) Chitra   Ranjit-ṭə   prasne   teerum kərə-la   dunna
     Chitra   Ranjit-DAT   problem   explain-PP   de.PAST
     'Chitra explained the problem to Ranjit.'[5]

It might be interesting to see that some ditransitive verbs with indirect objects, and semi-transitive verbs with dative objects cannot be admitted to the simple benefactive construction, as (74) and (75) respectively show.

(74) *Chitra   Ranjit-ṭə   pot-ak   yawə-la   dunna
     Chitra   Ranjit-DAT   book-INDF   send-PP   de.PAST
     'Chitra sent a book to Ranjit.'

(75) *Chitr   Ranjit-ṭə   prəsansaa kərə-la   dunna
     Chitra   Ranjit-DAT   praise-PP   de.PAST
     'Chitra praised Ranjit.'

Why these cannot be converted to the simple benefactive construction when their verbs are ditransitive or semi-transitive? These verbs are lexically subcategorized for dative

---

5. The English gloss does not make the benefactive features grammatically explicit.

constituents. They suggest that verbs for which dative constituents are lexically specified conflict with the simple benefactive construction, which has the independent right to impose its own valency by assigning the dative case to the new participant. There is an important assumption underlying this speculation: the simple benefactive construction affects the argument structure of verbs by increasing valency. Compare the (a–b) pairs in the following.

(76) a. Ranjit bootəlee æria
Ranjit bottle open.PAST
'Ranjit opened the bottle.'

b. Ranjit Chitra-ʈə bootəlee ærə-la dunna
Ranjit Chitra-DAT bottle open-PP *de*.PAST
'Ranjit opened the bottle for Chitra.'

(77) a. Chitra bittəree kæɖuwa
Chitra egg break.PAST
'Chitra broke the egg.'

b. Chitra Ranjit-ʈə bittəree kaɖə-la dunna
Chitra Ranjit-DAT egg break-PP *de*.PAST
'Chitra broke the egg for Ranjit.'

However, there are some transitive verbs that can have dative participants in appropriate environments, though they are not entitled to have a lexically specified dative argument.

(78) a. Chitra Ranjit-ʈə tee hadə-nəwa
Chitra Ranjit-DAT tea make-IND
'Chitra is making tea for Ranjit.'

b. Chitra Ranjit-ʈə tee hadə-la de-nəwa
Chitra Ranjit-DAT tea make-PP *de*-IND
'Chitra is making tea for Ranjit.'

(79) a. Ranjit taatta-ʈə kamisəy-ak gatta
Ranjit Chitra-DAT shirt-INDF buy.PAST
'Ranjit bought a shirt for his father.'

b. Ranjit taata-ʈə kamisəy-ak araŋ dunna
Ranjit father-DAT shirt-INDF buy.PP *de*.PAST
'Ranjit bought a shirt for his father.'

(80) a. taata Chitra-ʈə ambə kaɖə-nəwa
father Chitra-DAT mango pluck-IND
'Father is plucking mangoes for Chitra.'

b. taata Chitra-ʈə ambə kaɖə-la de-nəwa
father Chitra-DAT mango pluck-PP *de*-IND
'Father is plucking mangoes for Chitra.'

The verbs like *hadənəwa* 'make', *gatta* 'bought' and *kaḍənəwa* 'pluck' that only have agent and patient as lexically specified thematic roles may appear with an additional dative constituent, as shown by (a) sentences in (78–80) above. Next, by comparing the (b) sentences with the phenomenon of the optional valence availability exhibited by the (a) sentences, we can observe that the *denəwa* form has not contributed an increase in the number of arguments in the verb. This may lead one to conclude that the simple benefactive construction is not a valency increasing construction. At least regarding the pairs in (78–80), one might aptly state that the simple benefactive construction has developed from a formation similar to the applicative construction with an optionally added argument, rather than considering it to possess an independent valency-bearing capacity.

Some *denəwa* forms that follow this structure have been conventionalized as idioms. Examples: *kiəla denəwa* '(say and give =) teach, instruct', *paawa denəwa* '(put forth and give =) betray', which were not dealt with here. It may be pointed out further that the simple benefactive construction is not a causative construction in the strict sense of the word. The simple benefactive construction does not present a situation where the agent-causer causes another agent to act or another process to take place. The action is solely carried out by the participant denoted by the subject; only the result of the action is transferred to another participant which is marked in the dative as the endpoint of the action

2.3.3 *Indirect causative construction*

Causative situations are generally considered as including two possibilities: One has an agent-causer directly causing a patient-causee to perform an action or to undergo a change of state. In the other the agent is involved in some action or a series of actions indirectly, preparing the circumstances leading to some other event. While the former is linguistically expressed through lexical and morphological causative the latter, called indirect causation, is only realized through periphrastic causatives.

The unitary and composite structure of lexical/morphological causatives is totally compatible with the function of direct causation. By contrast, the periphrastic construction allows the two events, the causing event and the caused event, to stand separate as two clauses recognizable morpho-syntactically. The primary agent's action is denoted in the matrix form by the verb *salassənəwa* 'prepare' or *iḍə denəwa* 'allow, permit'; the individual lexical verbs denoting caused events are embedded in the matrix clause. The distance between two events is further indicated by the infinitive form used to combine the lexical verb with the matrix clause. Thus the verb complex for the indirect causative is [Verb-Infinitive form + *salassənəwa/iḍə denəwa*].

The following sentences will help understand the form of the nominal constituents appearing in indirect causatives.

(81) taatta gas kapa-nnə sælæssuwa
father trees cut-INF salassə.PAST
'Father caused the trees to be cut.'

(82) kærəli naayəkəya wiruddə kanḍaayəm-ee naayəkəya
rebel leader rival fraction-LOC leader
mara-nnə salassə-nəwa
kill-INF salassə.IND
'The rebel leader caused the rival faction leader to be killed.'

(83) guruwərəya lamain-ṭə ṭiiwii bala-nnə sælæssuwa
teacher children-DAT TV watch-INF salassə.PAST
'The teacher caused the children to watch TV.'

The verb complex with a transitive verb in (81) has an agent/causer constituent and an inanimate object. In (82) the two nominal constituents, both animate participants, represent agent/causer and patient. The sentence in (83) has three nominal constituents: the first appears as the subject representing agent/causer; the second appears in the dative representing the embedded subject; the third in the direct case represents the patient. As a comparison with (83) reveals, embedded subjects are missing in (81) and (82), which not only points to a possibility under the indirect causative construction but may also indicate some semantic motivation for the development of the construction. The example in (83) also shows that for an embedded subject the selected case is dative and its usual position is between the agent constituent and the patient constituent. This can be seen through the following example, too.

(84) mudəlali miniha-ṭə raa pera-nnə sælæssuwa
master man-DAT toddy tap-INF salassə.PAST
'The business master caused the man to tap toddy.'

It is understood that the agent represented by the subject constituent arranged for the referent of the dative constituent to carry out the action denoted by the verb phrase, which includes the object noun. However, the dative case is not the only possible choice for the embedded subject. Compare the two sentences in (85).

(85) a. Ranjit lamea-ṭə tanəbim-ee perəle-nnə sælæssuwa
Ranjit child-DAT lawn-LOC roll down-INF salassə.PAST
'Ranjit arranged for the child to roll down on the lawn.'

b. Ranjit lamea-wə puṭuw-en perəle-nnə sælæssuwa
Ranjit child-ACC chair-ABL roll down-INF salassə.PAST
'Ranjit caused the child to roll down from the chair.'

The sentence (85a) has the same structure as (84) in terms of case marking, the difference between the two sentences lying in the lexical verb: the former has an intransitive verb whereas the latter has a transitive verb. Now, sentence (85b) is different from (85a), and from (84) for that matter, in that its embedded subject is marked in the accusative despite the fact that the phonological verb form is the same in (85a) and (85b). A fundamental point to be revisited in this case is that the same phonological verb may split between the volitive and involitive distinction in Sinhala. The answer here appears to be that the two sentences have two different semantic structures as volitive and involitive indeed.[6] The embedded subject in (85b) is in the accusative case because the indirect causative construction allows involitive verbs to retain the original case marking of the embedded subject.

On the other hand, all embedded dative subjects should not be taken as belonging with volitive action verbs because, as elucidated before, involitive verbs often take dative subjects in Sinhala. When such clauses are embedded in indirect causative sentences, the embedded subject remains in the dative. An example is given in (86a), along with its embedded clause (86b).

(86) a. guruwərəya lamain-ṭə kurulu handə æhe-nnə sælæssuwa
teacher children-DAT bird sound hear-INF salassa.PAST
'The teacher arranged for the children to hear birds' chirping.'

b. lamain-ṭə kurulu handə æhe-nəwa
children-DAT bird sound hear.INVL-IND
'The children can hear birds' chirping.'

It should be noted that a range of verb types including involitive verbs, process verbs and stative verbs that cannot be inflected into morphological causatives because of some limitations are readily admitted as indirect causatives. Consider the following examples:

(87) miniha udee aṭə-ṭə boombe pipire-nnə sælæssuwa
man morning eight-DAT bomb blast.INVL-INF salassa.PAST
'The man caused the bomb to explode at eight in the morning.'

(88) lamai bamərə kærəke-nnə sælæssuwa
children windmill turn.INVL-INF salassa.PAST
'The children caused the windmill to turn.'

---

6. The embedded clauses of (85a) and (85b) would be independent clauses as in (1a) and (1b), respectively.

(1) a. lamea tanəbim-ee perəle-nəwa
child lawn-LOC roll down-IND
'The child rolls down on the lawn.'

b. lamea-wə puṭuw-en perəle-nəwa
child-ACC chair-ABL roll down-IND
'The child rolls down from the chair.'

(89) minniha   lamea-ṭə   asəniipə   wennə   sælæssuwa
     man   child-DAT   ill   be-INF   salassə.PAST
     'The man caused the child to get ill.'

(90) mantrii   lamea-ṭə   paasælə-ṭə   ætul   we-nnə   sælæssuwa
     MP   child-DAT   school-DAT   be   admitted-INF salassə.PAST
     'The MP caused the child to be admitted to the school.'

Our data shows that most of the animate participants selected as embedded subjects, whether volitional or non-volitional, appear in the dative case while some involuntary participants are marked in the accusative. In addition, as the following example shows, the embedded clause subject can also appear with the accidental agent marker *atin*.

(91) Ranjit   Chitra   atin   siinuwə   wæde-nnə   sælæssuwa
     Ranjit   Chitra   *atin* bell   ring.INVL-INF   *salassə*.PAST
     'Ranjit caused Chitra to accidentally ring the bell.'

Even in the underlying embedded clause Chitra is the accidental agent for the non-volitional event of bell-ringing. The matrix subject is not taken to initiate a voluntary action as long as the embedded subject remains marked by the *atin* phrase. Nor can it be modified by the causee marker *lauwa* as in a morphological causative sentence, as the following shows:

(92) *Ranjit   Chitra   lauwa   siinuwə   wæde-nnə   sælæssuwa
      Ranjit   Chitra   *lauwa* bell   ring.INVL-INF *salassə*.PAST

Marking the embedded agent with *lauwa* gives a more direct sense which is incompatible with the indirect causation and hence unfit to be embedded in the matrix of *sælæssənəwa* 'preparing or providing circumstances.' Further, since the verb complex for the indirect causative construction is not a composite structure but a periphrastic one with the verb *sælæssənəwa*, the *lauwa* phrase does not match up with the linguistic context.

Apart from this structural incompatibility, there is an important semantic reason underscoring the awkwardness. As observed before, one important assumption underlying the *lauwa/-ṭə kiəla* constituent is that there is some verbal transmission occurring from the external agent to the embedded agent. In case of indirect causation, however, no verbal transmission is implied; the network of contacts between the causing event and the caused event is never direct or clear-cut. Therefore the *lauwa* constituent cannot be used for the indirect causative construction.

Although the indirect causative construction was described using the main verb *salassənəwa* 'prepare', it should be noted that there is a range of verbs with varied nuances and varying degrees of grammaticalization generally used with the infinitive form of the lexical verb for indirect causative expression. Some of these are *idə denəwa* 'allow, permit', *idə arinəwa* 'allow, permit', *arinəwa* 'allow' (short form of *idə arinəwa*) and *denəwa* 'allow, let'. The following are examples.

(93) guruwərəya lamain-ṭə ṭiiwii bala-nnə idə de-nəwa
teacher children-DAT TV watch-INF permit-IND
'The teacher permits children to watch TV.'

(94) guruwərəya lamain-ṭə kataa baha kər nnə idə æri-nɔwa
teacher children-DAT talk-INF permit-IND
'The teacher allows children to talk.'

(95) Ranjit midul-e wal pælææṭi hæde-nnə æria
Ranjit yard-LOC weeds grow-INF let.PAST
'Ranjit allowed weeds to grow in the yard.'

(96) Ranjit Chitra-ṭə nida-nnə dunna
Ranjit Chitra-DAT sleep-INF let.PAST
'Ranjit let Chitra sleep.'

Their characteristics, limitations and semantics are not fully understood. At least some of them as exemplified by (95) and (96) seem to have developed as modal expressions.

All in all, causative constructions can be presented as a spectrum consisting of three basic types and several subtypes. In practical terms, different types are combined in cross-structural interaction to create an appropriate admixture of structures. This kind of interaction occurs between the passive and causative constructions, too. Identifying the full spectrum of possibilities helps us recognize the limitations, restrictions and premises of each construction.

CHAPTER 10

Expanded sentences

Two or more clauses are combined together to form an expanded sentence. Combination occurs in the form of coordination or subordination with the use of conjunctive endings, conjunctive particles, formal nouns, or case markers. Expanded sentences are categorized as compound, complex and mixed. A compound sentence, as traditionally accepted, consists of two or more coordinate clauses which are reversible and enumerable, that is the clauses can be put in the reverse order without any change in meaning and can be multiplied without limit. A complex sentence consists of one main clause and one subordinate clause that functions as an adverbial, adjectival or nominal constituent of the main clause. A mixed sentence consists of both compound and complex sentences. Simple sentences are expanded through coordination, subordination or both.

1. Compound sentences

Three types of coordination can be observed: (1) collateral coordination, (2) use of particles and (3) use of the conjunctive ending.

The collateral coordination is the simplest form of combining sentences. Two or more clauses are placed side by side without any inflectional suffix or particle to combine them.

(1) Ranjit gedərə e-nəwa   bat   ka-nəwa ʈiiwee balə-nəwa
    Ranjit home   come-IND rice   eat-IND TV   watch-IND
    'Ranjit comes home, has a meal and watches TV.'

(2) wælə   mære-nəwa alə   bahi-nəwa
    creeper die-IND   roots grow-IND
    'Roots grow while the creeper withers.'

(3) api wædə kərə-nnə ee gollo   paɖi   gan-nə
    we work do-INF   those people salary take-INF
    'We are to work and they are to get salaries.'

(4) e-nnə   ka-nnə   bo-nnə   winoodə we-nnə
    come-IMP eat-IMP drink-IMP enjoy-IMP
    'Come, eat, drink and enjoy (yourself).'

The examples given above all include coordinated clauses. In (1) the clauses are coordinated by identical noun deletion. When the clauses in a chain share the same subject it is deleted except the one of the initial clause. In (2) and (3) with no elements deleted, two clauses are placed side by side in each. They both express contrasts: in (2) the contrast is presented by declarative clauses whereas in (3) the contrast is emphasized by placing infinitive clauses in the focused position. Nothing is deleted in the process of coordination in (4); all the four clauses are imperative structures and the subject constituent is elliptical.

The noun-coordinating particle *saha* cannot be used as a clause-coordinator in Sinhala. Thus (5) in English cannot be rendered as (6) in Sinhala (Abhayasinghe 1992).

(5) Mr. Perera teaches in a government school and Mrs. Perera in a private one.

(6) *Perera mahatməya rajəy-ee   paasələ-k-ə   uganwə-nəwa
     Perera Mr.   government-LOC school-INDF-LOC teach-IND
     saha emə   mahatmiya pudgalika paasələ-k-ə   uganwənəwa
     and aforesaid Mrs.   private   school-INDF-LOC teach-IND
     'Mr. Perera teaches in a government school and Mrs. Perera in a private one.'

However, with some adjustment, as in (7), the sentence has become acceptable to a great extent in modern Sinhala.

(7) Perera mahatməya rajəy-ee   paasələ-k-ə   saha
     Perera Mr.   government-LOC school-INDF-LOC and
     emə   mahatmiya pudgalika paasələ-kə   uganwə-nəwa
     aforesaid Mrs.   private   school-INDF-LOC. teach-IND
     'Mr. Perera teaches in a government school and Mrs. Perera in a private one.'

This suggests that the Sinhala noun coordinator *saha* is increasingly being established as a clause-coordinator, perhaps under the influence of English (Abhayasinghe 1992).

It is often said that the relation between two or more clauses may be reversed without a change in truth-conditional meaning. However, when a compound sentence represents a temporal (i.e. 'and then'), as in (8), or logical (i.e. 'therefore') sequence, as in (9), the order may not be changed.

(8) miniha watə-pitə bæluwa   pəəs eka æhində gatta
     man   around   look.PAST purse one pick up.PAST
     'The man looked around and picked the purse up.'

(9) miniha mahansi unaa   wibaage   paas unaa
     man   make   efforts.PAST examination pass.PAST
     'The man worked hard and passed the examination.'

If the order is reversed in (8) or (9), the pragmatic meanings will not be conveyed properly, though the truth-conditional meanings still remain the same.

All the sentences given so far are examples of collateral coordination. They are characterized by the absence of any morpheme that explicitly marks the link between the clauses. The speaker simply moves from one clause to the next combining ideas into some lager sequence. In the written language they may be connected by a comma or a semicolon. While separate clauses may be marked by separate intonation units, a single sentence, however complex, may have only one illocutionary force. This follows from the fact that "illocutionary force is the outermost peripheral operator" pointed out by Foley and Van Valin (1984: 239).Accordingly, the above examples all are considered as compound sentences.

In fact, Sinhala has several conjunctive markers to combine clauses. One such device is the coordinating conjunction *-i,* which is doubly used, as in (10) through (12), or used after each NP, as in (13). The following use of the ending *-i* reveals that it is a clitic. If the nominal or verbal constituent ends in a consonant, the epenthetic vowel *u* is added before adding the clitic.

(10) amma   Ranjit-ṭə   kamiseku-i   Chitra-ṭə
     mother Ranjit-DAT shirt.INDF-CONJ   Chitra-DAT
     gauməku-i   araŋ   dunna
     gown.INDF-CONJ   buy.PP give.PAST
     'Mother bought a shirt for Ranjit and a gown for Chitra.'

(11) Chitra   niiti   piiṭə-en   upaadiə-ku-i   samaajə widyaa
     Chitra   law   faculty-ABL   degree-INDF-CONJ   social   sciences
     piiṭə-en   diploomawə-ku-i   gatta
     faculty-ABL   diploma-INDF-CONJ   get.PAST
     'Chitra obtained a degree from the Faculty of Law and a diploma from the Faculty of Social Sciences.'

(12) denna   gaha gan-nəwa-i   bænəgan-nəwa-i   iwərəy-ak   nææ
     two.ANIM   hit.REFL-IND-CONJ   scold.REFL-IND-CONJ   end-INDEF   no
     'There is no end to the beating and scolding between the two.'

(13) guruwəru-i   demaupiyo-i   laməinu-i   paarə   suddə kəlaa
     teachers-CONJ parents-CONJ children-CONJ   road   clean.PAST
     'The teachers, parents and children cleaned the road.'

In (10) *amma* 'mother' is the shared subject of the benefactive verb; unshared components of the original clauses are combined by adding the conjunction *-i* to the end of each. In (11) Chitra is the shared subject of the 'receiving' verb; each unshared component is linked by the clitic *-i*. In (12) the verbal compounds of the coordinated clauses represent unshared components and hence they are combined by adding the clitic *-i*. However, this compound sentence with two coordinated clauses is embedded in another clause, namely *iwərəyak næǣ* 'there is no end', to make a complex sentence. The verb phrase in (13) represents the shared component, and the three subjects representing unshared components are all linked by the conjunction.[1]

There is another clitic that functions in a similar way as a coordinating conjunction. This is the clitic *-t*. The Example (7), given before as a sentence increasingly becoming acceptable, can be put in a more traditional way by using this clitic, as follows.

(14) Perera   mahatməya   rajəy-ee   paasələ-ka-t
     Perera   Mr.   government-LOC   school-INDF.LOC-CONJ

     emə   mahatmiya   pudgalika   paasələ-ka-t   uganwə-nəwa
     aforesaid   Mrs.   private   school-INDF.LOC-CONJ   teach-IND

     'Mr. Perera teaches in a government school and Mrs. Perera in a private one.'

Further examples are given below.

(15) apə-ṭə   gewal   hada-nna-t   puluwan   kaḍanna-t   puluwan
     we-DAT   houses   make-INF-CONJ   can   break-INF-CONJ   can
     'We can build houses and also destroy houses.'

(16) mamə   uya-nna-t   oonæ   lamea   balaa   gan-na-t   oonæ
     I   cook-INF-CONJ   must   child   look   after-INF-CONJ   must
     'I must cook and also look after the child.'

Both (15) and (16) have modal expressions. In (15) the modal has its subject in the dative and in (16) in the nominative. The content of the potentiality denoted by *puluwan* (15) and that of the obligation denoted by *oonæ* (16) are divided by two infinitive clauses each of which with the conjunction *-t*. Thus the doubly used conjunction *-t* grammatically signals the incorporation of two component clauses into one single compound sentence. The double use of the conjunction *-t* can be distinguished from that of the conjunction *-i* in that the former has an emphatic overtone. Thus (15) has a particular overtone of speaker boast while (16) sounds complaining.

There are several disjunctive particles to form disjunctive coordination. The double use of the particle *hari* 'or' is widespread in the colloquial language.

(17) Ranjit   gedərə   næǣ   kaḍee   gihilla   hari   naa-nnə
     Ranjit   home   no   shop   go.PP   hari   bathe-INF

     gihilla   hari   we-nnə   oonæ
     go.PP   hari   be-INF   must

     'Ranjit is not at home: he must have gone shopping or gone to bathe.'

(18) pol geḍiə   arə genə   hari   bimə-ṭə   daa-la   hari
     coconut   take.PP   hari   ground-DAT   put-PP   hari

---

[1]. This sentence can also be considered as a coordinated noun phrase, with the three nouns combined at the phrase level.

ikmənəʈə   bahi-nnə
soon   descend-IMP
'Get down soon with the coconut in your hand or after throwing it down.'

The first part of sentence (17) says that Ranjit is not home, and the second part gives the supposed reason. Therefore the sentence ends with the epistemic modal expression *wenna oonæ* 'must be'. The supposition consists of two disjunctive clauses which are combined by adding the particle *hari* to each. The Example (18) is an imperative sentence in which the speaker's command to the addressee is to 'get down'. The imperative verb is modified by two perfective clauses; they are combined by adding the particle *hari* to each and incorporated into the imperative construction to form a complex sentence.

Another disjunctive particle, *nætnaŋ* 'or', is used between two clauses to coordinate them.

(19)   oyaa adə   ya-nnə   nætnaŋ ʈelipoon   kəra-nnə
       you   today go-IMP   nætnaŋ telephone   do-IMP
       'You go today or give them a call.'

(20)   bat   uyə-mu   də nætnaŋ paan   ka-mu   də?
       rice   cook-HORT   Q   nætnaŋ bread eat-HORT   Q
       'Shall we cook rice or eat bread?'

In (19) two imperative clauses and in (20) two interrogative hortative clauses are coordinated by the particle *nætnaŋ*. However, the disjunctive coordination of two interrogative clauses can also be achieved through juxtaposition.

(21)   oya ya-nəwa də mamə ya-nnə de?
       you go-IND   Q   I   go-INF Q
       'Will you go or shall I go?'

(22)   eyaa sindu kiə-nəwa də pirith   kiə-nəwa   də?
       he   songs sing-IND Q   chanting   recite-IND Q
       'Is he singing songs or chanting religious verses?'

When the particle *nætnaŋ* intervenes between two interrogative clauses, it seems to create a pragmatic distance between the two events denoted by the clauses. Compare the two sentences below:

(23)   a.   adə   e-nəwa   də natərə we-nəwa də
            today come-IND   Q   stay-IND   Q
            'Are you coming back today or staying there?'

       b.   adə   e-nəwa   də nætnaŋ natərə we-nəwa də
            today come-IND   Q   nætnaŋ stay-IND   Q
            'Are you coming back today, or going to stay there?'

(23a) coordinated by juxtaposing two interrogative clauses has continuity; it may also be mediated by a pause in between alternatively. (23b), by contrast, most probably will have a pause before shifting to the second clause. The exact place for the pause is between the end of the previous clause and the conjunction *nætnaŋ*. A speaker who wants to pose the disjunctive question in an emphatic tone will use (23b).

The separation of two clauses will be further emphasized when the conjunction *nætnaŋ* is accompanied by another particle, *ekkoo*; the pair is similar to the English 'either-or' construction.

(24) ekkoo alut gey-ak hadə-mu nætnaŋ parənə gee alut kərə-mu
ekkoo new house-INDF build-HORT nætnaŋ old house renew-HORT
'Let's either build a new house or refurbish the old house.'

(25) ekkoo gedərə daa-la æwilla nætnaŋ kaarek-ee æti
ekkoo home put-PP come.PP nætnaŋ car-LOC be.INFER
'Either I have left it at home or it might be in the car.'

The sentence in (24) expresses an either-or situation by coordinating two hortative clauses; the first one is preceded by *ekkoo* and the next one by *nætnaŋ*. The example in (25) is a compound sentence with missing subjects. The first clause represents a person-focused event with a transitive verb: its subject may be a first person, second person or third person noun. Assuming a context in which the speaker involves him/herself, one can easily adopt a first person subject. The second clause represents a state. The object noun of the first clause and the subject noun of the second clause, both having a common referent, are missing, left to be recovered from the context. There are no overt shared components in the two clauses; shared components exist in the context. The latent elements have to be understood, relying on the context in which the sentence is uttered. The speaker's successive thoughts on different possibilities are coordinated by putting them into the *ekkoo- nætnaŋ* template.

Interestingly, the negation of an either-or (*ekkoo- nætnaŋ*) situation, that is, neither-nor situation, is expressed by the conjunction *-t*, not by the same disjunctive particle. Observe the following Sinhala proverb:

(26) balla piduru ka-nne-t nææ
dog hay eat-NPT.FOC-CONJ no
gonaa-ţə ka-nnə de-nne-t nææ
bull-DAT eat-INF give-NPT.FOC-CONJ no
'The dog neither eats hey nor allows the bull to eat it.'

The first clause consists in a negative transitive sentence whose subject is shared by the second clause consisting in a negative causative sentence. When taken in the affirmative sense they may form a disjunctive coordination because they represent two disjunctive units, 'eating' and 'allowing to eat'. However, given the fact that the constructions are negative, and the two events find commonality in the negation, it is not difficult to consider that the two events remake themselves within the coordination of conjunction, rather than of disjunction. The important point is that the clauses consist of a single subject and a single auxiliary negation, which is a necessary condition for conjunctive coordination.

There are some other particles used to connect sentences in Sinhala such as *itin* 'then', *etəkoṭə* 'then', *iiṭə passe* 'then, after that', *ærat* 'besides, *eet* 'but', etc. Although they function as discourse particles indicating various relationships between sentences, it is not clear whether they contribute to clause coordination, creating compound sentences.

Yet another way of coordinating clauses is using an inflectional form of the verb as a conjunctive ending. There are mainly two verbal forms used for coordination in verbal categories. One is the Perfect Participle (PP) form. We have already seen that the PP can be used as a finite verb form, i.e. as a predicate of an independent clause, indicating some aspectual meanings. The same PP form is used to coordinate a sequence of verbal elements, with anticipatory ellipsis of tense and mood inflections and aspectual or modal auxiliaries. Given the fact that coordination is always between units of the same class, it is not surprising that the PP serves as a coordinator for sequences of elements, whether or not they could independently form a unit.

(27)   Ranjit   ṭaumə-ṭə   gihin   baisikəlee   natərə kərə-la   maakaṭ   ekə-ṭə   ætul unaa
       Ranjit   town-DAT   go.PP   bicycle   stop-PP   market   one-DAT enter.PAST
       'Ranjit went to the town, stopped the bicycle and entered the market.'

When those units which are equivalent in relation to each other show a sequence, temporal or otherwise, all such verbal forms are PPs except the verb that indicates the end of the sequence. Thus the units denoting 'going to the town' and 'stopping the bicycle' are represented by PP forms while the unit denoting the end of the sequence, i.e. 'entering the market', appears in the full form. The identical subjects are deleted, except the initial one. The coordination between full verb phrases thus occurs with a structure resulting from the reduction of their distinct tense forms. Here the PP does not represent perfect tense but only denotes an action completed prior to the finite action.

Another example is given below.

(28)   Ranjit   bænkuw-en   nay-ak   araŋ   gewaa gannə   bæruwə
       Ranjit   bank-ABL   loan-INDF   take-PP   pay.REFL.INF be unable-PP
       diwi   naha gatta
       commit suicide.PAST
       'Ranjit committed suicide being unable to repay the loan he took from the bank.'

The sequence of events that Ranjit has undergone consists of three units in which only the third unit has the past tense verb as an actual element, i.e. an element that remains overtly past tense, while the first two units have been combined to the former by the PP forms of the verbs. As for the topic, on the other hand, only the subject of the first unit appears as the actual element, allowing those of other units to be deleted.[2]

It is considered that in coordination the elements in a sequence must be equivalent to other elements of the sentence. Thus, as often found, coordinated sentences consist of a single subject and a single set of inflections, and for that matter a single set of auxiliaries. Is the following Sinhala sentence problematic in this respect ?

(29) Chitra-ṭə kuḍee amətəkə we-laa aapahu giyaa
Chita-DAT umbrella forget.INVL-PP back go.PAST
'Chitra left her umbrella and went back (to get it).'

Of the two units coordinated in (29), the first one has a latent verbal ending with anticipatory ellipsis of tense inflection, and the second one has a latent nominal constituent with retrospective ellipsis of subject. The latent nominal constituent and the actual nominal constituent are apparently non-equivalent in that the former is a dative constituent appearing with an involitive verb whereas the latter must be a nominative constituent, given that its verb is of the volitive-type. However, both constituents in such sentences are construed as subject in Sinhala and therefore the deletion of the second constituent poses no problem for coordination.

Another conjunctive coordinator is the Reduplicated from of the Perfect Participle base form (RPP). When the units to be coordinated represent simultaneously occurring events and the verbs are construed identically with a single subject, the verb forms belonging to the first, or the previous unit of the sequence are connected to it by the RPP from of the verb.

(30) Ranjit ṭiiwii balə-balə kæəmə ka-nəwa
Ranjit TV watch-RPP meals eat-IND
'Ranjit is eating while watching TV.'

(31) Chitra hinaa we-wii diiwa
Chitra laugh-RPP run.PAST
'Chitra ran while laughing.'

(32) lamea perəli-perəli hinaa we-nəwa
child roll-RPP laugh-IND
'The child is laughing while rolling over.'

---

2. Following Gair, one may also consider the *bæruwə*-ending unit as a quasi-verbal counterpart of the participial clauses (Gair 1970: 155).

While each of the three examples above expresses two concurrent events, it is common for speakers to see the event denoted by the finite verb as the main event; however, it would be difficult to assign a temporal order to the sequence. For pragmatic reasons, speakers tend to associate temporal sequencing to the coordinates from the opposite end in (32): for instance, the first unit will never be taken as initial but only as resulting from the event coded through the finite verb. This sense might be acquired by the RPP form through its grammaticalization as a manner adverb to the finite verb.

2. Complex sentences

Complex sentences fall into three categories by virtue of the character of subordinate clauses incorporated in them. Their characters are identified as nominal, adnominal, and adverbial. Nominal clauses function as subject, object, and complement. Adnominal clauses function as nominal modifiers and adverbial clauses as verbal modifiers. Various verbal forms, case markers, particles, or formal nouns are used for subordination.

In general, subordinate clauses precede main clauses, or take a position relative to the head noun of the main clause. In some circumstances, such as seeking an extra pragmatic effect, the subordinate clause may follow, rather than precede, the clause to which it is linked.

(33) a. api umbə boru kiya-nn-e næti wittiə dan-nəwa
we you lies tell-NPT-FOC no.ADJ fact know-IND
'We know that you don't tell lies.'

b. umbə boru kiya-nn-e næti wittiə api dan-nəwa
you lies tell-NPT-FOC no.ADJ fact we know-IND
'We know that you don't tell lies.'

c. api dan-nəwa umbə boru kiya-nn-e næti wittiə
we know-IND you lies tell-NPT-FOC no.ADJ fact
'We know that you don't tell lies.'

In all three sentences the object noun *wittiə* 'fact' is modified by an adnominal clause. The sentence in (33a), with unmarked word order SOV, has the subordinate clause in the unmarked object position, that is, in the preverbal position. In (33b), with OSV order, the object clause is preposed in the topic position for the sake of emphasis. In (33c) the same object clause has gone to the post-verbal position, that is, focused position, acquiring a greater pragmatic effect suited to an ironical comment about the addressee. In terms of pragmatic effect, (33c) might be the least unmarked expression. The above appearances of object clauses show that there is no strict constraint on placements of the object clause.

2.1 Nominal clauses

There is a variety of clause-nominalizing devices. The use of the nominalizing particle *ekə*, formal nouns such as *wittiə, wagə, bawə* and the quotative marker *kiəla* is widespread in subordination. All these clause-linking connectives traditionally called 'subordinating conjunctions' are added to the end of the embedded clause. Although the mood expressions attached to the verb are usually deleted before adding the subordinator, the linking can also be achieved by juxtaposing two clauses: the linkage is realized by sequential order alone, with no subordinate marker. In such cases the embedded verb does not undergo any change such as mood indicator deletion. Such nominalized clauses are found embedded in a sentence as subject, object, and subject- or object-complement.

The following examples include subordinated clauses juxtaposed to a main clause without any marker.

(34) eyaa wædə kərə-nawa honda-i
    he/she work do-IND good-AM
    Lit. 'His working is good.'
    'He works well.'

(35) Ranjit paaḍam kəlaa madi
    Ranjit study.PAST insufficient
    Lit. 'The extent that Ranjit studied is insufficient.'
    'Ranjit didn't study enough.'

(36) miniha ya-nəwa mamə dækka
    man go-IND I see.PAST
    'I saw him go.'

(37) kaudoo kææ gaha-nəwa matə æhuna
    somebody shout-IND I-DAT hear.INVL.PAST
    'I heard somebody shouting.'

Adjectives of a particular type may have embedded clauses as their subjects as in (34) and (35). Embedded clauses may appear as objects of sensory perception verbs like 'seeing' in (36) and 'hearing' in (37).

The nominalizer *ekə* joins with the adjectival form of the embedded verb, past or non-past, to form a subordinate clause and seems to work in a way similar to the English gerund or infinitive construction (See Chapter 1:1.4). In (38) and (39) the embedded clauses function as subjects.

(38) miniha eten-tə giə ekə hondə næe
    man there-DAT go.PT. ekə good no
    'It is not good that the man went there.'

(39) japaan-e rassaawal hoyə-nə ekə leesi næææ
    Japan-LOC jobs   find-NPT ekə easy no
    'It is not easy to find jobs in Japan.'

Formal nouns such as *wittiə, wagə, bawə* are used to build complement clauses. They are called formal nouns because they cannot stand by themselves without getting modified. Structurally they function as complementizers restructuring a clause as a complement of a complex sentence like the English *that* clause. Clauses embedded as complements may include verbal clauses, adjectival clauses, or non-verbal clauses. They function both as subject complements and object complements. In (40) below the embedded clause appears as the subject complement.

(40) Ranjit-ṭə   usas wiim-ak   læbunu wittiə
    Ranjit-DAT promotion-INDF receive.INVL.PT NM

    pattər-e-t   wæṭuna
    newspaper-LOC-too appear.PAST
    'The fact that Ranjit got a promotion even appeared in the newspaper.'

Generally mood markers are removed from the verb of the embedded clause and a complementizer is added to the verbal adjectival form. Most commonly, the main clause to which a complement clause is linked as subject expresses some comment supporting or negating the proposition of the latter.

(41) miniha horaa bawə ætta
    man   thief   NM   true
    'It is true that that man is the thief.'

(42) Ranjit liumə liə-pu   wagə pæhædili-i
    Ranjit letter write-PTAD   NM   clear.AM
    'It is clear that Ranjit wrote the letter.'

(43) ? Ranjit kaamәre-e hiṭiə   wagə/wittiə/bawə boru
      Ranjit room-LOC be.PTAD NM   lie
    'That Ranjit was in the room is a pack of lies.'

All three sentences have complement clauses as their subject. The sentences in (41) and (42) have predicates supporting the content of the complement clause. There is some thing odd with (43), whose predicate is meant to negate the proposition of the complement clause. Even though the predicate lexically expresses that it is untrue, the complement seems to remain "factive". This shows that the nominalizers given above add "factivity" to the clause, with a presupposition that its content is true, rather than just introducing subordinate clauses (cf. Kiparsky & Kiparsky 1971; Kuno 1973; Iwasaki 2002). To express the negation of a fact or low degree of factivity there is a particular type of expression, which will be introduced later.

Now let us look into how complement clauses are produced to be objects of predicates. In general, "content" verbs such as verbs of speech, knowledge, sign, report, discovery and forensic acts, as in (44) through (49) respectively, take as their object a complement clause with a formal noun such as *wittiə, wagə* and *bawə*.

(44) Ranjit gedərə ya-nnə akəmæti bawə kiiwa
Ranjit home go-INF reluctant that say.PAST
'Ranjit said that he would not like to go home.'

(45) Chitra chitrə andi-nə bawə Ranjit dan-nəwa
Chitra pictures draw-NPT that Ranjit know-IND
'Ranjit knows that Chitra draws pictures.'

(46) man mehe in-nə wittiə Chitra-ṭə angəwa-nnə epaa
I here be-NPT that Chitra-DAT imply-INF don't
'Don't indicate to Chitra that I am here.'

(47) labənə sati-e kæmpəs waha-nə wittiə upəkuləpəti
next week-LOC campus close-NPT that vice-chancellor
amaatyanshəyə-ṭə waartaa kəlaa
ministry-DAT report.PAST
'The vice-chancellor reported to the ministry that the university will be closed next week.'

(48) wenə yaturə-k-in dorə ærə-la tie-nə wittiə
another key-INDF-INS door open-PP be-NPT that
polisiə hoyaa gatta
police discover.PAST
'The police discovered that the door had been opened with another key.'

(49) Ranjit kaaryaaləyə-ṭə balen ætul wunu bawə
Ranjit office-DAT by force enter.PT that
niitigñəya oppu kəlaa
lawyer prove.PAST
'The lawyer proved that Ranjit had entered the office by force.'

In terms of linearity, the object clause is embedded between the subject constituent and the predicate of the main clause, and the identical subject of the embedded clause is deleted as in (44). In all the other sentences given above the embedded clause precedes the main clause. Content clauses are also incorporated by dative subject constructions as (50) and (51) show.

(50) putaa-ṭə upandinə tæægg-ak yæu-e næti wittiə
son-DAT birthday present-INDF send.PT-FOC no.ADJ that
ma-ṭə kalpanaa unaa
I-DAT think.INVL.PAST
'It occurred to me that I have not sent a birthday present to my son.'

(51) Chitra-ṭə   salli   dunnə   wiitiə ma-ṭə   amətəkə unaa
     Chitra-DAT   money   give.PT.ADJ   that   I-DAT   forget.INVL.PAST
     'I forgot that I had lent money to Chitra.'

The content-verb clauses linked to a main clause through the formal nouns *wittiə, wagə* or *bawə*, as shown above, are examples of what traditional grammar calls Indirect Speech. The formal nouns integrate the speaker's words, thoughts or ideas into a framework of indirect speech. Such content-verb clauses can also be embedded into the main clause according to the pattern known as Direct Speech. The quotative marker *kiəla* is used to embed reported speech or thought. The complementizer *kiəla* has developed from the perfect participle form of the verb *kiənəwa* 'say' with the original meaning of "having said". Though the two clauses are integrated into one complex sentence, they remain discrete thereafter as reporting clause and reported clause. For Example, (44) through (47) given above are changed to the direct speech pattern as follows:

(52) Ranjit   gedərə   ya-nnə   akəmæti-i   kiəla   kiiwa
     Ranjit   home   go-INF   reluctant-QM QM   say.PAST
     'Ranjit said, "I don't like to go home."'

(53) Chitra   chitrə   andi-nəwa   kiəla Ranjit dan-nəwa
     Chitra   pictures draw-NPT.IND   QM   Ranjit know-IND
     'Ranjit knows that Chitra draws pictures.'

(54) man mehe   in-nəwa   kiəla Chitra-ṭə   angəwa-nnə   epaa
     I   here   be-NPT.IND   QM   Chitra-DAT   imply-INF   don't
     'Don't indicate to Chitra that I am here.'

(55) labənə sati-e   kæmpəs waha-nəwa   kiəla upəkuləpəti
     next   week-LOC   campus close-NPT.IND QM   vice-chancellor
     amaatyanshəyə-ṭə   waartaa kəlaa
     ministry-DAT   report.PAST
     'The vice-chancellor reported to the ministry that the university will be closed next week.'

When the main clause has a verb denoting a speech or report activity it may include an optional constituent denoting an addressee or reportee, as in (55); (52) does not specify the addressee. The verb of the subordinate clause appears inflected for TAM in these sentences, which indicates that embedded clauses are not fully reduced clauses. Further, if the subordinate clause consists of a vowel-final adjectival predicate, as in (52), it must be ended with the assertion marker *-i* before joining the quotative marker. Such morphological characterizations suggest that the subordinate clause is at the low end of the scale of desententialization (Lehmann 1988).

The quotative-marker construction can also incorporate interrogative sentences and imperative sentences, as in (56) and (57).

(56) Chitra Ranjit-gen æhuwa heṭə paaṭiə-ṭə ya-nəwa də kiəla
    Chitra Ranjit-ABL ask.PAST tomorrow party-DAT go-IND Q QM
    'Chitra asked Ranjit whether he is going to the tomorrow's party.'

(57) Ranjit dorə waha-nnə kiəla Chitra-ṭə kiiwa
    Ranjit door close-IMP QM Chitra-DAT say.PAST
    'Ranjit asked Chitra to close the door.'

As the two examples above respectively show, the embedded clause may also be placed after, or in the middle of, the main clause.

As becomes explicit from the above data, the subordination realized through the quotative marker is not restricted to speech activities; it integrates a range of activities such as transmission of a message, verbal or otherwise, and cognitive activities or states such as thinking and knowing. Other verbs and adjectives capable of incorporating *kiəla* marked embedded clauses include *kæœ gahanəwa* 'shout', *kendiri gaanəwa* 'mutter', *illənəwa* 'request', *porondu wenəwa* 'promise', *wiswaasə kərənwa* 'believe', *bayai* 'be worried' and *sækai* 'doubt'. The embedded clause appears as the object complement of such predicates.

Of particular interest is that the embedded clause with a verb of 'speculation', i.e. thinking, imagining, expecting, doubting, fearing, or regretting, etc. is expressed through the *kiəla* construction as far as it denotes a sense of uncertainty. Observe the following example:

(58) api oyaa ei kiəla balaŋ hiṭia
    we you come.INFER QM expect.PAST
    'We were expecting that you would come.'

The embedded clause is the object complement of the verb 'expect'.

An embedded clause consisting in an interrogative pronoun may function as the object complement, as the following sentences show.

(59) eyaa monəwa kərə-nəwa də kiəla kawuruwat dan-ne næœ
    he what do-IND Q QM anybody know-NPT.FOC no
    'Nobody knows what he does.'

(60) puusa kohomə aawa də kiəla hitaa ga-nnə bæœ
    cat how come.PAST Q QM think.REFL-INF cannot
    '(I) can't think how the cat came (here).'

(61) kaudə aawe kiəla kiya-nnə
    who.Q come.FOC QM say-IMP
    '(Please) tell me who came.'

When an interrogative pronoun is present in the embedded clause, the interrogative particle *də* appears separately, as in (59) and (60), or attached to the pronoun, as in (61).[3]

2.2 Adnominal clauses

Adnominal clauses include verbal or adjectival sentences. The verb of the attributive clause is changed to an adjectival form of the present or past tense. This form indicates the tense of the embedded clause and need not agree with the main clause. Adjectival predicates do not inflect for tense. In terms of function, adnominal forms are analogous to the English relative pronouns such as *that*, *which*, and *who*. However, adnominal form does not agree in number or gender with the noun it modifies.

The following two sentences adapted from two Sinhala proverbs show the way things are.

(62) att-en   attə-ṭə   pani-nə   kurulla temii   nahinəwa
     branch-ABL branch-DAT jump-NPT.ADJ bird   get wet.PP perish.IND
     'The bird that hops from branch to branch will perish by getting soaked through.'

(63) gah-en   wæṭ-unu   minihaa-ṭə gonaa ænna
     tree-ABL fall-PT.ADJ man-DAT bull poke.PAST
     'The bull poked at the man who had fallen from the tree.'

In (62) the subject of the main clause is modified by an embedded clause whose verb is non-past. In (63) the dative object of the main clause is modified by an embedded clause with a past tense verb. The following three proverbs will provide further examples.

(64) kapa-nnə bæri   atə   simbi-nəwa
     cut-INF unable hand   kiss-IND
     'Kiss the hand which cannot be cut.'

(65) pir-unu   kal-ee   diə   nosælee
     get filled-PT.ADJ pot-LOC water no shake
     'A pot which is full of water does not shake.'

(66) hitə   giə   tænə   maaligaawə
     mind go.PT.ADJ place castle
     'The place your heart is in is your castle.'

---

3. For theoretical issues regarding wh-words and Q element, see Kishimoto 1991, Hagstrom 1998 and Henadeerage 2002.

The sentence in (64) has an adjectival clause attributive to the object noun of the main clause. In (65) a short verbal clause is attributive to the locative noun of the main clause. In (66) the 'place', denoting the subject of the main clause, is modified by a past tense verbal clause. The verbal adjectives of this kind of attributive clauses can be reduplicated to give a sense equivalent to the English 'Every …'. Consider the following examples.

(67) giə   giə   tænə   kææmə honda-i
      go.PT.ADJ go.PT.ADJ place food   good.AM
      'Every place (we) went we had nice food.'

(68) balə-pu   balə-pu   atə   senəgə pirila
      look-PT.ADJ   look-PT.ADJ   direction crowd   be filled.PP
      'Every direction we looked had large crowds.'

(69) taatta   kaḍə-nə   kaḍə-nə   geḍi   api ekətu kəlaa
      father   pluck-NPT.ADJ pluck-NPT.ADJ fruits we   collect.PAST
      'We collected every fruit that father plucked.'

Given that the verb is reduplicated, the embedded clause shows that something occurs repeatedly. In (67) the embedded clause modifies the noun indicating the location of the main clause. In (68) the repeated action is attributive to the noun indicating the orientation of the main event. In (69) the repeated action initiated by the agent depicted in the embedded clause modifies the object of the main clause. The noun 'fruits' is the shared object of both the embedded clause and the main clause.

Another type of attributive clause involves sensory perceptual nouns. Such nouns need some extra information to make the utterance fully informative, which is provided by attaching a subordinate clause.

(70) paarə digee   lee   wækkerichcchi salakunu tibuna
      road   along   blood flow.PT.ADJ   signs   be.PAST
      'There were marks showing that blood had flown along the road.'

(71) apə-ṭə   kaju   puchchə-na   suwənd-ak   dænuna
      we-DAT   cashew-nuts   fry-NPT.ADJ   smell-INDF feel.PAST
      'We felt the smell of cashew-nuts being fried.'

(72) mal weḍi   pupurə-nə   sadde   mehaa-ṭə   æhe-nəwa
      firework   burst-NPT.ADJ sound   here-DAT   hear.INVOL-IND
      'The sound of fireworks bursting could be heard from here.'

The words *salakunu* 'signs', *suwəndak* 'a smell' and *sadde* 'sound' in these sentences are exspanded by subordinate clauses.

Another type of attributive clause comprises an adjectival predicate as follows.

(73) eyaa hitə hondə ammaṇḍi-ak
      she   mind good   woman-INDF
      'She is a woman who is good in heart.'

(74) eekə swaabawikə sampat-walin hungak pohosat raṭ-ak
    it natural resources-PL.INS very rich country-INDF
    'It's a country which is very rich in natural resources.'

(75) aurudu panah-ak witərə parənə kaarek-ak hoyaa gan-nə oonæ
    years fifty-INDF about old car-INDF find.REFL-INF want
    'I am looking for a car which is about fifty years old.'

The predicate nouns in (73) and (74) and the object noun in (75) are modified by embedded clauses with adjectival predicates. However, given the fact that each modifier precedes its head and that postmodification is impossible in Sinhala, it would be difficult to judge their syntactic relations out of context. It might be reasonable to suppose that the whole construction consisting of modifiers and the head is a nominal phrase representing a syntactically undifferentiated relation rather than a clause.

2.3 Adverbial clauses

When the embedded clause shows an adverbial behavior being attributive to the main clause, it is called an adverbial clause. Subordination occurs through verbal endings, inflectional form plus particles, and case markers. Such clausal endings are generally called subordinators. The semantic correlates of these clauses include (1) time, (2) cause and reason, (3) condition, (4) concession, (5) purpose and intention, (6) proportion, and (7) manner. The following description is organized according to the semantic functions of the subordinate clauses.

Adverbial clauses of time formed by means of these subordinators are illustrated below:

Verbal endings: -hamə/haamə 'when'
              -ddi 'while, when' (See Chapter 5:1.1.2)
Particles: koṭə 'when, by'
         gamaŋ 'while, soon after'
         hæṭie 'soon after'
         tek/kal(kan)/turu 'till, until, as long as'
         passe 'after'
         issərə 'before'

The -haamə inflectional form always appears after the past tense form of a verb, though it indicates unspecified time, as shown by (76). By contrast, the -ddi subordinator attaches directly to the verbal root to indicate unspecified time, as in (77).

(76) mee paarə singappuuru gihaamə saari-ak araŋ e-nnə
    this time Singapore go.PT.when sari-INDF buy.PP come-IMP
    'Buy a sari for me when you go to Singapore this time.'

(77) a. Chitra uya-ddi Ranjit pattəree balə-nəwa
Chitra cook-while Ranjit newspaper read-IND
'While Chitra is cooking, Ranjit reads a newspaper.'

b. Chitra uya-ddi Ranjit nidaa gatta
Chitra cook-while Ranjit sleep.REFL.PAST
'While Chitra was cooking, Ranjit slept.'

c. Chitra eləwəlu kapa-ddi atə kæpuna
Chitra vegetable cut-while hand cut.INVL.PAST
'While Chitra was preparing vegetables, she cut her hand (involuntarily).'

In (77a) the adverbial clause denotes a non-past event and in (77b) a past event; in (77c) the subject of the embedded clause and the inalienable possessor of the main clause are identical.

The following examples show how the verbal forms join up with various particles in creating adverbial clauses of time. The use of the particle *koṭə* is shown in (78).

(78) a. lankaa-we ayə kataa kərə-nə koṭə oluwə heminsæree
Lanka-LOC people talk.NPT.ADJ when head slowly

depætta-ṭə wanəwə-nəwa
two sides-DAT move-IND

'Sri Lankan people move their head slowly from side to side when they talk.'

b. man iie wædə-ṭə ya-nə koṭə Chitra-wə hambə unaa
I yesterday work-DAT go-NPT.ADJ while Chitra-ACC meet.PAST
'While I was going to work yesterday, I met Chitra.'

c. man ya-nə koṭə Ranjit nidaa genə hiṭia
I go-NPT.ADJ when Ranjit sleep.REFL.PP be.PAST
'When I went there, Ranjit was sleeping.'

d. bas ekə e-nə koṭə apə-ṭə pa-in ya-nnə puluwan
bus one come-NPT.ADJ when we-DAT foot-INS go-INF can
Lit. 'We can go there on foot when the bus comes.'
'We can get there by the time the bus comes.'

The tense of the unspecified temporal clauses in (78) is determined by the tense form of the main clause. The sentences (a) and (b) have propositions with concurrent events in the non-past tense and the past tense, respectively. The sentences (c) and (d), on the other hand, do not denote concurrent events, despite the fact that the same subordinator is used for linking the clauses. Here the tense seems to be determined by the relation between the subordinate and main clauses. Thus, according to (c), at the time when the speaker arrived there, Ranjit had already gone to sleep and was still asleep. What we understand from (d) is that the speaker presumes that they can reach the destination by the time the bus arrives at the place of speaking.

The particle *gaman* has at least two different senses determined by the temporal relation of the subordinate clause to the main clause.

(79) a. man pansələ-țə ya-nə gaman Chitra-wə hambə we-nnam
I temple-DAT go-NPT.ADJ while Chitra-ACC meet-OPT
'I'll meet Chitra when I go to the temple.'

b. gedərə giə gaman man kool ek-ak de-nnam
home go.PT.ADJ as soon as I call one-INDF give-OPT
'I'll give you a call when I get home.'

c. gedərə giə hæție man kool ek-ak de-nnaam
home go.PT.ADJ as soon as I call one-INDF give-OPT
'I'll give you a call immediately after I get home.'

When the verb of the subordinate clause is in the non-past tense the *gaman* particle expresses concurrent events, as in (a) above, analogous to the English 'while' clause. When the verb of the subordinate clause is in the past tense, on the other hand, the relation between the two events expressed by the same particle appears to be similar to the English 'as soon as' expression, as in (b). There is another particle to express the same relationship as the latter, namely *hæție*, as in (c). However, there is no non-past clausal linkage with this particle.

Three other particle-subordinators expressing temporal clauses are exemplified below.

(80) siinuwə gaha-nə tek/kal/kan lamai balaa in-nəwa
bell beat-NPT.ADJ until children wait-IND
'The children are waiting till the bell rings.'

(81) man giyaa-țə passe oyaa e-nnə
I go.PAST-DAT after you come-IMP
'You come after I go' or 'Follow me after I leave.'

(82) man ya-nnə issərə eyaa æwilla hiția
I go-INF before he/she come.PP be.PAST
'He had come before I go there.'

The particles *tek/kal/kan* denoting a 'till/until' relationship follow the non-past tense verb of the subordinate clause; the particle *passe* 'after' can only join a past tense verb marked in the dative; the verb governed by the particle *issərə* 'before' takes the infinitive form. This implies not only that the subordinate verb is governed by the particles but also that the inflectional form correlates with the particle semantics. It can also be observed that the particles *passe* 'after' and *issərə* 'before' function as pragmatic particles as well as relational nouns which mark nominal and adverbial constituents, in the latter case, with regular case markers like dative, licensing constituents within the clausal boundary.

Adverbial clauses of cause and reason are mainly formed with case markers and inflection plus the particles *hinda* or *nisaa*. The case forms include the dative *-țə* and the instrumental/ablative *-in* which are suffixed to the past or non-past form of the subordinate verb. The particles occur with past or non-past adjectival forms of the verb.

(83) ikmənətə   aawa-in   no-temi   beeruna
      quickly   come.PAST-INS   not-get wet.PP   be saved.PAST
      'I was able to save myself without getting wet (from rain) since I came hurriedly.'

(84) a. oyaa   gee   suddə kərənəwa-tə   eyaa   gewa-nnə   oonæ
        you   house   clean-IND-DAT   he   pay-INF   must
        'He must pay you for your cleaning the house.'

     b. wahale   hada-la   dunna-tə   piŋ   siddə weewa
        roof   make-PP   give.PAST-DAT   merits   occur-OPT
        'May merits be with you (many thanks) for mending the roof for us.'

(85) a. Ranjit   nidi   hinda   api   kataa kəl-ee   næ
        Ranjit   asleep   since   we   call.PT-FOC   no
        'Since Ranjit was asleep we didn't call him.'

     b. Chitra   illuwə   hinda   maŋ   yaturə   dunna
        Chitra   ask.PT.ADJ   since   I   key   give.PAST
        'I gave the key (to her) since Chitra asked for it.'

(86) oyaa   kiə-nə   nisaa   maŋ   de-nnam
      you   say-NPT.ADJ   since   I   give-OPT
      'I'll give it (to him) since you say (to do so).'

The instrumental-marked subordinate clause in the past tense in (83), the dative-marked subordinate clause in the non-past tense in (84a) and the dative-marked subordinate clause in the past tense in (84b) all express causal relations with respect to the corresponding main clause. The sentences in (85) and (86) respectively appear with the particles *hinda* and *nisaa* expressing cause and reason. The particular stative predicate used in the subordinate clause in (85a) does not show inflectional characteristics. As seen in (85b) and (86), a verbal predicate inflects for the adjectival form, past or non-past, before linking with a particle to express cause and reason.

A causal relation can also be expressed by the perfect participle clause. In some cases the causal relation is implied rather than explicitly expressed. In some cases, however, the relation is more explicit.

(87) a. Ranjit   kakulə   kæpila   ispiritaale-tə   araŋ   giya
        Ranjit   leg   cut.INVL.PP   hospital-DAT   carry.PAST
        'Ranjit was taken to hospital because he had cut his leg/foot (involuntarily).'

     b. Chitra   gamee   gihin   Ranjit-tə   uya-nnə   we-laa
        Chitra   village   go.PP   Ranjit-DAT   cook.INF   become-PP
        'Ranjit has to cook because Chitra has gone to her home town.'

Although the speaker does not assert the causal relation, the construction consisting of a past participle clause and a main clause associated with a relevant context as given above expresses a sequential relation of cause and effect.

Another causal subordinator, which has not caught the attention of scholars, is the quotative particle *kiəla*, which is used with the formally finite form of the subordinate verb.

(88) a. adə   maamə e-nəwa   kiəla amma kæun   hadə-nəwa
         today uncle come-IND   QM   mother rice-cake make-IND
         'Mother is making rice-cakes hearing that uncle would come today.'

   b. man giyaa   kiəla wæḍ-ak   we-i   də
      I   go-PAST   QM   work-INDF become.INFER   Q
      Lit. 'Does it make any sense if I went there?'
      'Will my going there make any sense?'

   c. lamea wæṭe-i   kiəla maŋ allagatta
      child fall-INFER   QM   I   hold.PAST
      Lit. 'I held the child assuming that he may fall.'
      'I held the child so that he would not fall down.'

The subordinate clause marked by *kiəla* in this particular construction expresses the supposed reason for the event encoded by the main clause. In all the three sentences above the embedded events are reasons or motivations supposed by the subject participants of their main clauses. The quotative marker *kiəla* implies that the subordinate clause embodies thought or (unsaid) speech emanating from a participant of the consequent, i.e. the subject of the main clause. This is further demonstrated by the inferential expressions frequently used in this construction, as in (88b and c).

Conditional clauses are introduced by an inflectional form or a particle. The inflectional suffix is *-ot*; this inflectional form is realized through the past tense verb. The particle is *naŋ*, which is attached to the finite verb form of the subordinate clause.

(89) a. heṭə   wæssot   gamənə kal daa-mu
         tomorrow rain.COND   trip   postpone-HORT
         'Let's postpone the trip if it rains tomorrow.'

   b. oyaa koləmbə giyot   duwə-ṭə   maaləy-ak   araŋ   e-nnə
      you Colombo go.COND daughter-DAT necklace-INDF buy.PP come-IMP
      'If you go to Colombo, (please) buy a necklace for our daughter.'

   c. koləmbə rassaawa-ka-ṭə   giyot   aye   gamə-ṭə   e-nn-e   næ
      Colombo job-INDF-DAT   go.COND again village-DAT come-NPT-FOC   no
      'If you go to a job in Colombo, you'll not return to your native village.'

(90) a. oyaa rassawə-ṭə ya-nəwa naŋ mamə wædəkaarə-ek gan-nam
you job-DAT go-IND if I house-servant-INDF take-OPT
'I'll employ a house-servant if you go to work.'

b. oyaa koləmbə ya-nəwa naŋ duwə-ṭə maaləy-ak
you Colombo go.IND if daughter-DAT necklace-INDF
araŋ e-nnə
buy.PP come-IMP
'If you go to Colombo, (please) buy a necklace for our daughter.'

c. wææn ekə aawa naŋ apə-ṭa-t ya-nnə tibuna
van one come.PAST if we-DAT-too go-INF be.PAST
'If the van had come, we could have gone (joined), too.'

The examples in (89) show how conditional senses are expressed through the inflectional form of the subordinate verb whereas the sentences in (90) include conditional clauses introduced by the particle. Notice that the particle is linked with a past or non-past base. The expression of hypothetical conditions may be weak, strong or neutral depending on factors such as the form of the conditional subordinator, the type of the main clause, and the presence or absence of an identical subject. In some cases, a particle-mediated sentence cannot be transformed to an inflectionally formed sentence, and vice versa. This applies to (90c) in which a counterfactual statement is made through the main clause. In some cases, however, the subordinators are interchangeable, as demonstrated by the pair of (89b) and (90b). The semantic boundaries between the two types are not yet clear.

Adverbial clauses of concession are formed with the dative case marker -ṭə and the inflectional ending -at. The dative marker is suffixed to the past form of the subordinate verb, and the inflection for concession is invariably associated with the past base.

(91) a. Ranjit pansal giyaa-ṭə mal puuja kərə-nn-e nææ
Ranjit temple go.PAST-DAT flowers offer.NPT.FOC no
'Although Ranjit goes to the temple, he doesn't offer flowers.'

b. eya panti-e hiṭia-ṭə hitə wenə kohewat
she/he class-LOC be.PAST-DAT mind else somewhere
'Although he is in the class, his heart is in somewhere else.'

(92) a. man kataa kəlat eyaa næwətun-ee nææ
I call.CONC she/he stop.PT-FOC no
'Although I called him, he didn't stop'

b. oyaa epaa kiiwat mamə ya-nəwa
you no say.CONC I go-IND
'Even though you ask me not to, I'll be going.'

The subordinator appearing as the dative form, as in (91) or inflectional form, as in (92), expresses a clear incompatibility between the antecedent represented by the subordinate clause and the consequent represented by the main clause: notwithstanding a fact being expressed as the antecedent, the main clause maintains a second fact, which makes them concessive sentences.

Concessive clauses may share some features with conditional sentences by relating some antecedent conditions to a consequent. Such concessive conditionals obtain in the following sentences.

(93) a. wædə kəlat nætat ee gollan-ṭə paḍi
work do.CONC no.CONC those people-DAT salary
'Whether they work or not, they get their salary.'

b. kochchərə hambə kəlat hit-ee satuṭ-ak næe
how much earn.CONC mind-LOC happiness-INDF no
'No matter how much we earn, there is no happiness in our heart.'

Purpose clauses are expressed through the infinitive marker. The infinitive form in Sinhala, diachronically, is produced by adding the dative form to a nominalized verb (Geiger 1938). Since the dative is the vehicle for a semantic goal, the use of the dative/infinitive for expressing a goal, purpose or intention is a logical extension (Genetti 1986). These facts are resonant with the formation of purpose clauses. Look at the examples below.

(94) api perəhærə bala-nnə(ṭə) Kandy giyaa
we festival see-INF Kandy go.PAST
'We went to Kandy to see the Perahera Festival.'

(95) Chitra magulgedərə ya-nnə(ṭə) saari-ak gatta
Chitra wedding go-INF sari-INDF buy.PAST
'Chitra bought a sari to go to the wedding.'

(96) mage adəhasə kohomahari upaadi-ak gan-nə(ṭə)-i
my idea however degree-INDF get-INF-AM
'My idea is to get a degree at any cost.'

Infinitive clauses express a purpose or a motive for the events denoted by the main clauses. While in (94) and (95) intentions are situated anterior to concrete actions, in (96) the intention itself becomes the proposition: the postposed subordinate clause denotes the content of the intention.

Adverbial clauses of proportion are formed with the adjectival base of the verb plus the particles *hæṭiəṭə* and *tarəməṭə*.

(97) a. wædə kərə-nə hæṭiəṭə paḍi gewə-nəwa
work do-NPT.ADJ as salary pay-IND
'The salary is paid in proportion to the work you do.'

b. mahansi we-nə tarəməṭə aadaayəmə honda-i
work hard.NPT.ADJ to the extent income good-AM
'The harder you work the higher grows the income.'

Adverbial clauses of manner are expressed with the adjectival base of the verb plus the particle *widiəʈə*.

(98) eyaa   kiə-nə   widiəʈə   api   wæɖə kərə-mu
     she/he   say-NPT.ADJ   as   we   work-HORT
     'Let's work as she says.'

3. Mixed sentences

In the above description, for simplicity's sake, examples were deliberately restricted to biclausal sentences to help readers understand the clause linkages under discussion without overstraining them. However, it is not uncommon in actual discourse to express ideas with layered combinations of clauses, coordinated and subordinated, particularly in adult speech. Such a mixed sentence may include finite clauses as well as non-finite clauses.

Two examples are examined here. The following sentence incorporates three adverbial clauses with three coordinated clauses.

(99) wæɖə kaarə-ek   gatta-həmə   wæɖə kəlat   nætat
     house-servant-INDF take.PAST-when   work do.CONC no.CONC

     eyaa-ʈə   paɖi   gewa-nnə   oonæ   kææmə   de-nnə   oonæ
     she/he-DAT wage   pay-INF   must   food   give-INF   must

     asəniipə   un-ot   beet   araŋ   de-nnə   oonæ
     ill   be.PAST-COND   medicine buy.PP   give-INF   must
     'When we employ a house-servant, whether he works or not, we have to pay him a wage, feed him, and buy him medicine in case he becomes ill.'

First, we can find two adverbial clauses subordinated to the matrix sentence, namely, the temporal clause *wæɖə kaarəek gattahəmə* 'when we employ a house-servant' and the concessive conditional clause *wæɖə kəlat nætat* 'whether he works or not'. The object of the first adverbial clause ('house-servant') and the subject of the second adverbial clause are identical, and hence the latter is deleted. The matrix sentence consists of three conjoined clauses: *eyaa-ʈə paɖi gewannə oonæ* 'have to pay him a wage'; *kææmə dennə oonæ* 'give him food'; *beet araŋ dennə oonæ* 'buy him medicine'. The subject of neither clause appears overtly: given that the proposition is a general statement, the subject of the first clause ('we') is elliptical as it is pragmatically retrievable whereas in the two other clauses the ellipsis is due to the identical subject deletion rule. However, the three clauses are not equal in the sense that the last one is modified by an adverbial clause, namely the conditional clause *asəniipə unot* 'in case she/he becomes ill'.

The next sentence, as given below, includes one nominal clause, one adnominal clause and two adverbial clauses with two coordinated clauses and one subordinate clause.

(100) wahi-nəwa kiəla wædə-ṭə ya-nn-e nætuwə
 Rain-IND QM work-DAT go-NPT-FOC no.PP
 gedərə hiṭiə Ranjit wæssə pææuwa-ṭə passe
 home be.PT.ADJ Ranjit rain stop.PAST-DAT after
 mokədə kəranne kiəla kalpənaa kərə-nnə paṭan gatta
 what.Q do-NPT-FOC QM think-INF begin.PAST
 'Ranjit who stayed home without going to work because of rain began to think what he would do when the rain stops.'

The subject noun of the sentence, Ranjit, is modified by a relative clause. The verbal adjectival form functions as the subordinator. This adnominal clausal construction consists of two coordinated clauses: The two clauses *wædəṭə yanne nætuwə* 'doesn't go to work and' and *gedərə hiṭiə* 'stay at home' are coordinated by the perfect participle form attached to the former. It is preceded by an adverbial clause with the quotative marker *kiəla* functioning as the subordinator. This adverbial clause expresses the supposed reason for Ranjit's not going to work. Now Ranjit is thinking, according to the matrix sentence. The nominal clause 'what to do' attached by the quotative marker to the main verb 'thinking' is its object complement. There is another adverbial clause left, which appears between the subject and the verbal complex of the main clause, as *wæssə pææuwaṭə passe* 'after the rain stops'. Whether it modifies the main verb 'thinking' or the embedded clause 'what to do' is not clear. Depending on the locus of modification it may be interpreted either as 'when Ranjit started thinking the rain had stopped' or as 'Ranjit is thinking what to do after the rain.'

As becomes explicit by this description, Sinhala admits clause chaining, according to which a chain of clauses denoting a chain of events is produced through non-finite verb forms. One of the most convenient verbal forms that can be used as both coordinator and subordinator is the perfect participle form. As already mentioned, even the quotative marker *kiəla* has developed from a perfect participle form of the verb *kiənəwa* 'say'. Below is an extreme case of clause chaining:

(101) haamuduruwo gam-ee ipədilaa
 the Buddhist priest village-LOC born(PP)
 gam-ee pansal-en igenə genə
 village-LOC temple-ABL learn.PP
 looke gænə dænə gan-na-t oonæ kiəla
 world about know.REFL-INF-too must QM

  wishwa widyaale gihin
  university   go.PP
  upaadi-ak arə genə
  degree-INDF take.REFL.PP
  iitə passe iskoolə patwiim-ak araŋ
  then school appointment-INDF take.PP
  laməin-tə uganne-laa
  children-DAT teach-PP
  gamə-ṭa-t raṭə-ṭa-t   wisaalə seewə-ak kərə-la
  village-DAT-too country-DAT-too large service-INDF do-PP
  dæn wisraamə arə genə
  now retirement take.REFL.PP
  pansəl-ee wiweek-en in-nəwa
  temple-LOC rest-INS be-IND

'This Buddhist monk was born in the village, received education from the village temple, entered the university with the purported cause of knowing about the world, completed a degree, then got a teaching appointment at a school, taught children, did a great service to the village as well as to the country and now is restfully living in retirement at this temple.'

CHAPTER 11

Sentence and information structure

To understand the composition of a sentence comprehensively, we need to pay attention to the aspects of discourse and pragmatics and, in particular, information structure, and how they influence sentence formation. This chapter aims to describe such pragmatic aspects as the topic-comment organization and the focus phenomenon.

1. The topic-comment organization

Sinhala does not have a specific morpheme to mark the topic. The initial position of sentence is generally identified as the topic position. In a prototypical declarative sentence which expresses the speaker's judgment regarding information structure the first constituent of the clause, which is conflated with the grammatical subject, nominative or non-nominative, represents the topic component. While this part of the clause says what the message is basically going to be 'about', the rest of the clause provides the message or some state of affairs which constitutes a comment about the chosen element.

Some examples are provided below with sentences providing locational information. A locational sentence consists of at least two constituents: the nominative nominal denotes a located entity while the noun phrase with the locative marking represents locational information including orientation with respect to some other object. All the linguistic choices including the selection of NPs and their linear order are made in conformity with contextual factors such as speaker's purpose, the structure of information and the listener's sphere of knowledge, etc. Consider the following examples:

(1) lamai   piṭṭəni-e   in-nəwa
    children yard-LOC   be-IND
    'The children are in the yard.'

(2) pattəree   meese udə tiye-nəwa
    newspaper table on   be-IND
    'The newspaper is on the table.'

In these sentences the nominative constituent occupying the initial position of the clause establishes its referent as the element which the clause is going to be about. Note that these noun phrases are definite nouns in both sentences: the definiteness presupposes that the starting point of information is already known to the listener. Such noun phrases representing "old information" are typical topics, while the rest of the clause, consisting of the locative NP and the existential verb, gives "new information" about the located object and can be taken as comment. This structure of information will be evident from an examination of the contexts in which these sentences can be uttered naturally. The sentences (1) and (2) are appropriate as responses to the questions asked about the relevant located entities equivalent to (3) and (4), respectively.

(3) Where have all these children gone?
(4) Do you know where the newspaper is?

They will not be appropriate responses to the questions like

(3') Who are there in the yard in these late hours?
(4') Can you say what's on the table?

The person who is asking the questions in (3) or (4) obviously has the relevant located entities in his sphere of knowledge; only their whereabouts are not known to the speaker. Therefore it is reasonable to judge that the Sinhala sentences given above are used to convey some locational information about a known entity. Our explanation for the definiteness can be compared with the observations made by Clark 1978, which presents some basic insights into the discourse rules governing locational sentences. According to Clark, "The absence of indefinite nominals in initial position reflects a general discourse constraint in languages." (Clark 1978, p.88). This kind of locational sentences is called a Locative Construction. The word order will be

(5) a. [NP_{def} + LOCATIVE + v_{exist}] for SOV languages and
    b. [NP_{def} + V_{exist} + LOCATIVE] for SVO languages.

In contrast to the locative construction, there prevails another construction, referred to in the literature as Existential Construction, where the locative precedes the subject which is denoted by an indefinite nominal. The basic word order of existential sentences appears to be fixed universally:

(6) a. [LOCATIVE + NP_{indef} + V_{exist}] for SOV languages and
    b. [LOCATIVE + V_{exist} + NP_{indef}] for SVO languages.

The following examples will be illustrative:

(7') piṭṭəni-e   ball-ek   in-nəwa
      yard-LOC   dog-INDF   be-IND
      'There is a dog in the yard.'

(8') meese   udə   pattərə-ak   ti-una
      table   on   newspaper-INDF   be-PAST
      'There was a newspaper on the table.'

In existential sentences, as exemplified by (7) and (8) above, the locative NPs function as the 'starting point of the message' (Halliday 1985, p.39). They are not only the starting point of each clause but also considered as definite elements in that they are identified by the speaker and also identifiable by the listener. Thus the locative element constitutes the topic part of the sentence. The topic NP is followed by the nominative phrase marked for indefiniteness. This nominative constituent together with the existential verb bring new information and serve as the comment component.

The appearance of the locative phrase in the initial position in existential sentences accords with the Topic + Comment order. Kuno 1973 assumes that the locatives are preposed very early, at the level of the "deep" underlying structure, because of a general tendency in a continuous discourse to start sentences with old information and to introduce new information toward the end of the sentence. When the subject nominal is indefinite, the locative usually appears to be definite and moves to the initial position in existential sentences. Thus it seems to be a natural phenomenon for existential sentences to have locatives preposed; it would be awkward, on the other hand, for the locative to remain in a non-initial position. Compare the following (7′) and (8′) sentences below with (7) and (8) above:

(7′) ?ball-ek   piṭṭəni-e   in-nəwa
      dog-INDF   yard-LOC   be-IND
      'There is a dog in the yard.'

(8′) ?pattərə-ak   meese   udə   ti-una
      newspaper-INDF   table   on   be-PAST
      'There was a newspaper on the table.'

They are awkward because there is some confusion over which element is going to be the staring point or topic and which is going to be new information or comment part. The problematic (7′) and ((8′) sentences will sound natural if some morphosyntactic adjustment is made as in (7″) and (8″).

(7″) ball-ek   piṭṭəni-e   naŋ   in-nawa
      dog-INDF   yard-LOC   CONTR   be-IND
      'A dog – **in the yard,** there is one.'

(8″) pattərə-ak   meese   udə   naŋ   tie-nawa
      newpaper-INDF   table   on   CONTR   be-IND
      'A newspaper – **on the table,** there is one.'

What has been done here is adding the contrastive particle *naŋ* to the locative constituent. This suggests that the locative has become the focused constituent with the contrastive particle added after it.

Do the sentences in (7″) and (8″), then, defy the general discourse constraint that indefinite nominals are absent in initial position (Clark, 1978; Kuno, 1973)? As Chandralal 2005 has suggested, though the subject nominals are suffixed with an indefinite marker, they are not semantically indefinite. They are anaphoric, that is, continuing with something already introduced in the preceding discourse. This can be proved by an important fact related to intonation: there is a clear pause, "a thinking space", between the first constituent and the rest of the sentence. In this sense, the superficially indefinite nominals in (7″) and (8″) are effectively anaphoric: The subject nominal refers to a type of entity or a class familiar to both the speaker and the listener. Thus it can remain as the topic or be thematic owing it its anaphoric relation. This is also proved by the fact that these sentences will never be used discourse-initially. Therefore, we maintain that they follow the general principle of "old information first". Following Kuno 1973, we may also assume that the sentences were formed by postposing the locative phrase to allow it together with the particle *naŋ* to obtain a contrastive reading and the subject nominal to remain as topic.

The fact that an NP with an identifiable referent is anaphoric and semantically definite and hence can occur in the sentence-initial position is essentially a discourse process arising from the pragmatic presupposition including the conditions of "identifiability" and "salience" discussed in the literature (Chafe 1976; Lambrect1994, etc.). From situations void of such pragmatic conditions may emerge topic-less utterances which cannot be categorized as prototypical declarative sentences. Sentences uttered through immediate perception with some emotions, rather than with the intention of providing comments or additional information about a specific element chosen as topic, fall into this category. The sentences given in (7′) and (8′) as awkward can be converted to exclamatory sentences with appropriate lexical and semantic environments to sound completely natural as follows.

(9) ball-ek   taappe   udə   in-nəwa
     dog-INDF   wall   on   be-IND
     'There is a dog on the wall.'

(10) pattərə-ak   wahale   udə   tie-nəwa
     newspaper-INDF   roof   on   be-IND
     'There is a newspaper on the roof.'

These sentences cannot be divided into the elements of topic and comment. The speaker's perception is grasped as an entire scene through the words arranged lineally. Since such sentences only refer to the events occurring in the immediate context of situation, they cannot appear in the past tense. This nuance of meaning disappears when the locative phrase is preposed.

Existential sentences with preposed locatives can be used as deictic statements. The definiteness of the locative or its nature as a mutually apprehended element, which is directly related to deixis, is one of the most typically identified features in describing existential sentences. Observe the following existential sentences, equally identifiable as deictic expressions in the sense that they are used to indicate a particular situation, the speaker's perceptual cognition, to the addressee.

(11) oluw-e   roḍḍ-ak   (tie-nəwa)
      head-LOC   dust-INDF   (be-IND)
      'There is some dust on your head.'

(12) nikəṭ-e   bat   æṭəy-ak   (tie-nəwa)
      chin-LOC   rice   grain-INDF   (be-IND)
      'There is a grain of rice on your chin.' ('You have a crumb on your chin.')

(13) oyə   gah-ee   kaṭu   (tie-nəwa)
      that   tree-LOC   thorns   (be-IND)
      'There are thorns on that tree.'

A noteworthy feature regarding these sentences is that they appear in actual use without verbs. If these sentences are used to assert the existence of an entity in a given location, they function as existential sentences and require the presence of the existential verb. In such existential sentences the initial locative phrase represents the topic and the rest of the sentence including the existential verb represents the comment component. If these sentences are used as deictic statements reporting a perceptual experience in the immediate context to the addressee, they do not require the presence of an existential verb in surface form. The two nominal constituents seem to be adequate to achieve the purpose. In other words, the immediate expression of the location-located relation need not be structured according to the topic-comment organization.

When existential sentences are used to unambiguously express the existence of some entity, that is the sentence is in the ordinary declarative mode and is not deictic, the obligatory presence of the existential verb is required. Look at the following sentences.

(14) deiyo   in-nəwa
      gods   be-IND
      'Gods exist.'

(15) Indiyaaw-e   koṭi   in-nəwa
      India-LOC   tigers   be-IND
      'There are tigers in India.'

(16) kand-e   pansəl-ak   tie-nəwa
      mountain-LOC   temple-INDF   be-IND
      'There is a temple on the mountain.'

The main function of these sentences is to assert the existence of some entity. In that case, the existing entity, located place and the existential verb all comprise the composite structure of the topic-comment organization. These sentences will not be well-formed without existential verbs.

A similar differentiation can be observed with regards to locative sentences, too. First observe the situation when locative sentences are used as deictic statements.

When locative sentences are used to report a perceptual experience to the addressee in the immediate context, it is understood as occurring in the present, i.e. the speech time. Observe the following sentence:

(17) kannaḍiə   naləl-e
     glasses   forehead-LOC
     'The glasses are on your forehead.'

Sentence (17) sounds natural without the existential 'be' verb; its naturalness will be threatened if the 'be' verb is inserted. This means that the linear arrangement of the nominative constituent and the locative phrase is adequate to convey the perceptual experience of an immediate context, and the information need not wrapping up in the topic-comment cover.

When the speaker intends to express locational information regarding a particular entity using the locative construction, there are two options available to him depending on the context. For example, while (18a) will be an appropriate response to a question like *Where is the boss?*, the variant with the 'be' verb in (18b) cannot be used felicitously in the same context.

(18) a. mahatteya   kantooru-we
         boss   office-LOC
         'Boss is in the office.'

     b. mahatteya   kantooru-e   in-nəwa
         boss   office-LOC   be-IND
         'Boss is in the office.'

The variant in (18b) will be appropriate only as a response to a speculation such as *It seems that the boss is absent today*, because the function of the 'be' verb here is not just establishing the relation between the location and the located entity but also to assert the existence of the entity in the given location. In such a context the locative sentence should retain the existential verb. While a single locative constituent may form the comment against a nominative constituent representing the topic in some contexts, as in (18a), in another context the locative constituent and the existential verb together constitute the comment component, as in (18b).

If the locative construction is used to denote a locational situation in the declarative sense and not to express an immediate temporal context as in (17), it will require the topic-comment structure to cover the intended message as (17′) shows below.

(17′) kannaḍiyə   laachchu-e   tie-nəwa
      glasses   drawer-LOC   be-IND
      'The glasses are in the drawer.'

However, it is difficult to know whether a sentence turns out to be a transient locative, general locative, or a deictic locative without considering their correlated intonation patterns. How can we differentiate between the following three sentences?

(19) a. kurulla at-ee
      bird   hand-LOC
      'The bird is on his hand.'

   b. kurulla kuuḍu-we in-nəwa
      bird   nest-LOC be-IND
      'The bird is in the nest.'

   c. kurulla at-ee   in-nəwa
      bird   hand-LOC be-IND
      'The bird is on his hand.'

The example in (19a) may denote a transient location which allows the drop of the existential verb whereas sentence (19b) denotes a locational situation perceived as a more general state. Still it will be difficult to decide the state of (19c): it might be an exclamatory or a deictic expression. In (19a) the intonation nucleus will be with the locative phrase that introduces new information whereas in (19b) the intonation nucleus may pattern with the 'be' verb, which is used to assert the existence of the located entity in the given location, or it may be distributed over the locative phrase and the 'be' verb equally. In (19c) the intonation nucleus may spread across the whole sentence equally. These facts point to the comment component of each sentence: in (19a) the comment is the locative phrase and in (19b) it is the locative phrase plus the existential verb; (19c) does not follow the topic-comment pattern. The exact information contained in the individual sentences is therefore determined by contextual factors including the speaker's purpose and judgment on the scene.

Although our discussion was centered around the patterns of locative sentences, topic/comment organization can be observed with some other constructions, too. Let us take, for example, the dative subject construction. The dative subject will function as the topic, and the rest of the clause will represent the comment.

(20) Ranjit-ṭə taraha giyaa
     Ranjit-DAT anger go.PAST
     'Ranjit got angry.'

(21) Chitrə-ṭə pattəree pæægunaa
     Chitrə-DAT newspaper step on.INVL.PAST
     'Chitra stepped on the newspaper inadvertently.'

(22) ma-ṭə put-ek in-nəwa
     I-DAT son-INDF be-IND
     'I have a son.'

The dative subjects denoting the participant of an emotional experience in (20), an involuntary participant in (21) and a possessor in (22) are chosen as topic since they are salient participants of the events. The rest of the clause, including nouns denoting an emotion, object or an animate being and verbs of motion, involitive/existential states, represents the comment.

While the subject becomes the unmarked or 'default' topic, the use of another element of the sentence in the topic position is possible as a marked option.

(23) hændææwə-ṭə maŋ e-nnam
      evening-DAT   I   come-OPT
      'In the evening I'll visit you.'

The adverbial constituent, the first element of the sentence, has become the topic in this sentence.

From the beginning our stance has been that there is no particular morpheme to mark the topic in Sinhala but a caveat should be added. In informal, non-standard language a nominal constituent may be marked as topic by the postposition *æwilla*.[1]

(24) api æwilla horəṭə   wædə kərənə minissu newei
      we   TM   dishonestly work.NPT   people   no
      'We are not the kind of people that work dishonestly.'

Another morphological marker of topic, *naŋ*, gives the sentence both topic and contrastive readings.

(25) Ranjit naŋ paas unaa
      Ranjit TM   pass.PAST
      'As for Ranjit, he passed (the exam).'

While all the examples given so far have nominal constituents for topics, it is also possible that clauses be chosen as topics.

(26) wædə kəra-nnə amaaru-i
      work-INF   hard-AM
      Lit. 'Working is hard.'
      'It is hard to work.'

(27) kiya-nnə naŋ leesi-i
      say-INF   TM   easy-AM
      Lit. 'Saying is easy.'
      'Easier said.'

---

1. The origin of the postposition can be traced to the verb *enəwa*. *æwilla* is the past participle form of this verb.

In these sentences the first element, a verbal clause, is chosen as the topic.

As this description reveals, the topic-comment organization in Sinhala plays a fundamental role in shaping morpho-syntactic aspects of sentences and it seems crucially involved with semantic, pragmatic and discourse-related factors, such as context, identifiability, the definite/indefinite distinction, anaphoric relations, deixis, salience, perceptual information, etc.

2. The focus structure

The Sinhala focused sentence construction has a prominent role in its grammar. It has a wide-ranging marking system: focus may be marked morphologically, syntactically, or suprasegmentally. Known as 'cleft', 'pseudo-cleft', 'emphatic' or 'focused' construction, it has been treated with particular attention in a number of studies (Gair 1970 and 1983; Fernando 1973; De Abrew 1981; Kishimoto 1991; Kariyakarawana 1992; Hagstrom 1998; Henadeerage 2002).

Sinhala uses a special marking of the tensed verb for focus construction; the focus affix *-nne* is used for the present and *-e* for the past. The following examples show how focus appears in sentences. Observe that the example in (28) is a neutral sentence, that is, since the verb is not marked for special emphasis, no constituent is focused. In other words, its verb is identical with focus.

(28)   Ranjit   wiidurua   binda
       Ranjit   glass   break.PAST
       'Ranjit broke the glass.'

In contrast, (29a through g) are all focused sentences. When the focus form appears on the verbal predicate it indicates that one of the constituents of the clause, an element external to the verb, is focused. Notice the difference in verb form: the ending *-a/aa* appears on a finite tensed verb in a neutral sentence like (28) while the verb ends in *-e* in focused sentences like (29a-g).

(29)   a.   Ranjit   wiidurua   bind-e
            Ranjit   glass   break.PAST-FOC
            'It was Ranjit that broke the glass.' or
            'It was the glass that Ranjit broke.'

       b.   Ranjit   tamai   wiidurua   bind-e
            Ranjit   FM   glass   break.PAST-FOC
            'It was indeed Ranjit that broke the glass.'

c. Ranjit   wiidurəə   tamai   bind-e
   Ranjit   glass   FM   break.PAST-FOC
   'It was indeed the glass that Ranjit broke.'

d. wiidurəə   bind-e   Ranjit
   glass   break.PAST-FOC   Ranjit
   'It was Ranjit that broke the glass.'

e. Ranjit   bind-e   wiidurəə
   Ranjit   break.PAST-FOC   glass
   'It was the glass that Ranjit broke.'

f. RANJIT   wiidurəə   bind-e
   Ranjit   glass   break.PAST-FOC
   'It was Ranjit that broke the glass.'

g. Ranjit   WIIDURƏƏ   bind-e
   Ranjit   glass   break.PAST-FOC
   'It was the glass that Ranjit broke.'

For (a), two possible readings are available. The readings are associated with different choices of focus: one with Ranjit and the other with the glass. The sentences (b) and (c) show morphologically marked focus: the particle *tamai* added to the relevant constituent indicates association with focus. Rightward movement of the focused constituent leads to nullifying ambiguity, as in (d) and (e); they are examples of structurally marked focus, i.e. through verb marking plus phrase structure. Ambiguity can also be removed with emphatic stress, as in (f) and (g), which is indicated by capital letters. Association with focus is expressed through intonation in such cases.

Three aspects of focus marking in Sinhala are summarized by Gair and Sumangala (1991) as follows:

Focus marking in Sinhala:

a. -E (Emphatic form or focus affix) is structure-specific, and is not a form with general nominal distributions,
b. It indicates that the focus is external to, i.e. does not include, the verb. That is, it requires a verb external focus,
c. is in complementary distribution with the most common finite verbal affix -A, and like it, follows tense.

By analyzing the focused sentence construction, we can show that some semantic and pragmatic characteristics are systematically related to the form of the sentence though they may not appear overtly. Crucial to the discussion are the two semantic notions of *focus* and *presupposition*. As pointed out by Jackendoff 1972, the division of the semantic representation into focus and presupposition is reflected in the syntactic structure of the sentence. The focus of a sentence is the part of it that presents new information and is often marked by stress, while the presuppositions are the propositions assumed by the speaker to be shared by him and the hearer.

This suggests that the focus structure has something in common with the topic-comment organization. The topic comprises part of the presupposition including context-construable information. The comment, on the other hand, presents new information which is available for the subsequent development in the discourse. The comment part *wiiduruə binda* 'broke the glass' in (28) may include a kind of focus sometimes referred to as presentational focus. However, this type of focus is to be distinguished from contrastive focus presented in (29a through g) whose focused constituent is selected as the appropriate variable after rejecting a class of possible contrasts with the focus. For example, for (29b) the reading available is that it was not somebody else but Ranjit that broke the glass; in (29c) the noninvolvement of an alternative participant is contrasted with the object constituent 'It was nothing else but the glass that Ranjit broke.' The class of possible contrasts represents the range of information over which communication participants, the speaker or the hearer, are uncertain. The semantic function of the focus is providing this unpredictable information by choosing the appropriate variable.

Let us look at some important characteristics of Sinhala focused sentences. As seen in (29b) and (29c) above, the focused constituent is marked by the particle *tamai*. Apart from *tamai*, there is a range of focus-marking particles which include the interrogative *də* 'question', the emphatic *yi*, *lu* 'hearsay', *naŋ* 'if', *ne* 'n'est-ce pas', focus negation *newei*, and dubitative *yæ*. Their occurrence is restricted to the focus: immediately following the verb of a neutral sentence or the focus of a focused sentence. In the latter case, since they appear on a constituent other than the verb, the verb invariably changes to the focus form. When such a particle is added to a constituent, it indicates there is some thing new to the hearer and constitutes part of the focus.

Not only nominal constituents but even some adverbial particles can be focused with these particles. Look at the following examples.

(30) a. Ranjit-ţə passe də oyaa giyee
Ranjit-DAT after Q you go.PAST.FOC
'Was it after Ranjit that you left?'

b. Ranjit-ţə passe tamai maŋ giyee
Ranjit-DAT after FM I go.PAST.FOC
'It was indeed after Ranjit that I left.'

When the focus marker follows a finite verb, the verb or the whole proposition may be focused. In such cases, as mentioned before, the verb appears in the basic form without inflecting into the focus form.

(31) a. man giyaa tamai
I go.PAST FM
'I did go.'

b. Ranjit kaḍee-ṭə giyaa tamai
Ranjit shop-DAT go.PAST FM
'It certainly was the case that Ranjit went to the shop.'

When the indicative verb bears focus, as in (31a), this is indicated by the emphatic stress accompanying it. However, the stress on the verb, or for that matter on any single constituent, renders the sentence unacceptable for the given reading. The *tamai* construction has acquired further nuances in the colloquial language. When used with a deleted subject it expresses an ironic comment about the addressee's action.

(32) A: maŋ wattə suddə kəlaa
I land clear.PAST
'I cleared the land.'

B: suddə kəlaa tamai
clear.PAST FOC
'You did the clearing!'

The B's response is ironic: the speaker's voice would make it obvious that he or she is not pleased with A's job. To B, it seems that A has not done the job well or has done something unnecessary, say, by uprooting some useful plants. Under the shared presupposition, the two speakers implicitly agree that the clearing had not been done before. A's utterance is a neutral sentence in which 'I' is the topic and 'cleared the land' is the comment. The speaker assumed that it is information new to B. B's utterance as a focused sentence has a presupposition in which he agrees only that A has done the job to some extent, but implies that the job is not complete, or done with some harm. A third person listening to the dialogue will understand that the two speakers do not share the same presupposition. Even A will understand that there is an irony in B's response because the verb he used as part of new information, with the association of *tamai* at the hand of B, implies that there is something unusual or unexpected about his own action.

We have seen before that yes/no questions are formed by placing the *də* particle after a predicate. The sentence in (33a) given below is such a neutral question. In forming focused questions, that is when any constituent other than the verb is chosen for questioning, this is marked with *də* and the relevant verb needs marking with the focus form as in (33b) and (33c). Variable orders are possible as shown in (33d) and (33e).

(33) a. Ranjit sudu kalisaŋ andi-nəwa də
Ranjit white slacks wear-IND Q
'Does Ranjit wear white slacks?'

b. sudu kalisaŋ andi-nne Ranjit də
white slacks wear-NPT.FOC Ranjit Q
'Is it Ranjit that wears white slacks?'

c. Ranjit andi-nne sudu kalisaŋ də
Ranjit wear-NPT.FOC white slacks Q
'Is it white slacks that Ranjit wears?'

d. Ranjit də sudu kalisaŋ andi-nne
Ranjit Q white slacks wear-NPT.FOC
'Is it Ranjit that wears white slacks?'

e. sudu kalisaŋ də Ranjit andi-nne
white slacks Q Ranjit wear-NPT.FOC
'Is it white slacks that Ranjit wears?'

The sentence pairs (b) and (d), and (c) and (e) represent variants of the same question. When the focused constituent is moved, it should be accompanied by the *də* particle.

In forming WH questions, WH forms are always accompanied by the question particle *də*.² The co-occurrence of the WH form with the particle *də* indicates that the focusing of the WH constituent is virtually obligatory. The lexicographic treatment of the lexical forms with the question particle like *kaudə* 'who' and *mokaddə* 'what' as composite structures conforms to the native intuition. The pair in (34a and b) with variant orders illustrates the focused situation in WH questions. In both the verb appears in the focus form. The examples in (35a and b) show that a sentence is ungrammatical when the WH form is not accompanied by the question marker *də*, whether or not the verb is in the focus form.

(34) a. Ranjit genaawe monəwa-də
Ranjit bring.PT.FOC what-Q
'What did Ranjit bring?'

b. Ranjit monəwa-də genaawe
Ranjit what-Q bring.PT.FOC
'What did Ranjit bring?'

(35) a. *Ranjit monəwa genaawa də
Ranjit what bring.PAST Q
'What did Ranjit bring?'

b. *Ranjit monəwa genaawe də
Ranjit what bring.PT.FOC Q
'What did Ranjit bring?'

---

2. Strictly speaking, the Sinhala WH forms are K/M forms like *kauru* 'who', *kookə* 'which', *mokak* 'what' (sg.) and *monəwa* 'what' (pl.).

There are exceptions to this rule: we can find three instances in which a WH constituent appears not focused. One is a type of embedded sentences we have already discussed (See Chapter 10). We have seen that an embedded clause consisting in an interrogative pronoun may function as the object complement of a verb expressing doubt or suspicion. In such an embedded clause the question marker *də* need not immediately follow the WH word, as shown in (36).

    (36)   Ranjit   monəwa   genaawa   də   dan-ne   næǣ
             Ranjit   what   bring.PAST   Q   know-NPT.FOC no
           '(We) don't know what Ranjit brought'

In this sentence the WH word does not express a straightforward question and the verb in the main clause expresses uncertainty or doubts about the whole proposition, not just about one focused constituent. The other two instances in which the WH word is not focused are exemplified by (37) and (38).

    (37)   monəwa   gee-nnə   də
             what   bring.INF   Q
           'What to bring?'

    (38)   kohee   ya-nəwa   də
             where   go-IND   Q
           'Where (on earth) are you going?'

Although the utterance in (37) appears as an independent clause it can be considered as having originated as an object complement of an imaginative or suspective expression. The speaker's imagination or suspicion concerns the whole proposition, not merely one constituent. The example in (38) represents a similar situation: the speaker is wondering about the other person's movement and expressing some annoyance. Incidentally, these expressions show that WH formation is used for some other functions apart from the focusing.

A clarification that must be added at this point is that this description does not deny the occurrence of WH focus in embedded questions. In fact, a WH form appears focused with the co-occurring *də* within an embedded clause, as in (39).

    (39)   Ranjit   monəwa-də   genaawe   kiəla   Chitra   æhuwa
             Ranjit   what-Q   bring.PT.FOC that   Chitra   ask.PAST
           'Chitra asked what Ranjit brought.'

Note that the WH form is immediately followed by *də* and the embedded verb is in the focus form. On the other hand, when the focus occurs in the higher sentence with a wide scope reading, there are two possibilities: one is with the WH form remaining in situ in the lower sentence, as in (40), and the other is with the WH form moving to the higher sentence, as in (41). Variant orders are possible in the latter case.

(40) [Ranjit monəwa-də genaawa] kiəla Chitra hituwe
Ranjit what-Q bring.PAST that Chitra think.PT.FOC
'What did Chitra think that Ranjit brought?'

(41) a. [Ranjit genaawa] kiəla Chitra hituwe monəwa də
Ranjit bring.PAST that Chitra think.PT.FOC what Q
'What did Chitra think that Ranjit brought.'

b. monəwa də [Ranjit genaawa] kiəla Chitra hituwe
what Q Ranjit bring.PAST that Chitra think.PT.FOC
'What did Chitra think that Ranjit brought.'

c. monəwa də Chitra hituwe [Ranjit genaawa] kiəla
what Q Chitra think.PT.FOC Ranjit bring.PAST that
'What did Chitra think that Ranjit brought.'

The main verb is marked with the focus form in all the sentences in (40) and (41). However, only in (40) is the WH form situated in the embedded clause; in all the others it is moved out from the embedded clause. These examples also show that focus is not bound within a clause; it can move across clauses.

Focus can be said to be unbounded in the sense that focusing within a lower clause does not hinder further focusing. Look at the following sentence.

(42) [maŋ monəwa də yæuwe] kiəla
I what Q send.PT.FOC that
oyaa æhuwe amma-țə də
you ask.PT.FOC mother-DAT Q
Lit. 'Was it to mother that you asked what it was that I sent?'

In this sentence focusing has occurred out of a once focused lower clause. The matrix clause is *oyaa æhuwe* 'you asked'; the verb is marked with the focus form. The focused element *ammațə* followed by the question particle *də* bears the case marking of dative which is inappropriate with the main verb. The Sinhala verb *ahanəwa* 'ask' does not subcategorize for a dative constituent; the person asked is invariably marked with the ablative. This clearly shows that the dative constituent originally does not belong to the main clause but has moved from the lower clause. The verb of the lower clause *maŋ monəwa də yæuwe* 'what I sent' is marked with the focus form and its direct object, the WH form, is marked with the question particle to indicate its focused status. The verb *yawənəwa* 'send' takes its indirect object marked with the dative. Now it is obvious that the focused constituent appearing in the dative with rightward placement owes its morphological identity to the lower verb, and its present position to the matrix verb. Thus double focusing occurs through the lower verb and the higher verb as well.

To interpret focus within multi-clause sentences, two combinatory factors should be taken into consideration: the place the focus form appears, i.e. whether on the matrix verb or the embedded verb, and the clause the focus constituent belongs to (Henadeerage 2002). Even when a constituent belonging to the embedded clause is focused in form, the focus interpretation varies according to where the focus form appears. The following pair of sentences (from Henadeerage 2002) includes the same embedded clause constituent marked for focus by *tamai* (43) or *də* (44) while bearing different interpretations between the (a) and (b) versions.

(43) a. Gune [janaadipati boruw-ak tamai kiuwe] kiəla hituwa
Gune President lie.INDF FM say.PT.FOC that think.PAST
'Gune thought that it was a lie that the president told.'

b. Gune [janaadipati boruw-ak tamai kiuwa] kiəla hituwe
Gune President lie.INDF FM say.PAST that think.PT.FOC
'It was a lie that Gune thought the president told.'

(44) a. Gune [janaadipati boruwak də kiuwe] kiəla hituwa
Gune President lie.INDF Q say.PT.FOC that think.PAST
'Gune wondered if it was a lie that the president told.'

b. Gune [janaadipati boruwak də kiuwa] kiəla hituwe
Gune President lie.INDF Q say.PAST that think.PT.FOC
'Was it a lie that Gune thought that the president told?'

Notice that the (a) sentences, with the focus form on the embedded verb, are interpreted for embedded focus while the (b) sentences, with the emphatic form on the matrix verb, are taken for the matrix focus interpretation. Thus the focus verb form is crucial for potential focus interpretation. The scope of the presupposition is shaped by where the focus form appears; depending on the focus form, therefore, the sentences are taken as based on different presuppositions. The presupposition for (43a) is that the President said something and the focus is that it is not true. The presupposition for (43b), on the other hand, is that Gune thought that the President said something, and the focus that it is not true in that case has a wider scope including both embedded and matrix clauses.

Multiple foci are allowed even within a single clause although restrictions exist depending on the focus markers. WH forms accompanied by the question marker *də* allow multiple foci in a single clause, as in (45). Two focused constituents can occur in a single clause when one is marked by a focus marker and the other by a question marker, as in (46). Multiple foci through focus particles excluding question markers are generally not allowed, as shown in (47).

(45) [maŋ kaa-tə də monəwa də yawa-nne] kiəla eyaa nitərəmə
I who-DAT Q what Q send.NPT.FOC that she/he always
hoyə-nəwa
search-IND
'He always checks whether it is to whom and what that I send.'

(46) [maŋ tamai monəwa də yawa-nne] kiəla
    I   FM   what   Q send.NPT.FOC that
    kaurut   hoya-nne
    everybody search.NPT.FOC
    'It is me that everybody checks as to what is sent.'

(47) a. *[maŋ tamai salli tamai yawa-nne] kiəla kaurut
        I   FM   money FM   send.NPT.FOC that everybody
        hoya-nne
        search.NPT.FOC
        'It is indeed me that definitely sends money that everybody checks.'
     b. *maŋ tamai salli witərai yawa-nne
         I   FM   money FM   send.NPT.FOC
         'It is indeed only me that only sends money.'

In (45) the lower verb is marked with the emphatic form and two WH constituents are focused by the question marker *də*. In (46) both the lower verb and the higher verb are marked with the focus form and two constituents are focused within the lower clause. Unlike in (45), however, one constituent, namely the one that denotes the subject of the lower verb, bears focus relation to the higher verb while residing in terms of position within the lower clause, i.e. without rightward movement. It seems that the existence of multiple foci is supported by a multi-clause sentence. Because of the multi-clausal nature, it becomes possible that a predicate is identified and appropriately marked for each focused constituent. The example in (47) shows that multiple foci are unacceptable in a single clause through non-interrogative focus particles, regardless of whether the same focus particle is used (a) or two different focus particles are deployed (b), and no matter whether the single clause remains embedded (a) or independent (b). The sentence in (47a) is ungrammatical despite the fact that the two verbs are appropriately marked with the focus form for two focused constituents, which is in accordance with the principle that non-interrogative focus particles are non-iterative.

Since it was mentioned above that there is a relation between focus and the interpretation of negation, how negation is realized in Sinhala is briefly sketched here. The verbal negator, *nææ*, occurs with the focus form of the verb in unmarked sentences, as in (48). It occurs at the end of the clause.

(48) a. Ranjit bo-nne   nææ
        Ranjit drink-NPT.FOC   no
        'Ranjit doesn't drink.'
     b. Ranjit wiidurua binde   nææ
        Ranjit glass   break.PT.FOC no
        'Ranjit didn't break the glass.'

Another form used as a nominal negator, *newei*, also functions as a focal negator. *Newei* occurs at the end of a focused constituent negating constituent focus, as in (49), or at the end of a sentence negating sentence focus, as in (50). Thus the particle appears as a focus marking form for the preceding elements.

(49) a. Ranjit newei wiidurəə bind-e
Ranjit FN glass break.PT-FOC
'Ranjit was not the one who broke the glass.'

b. Ranjit wiidurəə newei bind-e
Ranjit glass FN break.PT-FOC
'It was not the glass that Ranjit broke.'

(50) Ranjit wiidurəə binda newei
Ranjit glass break.PAST FN
'It was not the case that Ranjit broke the glass.'

The fact that these sentences contain focused constituents can be demonstrated by comparing each of the *newei* marked constituents with a coherent set of possible contrasts. For example, (49a) can be modified by adding an extra subject as *Ranjit newei wiidurəə binde, Chitra* 'It was not Ranjit that broke the glass, it was Chitra'; (49b) can be modified by adding an extra object as *Ranjit wiidurəə newei binde, chiminiə* 'It was not the glass that Ranjit broke, it was the chimney'; (50) can have the following alternative: *Ranjit wiidurəə binda newei, kædichchə wiiduruwə æhinda* 'It was not the case that Ranjit broke the glass but it was that he picked up the broken glass.' Such possible contrasts are posited in accordance with the condition "that the variable will have the same functional semantic form as the focus" (Jackendoff 1972).

The fact that these sentences contain focused constituents can also be substantiated by associated intonation contours. Since emphatic stress is generally assigned along with the focus marker, the focused constituents can be shown to have received emphatic stress. Further, it will be relevant to see that the meanings of these focused sentences can be expressed by a neutral sentence like (48b) with appropriate assignment of emphatic stress. Thus the sentences (49a and b) will be equal to (51a and b) respectively in focus relation. (Focused constituents are given in caps)

(51) a. RANJIT wiidurəə binde næǽ
Ranjit glass break.PT.FOC no
'RANJIT didn't break the glass.'

b. Ranjit WIIDURUƏ binde næǽ
Ranjit glass break.PT.FOC no
'Ranjit didn't break the GLASS.'

The focus shifts with contrastive stress. No specific noun phrase can be stressed for (50) since it contains sentence focus. The difference in the contrastive stress in (51), or in the negation associated with the focus in (49) and (50) is based on different presuppositions. For example, the presuppositions for (49a), (49b) and (50) can be identified as follow.

(49a′)   Somebody has broken the glass.
(49b′)   Ranjit has broken something.
(50′)   There is an opinion that Ranjit has broken the glass.

The negation in the respective sentences associates with focus by making assertions against these presuppositions.

There is a subtype of focused sentences appearing with deictic pronouns. Such sentences express varied nuances.

(52)   arə   e-nne   Ranjit!
       that   come.NPT.FOC   Ranjit
       'There comes Ranjit!'

If the emphatic stress is assigned to *Ranjit*, this sentence can be taken as a focused sentence with contrastive focus falling under the same category as discussed so far. However, in the particular sentence type introduced here the initial part, *arə enne* 'there comes', is associated with emphatic stress. This verbal phrase undergoes association with focus by virtue of stress assignment. It is *Ranjit* that forms part of the presupposition. The sentence says that just when Ranjit was under discussion in the discourse at hand, he actually arrived. By being deictic in nature, it performs an exclamatory function with presentational focus rather than contrastive focus.

This subtype of focused sentence construction has also been conventionalized as follows:

(53)   a.   oyə   hadanne!
            that   make.NPT.FOC
            '(They) are making it!'

       b.   oyə   kiiwe!
            that   say.PT.FOC
            'Did you hear? What a saying!'

By using (53a), the speaker expresses his or her reluctance to accept the success of the action referred to. The utterance in (53b) is used by a speaker when someone has said something unexpected, strange or interesting. These sentences should be taken as exclamatory utterances by considering their nature of contexts and interpretations. Although they have verbs marked with the focus form, no specific constituent is focused; the focus seems to apply to the entire sentence. Neither can they be interpreted along the division of focus and presupposition.

The focus construction in Sinhala plays a crucial part in the grammatical structure through its interaction with some important grammatical processes such as WH question formation and negation and the morpho-syntactic phenomena like the appearance of the focus form. Its involvement with pragmatic aspects and contextual meanings spreads to wider domains including the "reanalysis" of the construction.

CHAPTER 12

Discourse and grammar

This chapter discusses some structural aspects of discourse. Discourse is considered as reflecting a composite structure interwoven with the linguistic text and extra-linguistic information. This presupposes that discourse structures cannot be understood without reference to linguistic and non-linguistic context. Deixis plays a prominent role in integrating contextual information within language. How the deictic system works in Sinhala is explicated in the following sections, mainly focusing on local and personal deixis.

Demonstratives, as part of deictic system, encode information from a dimension directly relevant to the context of discourse. Primarily, the speaker occupies the most important place in the context although the hearer as well plays an important part. The spatial distance between the referent object and speaker and/or hearer is taken as the main criterion for the choice of deixis. This distance is dichotomized into proximal and distal. There may be information proximal to the speaker, to the hearer, or to both speaker and hearer. There may also be information distal from both speaker and hearer. Information is thus located within the spatio-temporal context.

There are some other elements of the discourse regarding which the accurate identification of information will be required for effective communication. To bridge this gap there are demonstratives which are used to indicate not only spatial distance but discourse status also. The same forms used for situating objects, persons, etc. in space are also used to identify referents in discourse. Accordingly, the function of the Sinhala demonstratives can be broadly divided into two aspects: expressing spatial deixis and expressing discourse deixis.

1. Deictic system of demonstratives

Sinhala has several four-member sets of forms with varying functions to express deixis. First, there is a set of determiners that express four distinct deictic properties. This distinction is phonologically marked in the first syllable of the deictic form: *m-*, *o-*, *a-*, and *e-*. The first two are proximal: the contrast is between near-speaker and near-hearer. The second two are distal: the contrast is based on spatial distance plus visibility.

Table 1. Determiners and their deictic properties

Deictic property	Deictic form	Deictic Meaning
Proximal 1 (1P)	*mee*	'this, these': proximal to speaker, or to both speaker and hearer
Proximal 2 (2P)	*oyə*	'that, those': proximal to hearer
Distal 1 (1D)	*arə*	'that, those'(over there); distal from both speaker and hearer; in sight
Distal 2 (2D)	*ee*	'that, those': outside the speaker/hearer's reach or not in the speech situation

Demonstrative deictics characterize the location of participants in the narrated event with reference to the speech event. The distinction is based on the opposition of proximal vs. distal with respect to the location of the persons involved in the speech event. Two points of proximal contrast (1P and 2P) and another two points of distal contrast (1D and 2D) are encoded in Sinhala. This shows that the system depends on an evaluation of distance from the reference points of the speaker's location as well as the hearer's location at the moment of utterance. In the canonical case, *mee* represents a referent evaluated as being nearer to the speaker and *oyə* as nearer to the hearer. In deciding distal contrast, in addition to the spatial orientation point, another relational feature seems to work. The contrast depends upon whether the referent is located in the field of vision. *Arə* (1D) is selected when the referent is evaluated as being distal from both the speaker and the hearer and being in the field of vision. The feature EXCLUSIVE also seems to be relevant in spatial deixis. 1D can be characterized as that part of the deictic field which includes the interlocutors, both the speaker and the hearer, while *ee* (2D) can be considered as that part of a deictic field which does not include the interlocutors. Thus the Sinhala deictic system becomes complete with 'that exclusive' (2D) added to the more common three-way distinction of 'this very near' (1P), 'that yonder' (2P), and 'that distant' (1D). The ultimate opposition is represented by two-terms expressions such as *ehe-mehe* 'here and there' (Lit. 'there and here') *eekə-meekə* 'this and that' (Lit. 'that thing and this thing').

These spatial deictic demonstratives are used in the nominal, adjectival or adverbial form to indicate an object, animal, person, place, direction, or events in the spatio-temporal context of speech. The paradigm of deictic demonstratives is given in Table 2.

As shown in the table below, Sinhala uses a four-way deictic system, with further distinctions in terms of number, gender, social relations, and discourse roles. It might seem interesting that human person forms do not distinguish singular from plural number or masculine from feminine gender while animal forms split into

Table 2. Deictic demonstrative expressions

	Speaker-proximate	Hearer-proximate	Distal/visible	Distal/non-situational
Adectival	mee	oyə	arə	ee
Nominal				
Object (SG)	meekə	ookə	arəkə	eekə
(PL)	meewa	oowa	arəwa	eewa
Animal: 1. SG.;M	meeka	ooka	arəka	eeka
SG; F	meeki	ooki	arəki	eeki
2. SG	muu	–	aruu	(uu)
PL	muŋ	ouŋ	aruŋ	euŋ(uŋ)
Human	meyaa	oyaa	arəya	eyaa
Location 1.	metənə	otənə	atənə	etənə
2.	mehe	ohe	arəhe	ehe
Direction	mehaa	ohaa	arəha	ehaa
Degree	mechchərə	ochchərə	achchərə	echchərə
Adverbial				
Manner	mehemə	ohomə	arəhemə	ehemə
Presentation	mennə	onnə	annə	–

these distinctions. Person nouns, i.e. personal pronouns, however, are marked by a plural suffix to indicate plurality as in *oyaa-la* 'you (pl.)' and *meyaa-la* 'these persons', though not indicated in the paradigm. Animal forms may also be used for the human category in a derogatory sense.

Some sets are incomplete, lacking forms within one or two categories. Differences existing between forms peculiar to some sets with respect to the same deictic element are not unique. The hearer-proximate human form, *oyaa*, for example, has been established as the second person pronoun, taking it as indicating the addressee him/herself, rather than somebody nearer to the addressee. Also, the hearer-proximate second locational noun form, *ohe*, is also used as the second person pronoun in some dialects. These two second person pronominal uses have different values in terms of social deixis, depending on the regional dialect.[1]

Deictic expressions may be used to specify referents independently by themselves or in conjunction with other linguistic forms. Adjectival forms, serving as determiners,

---

1. Some honorific terms and temporal forms were not included in the paradigm given in Table 2.

represent the latter type and occur attributively to nouns as in *mee potə* 'this book' and *oyə balla* 'that dog'. Nominal forms, on the other hand, occur as pronouns independently as in *meekə hondai* 'This is good' and *ooka hapaawi* 'That one (i.e. dog) might bite'. The nominal form indicating degree may occur in adverbial form, too. Adverbial forms modify verbs, adjectives, or sentences, as in *mehemə liyannə* 'Write this way', *mehemə hondai* 'This way is good' and *mennə enəwa* 'Here comes'.

To this four-member set of demonstratives may be added as a fifth member a set of interrogatives whose first syllable is marked with *m-* or *k-* as in *mokə* (what), *kookə* (which), *kauru* (who) and *kohe* (where) to form the deictic-interrogative organization in Sinhala.

2. The deictic parameter

However, in general, what motivates the use of a particular form can be delineated in terms of the proximal/distal parameter. If a question includes a word from the 1P series, referring to something close to the speaker, the answer will have a word from the 2P series, indicating that the object is closer to the partner, as in (1). If the question includes a word from the 2P series, signaling that the referent is close to the hearer, the answer will have a word from the 1P series, indicating that the object is closer to the responder, as in (2).

(1) A: meekə mokaddə?
       this   what.Q
       'What's this?'

    B: ookə laiṭərə-ak
       that lighter-INDF
       'That's a lighter.'

(2) A: ookə mokaddə?
       that what.Q
       'What's that?'

    B: meekə ḍəəri-ak
       this diary-INDF
       'This is a diary.'

When an echo question is made after a question with a 1D series word, the same form is used because the referent is away from both interlocutors. However, it is answered with a 2D series word, shifting to the anaphoric use, as in (3).

(3) A: arəkə   kiiyədə?
       that one (over there) how much
       'How much is that one (over there)?'

B: arəkə   də
    that one (over there)   Q
    'That one (over there)?'
    eekə   rupial   pənaha-i
    that   rupee   fifty-AM
    'It's fifty rupees.'

In weather-talk, different forms may be used depending on the location of the interlocutors from whose reference point the distance is evaluated.

(4) A: mee   palaatə   hari   rasne-i   needə?
        this   province very   hot-AM   isn't it
        'This region is very hot, isn't it?'

    B: mehaa-ţə   wæssə   hinga-i   ne
        here-DAT   rain   scarce-AM   ne[2]
        'We don't get much rain in this region; that's why (it's hot).'

(5) A: ee   pættə-ţa-t   wahi-nəwa   æti   needə?
        that   area-DAT-too   rain-IND   might   isn't it
        'It might be raining in that region, too, isn't it?'

    B: ehaa-ţə   wæssə   næǣ
        there-DAT   rain   no
        'No, it was not raining there.'

(6) (a telephone conversation)

    A: ohaa-ţa-t   wahinəwa   də
        there-DAT-too   rain-IND   Q
        'Is it raining there, too?'

    B: næǣ,   mehaa-ţə   wahi-nn-e   næǣ
        no   here-DAT   rain-NPT-FOC   not
        'No, it doesn't rain here.'

In (4) interlocutors talk about the same region where they happen to remain at the speech time. While the place of utterance and the referent of the deixis coincide, there is no difference in distance between the referent as assumed and the each interlocutor. This motivates the same deixis of 1P series. In (5) the deictic field is defined by the interlocutors located in one and the same place and the referent denoting another place away from the both interlocutors. Thus the use of 2D series is justified. The conversation in (6) involves the interlocutors coming from different locations. The first speaker uses the deixis of 2P, indicating the referent belongs to the hearer's domain

---

2. *ne* is an interactional particle used in the clause final position to elicit addressee's consent or attention or to add emphasis to an statement.

whereas the response includes the deixis of 1P as the referent represents the speaker's domain, with the shift of the speaker.

3. Functions of deictic expressions

We can now consider how different forms are used in actual discourse. Fillmore (1982) divided deictic expressions into three different functions, as identifying, informing, and acknowledging. This function-based distinction is followed here to describe various uses of deictic categories.

3.1 Identifying function

The appropriate deixis is selected for uniquely identifying a referent from among a number of potential referents, according to its relative distance from the speaker and the hearer. The following examples illustrate the use of the primary deixis of proximal relation (1P):

(7) a. meekə pot-ak
       this book-INDF
       'This is a book.'

   b. mee pintuurə pot-ee tie-nn-e katandərə
      this picture book-LOC be-NPT-FOC stories
      'This picture book has stories.'

   c. mee liumə baappə-laa-gen
      this letter uncle-PL-ABL
      'This letter is from our uncle and his family.'

   d. meewa piṭəraṭə baḍu
      these foreign commodities
      'These are imported commodities.'

   e. meyaa tamai sarungəlee hædu-e
      this person FM kite make.PAST.FOC
      'It is this person who made the kite.'

The objects are identified by using the nominal forms in the singular as in (7a) and in the plural as in (7d). The Examples (7b) and (7c) use adjectival forms to identify the referents. The Example (7e) shows how a person is identified by using the participant dimension. Participant dimension includes both interlocutors and non-interlocutors (Grenoble 1998). The personal pronoun *meyaa* is generally used in Sinhala to denote a non-interlocutor or non-participant in the speech act.

However, the actual pragmatic forces behind these uses are best illustrated by their individual contexts. The following type of utterance, for example, is typically used in introducing someone who is very close to the speaker.

(8)   mee   apee   malli
         this   our   younger brother
         'This is my younger brother.'

Using the adjectival form of 1P, rather than the personal noun, is the accepted convention in such situations and which is motivated by the fact that the referent is psychologically as well as physically close to the speaker. Using the personal pronoun *meyaa*, as in (9), is acceptable under certain conditions.

(9)   a.   meyaa   apee   malli
              this person   our   younger brother
              'This is my younger brother.'

       b.   *meyaa   apee   taatta
              this person   our   father
              'This is my father.'

There seems to be a subtle difference between the adjectival form and the pronoun in use. As (9b) shows, personal pronouns have restrictions such as that they cannot be used for persons higher in position relative to the speaker. The sentence in (9a) is acceptable since the personal pronoun is used to indicate the younger brother of the speaker. Further, the use of the personal pronoun gives an unnecessary emphasis to the referent (cf. (7e)) and therefore may not be appropriate for an introductory expression, depending on circumstances. Consider the morphosyntactic difference in the two uses. By using the pronoun, the referent is treated as an entity and cited in the nominative case. The subject-predicate relation denotes the topic-comment relation. These particularities are omitted by using the adjectival form to indicate the person. Thus type of form can be taken as iconic of the relationship between the speaker and the referent. In contrast to the adjectival form, the personal pronoun may indicate a more distance-centered, neutral relationship between the speaker and the referent.

     It is also interesting to find that the proximal personal pronoun *meyaa* can be used to refer to the hearer himself like a second person pronoun.

(10)   meyaa   kau-də
          this person   who-Q
          'Who are you?'

The utterance has some restrictions: it is generally used when the addressee is not the only hearer at the moment of speech. It is not the case that the speaker addresses just a single addressee. The addressee circle includes several people, out of whom anybody can answer the question. It might be that the referent was not the intended addressee originally. This type of situation where there are a number of possibilities for the recipient of a speech event may be grasped by the concept Goffman (1981) introduced as "footing".

Such different participant roles are not lexicalized in Sinhala. Another context in which the personal pronoun *meyaa* is used to refer to the addressee is exemplified by (11):

(11) monəwa də, anee, kəra-nn-e meyaa?
 what Q dear do-NPT-FOC this person
 'What are you doing, my dear?'

The use of the proximal pronoun in this way indicates that the addressee is psychologically close to the speaker. Thus, person deixis is used both as a locating expression as well as for encoding participant roles in the discourse.

Next, 2P deixis, i.e. hearer-proximate relation, is illustrated by the following set of examples.

(12) a. oyə pattəree araŋ e-nnə, putaa
 that paper bring-IMP son
 '(My dear) son, bring that newspaper.'

 b. oyə paare ya-nnə epaa, kaṭu
 that way.LOC go-INF don't thorns
 'Don't go by that way; there are thorns.'

 c. ookə-ṭə tawə miris ṭikak daa-nnə
 that one-DAT more chilli a bit put-IMP
 'Add some more chilli to that one (pot).'

 d. oowa magul gedərə-ṭə araŋ y-nnə hadə-pu mal
 those wedding-DAT take-INF make-PTAD flowers
 'Those are the flowers made for taking to the wedding.'

 e. oyaa heṭa-t e-nəwa də
 you tomorrow-too come-IND Q
 'Will you come tomorrow, too?'

The Examples (12a) and (12b), with adjectival forms, and (12c) and (12d), respectively with singular and plural nominal forms, show that the referents are objects close to the hearer. The sentence (12e) is an example of the specialized use of the person deictic as a second person pronoun. It is never used as a third person pronoun which makes it intrinsically different from other members of the category of person deixis,. That is, *oyaa* is always used to denote the discourse role of addressee, not to locate a person.

Even an action can be located with respect to interlocutors, in terms of the proximal/distal parameter.

(13) itin mokədə oyə hati dama-nn-e?
 so why that breathe heavily-NPT-FOC
 'So why are you breathing heavily?'

(14) too kohe-də mee duwa-nn-e?
 you where-Q this run-NPT-FOC
 'Where are you (derogatory) running?'

That the speaker understands the action as occurring in the hearer's domain motivates the use of 2P in (13). On the contrary, in (14) the speaker seems to have put the hearer's action into his own domain, as depicted by the deixis of 1P, by virtue of grasping the action with his visual senses. The distinction reveals that determination of boundaries between the 1P ('*mee*') and the 2P ('*oyə*') depends not only on physical location, but also on the speaker's perspective or perceived distance.

1D deixis is used to indicate that the referents are away from both the speaker and the hearer, but in sight, in the following way.

(15) a. arə ʈii shəəʈ ekə kiiya də?
　　　　that t shirt one how much Q
　　　　'How much is that T shirt?'

     b. arəkə laabə də?
　　　　that one cheap Q
　　　　'Is that one over there cheap?'

     c. arəwa-ʈə waḍaa meewa honda-i
　　　　those-DAT than these good-AM
　　　　'These things are better than those things over there.'

     d. arəya kaudə?
　　　　that person who
　　　　'Who's that person over there?'

1D deixis can be ambiguous, though in a limited sense, indicating an immediate spatial context or a place away from the deictic center. Observe the directional term *areha* 'that way (direction)' in the following sentence.

(16) areha-ʈə ya-nnə
　　　that way-DAT GO-IMP
　　　'Go away.'

Through this imperative sentence, the addressee is ordered to move a little away albeit within the space of the speaker's sight, or, on the other hand, further away, out of the social space of the conversation.

2D deixis is controversially different in function from the three other demonstrative series. As the 'most distal' category, it seems to denote objects away from both speaker and hearer, and further out of sight. However, as an implication, we can take the form as denoting 'that (those) we are talking about' or 'that (those) in question' (Fairbank, Gair & De Silva 1981: 21). Another observation strongly rejects the deictic use of the category: "The *e*-forms, on the other hand, are never used in spatial terms and are restricted to anaphoric use" (Gair 1991a: 451). There are, however, some data that do not agree with this strong claim.

(17) (The speaker is asking someone sitting on the bench to make space.)
poḍḍAk   ehaa-ṭa   we-nnə
a little   there-DAT be-IMP
'Move a bit away.'

The form *ehaa* does indicate space. Contrary to the initial definition of 2D deixis, the space indicated in (17) is within the immediate speech situation. However, it is neutral with regard to the speaker-hearer axis.[3]

(18) (A householder is blaming a housemaid.)
ee   gedərə-ṭa-i   mee   gedərə-ṭai   gihin
that   house-DAT-too   this   house-DAT-too go-PP
kataa   kərə-kərə   in-nəwa misak ....
talk   do-do   be-IND except
'....apart from your going to this house and that house and just keeping on chatting.'

In this case *ee* and *mee* as well denote spaces in the physical environment but do not refer to a specific space. They are neutral with regard to the speaker-hearer axis. Their use is not anaphoric since the forms do not refer to objects linguistically introduced beforehand.

Of particular interest is the fact that the proximal *mee* and the distal *ee* are occurring in juxtaposition in (18), which does not seem to be accidental. When used in explicit opposition in this way, demonstrative expressions work as a distance-oriented system, i.e. being distinguished by the proximal-distal feature and not as a person-oriented system, i.e. not being distinguished by the speaker-hearer domain distinction. However, they express a range of distances, rather than signaling the actual distance. This distribution also shows how 2D deixis differs in function from the three other demonstrative series.

(19) a. læællə   ehaa-ṭa   mehaa-ṭa   wenəwa
        plank   there-DAT   here-DAT   be-IND
        'The plank moves here and there (is not stable).'

   b. ehe   mehe ya-nn-e   nætuwə in-nə
        there   here go-NPT-FOC   without be-IMP
        'Be (in this place) without going here and there.'

   c. atənə   metənə   tiə-pu-hamə   baḍu   næti   we-nəwa
        there   here   put-PTAD-when   things be   lost-IND
        'Things are lost when you put them here and there.'

   d. eyaa   ek-ak   kiə-nəwa;   meyaa   ekak   kiə-nəwa
        that person one-INDF   say-IND   this person one-INDF   say-IND
        'This person says one thing and that person says another.'

---

3. Gair's contention that this as an exceptional case might be right.

In all these examples the demonstrative expressions, used in juxtaposition, are neutral with regard to the speaker-hearer axis. Moreover, they are also neutral with regard to spatial distance: the forms do not necessarily signal the distance of the referents. Nor do they fulfill a specific identifying function, picking out each referent from a set of possible referents. The fact that the use of demonstratives in contrastive contexts, as in (19d), differs from their non-contrastive use is discussed in Wilkins 1999 and Margetts 2004.

However, an instance that shows how 2D deixis is not used for simply referring to something previously introduced in the discourse and that it is therefore not anaphoric is given below.

(20) a. mokaddə   ee   sadde?
         what.Q   that   sound
         'What's that sound?'

    b   mokaddə   ee   æhe-nn-e?
         what.Q   that   hear-NPT-FOC
         'What's that we hear?'

As (20) shows, non-visual stimulus sources such as sound and smell are signaled by the *ee* form even when they were not linguistically introduced to the discourse.

3.2 Acknowledging function

Rather than signaling a precise distance, 2D deixis is frequently used to fulfill an acknowledging function which involves 'presupposing' the ground or the point of reference against which a referent is associated, according to Fillmore (1982).

(21) A: polee   eləwəlu   ganaŋ   də?
         fair.LOC   vegetables expensive Q
         'Are the vegetables expensive at the fair?'

    B: ee   taram   ganaŋ   næe
         that   extent   expensive   no
         'No, not so expensive.'

(22) A: hungak   durə   də
         a lot   far   Q
         'Is it very far?'

    B: echchərə   durə   næe
         so   far   not
         'Not so far.'

In these examples B presupposes that A asks the question assuming that the vegetables are expensive (21) and that it is very far (22). Accordingly B uses a deictic expression of degree to negate A's assumption. One may argue that this is an anaphoric use. But B's response is not so much to a linguistically established fact as to a presupposed fact. Further, the deictic expression does not convey the exact degree or distance but signals a subjective measure of the given attribute. We have shown that 2D deixis is mostly neutral with regard to spatial distance. This may be correlated to the fact that this distal demonstrative series is predominantly of anaphoric use, which will be illustrated later. The preceding examples given in (18 &19) and (21 &22) also show that 2D deixis involves discourse-related notions such as individuation and specificity. A closer look at the examples reveals that the state of affairs they express lack individuation and specificity.

3.3   Informing function

Deixis also has an informing function. The informing function provides information about the location of the referent. Such deictic expressions are used when the speaker wants to tell the hearer where the particular referent is, or when presenting something to the hearer. Presentatives are prototypical deictic expressions used for the informing function. Only *mennə*, the most proximate presentative, is used as an actual presentative, i.e. when the speaker hands something to the hearer. This is naturally bound with the proximality which is an essential condition for presentation. This also explains why the most distal series, i.e. 2D, does not have a presentative form. The following examples are illustrative (The presentatives, lacking appropriate English glosses, are indicated in italics):

(23) a. mennə   putaa-ʈa-t   salli
         mennə   son-DAT-too   money
         'Here you are, son, some money to you, too.'

    b.   onnə   yaturə
         onnə   key
         'Here you go, take the key.'

The example in (23a) represents a situation in which the speaker politely hands money to the addressee. The utterance in (23b), on the other hand, may indicate a situation involved with lack of empathy or with anger where the speaker leaves the key on a table or throws it at the recipient. These deictic expressions are usually accompanied by appropriate gestures accordingly.

   Presentatives are also used to demonstrate something.

(24) a. (The interlocutors are walking in the zoo.)
         mennə   akke   monəru
         mennə   elder sister.VOC   peacocks
         'Here are the peacocks, elder sister.'

    b.   annə   paraale   udə   mii-ek
         annə   rafter   on   rat-INDF
         'Look, there's a rat on the rafter.'

c. (The interlocutors have been waiting for the bus.)
   annə bas ekə e-nəwa
   annə bus one come-IND
   'Here it is, the bus's coming.'

Apart from their presentative use, demonstrative pronouns which are primarily used for identifying are also used to achieve an informing function.

(25) a. arə   tie-nn-e   miris   paatti-ak
         that   be-NPT-FOC   chilli patch-INDF
         'That one (over there) is a patch of chilli plants.'

   b. mee   in-n-e   monəru
       this   be-NPT-FOC   peacocks
       'Here are the peacocks.'

As the examples in (25a) and (25b) show, different deictic forms are used to point to a referent, signaling to the addressee to focus attention on it.

Since the *arə* form indicates something in sight, it is also used to point out something, as in (26).

(26) a. mokaddə   arə   atənə   dilise-nn-e?
         what-Q   that   there   shine-NPT-FOC
         'What is that over there shining?'

   b. arə,   miniha   atə   wanə-nəwa
       there   man   hand   wave-IND
       'There, he is waving (to us).'

   c. arə,   arə,   pol gahee   karəṭiə-ṭə   uḍin,   needə   taatte
       there,   there,   coconut tree-LOC   top-DAT   above   isn't it father
       'There, dad, it is above the top of the coconut tree, isn't it?'

Though homophonic with the adjectival forms, the deictic expressions in these examples occur as attention-drawing exclamations rather than attributively. By its repetition as in (26c) the form can express the speaker's excitement or surprise.

3.4 Expressive function

We might also add the expressive function (Popper 1972 and Leech 1983) to the function-based analysis of deictic expressions. This aspect of deictic expressions is also described as the "affective" use. The deictic expressions of the 2P series can be used with affective meaning, which conveys the speaker's subjective evaluation of some particular reference entity including negative or derogatory overtones.

(27) a. oyə   tie nə   kaḍee-k-in   arən   e-nna
         that   be-NPT   shop-INDF-ABL   buy.PP   come-IMP
         'Buy and bring it from whatever shop available.'

b. oyə baaldiə aiŋ kərə gan-nəwa
   that bucket remove.PP take-IND
   'Remove that bucket.'

c. oyə kataawə aye paarak ma-ge kanə-ṭə æhun-ot
   that talk next time.INDF I-GEN ear-DAT hear.PAST-COND
   umbe oluwə pələ-nəwa
   your (derogatory) head split-IND
   'If I hear that word again, I'll split your head.'

The distance indicated by the 2P deictic is not strictly spatial, as shown by these examples. Rather, the sense of distance is used metaphorically to indicate the speaker's psychological distance (27a), dislike (27b) and anger (27c). This is in accordance with the cross-linguistic tendency of signaling empathy, or lack of empathy through the concept of distance (Brown and Levinson 1987: 205; Fillmore 1982: 44).

Although different communicative functions were treated separately here, there is no clear-cut form-function isomorphy regarding deictic expressions. One and the same form can be used to perform different communicative functions, and different forms are used to indicate the same referent.

The same form can be used irrespective of the relative distance of the reference.

(28)   (The two interlocutors are helping a small child to walk to the school.)
       Kamani mee atə alla ga-nnə, mamə mee atə alla ga-nnam
       Kamani this hand hold-IMP I this hand hold-OPT
       'Kamani, you hold this hand and I'll hold that hand.'

Given that the two proximal deictics refer to the two hands of the child and that the two interlocutors involved are not in the same position, the relative distance of the referents with regard to the speaker-hearer axis cannot be the same. Nevertheless, the same 1D deictic is used by the speaker. The crucial point here might be the speaker's subjective position relative to the referent rather than the actual distance per se.

Two different deictic forms may combine together to express an admixture of functions if they represent the same deictic property. A proximal or distal deictic form combines with another deictic that also signals proximity or distance in the following way.

(29) a. onnə oyə kabəḍ ek-en tia-nnə
        onnə that cupboard one-ABL put-IMP
        'Leave it in that cupboard.'

     b. annə arə leḍaa-ge seelain bootələyə galəwə-nəwa needə
        annə that patient-GEN saline bottle remove-IND aren't they
        'Look, they are removing the saline bottle from that patient, aren't they?'

In (29a) two 2P deictics are combined, conveying the speaker's casual attitude, while in (29b) two 1D deictics, distal presentative and distal demonstrative, are used together, thereby adding presentative/directive force into the informing function. Different deictic expressions are thus combined together to express meanings linked with different tiers.

4. Locative expressions

There seems to be some form-function isomorphy regarding alternative forms. This can be seen in the functional difference between alternate locative expressions of the 2P series (Kano, 1994). Sinhala has two demonstrative terms for location within each series (See Table 2). The two forms for the 2P series with the stem vowel 'o-': *otənə* and *ohee*, differ in distribution with respect to the feature 'specificity'. For instance, *otənə* denotes a specific place while *ohee* indicates a vague place. When someone gives a direction to another person to dig a hole in a specific place on the ground, for example, he may say something like (30). The use of *ohe* is unacceptable in this context.

(30) otənə/*ohee wala-k kappa-nnə
     there   hole-INDF cut-IMP
    'Dig a hole there (in the place you are standing).'

Ohe can be used to denote a vague place in the following way.

(31) A: koo malli?
        where younger brother
        'Where's your younger brother?'

     B: ohee/*otənə hiṭia
        there   was
        'He was around.'

The same unspecific form is used to suggest the speaker's attitude of indifference towards, or dislike of, the reference entity.

(32) A: loku putaa koo?
        big   son   where
        'Where's the elder son?'

     B: onnə ohee in-n-e
        onnə there be-NPT-FOC
        'He's just around.'

B's answer carries a negative evaluation of the whereabouts of the indicated person, sounding as if he is doing nothing and just exists without a clear direction or purpose.[4] The 2P expressions, in particular those marked with the phonological features of *o-h*, are

---

4. In Sinhala *ohee innəwa* 'just being there' has developed as a humble greeting analogous to the English 'I'm fine', given in response to 'How are you?'.

metaphorically used to encode the speaker's perspective and lack of empathy. They have taken on special semantic features implying that the participant is idling his time away.

5. Demonstratives as discourse deictic

We have already mentioned in passing how primary deixis is used metaphorically to signal the speaker's emotional and attitude-wise distance. The spatiotemporal and participant dimensions of primary deixis are often metaphorically extended into new uses, mapping with textual and thematic dimensions. These secondary uses of deictics include locating referents in the text, determining the information status of different elements of the discourse, and establishing the thematic status of participants in the discourse.

While the whole discourse is metaphorically viewed as a spatial entity having directions and a trajectory, etc., its various parts related to the text and the textual content have to be properly indexed by deictics, in a way that the interlocutors can track the information flow. Using such a reference schema, the interlocutors may connect prior parts of the text as well as upcoming text, integrating what has already been established in the discourse and, sometimes, even what will appear in the future discourse, into the text meaningfully. Therefore, discourse deictics play a crucial role in information tracking in the ongoing discourse.

5.1 Anaphoric use

In Sinhala, while all four series of demonstratives play the dual role of spatial deictics and discourse deictics, the *e*-series of 2D in particular is widely used for discourse reference. This has led Gair (1991) to consider that the forms of the *e*-series are specialized in the anaphoric function and their primary domain of reference is code-message. One can see how spatial deictics and discourse deictics interplay to create a cohesive text in the following dialogues.

(33) (A conversation between a child and his uncle when they visit a sanctuary.)
 A: arə mokeddə, baappe?
   that what(anim.).Q uncle
   'What's that (over there), uncle?'

 B: ee sarpə-ek, putaa
   that snake-INDF son
   'That's a snake, son.'

(34) A. arə tie-nn-e miris paatti-ak
   that be-NPT-FOC chilli patch-INDF
   'That one (over there) is a patch of chilli plants.'

B. ee   paatti-e   tie-nn-e   miris   pælə   witərak   də?
    that patch-LOC   be-NPT-FOC chilli plants only   Q
    'Are there only chilli plants in that patch?'

A's utterance presents a question in (33) referring to an animal and contains a statement in (34) referring to an object, both of which are indicated by the adjectival form of 1D, the spatial deictic *ara*, signaling the referent is located away from both the speaker and the hearer. Typically the response is not given with the same form. B's response has the word *ee* from the 2D series, which is neutral with regard to speaker or hearer or spatial distance. This is an example of anaphoric deictics, which helps us to look back in the text and link the reference point with the referents in the prior co-text. The interlocutors are guided by these signposts to refer to prior parts of the text and correctly follow the discourse.

The *me-* series demonstratives of 1P may also occur as signposts for referent tracking. The following two sentences that constitute a part of a narrative are illustrative:

(35) a. mee   daruwa   loku   we-nnə   we-nnə
         this child   big   become-INF   become-INF
         tawat bohomə   pudumə   wædə   kəlaa
         more   very   wonderful work   do.PAST
         'The more the boy grew up, the more wonderful things he did.'

    b. mee   lamea-ge   pudumə   wædə   gænə   ratee   minissu
        this child-GEN   wonderful jobs   about country.LOC people
        kataa unaa
        talk.PAST
        'The people of the country talked about the wonderful things the child did.'

The two sentences appear towards the end of the narrative. The narrator adds them after telling about a series of heroic acts done by a child. The adjectival form *mee* of the 1P demonstrative, used with a noun, refers back to the hero of the story and signals the continuation of the previously established discourse topic. The particular deictic not only helps the listeners track the discourse referent in terms of thematic status but also implies, by virtue of its proximal feature, some empathy or a kind of identification of the narrator with the particular participant in the narrated event. This can be contrasted with the use of the adjectival form *ee* of the 2D demonstrative.

(36) issərə   ekə   kælææwakə   chuuti   kurulu   ranchuw-ak   hitia
     before   one   forest.INDF.LOC tiny   birds   flock-INDF   was
     'There once was a flock of tiny birds in a forest.'

     ee   kælææwə   langə   kumbur-ak   tibuna
     that   forest   near   rice-field-INDF was
     'There was a rice-field close to the forest.'

(37) issərə   weeyan-ţə   gewal   tibun-e   næǣ
     before   white-ants-DAT   houses   be.PT-FOC   no
     'Before, white-ants didn't have their own houses.'

   un   hiţi-e   diraapu   gas-wələ   witərai
   they   be.PT-FOC   decay.PTAD   trees-LOC   FM
   'It is only in decayed trees that they lived.'

   dawəs-ak   weeyeku-ţə   badəgini   we-laa
   day-INDF   white-ant.INDF-DAT   hungry   be-PP
   kǣǣmə   soya-nnə   giyaa
   food   search-INF   GO.PAST
   'One day a white-ant felt hungry and went out in search of food.'

   ee   welaawe-mə   wæssə-ku-t   paţan gatta
   that   time-EMPH   rain.INDF-too   begin.PAST
   'Exactly at that time it began to rain.'

(38) dawəs-ak   sinhə-ek   taman-ge   guhaawe   nidaa genə   hiţia
     day-INDF   lion-INDF   self-GEN   den.LOC   sleep.PP   was
     'One day a lion was sleeping in his den.'
     ....

   ee   sinhaya   iiţə   passe   ekə   dawəsəkə   kælee
   that   lion   after   that   one   day.INDF.LOC   jungle.LOC
   goduru   hoyaagenə   giyaa
   prey   search.PP   GO.PAST
   'Then, one day the lion wandered off the jungle in search of prey.'

In (36) the adjectival form *ee* of the 2D demonstrative with the noun stands in relation of anaphora; it relates back to the antecedent phrase *ekə kælæǣwəkə* 'in a forest' mentioned in the previous sentence. In (37) the adjectival form *ee* of the 2D demonstrative with the word *welaawe* 'at the time' and the emphatic marker refers back to the time when the white-ant went out in search of food mentioned in the previous line. In (38) the adjectival form *ee* of the 2D demonstrative with the accompanied noun refers back to the lion mentioned in the previous discourse. The selection of the particular demonstrative series, i.e. with the distal perspective, has allowed the narrators to tell the narrative with a detached attitude, without any identification with the discourse referents. An associated fact that must be added here is that the demonstrative *oyə* of the 2P series will be more appropriate if the narrator wants to suggest that the discourse participants in the narrated event behave with dislike or resentment towards the indicated object, person, or action. This correlates with the distanced subjective attitude towards the referent or the addressee expressed by the spatial deictic of the proximal demonstrative based on the notion of hearer-proximality, as discussed in the previous section.

Another distal series (1D), *arə*, which indexes information more neutral with respect to the speaker and hearer, is also commonly used for anaphoric reference. The antecedents may denote participants, events or things. In fact, there are certain pragmatic constraints or contexts where the demonstrative is acceptable: the 1D deictics are only allowed when the interlocutors or discourse participants have mutually established the referent in their memory, i.e. they should be familiar with the topic of the discourse.

(39) a. **arəkə**   genaawa   də?
       that one   bring.PAST   Q
       'Did you bring it?'

   b. **arə**   **kataawə**   kaa-ʈə-wat   kiya-nnə   epaa
       that   story   whom-DAT-even   tell-INF   don't
       'Don't tell that story to anybody.'

(40) a. anik   keləwərə   **arə**   **maha**   unə   **pandurə**   waʈə kərə-la   bænda
       other   end   that   big   bamboo   bush   round-PP   tie-PAST
       '(They) tied the other end (of the creeper) round the big bamboo bush.'

   b. **arə**   **edaa**   panə   beera   genə   giə   miiya
       that   that   day   life   save.take.PP   go.PT   rat

       duwə genə   aawa
       run.take.PP   come.PAST
       'The rat that had run away saving his life the other day appeared there soon.'

(41) A. Piyaseeli   oyaa   piyaanoo   gaha-nnə   dan-nəwa   də?
       Piyaseeli   you   piano   play-INF   know-IND   Q
       'Piyaseeli, do you know how to play the piano?'

   B: **ee** mokaddə?
       '(Piano?) What's that?'

   A: æi,   **arə**   api   sindu   gahanə   ekə.
       yeah   that   we   songs   play   one
       'Yeah, the one we play songs.'

In (39a) and (39b) the demonstratives refer to something with which the interlocutors are familiar. In (40a) and (40b) the demonstratives are used, respectively, to refer to an object and a participant previously mentioned in the narrated event. When the interlocutor A in (41) asks a question about the piano, B does not hide her feeling of surprise and her ignorance of the object; she distances herself from the object with the distal (2D) demonstrative *ee*. However, A is quick to remind her that they have played the instrument before: the use of *arə* implies that they are talking about something which they had been involved in earlier, not about something unheard of or strange.

5.2 Other uses of discourse deixis

The *arə* form of the 1D deixis can be used to imply a strong emotional attachment to the referent. This is analogous to the Japanese use of the *a-* series demonstrative

(Kuroda 1992: 91–104). The following is an excerpt from a conversation occurring between a patient and a visitor at a hospital.

(42)   A.   dostərə   mahatwəru   særə   də?
            doctor   gentlemen   strict Q
            'Are the doctors strict?'

       B: næӕ   næӕ ...
            no   no
            'No, never, ...'

       A: mama-t   aasa-i   mehemə   waaṭṭUwə-kə
            I-too   fond-AM   like this   ward-INDF.LOC
            dawəs-ak   dek-ak   in-nə
            day-INDF   two-INDF   be-INF
            'I, too, would like to spend one or two days in a ward like this.'

       B: ou   eekə   puduməy-ak   yæ?
            yes   that   wonder-INDF   isn't it
            arə   gedərə   ayə   wagee   dan-nə   andunə-nə   ayə
            that   home   people   like   know-NPT   know-NPT   people
            næti   unaa-ṭə,   dawəs-ak   dek-ak   in-nə   koṭə
            no   be.PAST-DAT   day-INDF   two-INDF   be-NPT   when
            nikammə   gedərə   wagee   purudu   we-nəwa
            without effort   home   like   get   used-IND
            'Yeah, no wonder. Although there are no people so close to you as your kith and kin at home, still you'll get used and feel at home automatically when you spend one or two days there.'

Although the speaker B attempts to evaluate the friendly atmosphere of the hospital and the easiness with which one can get used to it, the use of the demonstrative *arə* signals his emotional attachment to the people at home. The demonstrative in this case does not show any connection with an earlier statement or antecedent word or phrase; its use is rather motivated by a common human knowledge that allows us to presuppose the comfort one feels at home surrounded by people with whom one is connected by family relationship. This again correlates with the acknowledging function of spatial deictics pointed out by Fillmore (1982).

The locative form *ohe* of the 2P deixis is used to encode the non-attention of the speaker to a third participant. Observe the following dialogue.

(43)   A: amme,   annə   Sunil   ambə   kaḍə-nəwa
            mother   annə   Sunil   mango   pluck-IND
            'Mom, look, Sunil is plucking mangoes there.'

B: ohe   kaḍə-puwaawe
   there   pluck-PERM
   'Just let him pluck.'

In B's response the locative form *ohe* used with the permissive from of the verb has nothing to do with space. By using the presentative form of the 1D deixis, the speaker A has already indicated that Sunil's action is taking place away from both the interlocutors. The speaker B uses the *ohe* form to communicate to A his inner attitude. The *ohe* form signals 'just ignore it.'

5.3 Cataphoric use

Demonstratives are also used for cataphoric reference. Fillmore (1982) has suggested that perhaps most frequently a +proximal deictic will be used for text-referring cataphora, and a –proximal deictic for text-referring anaphora. Partially proving this prediction, in Sinhala the –proximal deictic is used anaphorically, as already shown, and the +proximal deictic *mee* is used either cataphorically or anaphorically. The following example, an excerpt from a school textbook, illustrates the use of the demonstrative *mee* as a spatial deictic, as a backward looking device, i.e. anaphorically, and as a forward-looking device, i.e. cataphorically.

(44) mamə   adə   **mee**   laməin-ṭə   bala-nnə
     I   today   this   children-DAT   see-INF

   pintuurə pot-ak   genaawa
   picture   book-INDF   bring.PAST

   mee   **pintuurə** **potee**   tie-nn-e   katandərə
   this   picture   book.LOC   be-NPT-FOC   stories

   api   issərə   welaamə   pintuurə   bal-mu
   we   first   of all   pictures   see-HORT

   lamai   pintuurə   bæluwa
   children   pictures   see.PAST

   pasuwə   gurutumii   **mee**   katandərəya   kiiwa
   later   teacher   this   story   tell.PAST
   ...

   'Today I brought a picture book for these children to read. This picture book has stories. First, let's see the pictures. The children looked at the pictures. Then the teacher told this story. ...'

The first *me-* series demonstrative (*mee*) is used as a spatial deictic since the teacher addresses the children in the class before her. The second *me-* series demonstrative can be taken as used both spatially and anaphorically: the picture book is deictically located in the speaker's domain when she introduces it to the children, and the deictic expression simultaneously refers back to the picture book the speaker has already mentioned in the discourse. The third *me-* series demonstrative refers forward to the subsequent discourse, the story the speaker is going to tell, and the text continues with the narrative. Thus, the same speaker-centered demonstrative is used both anaphorically and cataphorically, referring to a previously introduced discourse topic or introducing an upcoming text.

6. Encoding discourse units

A crucial point to note regarding the example in (44) is that the cataphoric deictic is identified, not just with a word or phrase that follows, but with a story, a larger upper-level discourse topic that follows. Notice this text is structured as consisting of, at least, two different subtopical units, rather than having a single, central topic running through the text. This correctly points to the fact that the discourse reference of a deictic does not necessarily relate to a lexical item but may refer to an entity of textual information larger than the content of a word or phrase. How deictics metalinguistically refer to discourse units, i.e. larger segments of discourse, can be understood by observing the deictic features in (45) below.

(45) dawəs-ak   sinhə-ek   taman-ge   guhaawe   nidaa genə   hiṭia
      day-INDF   lion-INDF self-GEN   den.LOC   sleep.PP   was
      'One day a lion was sleeping in his den.'
      ....
      miiya   yantam   panə   beeragenə   giyaa
      rat   finally life   save.REF.PP go.PAST
      'The rat finally went away by saving his own life.'

      ee   sinhaya   iiṭə   passe   ekə   dawəsakə   kælee
      that   lion   after   that   one   day.INDF.LOC   jungle.LOC
      goduru   hoyaagenə   giyaa
      prey   search.PP   go.PAST
      'Then, one day the lion wandered off the jungle in search of prey.'

      [edaa   uu   lanu-wəlin   kələ   dælək-in   saadə-pu
      that day   it   string-PL.DAT make.PT   net-INDF-INS   made-PTAD
      ugulakə-ṭə   asu unaa
      trap.INDF-DAT   be caught.PAST
      'On that day it got caught in a trap made from a net of strings.'

      kælee   siṭiə   satun   bohoo   denek   æwit
      jungle.LOC   be.PT   animals   many   ones   come.PP
      sinhaya   beera ga-nnə   hæduwa
      lion   save-INF   try.PAST
      'Many of the animals who were in the jungle came and tried to save the lion.'

ee	wunaaʈə	beera ga-nnə	bæri	unaa
but		save-INF	unable	be.PAST

'But they couldn't save it.']

mee	**kaləbələyə**	æhila	**arə**	**edaa**	**panə**	**beera genə**	**giə**	**miiya**
this	commotion	hear.PP	that	that day	life	save.REF.PP	go.PT	rat

duwə genə	æwit	ee	dælə	kapə-la	sinhaya	beeruwa
running	come.PP	that	net	cut-PP	lion	save.PAST

'**The rat that had run away to save his life on the other day**, after hearing **this commotion**, appeared there soon and saved the lion by biting through the net.'

While there are several deictic expressions used in the text, some of which having already been discussed, we will restrict the discussion to the underlined expressions appearing in the last section of the narrative. Mainly, the focus will be on the adjectival *mee* of the 1P demonstrative attributively used with the noun *kaləbələyə* 'commotion'. If it stands in a relation of anaphora to the co-text, what is the antecedent it relates back to? There is no noun or noun phrase with which it can be identified anaphorically, or cataphorically for that matter. However, there is an information unit already introduced and also inferred from the co-text to which the present linguistic text relates: this is the segment shown in brackets in the text. The series of events including the lion's getting caught in a trap, the animals' gathering and their attempts to rescue the lion, and their failure is abstracted from the previous text, paraphrased as *kaləbələyə* 'commotion' and brought into the foreground by the proximal deictic of *mee*. Thus the referent of the demonstrative expression is to be identified from the previous discourse unit. The deictic form contrasts with the distal form *arə*, appearing on the same line of the text which is used to reintroduce an old participant, the rat. The *arə* form is of recognitional use here, indicating that the listener is able to identify the referent based on specific shared knowledge (Diessel 1999: 91).

As we have seen, the exophoric or situataional deixis indexes entities in the text setting or in the participant framework, while the endophoric or discourse deixis links text and co-text through anaphoric and cataphoric uses and brings new participants into the discourse or reintroduces old ones. For the sake of exposition, we have treated exophoric deixis and endophoric deixis separately. In the actual discourse, the two types of deictics co-occur, with different functions intersecting.

(46) A:

arə	bala-nnə,	aiye,		ahasə	diha	wisaalə	ran	tæʈi-ak
that	look-INF	elder brother		sky	at	big	gold	plate-INDF

'Elder brother, there, look at the sky, a big gold plate!'

B:

ohomə	tamai,	nangi,	wesak	pooyə-ʈə
such	FM	younger sister	Vesak	full moon day-DAT

paayə-nə	handə
rise-NPT	moon

'Younger sister, **such** is the moon rising on the Vesak full moon day.'

A: aiye,   api pansal   giyaa-ʈə   passe
   elder brother we   temple   go.PAST-DAT   after
   ya-mu-də   toraŋ   bala-nnə
   go-HORT-Q   decoration   see-INF
   'Elder brother, after going to temple, shall we go to see the Vesak festival decorations?'

B: <u>ehemə</u> naŋ amma-gen   aha-mu
   so   if   mother-ABL   ask-HORT
   'In that case let's (first) get mom's permission.'

The demonstrative *arə*, with distal sense, is clearly a spatial and situational deictic. The use of *ohomə*, though with some speaker-hearer linkage, is anaphoric: it relates back to what A said, and is hence a hearer-based form. Next time, the speaker B uses the distal deictic *ehemə* with anaphoric reference to 'going to see the Vesak festival decorations' seemingly found earlier in prior text; being neutral with regard to participant framework or situation, it is endophoric.

7. Tracking the thematic flow of discourse

The deictic frame of reference, including the information status of participants and the thematic structure of the content, constantly keeps changing as the discourse progresses. Further, since the discourse may consist of several segments such as thematically related subtopics or episodes, certain linguistic devices, whether deictic or non-deictic in nature, are indispensable for tracking the information flow of the discourse. In Sinhala, presentative demonstratives are used for such functions as topic continuation, topic changes or cross-boundary topical movement.

(47) onnə   aayet   dawəsəkə   amma-ʈa-i   taatta-ʈa-i
     that   again   day.INDF.LOC   mother-DAT-too   father-DAT-too
     kumbure   wædə kəra-nnə   ya-nnə oonæ unaa
     rice-field.LOC   work-INF   go-INF want be.PAST
     'Then, again, one day the father and the mother wanted to go to work at the rice-field.'

(48) onnə api dæn in-n-e   Anuradhapura-e
     that we   now be-NPT-FOC Anuradhapura-LOC
     '**Here we are!** Now we are at Anuradhapura.'

In (47) the presentative is used to facilitate the progress of the discourse even when little new information is introduced, signaling that the repetition of the same event occurs as a necessary step of the narrative event. The sentence in (48) is an utterance by one of the interlocutors going on a bus tour. The presentative marks a clearly delineated topical boundary, indicating that they have arrived in a new place, thereby grounding the discourse to the frame of reference and linking it to the new setting.

The use of the hearer-based *onnə* in these sentences can also be taken as an example of shifted deixis which occurs when the narrator's space and time interfere with the space and time of the narrative (Bril 2004). With the shifted deixis, the event is narrated as if it were happening at the time of speaking, before the very eyes of the listener.

We have seen how discourse deictics direct the thematic flow of the discourse. In a prototypical case, a specific participant is introduced as central to the discourse topic by means of a full noun, and is tracked at the local level cohesively (Chafe 1987, 1994; Lambrecht 1994). Key devices to track thematic participants include pronouns, demonstratives, and zero anaphora. The preferred marking for the thematic participant of the discourse topic in Sinhala is zero anaphora. In the colloquial language, in particular, zero anaphora is a signal of the continuation of the current topic, and the tendency toward overt marking is followed in more formal literary styles. The following excerpt from a written narrative shows how the uninterrupted discourse topic extends over several lines while simply being marked by zero anaphora.

(49) 1. iisərə   ekə   kælææwəkə   chuuṭi   kurulu   ranchuw-ak   hiṭia
        before   one   forest.INDF.LOC   tiny   birds   flock-INDF   was
        'There once was a flock of tiny birds in a forest.'

   2. ee   kælææwə   langə   kumburak   tibuna
       that forest   near   rice-field-INDF   was
       'There was a rice-field close to the forest.'

   3. kurulu   ranchuwə   mee   kumburə-ṭə   e-nəwa
       bird   flock   this   rice-field-DAT   come-IND
       'The flock of birds comes to the rice-field.'

   4. **un**   kumburə-ṭə   e-nn-e   kumbur-e   tie-nə
       they   rice-field-DAT   come-NPT-FOC   rice-field-LOC   be-NPT
       wii   kanna-i
       paddy   eat-INF-AM
       'It is to eat paddy there that **they** come to the rice-field.'

   5. (ø) wii   ka-kaa   ində-la   hawas   unaamə
       paddy   eat-eat   be-PP   late afternoon   be.PAST.TEMP
       ø kælææwə   pættə-ṭə   igilii   ya-nəwa
       forest   direction-DAT   fly.PP   go-IND
       'They would be there eating paddy and fly off towards the forest when it is late in the afternoon.'

   6. ø aayet   pahuwədaa   udee-ṭa-t   wii   ka-nnə
       again   next day   morning-DAT-too   paddy   eat-INF
       kumburəṭə   enəwa
       rice-field-DAT   come-IND
       'Again, they come to the paddy-field to eat paddy next morning.'

7. ø mehemə   hæmədaamə   æwit   wii   kææwa
   this way   everyday   come-PP   paddy   eat.PAST
   'In this way they came and ate paddy everyday.'

8. kumbure   tie-nə   wii   ʈikə ʈikə   adu wennə
   paddy-field-LOC   be-NPT   paddy   little by little   decrease-INF
   paʈan gatta
   begin.PAST
   'Little by little, the paddy in the paddy-field began to become smaller in amount.'

The thematic participant is introduced in the first sentence by a noun phrase with an indefinite marker as a new topic, as *chuuʈi kurulu ranchuwak* 'a flock of tiny birds'. After introducing a new subtopic related to the main topic with the anaphoric demonstrative *ee* in the second sentence, an event relating the subtopic (identified by *mee*) to the main topic is narrated in the third sentence. Sentence 4 presents additional information relating to the event depicted in the previous sentence, rather than continuing the series of events.[5] The focus construction which identifies this additional information status triggers the use of the pronoun *un* whose feature specifies the semantic category of animals. The thematic participant of sentences 5, 6, and 7, all continuing the same topic with a series of events is marked by anaphoric zero. Like a pronoun, which is identified from a preceding or following phrase, an ellipsis typically relies either on the context in which a sentence is uttered or on some word or words preceding within the sentence. The listener/reader easily identifies the agent of these events with the main protagonist already established in the narrative.[6]

However, even when there is neither a change in the thematic participant nor a sign of entering a new episode anaphoric pronouns or full noun phrases can still be used if the discourse topic is interrupted by some discursive force.

(50)
1. dawəs-ak   **koʈi**   **raaləhaami**-ʈə   hondəʈəmə   badəgini   unaa
   day-INDF   tiger   master-DAT   very much   hungry   be.PAST
   'One day **Master Tiger** was very hungry.'

---

5. In describing the birds' coming to the rice-field the writer has repeatedly used the word *kumburə* 'rice-field' in sentence 3 and 4. This might be because the written text is meant for children. However, the present author believes that the word *kumburəʈə* in sentence 4 is redundant and can be omitted without any harm to the thematic flow.

6. The change in time reference, the shift from the past tense to the present tense and again from the present to the past, shows obvious deictic functions. However, we do not intend to extend the discussion to this area.

2. dæn   naŋ   irə   eliya-t   aḍu-i,   ræe   we-nna-t   langa-i
   now   TOP   sun   light-too   less-AM   night be-INF-too   close-AM
   kohe hari   gihin   kæǣmak   soyaa gan-nə   oonæ
   wherever   go.PP   food.INDF   search.INF   want

   'Now there's less sunlight; soon it'll get dark; going wherever possible, I need to find some food.'

3. mehemə   hitə-la   **koṭi**   **raaləhaami**   nægiṭə-laa   hemin   hemin
   this way think-PP   tiger   master   stand up-PP   slowly   slowly
   gal guhaaw-en   eliya-ṭə   aawa
   cave-ABL   outside-DAT   COM.PAST

   'Thinking so, **Master Tiger** stood up and slowly came out from the cave.'

Despite the fact that the continuation of the current discourse topic is obvious, the same thematic participant has been indicated by the full noun phrase in sentence 3 as it was in sentence 1. However, one can observe that the narration given in sentences 1 and 3 was interrupted by some complex information given in the sentence 2 in the form of a direct speech expressing the protagonist's thoughts and feelings. This goes to prove that the overt marking of discourse topic is acceptable or rather necessary to regulate the flow of information in the overall discourse after an inner monologue or direct speech.

CHAPTER 13

Pragmatics and grammar

Pragmatics as the subject of this chapter includes both aspects of sociopragmatics, i.e. discourse as social interaction as well as pragmalinguistics, i.e. the more linguistic aspects of discourse. These terms refer to the meanings of utterances that cannot easily be conveyed by individual lexical items or by the semantics of individual clause-level structures. First we will analyze some grammatical categories like modality, interrogation, and negation, which are important in terms of the pragmatic force of utterances. Social deixis and honorifics will be another area to be discussed.

1. Modality

Modality is one of the most context-sensitive grammatical features incorporating speaker-based or hearer-based felicity conditions. There are different types of modality, such as speech-act centered, agent-oriented, and epistemic modality. The acquisition of basic concepts underlying these notions remains a prerequisite for the acquisition of language in general.

1.1 Imperative mood

Speech-act centered modality can be realized through the imperative mood. Imperative verbs are used to achieve the social goal of getting things done by ordering, asking, demanding, or begging in a situation where the illocutionary function may remain competitive. Depending on the particular situation and the nature of the speaker-hearer relation involved, a speaker tends to select an appropriate imperative form from options available with varying degrees of directness and politeness.

The ordinary imperative verb form with affirmative sense is homophonous with the infinitive form.[1] Affirmative imperatives are followed by the negative particle *epaa* to give the negative sense.

---

1. Bolinger (1977:152–82) has provided evidence for the syntactic and semantic identity of the imperative and the infinitive.

Affirmative imperatives
udə balannə 'look up'
meekə adinnə 'pull this'
ʈikak hinaawennə 'smile'
(Lit. 'Laugh a bit')

Negative imperatives
udə balannə epaa 'Don't look up'
meekə adinnə epaa 'Don't pull this'
hinaawennə eppa 'Don't laugh'

The form serves as the standard use for directives;[2] it cannot be considered to have grammaticalized as an indicator of social deictic information. For instance, the same form, when used with an honorific pronoun or a polite title of address, turns out to be in the respectful grade.

(1) obətumaa ya-nnə
 you(honorific) go-IMP
 'Will you please go.' or 'You may go.'

(2) mahatteya ætulə-ʈə e-nnə
 gentleman inside-DAT come-IMP
 'Please come in, Sir.'

Imperative clauses in Sinhala can be considered as representing three different grades: (a) respectful (b) ordinary and (c) disrespectful, though there are no clear-cut grammatical devices corresponding to all of them. Within each grade, there are further different degrees of respect, politeness or indirectness. Using an optionality scale, different forms are employed to suit the social status of participants and to maintain the appropriate level of politeness. One such means to indicate extreme respect is adding a word meaning 'good' to the end of the imperative form. However, there are further lexical devices to increase the degree of respect towards an addressee which are used in combination with imperative verb forms, as in the following examples:

(3) obə wahanse issella waḍi-nnə hondai.
 you (honorific) before go(honorific)-IMP good
 'Will you please go ahead (and we'll walk behind you).'

(4) baləsampannə dewiraajayan wahansə saturu
 powerful king of gods (honorific address) enemy
 uwəduru-walin magee puttaa araksaa kərə denu mænəwi
 dangers-PL.ABL I-GEN son protect.PP give.IMP good
 'The great, powerful king of gods, I beg you to kindly protect my son from the dangers of enemies.'

---

2. There are some regional variations to this form: one, particularly prevailing among the highlanders of the country, is marked by the ending *-nʈə* instead of *-nnə* as in *balanʈə* 'look', *adinʈə* 'pull' and *hinaawenʈə* 'laugh', and another has the ending *-ḍə* as in *balanḍə* 'look', *adinḍə* 'pull' and *hinaawenḍə* 'laugh'.

Wahanse is a super-honorific form added to a personal pronoun and used as a term of reference as in (3) or added to a common noun and used as a term of address as in (4). The imperative form *waḍinnə* in (3) is from the honorific verb *waḍinəwa* 'go or come' used for Buddhist monks or gods (see Table 2 in this chapter). The super-honorific form of the imperative verb with the term 'good' to the right of it can be considered as a lexical strategy evoking an inference of indirectness endowed with the (pragmatic) force derived from the (semantic) sense. That sense is seen in lexical structures such as (5) below.

(5) a. mee   waturə   bo-nnə   honda-i
       this   water   drink-INF   good-AM
       'This water is good for drinking.'

   b. ehemə   kiya-nnə   narəka-i
      so   say-INF   bad-AM
      'It is bad to say such a thing.'

A somewhat similar imperative expression used in particular between a husband and a wife, more precisely between parents, indicates an important kind of politeness prevailing in the traditional Sinhala-speaking society and is essentially mutual, not asymmetrical. The expression consists of the past tense form of the verb followed by the conditional particle *naŋ*.

(6) a. mehaa-ṭə   aawa   naŋ
       here-DAT   come-PAST   if
       'Please come here.'
       Lit. '(It would be nice) if you came here.'

   b. wedə mahattea   langə-ṭə   giyaa   naŋ
      native physician   near-DAT   go.PAST   if
      'How about going to see the doctor?'
      Lit. 'It would be nice if you were to go to see the doctor.'

In terms of illocutionary force, the above utterances are directive in that the speakers use them to produce some effect through the expected action by the hearer, but they are not impositive in that they do not carry the perlocutionary effect of forcing or threatening the partner into the action.[3]

Disrespectful or non-polite forms of imperatives are made by adding *-pan* and *-piə* to the verbal root. The former is used to give orders to equals or inferiors; among equals it is often used to express intimacy, particularly in informal situations. The latter form is restricted to giving orders to inferiors. Both have their respective plural forms: *-palla* for the former and *-piyaw* for the latter.

---

3. This might go against the idea that illocutionary act and perlocutionary act are simultaneously performed in realizing a speech act as envisioned by Austin (1962).

	Singular	**Plural**
Intermediate:	baləpan	baləpalla 'see'
	ædəpan	ædəpalla 'draw or pull'
Inferior:	baləpiə	baləpiyaw 'see'
	ædəpiə	ædəpiyaw 'draw or pull'

The degree of respect or disrespect they express may vary with the particular context:

(7) a. balə-pan Ranjit e-nəwa-də kiəla
     see-IMP Ranjit come-IND-Q that
     'See whether Ranjit is coming.'

   b. ædə-pan putaa tawə ṭika-i kandə
     draw-IMP son more little-AM hill
     'Push on, son; not much more hill to go.'

(8) a. lanuwə ædə-piə buuruwa
     string draw-IMP donkey
     'Pull on the rope, you stupid ass.'

   b. kiə-piə aye paarak togě oluwə palə-nəwa
     say-IMP once again you.GEN head split-IND
     'Say that again and I'll split your head.'

The sentence in (7a) can be used in a context where the hearer is inferior or equal to the speaker. This means that the *-pan* form can be asymmetric or symmetric depending on the context. When asymmetric, for example, in a master-servant relationship, it is only used by the master towards the servant. In a symmetric case, on the other hand, for example, in a circle of close friends, it can be used by any of its members. The flexibility of the use of this form is further shown by (7b), in which the imperative verb is used with the kinship term *putaa* 'son'. If a native speaker of Sinhala is asked to provide an appropriate context for this sentence, he or she may easily imagine the friendly manner in which a master addresses his servant or the bull which is pulling a cart along a hilly road. The utterance in (8a) is explicitly disrespectful because of its use of the inferior imperative form together with the metaphorical use of a noun of the animal category, donkey, in a derogatory sense towards a human. If (7b) conveys the speaker's positive evaluation of the partner, (8a) only expresses the speaker's bad evaluation towards the hearer. When the inferior imperative verb is used with a declarative clause including a threat or a curse towards the hearer, as in (8b), it shows a situation of conflict and conveys the speaker's antipathy towards the hearer. Also note the speaker's elocutionary goal is antithetic to the surface meaning of the imperative verb in (8b): the speaker verbally orders the partner to say something while expecting him or her not to (say anything).

The stem of the verb in its bare form is also used as an imperative, giving an abrupt order or a command. Thus verb stems such as *balə* 'look', *gaha* 'hit', *kapə* 'cut' and *gan* 'take', when used as imperatives, are associated with the general illocutionary type of impositives and are impolite. Imperatives being non-indicative, their representation by the base form of the verb, without inflectional endings, is not particular to Sinhala, but can be seen in languages like English, too. What is rather uncommon is that even the indicative construction can be used in Sinhala with the illocutionary force of an imperative. The non-past tense form of the indicative mood is used as imperatives and may also inflect for plural form to show the plurality of hearers by whom the propositional content is to be fulfilled. The use of the indicative form enəwa 'come' in an imperative construction is exemplified below:

(9) a. mehe e-nəwa
here come-IND
'Come here.'
b. mehe enəwə-la
here come-IND-PL
'Come here (everybody).'

Both the stem form and the indicative form of the verb in the imperative function are presumed to be in non-polite use.

1.2 Permissive mood

Permissive forms used for asking for, and giving, permission constitute another speech-act related modal. The implicit agent or affectee can be first person, second person or third person. In asking for permission, the speaker designated by the first person pronoun will be the implicit agent of the speech event. The imperative/infinitive form followed by with the interrogative marker serves as the permissive verb. A request for permission is presumed to be polite when the relevant state of affairs is not in the speaker's domain of activity or the given state of affairs is under the authority of the hearer. Therefore, the interrogative marker is obligatory.

(10) ehenam mamə niwaaḍu gan-nə də?
then I leave take-IMP Q
'Then, can I take leave?'

An indicative form with rising intonation can be used for the speech act of permission, albeit with the risk of being impolite.

(11) ehenam mamə niwaaḍu gan-nəwa
then I leave take-IND
'Then, I take leave, is that OK?'

In such a situation the speaker may be seen as not showing respect to the hearer but seeking confirmation for an already taken decision. The sentence is acceptable when it is used by a member of a peer group. In seeking permission from someone in authority, a more indirect expression loaded with a few "mitigators" or polite markers will be used, as in (12).

(12) səər, man niwaaḍu gatta-ṭə kamak nædda?
sir I leave take.PAST-DAT doesn't matter.Q
'Sir, would you mind my taking leave, by any chance?'

In response to the utterance in (12), the relevant person may use the verb in the imperative form of the ordinary grade, as in (13a), or the equivalent periphrastic form, as in (13b).

(13) a. ehenam Ranjit niwaaḍu gan-nə
then Ranjit leave take-IMP
'You (can) take leave then, Ranjit.'

b. ehenam Ranjit niwaaḍu gatta-ṭə kamak næx
then Ranjit leave take.PAST-DAT doesn't matter
'You can take leave then, Ranjit.'

In giving permission following the above patterns, the implicit agent may be designated by the second person pronoun, indicating a more informal or intimate relationship between the participants.

Another kind of permissive verb takes third person nouns as implicit agents or affectees. There are three forms in this category, ending in *-dden*, *-we* and *-den*. For example, the verb *balənəwa* 'look' may appear in one of the following three forms to mean 'let him/her look': *baladden, bæluwaawe, bæluwəden*. These forms are different, in function and distribution, from the permissive verbs introduced before. Given that the implicit agent is a third person, it is impossible to assume that the speaker gives permission to the hearer. Instead, the speaker B's response to A is that A wants B to let C continue the action or to ignore C's action. The resultant utterance conveys the speaker's evaluation towards the third person, not towards the hearer. Hence this permissive construction represents a speech act in a marginal sense. Observe the example in (14).

(14) A: annə lameya ṭiiwii balə-nəwa
there child TV watch-IND
'You know, the child is watching TV.'

B: ohe bæluwaawe
there watch.PERM
'Let him watch' or 'Just ignore.'

1.3 Offer

Offer is another type of speech-act related modal in which the speaker signals that he/she is ready to commit him/herself to attempting some action and asks the hearer if he/she wishes to join it. Hortative forms of verbs followed by the interrogative marker are used for this purpose. Since both the speaker and the hearer are to be involved in the proposed action, the implicit agent is designated by the first person plural noun, though it avoids overt appearance in most cases.

(15) a. Ranjit-ṭə   kool   ek-ak   de-mu   də
        Ranjit-DAT call   one-INDF   give-HORT   Q
        'Shall we call Ranjit?'

    b. tee   ek-ak   bo-mu   də
        tea   one-INDF   drink-HORT   Q
        'Let's have a cup of tea.'

As in (15b), an offer may convey an invitation. Because of the strategy of maximizing the cost to oneself, morphologically realized through the hortative form (-*mu*), and minimizing the cost to the other, through the non-intruding interrogative marker *də*, offers are considered as intrinsically polite utterances. However, they may convey impolite messages or be offensive, if given without proper consideration to the relevant place and context.

1.4 Optative mood

Expressions of the optative mood, another speech-act related modal, are used for a variety of illocutionary acts: wishing, cursing, and greeting, etc. By using them, the speaker communicates to the hearer that there is some action the former wishes to occur to the latter.

(16) Wishing:
      tawə   tawa-t   diunu   weewaa
      more   more-too   develop-OPT
      Lit 'May you increase your chances of future success.'
      'I wish you success.'

(17) Cursing
      too   gaha   mula   wæṭi-yan
      you (derog)   tree   foot   fall-OPT
      'May you topple over under the tree.'

Optative forms are generally used for greetings in letter-writing, public broadcasts and addresses such as *sæpə weewaa* 'May you be healthy', *jayə weewaa* 'Be victory with you' and *subə udææsənak weewaa* 'Good morning'. *Weewaa* in these utterances is the optative form of the verb *wenəwa* 'be or become'.

In more colloquial use, however, imperative forms are used for the purpose, particularly for cursing.

(18) Cursing
    a. ooka-ṭə   hond-ak   naŋ   we-nnə   epaa
        he(derog)-DAT   good-INDF   TOP   be-IMP   don't
        'Never ever be good with him.'

b. muu-wə   diwia   kaa-piə
   this person(derog)-ACC leopard eat-IMP
   'Let him be eaten by a leopard.'

With the cost to the other maximized, they are intrinsically impolite.

1.5 Epistemic modality

Some utterances are marked for epistemically modified inferences. By means of referring to participants' knowledge states, epistemic modality makes explicit the speaker's commitment to the information conveyed. When the speaker utters something he knows very well, this is indicated by choosing a declarative construction. When he does not have such certainty, he will modify his statement to suit the level of perceived factivity.

The example in (19a) contains a simple declarative statement while the sentence in (19b) has the statement modified by an adverb of affirmation. The highest degree of certainty is expressed by adding -*mai* to the right of the indicative construction, as in (19c).

(19) a. miniha e-nəwa
       man   come-IND
       'He will come.'

   b. pæhædiliwəmə miniha e-nəwa
      clearly   man   come-IND
      'Definitely he will come.'

   c. miniha e-nəwa-mai
      man   come-IND-mai
      'He will surely come.'

A construction with the modal form *oonæ* added to the infinitive form of the verb is selected if the speaker wants to qualify the statement with high degree of certainty, as in (20). The example in (21) shows that the degree of certainty decreases with the modal form *puluwan*.

(20) dæn miniha e-nnə   oonæ
     now man   come-INF must
     'He must come now.'

(21) aye   e-nn-e   næ kiiwa-tə miniha e-nnə   puluwan
     again come-NPT-FOC   no said-DAT man   come-INF might
     'Though he said that he would not come again, he might yet come.'

Another modal form expressing the speaker's attitude towards a state of affairs is the *æti* form which seems to appear in a variety of linguistic and non-linguistic contexts. In (22a and b) it appears without a verbal predicate. As becomes explicit from the linguistic context, it substitutes for a 'be' verb. The infinitive form of the 'be' verb plus *æti* has become a composite structure to mean 'probably might' as in (22c). In (22d and e) *æti* has been added to an indicative construction and a past participle construction, respectively. Each construction can exist independently without the *æti* form. It is only when the modal form is added that the speaker's judgment to the proposition is expressed. In (22f) the *æti* form has been added to the dependent infinitive form to express the speaker's inference based on subjective assessment towards the situation.

(22) a. dæn miniha gedərə æti
now man home æti
'He might be home now.'

b. mee welaawə-ţə bas nætuwə æti
this time-DAT buses no æti
'There might not be buses at this time.'

c. miniha ţoiləţ ekee we-nnə æti
man toilet one.LOC be-INF æti
'Maybe he is in toilet.'

d. miniha dæn ya-nəwa æti
man now go-IND æti
'He might be going now.'

e. dæn miniha gedərə gihin æti
now man home go.PP æti
'By now he might have gone home.'

f. miniha gedərə ya-nnə æti
man home go-INF æti
'He must have gone home.'

The use of the modal form *æti* cannot be described without referring to deictic features and pragmatic inferences. The base form of the verb remains unchanged in some cases like (d) while in other cases it changes to the infinitive form as in (f)). The former case is time-framed and indicates some evidentiality whereas the latter case denotes a pure speculation about the event, devoid of time deixis.

When the speaker's inference is based on some evidence, this evidentiality is expressed through the particle *waage*.

(23) a. miniha aapahu ya-nəwa waage
man back go-IND waage
'It seems that he is returning.'

b. miniha aapahu gihin waage
man back go-PP waage
'It seems that he has already returned.'

c. adə wahi-i waage
today rain-INFER waage
'It seems that it will rain today.'

To mark hearsay evidentiality, the clitic *-lu* is attached to the proposition.

(24) a. adə ehe paaṭi-ak-lu
today there party-INDF-lu
'We hear there's a party today.'

b. miniha pagaa gan-nəwa-lu
man bribe take-IND-lu
'It is said he takes bribes.'

The hearsay evidential *-lu* is used with the dependent *wh*-word *monəwa* 'what' to bring an implication of incredulity.

(25) A: maŋ niwaaḍuwə-kə-ṭə aawa newei,
I holiday-INDF-DAT come.PAST not

rassaaw-en aswe-laa aawe
job-ABL resign-PP come.PAST.FOC

'It is not that I came on holiday; I came here after quitting my job.'

B: monəwa-lu
what-lu
'What?' Are you kidding?'

2. Interrogation

While positive affirmative propositions are factual by virtue of the truth values associated with them, their negative and interrogative counterparts do not necessarily reflect their logical equivalents. This linguistic universal applies to Sinhala, too. Look at the interrogative sentence in (26b) syntactically based on the indicative sentence in (26a).

(26) a. ambə kanəwa
mango eat-IND
'(They) are eating mango.'

b. ambə ka-nəwa də?
mango eat-IND Q
'Do they eat mango?', 'Do you eat mango?' or 'Do you want to eat mango?'

The function of (26b) is not just interrogating the propositional content of (26a). Suppose the speaker is peeling a mango; normally, inquiring whether someone eats mango in such a situation is equivalent to readiness to offer a piece of it. Such an inquiry without readiness of offering is nonsense, or is taken as playing games. However, since questions are underspecified in comparison with propositions, answers may be interpreted variously. A person, while peeling a mango, may ask a hearer the question (26b) and, if receives 'yes' from the hearer, may say, as the joke goes in Sinhala culture, 'Oh, you are eating; then you need not any more', pretending not to understand the pragmatic inference and only taking 'yes' as the logical equivalent of (26a). The confusion, or the joke in this case arises from the fact that some interrogative utterances may perform multiple functions such as a question and an offer, as in (26b). In other words, they may serve to express propositions, and also to perform actions.

The following types of questions are to be distinguished from ordinary yes-no questions.

(27) Requesting
poḍḍak mehaa-ṭə æwit ya-nəwa də?
a little here-DAT come.PP go-IND Q
Can you come here for a while?'

(28) Suggesting
narəkə-də mee paarə parlimeentuwə-ṭə idiripat unot?
bad-Q this time parliament-DAT offer as a candidate. COND
'Is it bad/Isn't it good, if you contest for the parliament this time?'

(29) Expressing incredulity
itiŋ mahattəyo, meewa maha polowə uhulə-nə apəraadə də?
so gentleman these great earth bear-NPT crime Q
'Tell me now! Will the earth bear these crimes, Sir?'

The following *wh*-type (*ko/mo*-type in Sinhala) questions also involve some non-propositional considerations.

(30) rassaaw-ak hoyaa gan-nə ekə kochchərə amaaru də
job-INDF find-NPT NM how much difficult Q
How difficult is it to find a job?'

(31) ooka hadaa gan-nə kochchərə mahansi unaa də
that person bring up-INF how much make efforts.PAST Q
'How much effort I have made to bring up that child!'

(32) haa-nəwa kiəla aaranchi unot kii denek
plough-IND that get the news-COND how many people
udauwə-ṭə e-nəwa də
support-DAT come-IND Q
'How many people used to come over for support when they got the news that someone's field is going to be ploughed.

(33) hæbæætə oyə læætərə monə taram rasə kæænak də
     really that læætərə how much delicious food.INDF Q
     'What a delicious food læætərə is!'

(34) minissu handə-ṭə giyaa kiiwamə aaye ehenam tawat monəwa də
     people moon-DAT go.PAST say.TEMP again if so more what   Q
     'Is there anything more (surprising) after having heard that people went to the moon.'

The utterances in (30) and (31) convey the speaker's sense of despair towards the state of affairs. Through the utterances in (32) and (33) which convey some positive evaluations of the situations referred to the speakers vent their nostalgia for the good old days. The interrogative sentence in (34) metaphorically expresses the speaker's detached attitude towards the state of affairs; its perlocutionary goal is persuading the listener that one should not be perplexed by bygone or upcoming social transformations.

3. Negation

Some aspects of negation can be accounted for on the level of logical/semantic structure. For example, the question in (35) can be replied to with either of the two negative lexical patterns, (a) or (b).

(35) A: umbə-ṭə salli oonæ də
        you-DAT money want Q
        'Do you want money?'
     B: a. oonæ næœ
           want no
           'No, I don't.'
        b. epaa
           don't
           'No, I don't.'

The use of the negative particle *epaa* as in (b) is considered as a strong denial of an offer in comparison with answer (a) which has *oonæ* 'want' followed by the negative marker *næœ*. This is because the negative marker serves as a form of understatement whereas the independent negative particle represents the syntactically positive equivalent.

However, facts related to negation cannot always be accounted for on the logical/semantic basis because negative sentences can be interpreted as having negative propositions and also as carrying additional implicatures. The negative question in (36) can either be used as a genuine request for reasons, or as a threatening command to get the hearer to do something.

(36) mokədə kərə-nnə bæri?
    why   do-INF   cannot
    'Why can't you do that?'

An indicative sentence with negation can be used in a non-indicative, i.e. imperative context.

(37) kaaməree-ṭə ya-nn-e næː
    room-DAT   go-NPT-FOC no
    'You are not supposed to go into the room.'
    Lit. 'You will not go to the room.'

Though the imperative mood is not used, when uttered with the appropriate intonation, this sentence is taken as a command to the hearer.
Observe the following dialogue where the negative particle is used as a suggestion.

(38)   From the novel Nil Mal Wilə (Ratnayaka, 1997:139)

    A: putaa, kohe-wat   gamən-ak   ya-nṭə-wæi?
        son   where-even journey-INDF go-INF-Q
        'Son, are you going away?'

    B: ou, maŋ Kurunegala ya-nəwa
        yes   I   Kurunegala go-IND
        'Yes, I am going to Kurunegala.'

    A: arə kuḍee-wat   ænnə ya-nn-e   nætuə
        that umbrella-even carry-NPT-FOC without
        'Even without carrying an umbrella?'

By using the negative form, A suggests to B to carry an umbrella when the latter goes out.
Negation involved in the expression of opinion or attitudes contains some evaluation of the state of affairs.

(39) hæbææṭə oyə læætərə monə tarəm rasə   kææmak   də
     really   that læætərə how much delicious food-INDF Q
     'What a delicious food læætərə is!'

     mee minissu mokədə dan-ne   næː euwa hada-nn-e   nætte
     these people why   know-NPT.FOC no those make-NPT-FOC no.FOC
     'I don't know why people don't make them (any more).'

In the second sentence in (39) the matrix clause *danne næː* 'don't know' with the elliptical first person subject expresses the speaker's subjective attitude towards the situation, rather than just carrying the propositional negation. The contrast makes it explicit: After impressively talking about a delicious food in the previous sentence, the speaker laments that people are not interested in it any more.

The colloquial negation marker *yæ*, which is a sentence final particle, adds different meanings and nuances to a statement. When added to an affirmative statement, it may function as a negative tag with an implication of incredulity or with an added emphasis.

(40) a. eyaa-ṭə kumburu wæḍə kəra-nnə puluwan-yæ
he-DAT rice-field work do-INF can-yæ
'He can't do rice-farming, can he?'

b. itiŋ etənə indaŋ maha durak-yæ
so there from great distance.INDF-yæ
'Yeah, but from there it's not so far, is it?'

c. mee wagee wiyədam-yæ polisi-e mahatturu awamə
this like expenses-yæ police-LOC gentlemen come.TEMP
api kəra-nn-e
we do-NPT-FOC
'This is not the kind of expenses that we bear when police officers come here!'

In these examples the negative tag is added for emphasis. In (40c) the speaker boasts that the expenses they bear for entertaining police officers are bigger compared to the present meager amount. By adding *yæ* to a negative sentence, the negative sense is canceled and the opposite polarity is emphasized, as in the following examples.

(41) a. api nodan-nəwa-yæ eyaa-ge witti
we NEG.know-IND-yæ he/she-GEN news
'Don't we know about him?!'

b. eekə-ṭə gamee æwidi-nnə epaa-yæ
that-DAT village.LOC walk around-INF don't-yæ
'For that (purpose), we need to go around the village, don't you know?'

c. eewa ka-nṭə oonnaŋ e-nnə epaa-yæ
those eat-INF want.COND come-INF don't-yæ
'If you want to eat them, you must come along.'

The use of the *yæ* particle turns the statement into a sarcastic expression in (41a), adds a particular overtone of speaker's disagreement with the hearer in (41b), and carries an overtone of complaint in (41c). As the examples in (40) and (41) show, *yæ* is a pragmatic particle whose meaning is best explicated in terms of non-propositional, pragmatic concepts; it commonly marks an information gap between the speaker and the hearer. Therefore *yæ* is not simply a negative marker, but serves as a marker of information status.

4. Social deixis and honorifics

Social deixis concerns "that aspect of sentences which reflect or establish or are determined by certain realities of the social situation in which the speech act occurs" (Fillmore, 1975:76). Levinson (1983) narrowed down the concept of social deixis to "those aspects of language structure that encode the social identities of participants (properly, incumbents of participant-roles), or the social relationship between them, or between one of them and persons and entities referred to". Accordingly, speech levels and honorifics are considered as grammaticalized aspects of language use that depend on relations between speaker, addressee, referent, and speech setting.

The most notable linguistic forms that reflect social relationships are pronouns, titles of address and other reference terms. Second person pronouns in Sinhala are identified as consisting of seven grades, each having a corresponding imperative concord (De Silva, 1976b). The following table shows second person pronouns beginning from the most respectful level (1) and going down to the most disrespectful level (7).

Table 1. Gradation of Second Person Pronouns

GRADE	SECOND PERSON PRONOUN
1	*obə wahanse*
2	*tamunnnanse*
3	*munnæhe > unnæhe > mehee > ohee**
4	*meyaa, oyaa*
5	*tamuse*
6	*umbə*
7	*too*

* > indicates that left item is higher in rank than the right item.

The grade 1 pronoun is specifically reserved for addressing a Buddhist priest. The grade 2 pronoun may be used for a Buddhist priest or a person to whom a high degree of respect must be shown. The four forms given for grade 3 are arranged in a descending order of respect. The hierarchical distance between them is somewhat blurred: they may be used for people equal in status or marginally superior, particularly in a setting that requires some level of formality. *Munnæhe* and *unnæhe* are more respectful than *mehee* and *ohee*. However, forms with *m-* 'this', like *munnæhe*, are regarded as more respectful than those without it like *unnæhe*. Strictly speaking, forms with *m-* are third person pronouns used for addressing participants with some respect. The grade 4 pronouns are used to address equals.[4] Use of the grade 5 form indicates that the addressee is regarded by the speaker to be slightly inferior in rank. A husband may address his wife as *tamuse* according her equality or marginal inferiority. The grade 6 form *umbə* is used towards inferiors and among equals as well in informal settings. The grade 7 form *too* is used to address people of lower rank or to express resentment. *Obə*, which is not included in the grade paradigm, is used as a neutral second person pronoun in school textbooks, in the literary language or the media, but is never heard in daily

---

4. There is some individual variation in the use of *oyaa* and *ohee*. There are also important regional restrictions: in the southern dialect *meyaa* and *oyaa* of grade 4 are not used for addressing equals; instead *mehee* and *ohee* of the lowest rank of grade 3 are considered as appropriate for addressing equals.

conversational language. However, *obətuma,* its respectful form is used to address people of higher rank, and comes between grade 2 and 3 in the paradigm (cf. Example 1).

Except in circumstances that require a higher degree of respect towards the addressee, or in situations that need to treat the addressee with the least respect, the use of second person pronouns is very restricted in actual conversation. Instead, personal names, kinship terms, titles and their combinations are used with much frequency. When addressing people of equal status or inferior status, personal names are used without titles. Shortened forms of personal names or initials are used to express solidarity or intimacy. For example, the shortened form *Gune* for Gunasekara or the initials *T.M.* for the surname Thilakaratne Mudiyanselage may be used as address forms. Babies are not addressed by personal names, but pets are.

Titles like *mahattea* 'gentleman', *noona* 'lady', *səər* 'sir', *mædəm* 'madam', and *haamuduruwo* 'Buddhist monk' are used independently or attached to personal names. Titles as variables follow personal names. *Ranjit mahattea, Premadasa mædəm* and *dhammaratana haamuduruo* are examples. The titles *səər* and *mædəm* borrowed from English are regarded as more respectful than *mahattea* and *noona.* The second person pronoun of grade 3, *unnæhe* given above, is used as a polite form with a trade title as *baas unnæhe* 'Mr. mason' or as a honorific title with a personal name as *Piyadasa unnæhe.* Some respectful professional titles are *dostərə mahattea* 'doctor', *injineeru mahattea* 'enjineer', *wedə mahattea* 'native phisician', *kapu mahattea* 'match maker', *nækət raalə* 'astrologer', *kaʈʈəndi raalə* 'exorcist', and *kapu raalə* 'lay-priest of a local shrine'.

Kinship terms like *amma* 'mother', *taatta* 'father', *ayya* 'elder brother', *akka* 'elder sister', *nangi* 'younger sister', *malli* 'younger brother', *nænda* 'father's sister', *punchi amma* 'mother's younger sister', *maama* 'mother's brother', *baappa* 'father's younger brother', *siiya* 'grandfather' and *kiri-amma* 'grandmother' are used to address relatives appropriately. When used as address forms, some of them are changed to the vocative form as *amme* 'mother' and *taatte* 'father'. There is a fictive use of kinship terms in which they are used to address people who are not bound by any kinship relationship. Young people freely use sibling terms to address each other to establish solidarity or express familiarity even in situations of first encounters. Young ones may address elderly ladies as *amma* 'mother' or *nænda* 'aunt' and elderly men as *maama* 'uncle'. It is not customary for young people to address elderly people by personal names. Instead, the use of kinship terms like *nænda* 'aunt' and *maama* 'uncle' following the personal name is considered as the polite way of addressing elderly ones even though they are not relatives.

There are several sets of honorific suffixes that can be considered as the most grammaticalized forms of respect. They are used in formal settings both as referent and addressee honorifics. One such set includes *-anu* (masculine) and *-ani* (feminine) which are added to common nouns or kinship terms. For example, *putənu* for *putaa* 'son' and *duwəni* for *duwə* 'daughter' can be heard in formal situations, for example, in an address delivered in a wedding ceremony. In that case the 'target' of respect includes both the son and daughter and their parents. Another set of suffixes, which are generally added to professional titles, are -wərə (mas.), -wəri (fem.), -wəru (pl.), -tumaa (mas.) and -tumii (fem.). Guruwərəya 'teacher', waidyəwəriə 'female doctor', guruwəru 'teachers', janaadipatitumaa 'President (male)' and widuhalpatitimiə 'principal (fem.)' are examples.

Another device for encoding respect is inflecting the noun designating the 'target' of respect for plurality. The plural suffix -o is added to a common noun, a professional title or a personal name. The plural form of pronouns does not indicate respect. Examples:

> putənu 'son (+ honorific suffix)' + o > putənuo
> haamuduru 'monk' + o > haamuduruo
> rajjuru 'king' + o > rajjuruo
> Sirimaa (name) + o > Sirimaao
> Martin Wichramasinghe (name) + o > Martin Wichremasingheyo

These nouns with the plural suffix referring to a person with due respect in a formal context such as putənuo 'the son', or referring to people of highly respected status, such as haamuduruo 'the monk', rajjuruo 'the king' each denote singular entities. To denote plurality, they take plural number inflection as putənuwəru 'the sons', haamuduruwəru 'the monks' and rajjuruwəru 'the kings'. The aggregation of honorifics in an expression like putənuo above is acceptable.

Wahanse is a high honorific applied to a priest or to religious objects regarded with great respect. Examples:

> sangaya wahanse 'Buddhist priests'
> pot wahanse 'book of religious sutras'
> daatuun wahanse 'sacred relics'
> bodiin wahanse 'sacred Bodhi tree'

Sinhala has a respectful indefinite form which helps to understand or establish a 'speech level': instead of the ordinary indefinite suffix -ek/-ak, the respect form *kenek* is applied to certain honorific titles and respectful terms. They include professional or honorific titles, kinship terms specifying older relatives, certain nouns designating superiors and occupational terms. *raaləhaami kenek* 'a police officer', *leekam kenek* 'a secretary', *amma kenek* 'a mother', *maama kenek* 'an uncle', *dostərə kenek* 'a doctor', *baas kenek* 'a mason'. However, the noun *haamuduruo* 'Buddhist monk' has a specific respectful indefinite form indicating a higher level of respect, which is *namak*.

There are many language forms reserved for Buddhist monks regarded as authorized speakers and authorized recipients. As already mentioned, special forms are used when addressing or referring to Buddhist monks. The second person pronoun *obə wahanse* or the honorific title *swamiin wahanse* are used as address terms. The common noun *haamuduruo* is also used for addressing. There is a set of special verbs and nouns to use when referring to Buddhist monks. The following is a list of such honorific terms.

Table 2. Special Honorific Words

Meaning	Non-honorific	Special honorific
'eat'	kanəwa	waləndənəwa
'drink'	bonəwa	waləndənəwa
'go'	yanəwa	waḍinəwa
'come'	enəwa	waḍinəwa
'be'	innəwa	wæḍəinnəwa
'sleep'	nidənəwa	sætəpenəwa
'tell'	kiənəwa	deesənaa kərənəwa, wadaarənəwa
'die'	mærenəwa	apəwat wenəwa
'rice'	bat	daane
'drinks'	biimə	gilampasə
'desserts'	aturupasə	awulupat
'chewing'	bulat wiṭə	dæhæt wiṭə
'yes'	ou	ehei

Someone may address a monk and say,

    obə wahanse issella waḍinnə
    you hon. title earlier go.hon.IMP
    'You may go earlier.'

Also, someone may say, referring to a monk,

    haamuduruwo daane waləndənəwa
    monk.hon rice eat.hon.IND
    'The monk is eating rice.'

Of particular interest is the fact that a monk may say, referring to himself in honorific terms,

    mam tawəmə wælənduwe næǣ
    I yet eat.hon.PAST.FOC no
    'I haven't eaten yet.'

These special honorific expressions are never relational: that is, they must be used when addressing a monk even by his parents and even by his teacher if the latter is a layman. The last example given above is the result of a referent honorific pattern in which the referent happens to be the speaker himself. Thus the Sinhala system of special honorifics, as reserved for Buddhist monks, is an absolute honorific system in which the referent is invariably respected regardless of the rank of the speaker. Under such honorific terms, all other expressions are ranked subordinate.

Although Sinhala has an absolute honorific system and some inherently respectful expressions, the language neither has an elaborate honorific system nor is it rich in subtle politeness features encoded in either its structure or its use. For example,

Sinhala cannot express the degree of politeness with the same elocutionary force as conveyed by the polite English sentence '*I don't suppose that you would by any chance be able to lend me some cash, would you?*' (example from Levinson 1983). There is also no specific means to lower the status of the speaker or his "in-group" member thereby raising the level of respect towards the addressee, as is done in Japanese. Conversely, in Sinhala, it is possible to use the honorific titles *mahattea* (male) and *noona* (female) in referring to one's husband or wife while speaking with an "out-group" member. Without being much puzzled by variable choices in the use of expressions, one can safely make an order or a request by using the standard imperative ending in *-nnə*. However, it is customary to use a "mitigator" or a politeness marker like *poḍḍak* or *ṭikak* 'a little' in addressing an out-group member in particular.

(42) a. poḍḍak ain we-nnə
   a little move away-IMP
   'Please move away a little.'

 b. mee bææg ekə ṭikak balaa ga-nnə
   this bag one a little take care-IMP
   'Please take care of this bag for a moment.'

It will be more polite to make the request in the interrogative form, as in (43).

(43) a. poḍḍak ain we-nəwa də
   a little move away-IND Q
   'Excuse me. May I go through?'

 b. mee bææg ekə ṭikak balaa ga-nnəwa də
   this bag one a little take care-IND Q
   'Could you please take care of this bag for a moment?'

When addressing an in-group member, some people add the suffix *-ko* to the imperative form; it also expresses intimacy or affection rather than mere politeness and may also add extra force to the request.

(44) mee liumə ṭaip kərə-la de-nnə-ko
   this letter type-PP give-IMP-ko
   'Please type this letter for me.' or 'Do type this letter for me.'

The exact elocutionary force of a sentence like (44) with the *-ko* imperative largely depends on the accompanying intonation.

Finally, there are various kinds of registers carrying different indexical features, associated with various styles of meaning and indicating different contextual configurations. One has to learn different sets of registers including the expressions and lexico-grammatical features which allow us to determine whether an utterance is to be considered as formal or relaxed, refined or rough, whether or not it connotes social prestige, etc., some of which are to be exemplified in the following chapter.

CHAPTER 14

Sample texts

This chapter presents two example texts. One is a local legend and the other is part of a novel.

Legend: "How Appuwa became king"

This is a popular story current among the local peasantry in the North-Western Province of Sri Lanka. Kurunegala, an ancient city in the Northwestern Province of Sri Lanka, is located at the foot of a giant rock called Etugala which means 'Elephant rock' in Sinhala. The area has several massive rocks and hills to adorn its landscape. Many tales mingled with romance, tragedy and heroism have been woven around these mountains and rocks. One popular story, "How Appuwa Became King", whose origin is attributed to the period of Dambadeniya, towards the end of the thirteenth century, is a legend about a peasant hero admired by the local community.

mii-ṭə	awurudu	hatsiiyə-kə-ṭə	witərə	issərə	Lanka-we
this-DAT	years	seven hundred-INDF-DAT	about	before	Sri Lanka-LOC

Yapahuwa	kiyəla	punchi	raajədhaaaniy-ak	tibuna
Yapahuwa	called	small	kingdom-INDF	was

'About seven hundred years ago, there was a small kingdom called Yapahuwa in Sri Lanka.'

mee	raajjyə	paalənəyə	kəlee	Buwənekəba	kiyəla	raja	kenek
this	kingdom	rule-PT-FOC		Buwanekaba	named	king	one

'The kingdom was ruled by a king named Buwanekaba.'

saturu	uwəduru-wal-in	tamanwə	rækə	gannə-ṭə
enemy	disaster-PL-ABL	oneself-ACC	protect.REFL.INF-DAT	

rajətumaa	kandak	udə	alut	maaligaaw-ak	idikerewuwa
king	mountain-INDF	on	new	castle-INDF	construct.CAUS.PAST

'To defend himself against rival forces, the king built his palace on the top of a mountain.'

rajə-tumaa	eekə-ṭə	tooraa	gatt-e	Weeragala	kiyənə	kanda-i
king-HON	that-DAT	select.REFL.PT-FOC		Weeragala	named	mountain-AM

'It was the mountain called Weeragala that the king selected the for the purpose.'

agə	mehesiə	ætulu	pariwaarə	biswun	hæṭə pas	denek	ekkə
chief	queen	including	surrounding	queens	sixty-five	people	with

rajə-tumaa	alut	maalig-ee	padinchiyə-ṭə	giyaa
king-HON	new	castle-LOC	residing-DAT	went

'The king moved to the new castle with his queen consort and sixty-five deputy queens.'

rajə-tumaa	Weeragala	padinchiyə-ṭə	aapu	ekə	gænə	manaapəyak
king-HON	Weeragala	residing-DAT	come.PTAD	one	about	like-INDF

dækku-we	næti	ken-ek	hiṭiya
show.PT-FOC	NEG	person-INDF	was

'There was a person who was not happy with the king's new arrival into Weeragala.'

ee	palaat-ee	ratee	raala-i	ee
that	area-LOC	local	chieftain-AM	that

'That was the local chieftain of that area.'

Galabedderala	Agbo	kumaarəyaa-ṭə	gatu	kiə-la
Galabedderaala	Agbo	prince-DAT	telltale	say-PP

rajə-tumaa-t	kumaarəyaa-t	atərə	haturukəm-ak	awileuwa
king-HON-too	prince-too	between	dispute-INDF	kindle.PAST

'Galabadderala created a dispute between the king and the prince Agbo by telling telltale to the prince.'

Agbo	kumaaraya	tamanṭə	wiruddəwə	kæræll-ak	gaha-nnə
Agbo	prince	oneself-DAT	against	rebellion-INDF	strike-INF

suudaanam we-nə	wittiə	dænə gatta	rajə-tumaa
prepare-NPT	fact	come to know.PT.	king-HON

saturaa	winaasə kərə-nnə	wahaamə	hamudaawə	ræskəla
enemy	destroy-INF	promptly	army	gather.PAST

'The king heard the news that the Prince Agbo was organizing a rebellion and promptly gathered his troops to destroy the enemy.'

ikmənimmə	hamudaa	dekə	atərə	yuddəy-ak	ætiunaa
soon	armies	two	between	war-INDF	arise.PAST

'Soon a war broke out between the two armies.'

rajə-tumaa-ge	agə	mehesiə-ṭə	ee wənə wiṭə	ladəru	put-ek	hiṭiya
king-HON-GEN	top	queen-DAT	by then	baby	boy-INDF	was

'By then the queen consort had a baby boy.'

yudde-ṭə	piṭat we-nnə	issella	rajə-tumaa	bisoo-wər-un-ṭə
war-DAT	leave-INF	before	king-HON	queen-HON-PL-DAT

karunu	pæhædili kəlaa
matters	clarify.PAST

'Before leaving for the battlefield, the king described the situation to the queens.'

"mamə kærəllə mardənəyə kəra-nnə yanəwa"
I   rebellion   put down-INF   go-IND
'I will go to put down the rebellion.'

"yudde awəsan we-nə koṭə paniwiḍə kaarə-ek ee-wi"
war   finish-NPT   when messenger-INDF   come-INFER
'When the war draws to a close, there will be a messenger.'

"maŋ dinu.ot   sudu   koḍi-yak   osəwa-awi
I   win.PT-COND white flag-INDF   raise-INFER
pærədun-ot   kalu kodi-yak   osəwa-awi"
lose.PT-COND   black flag-INDF raise-INFER
'If I win he will raise a white flag and if I lose the battle a black flag will be raised.'

iilangə dawas-e   Buwanekaba raju-ge   seenaawa-t Agbo kumaarəya-ge
next   day-LOC   Buwanekaba king-GEN   army-and   Agbo prince-GEN
seenaawa-t atərə   yudde paṭan gatta
army-and   between war   start.PAST
'On the following day the war broke out between King Buwanekaba's army and Prince Agbo's army.'

yudd-en   Agbo kumaarəya miyəgiyaa Buwanekaba rajə   jayə gatta
battle-ABL   Agbo prince   die-PAST   Buwanekaba king   win.PAST
'Prince Agbo was killed in the battle while King Buwanekaba achieved victory.'

koḍi   baarə   paniwiḍəkaarəya purə-wərə-yə-ṭə   gihin
flags in charge   emissary   city-HON-SG-DAT   go.PP
bisoo-wər-un-ṭa-t   raṭə wæsiyan-ṭa-t   yudde pratipalə
queen-HON-PL-DAT-and   citizens-DAT-and   war   result
dænum de-nnə   piṭat unaa
inform-INF   leave.PAST
'The royal emissary in charge of flags left for the royal city to announce the result of the battle to the queens as well as the citizens.'

paniwiḍəkaarəya atərəmagədii raapolə-kə   natərə we-laa
messenger   on the way   toddy-booth-INDF.LOC stop-PP
raa   bii-la   weriunaa
toddy drink-PP   be drunk-PAST
'On the way, the messenger stopped at a toddy booth, drank toddy and got drunk.'

wihiluw-ak   kəra-nnə   hitaagenə   miniha kalu   koḍiə   issuwa
joke-INDF   do-INF   think.REFL.PP   man   black flag   raise-PAST
'Thinking to make fun, he raised the black flag.'

kalu   koḍiə   dækkə   bisoo-wəru   hituwa
black   flag   see-PT   queen-HON.PL   think.PAST
rajətumaa yudd-en   paraadə una-i   kiyala
king   battle-ABL   be defeated.PAST-AM   that
'Seeing the black flag, the queens thought that the king was defeated in the battle.'

aneee!	bisoo-wəru	hæṭə	pas	denaa-mə	bælumgal-en	pænə-la
alas!	Queen-HON.PL	sixty	five	people-EM	lookout-rock-ABL	jump-PP

siyə diwi   nasaa gatta
commit   suicide-PAST

'Alas! All the sixty-five queens jumped off the Lookout Rock and committed suicide.'

saṭən-in	jayə arəŋ	rajə	pərəhar-en	maaligaawə-ṭə	aapu
battle-ABL	win.PP	royal	procession-INS	palace-DAT	come.PTAD

rajətumaa	mee	winaase	dækə-la	kampaawe-laa
king	this	disaster	see-PP	be shocked-PP

gal-en   pænə-la   siyə diwi nasaa gatta
rock-ABL   jump-PP   commit suicide.PAST

'The victorious king returned to the palace with pomp and ceremony but was shocked to see this disaster and jumped off the rock committing suicide.'

edaa	maaligaa-we	ituru un-ee	bilindu	put	kumara	witərai
that day	palace-LOC	be left.PT-FOC	baby	son	prince	only

'On that day only the baby prince was left alone in the palace.'

waasənaawəṭə	eten-ṭə	aapu	maaligaa-we	redinænda
fortunately	there-DAT	come.PTAD	palace-LOC	laundress

punchi   kumaarəya-wa   dækka
little   prince-ACC   see.PAST

'Fortunately, the laundress of the palace arrived there in time and saw the little prince.'

redinænda	daruwa-wə	redikəḍə-kə	otaagenə
laundress	child-ACC	piece of cloth-INDF.LOC	wrap up.REFL.PP

hangagenə   maligaa-wen   pænəla   giyaa
hide.REFL.PP palace-ABL   flee-PP go.PAST

'Having hurriedly wrapped the child in a cloth she concealed it and fled from the palace.'

edaa	redinænda	daruwa-wə	hangə-pu	tænə	Hengawatta	nam-in
that day	laundress	child-ACC	hide.PT	place	Hengawtta	name-INS

prasidda unaa
be known.PAST

'The place she hid the baby on that day became known as Henga-watta ('Hide-yard').'

antimiṭə	Kalundawe	gaməraala	atəṭə	lamea-wə	giyaa
finally	kalundawa	village headman	hand-DAT	child-ACC	go.PAST

'Eventually, the child came into the possession of the village-headman of Kalundewa.'

lamea	Appuwa	kiənə	nam-in	saamaanya	gam-ee	lame-yek
child	Appuwa	called	name-INS	ordinary	village-LOC	child-INDF

hæṭiyəṭə   hadaa waḍaa gatta
as   bring up.PAST

'The child was named Appuwa and was brought up as an ordinary village boy.'

kaalə-yak	yanə	koṭə	Appuwa	hæḍi ḍæḍi	tarunə-yek	unaa
time-INDF	go	when	Appuwa	robust	youth-INDF	become.PAST

'Some years passed and Appuwa grew up to be a robust young man.'

oyə	gaməraalə-ṭə	duu-la	denn-ek	hiṭiya
that	village headman-DAT	daughter-PL	two-INDF	be-PAST

'The village headman had two daughters.'

wæḍimal	duwə	Kalu ethana,	baalə	duwə	Sirimal etəna
elder	daughter	Kalu-ethana	younger	daughter	Sirimal-ethana

'The elder daughter was Kalue-thana and the younger daughter was Sirimal-ethana.'

Kalu ethana	særa-i,	baalə	duwə	Sirimal etəna
Kalu-ethana	rough-AM	younger	daughter	Sirimal-ethana

Appuwa-ṭə	karunaawanta-i
Appuwa-DAT	kind-AM

'The elder daughter, Kalu ethana, was rude to Appuwa while the younger daughter, Sirimal ethana, was kind to him.'

Sirimalethana	Appuwa-ṭə	nitərəmə	gaurawə-en	sæləkuwa
Sirimal-ethana	Appuwa-DAT	always	respect-INS	treat.PAST

'Sirimal-ethana always looked up to him.'

itin	gaməraalə	Sirimalethana-wə	Appuwa-ṭə	bandə-la	dunna
so	village headman	Sirimal-ethana-ACC	Appuwa-DAT	marry.PP	give.PAST

'So the village headman married her to Appuwa.'

mee	denna	bændə-la	alut	gedərakə	padinchiə-ṭə giyaa
these	two people	marry-PP	new	house-INDF.LOC	settle down.PAST

'After their marriage, Appuwa and Sirimal Ehtana settled down in a new house.'

gaməraalə-gen	oun-ṭə	idəm-ak-ui	kumbur-ak-ui
village headman-ABL	them-DAT	land-INDF-and	field-INDF-and

hambə	una
be received.PAST	

'They received a plot of land and a rice field from the village headman.'

mee	wenə	koṭə	Kurunegala	raajədhaaniə	paalənee kəl-ee
this	be	when	Kurunegala	kingdom	control.PT-FOC

Wath-himi	kumaarəya-i
Wath-himi	prince-AM

'By this time, it was prince Wath-himi that was ruling the Kurunegala kingdom.'

arə	miyə giya	Buwanekaba	rajjuruwan-ṭə	muslim	bisow-ak	hiṭiya.
that	die-PT	Buwanekabaa	king.HON-DAT	Muslim	queen-INDF	be.PAST

'The late king Buwanekaba had a queen of Muslim origin.'

æyə-ṭə	upan	kumaarəya	tamai	Wath-himi	kiya-nn-e
she-DAT	born	prince	FM	Wath-himi	say-NPT.FOC

'It was the prince born to this queen that was called Wath-himi'

awaasənaawə-ṭə	muslim	kumaarəy-ek	sinhaasən-ee	in-nə	ekə
bad luck-DAT	Muslim	prince-INDF	throne-LOC	be-INF	that

æməti-waru	rissuw-e	næ̈
minister-PL.HON	like.PT-FOC	no

'Unfortunately, his ministers didn't like the fact that a son of Muslim origin remains in the throne.'

kumaarəya-wə	mara-nnə	kumantrənə-yak	diyat keruna
prince-ACC	kill-INF	plot-INDF	launch.INVL.PAST

'They were plotting a coup to kill the prince.'

Kurunegala	Etugala	mudun-ee	pawatta-na	pirit	deesənaawə-ṭə
Kurunegala	Elephant Rock	top-LOC	hold.NPT	pirit	chanting-DAT

Wath-himi	kumaarəyaṭa-t	aaraadənaa kəlaa
Wath-himi	prince-DAT-too	invite.PAST

'The prince was invited to a Pirit chanting ceremony held at the top of the Elephant Rock in Kurunegala.'

æməti-wəru	sælasum kərə-la	tibunu	widiyə-ṭə	indəgenə hiṭiə
minister-PL.HON	plan do-PP	be.PT	way-DAT	be seated.PT

aasənəya-t	ekkəmə	rajə-tumaa	gal parwətə-yen	pahalə-ṭə
seat-too	together	king-HON	stone rock-ABL	below-DAT

pərəlaa	dæmma
push-PP	put.PAST

'As had been plotted by the ministers, the king was pushed off the rock together with the seat he was sitting.'

Wath-himi	kumaarəyaa-ge	maran-en	passea	raṭee	rajəkəmə-ṭə
Wath-himi	prince-GEN	death-ABL	after	country-LOC	kingship-DAT

suduss-ek	tooraga-nnə	eka-i	iilangə	prasne
suitable-INDF	select-INF	one-AM	next	question

'The next step was to find a suitable successor to the throne vacated by the death of Prince Wath-himi.'

mee kaariyə	baarə un-ee	mangələ	hastiraajəyaa-ṭa-i
this task	be entrusted-FOC	auspicious	royal elephant-DAT-AM

'It was the royal elephant that the task was entrusted to.'

rajəwaasələ	magula ætaa	kauruhari	idiriye	dangahala	wændot
royal palace	royal elephant	somebody	before	kneel down-PP	greet-COND

ee tænatta	raṭ-ee	rajəkəmə-ṭə	patwe-nəwa	kiyala
that person	country-LOC	kingship-DAT	be appointed-IND	that

sampərədaay-ak	ee	kaal-e	tiuna
tradition-INDF	that	time-LOC	be-PAST

'Tradition goes that the person before whom the royal elephant would kneel down and greet him is to be crowned king.'

æməti-wəru	pærəni	chaaritərree	hæṭiyə-ṭə	wædə	kəlaa
minister-PL.HON	ancient	custom	way-DAT	work.PAST	

'The ministers followed the procedures laid down by the ancient custom.'

mangul ætaa	sarəsə-laa	berə	sak	handə	mædde
royal elephant	decorate-PP	drum	conch	sound	midst

peræhær-ee	yæuwa
procession-LOC	go.CAUS.PAST

'They decorated the royal elephant and dispatched him in procession amidst the sounds of drums and conch.'

edaa	Appuwa	kumbur-e	wædə
that day	Appuwa	rice-field-LOC	work

'On that day Appuwa was working in his rice-field.'

Ranbamaraketa	kiyənə	kumburə	haa-nəwa
Ranbamaraketa	called	rice-field	plough-IND

'He was ploughing the rice-field called Ranbamaraketa.'

Sirimala ethana	dawal	æmbulə	genaawa
Sirimal-ethana	day	pot meal	bring-PAST

'Sirimal-ethana brought the pot meal (to the rice-field).'

Appuwa	dawal	kææmə	araŋ	mahansiə	niwaa gannə
Appuwa	day	meal	take.PP	fatigue	get over-INF

birində-ge	ukel-e	oluwə	tiyaagenə	ṭikak	nidaagatta
wife-GEN	lap-LOC	head	lay.REFL.PP	a little	sleep.REFL-PAST

'After having had his lunch, Appuwa slept a little with his head on his wife's lap to get over his fatigue.'

ṭikə	welaaw-ak-in	Appuwa	hiinəyak	dækka
little	time-INDF-INS	Appuwa	dream-INDF	see.PAST

'After a while Appuwa saw a dream.'

nagule	miiyak	bændə.la
plough-LOC	bee-hive-INDF	build.PP

'There was a bee-hive built on his plough.'

Appuwa	ikmənətə	nægitə-la	Sirimal ethana-tə	hiine	gænə	kiiwa
Appuwa	suddenly	wake up-PP	Sirimal-ethana-DAT	dream	about	tell.PAST

'Suddenly Appuwa awakened from his nap and told his wife about the dream.'

Sirimal ethana	hiine	teerum kəlaa
Sirimal-ethana	dream	interpret.PAST

'Sirimal-ethana interpreted the dream.'

ehenam	kisimə	anumaanəyak	nǽæ	oyaa	rajə	we-nəwa	maŋ	agəbisowə
then	any	doubt-INDF	no	you	king	become-IND	I	top queen

"Then there is no doubt. You are becoming king! I am to be the queen consort!!"

kiya-la	Sirimal	ethana	hinaa unaa
say-PP	Sirimal	ethana	laugh.PAST

'Said Sirimal-ethana laughing.'

mee	kataawə	ya-ddi	ǽæt-in	berə	saddəy-ak	æhe-nnə	patan gatta
this	talk	go-while	far-ABL	drum	sound-INDF	hear-INF	begin-PAST

'While the conversation was going on, they heard the throb of distant drums.'

dennaa-tə	æs	adəhaa	gan-nə	bæriunaa
Two(anim.)-DAT	eye	believe.REFL-INF	be impossible.PAST

'The two couldn't believe their eyes.'

mangələ hasti raajəya	welyaayə	mædden	mee	gollə	dihaa-tə
royal elephant	terrace of rice-field	through	these	people	direction-DAT

garugaaambiirə	taaletə	e-nəwa
solemn	style-DAT	come-IND

'The royal elephant was stepping solemnly through the rice-fields in their direction!'

pitipassen	æməti-wəru	kandaayəm-ak	ekkə	loku	perahærak.
behind	minister-HON(PL)	group-INDF	together	big	procession-INDF

'Behind him a grand parade was marching along with a cabinet of ministers following it.'

kumburə-tə	aapu	mangələ hastiraajəya	Appuwa	idirie	danə
rice-field-DAT	come.PT	royal elephant	Appuwa	before	kneel

gahala	namaskaarə kəlaa
down-PP	greet.PAST

'The royal tusker came forward to the rice-field, knelt down before Appuwa and greeted him.'

Appuwa	suwəndə	pæn-in	naa-wə-laa	salupili	andə-wə-la	ætaa
Appuwa	fragrant	water-INS	bathe-CAUS-PP	garment	wear-CAUS-PP	elephant

pit-ee	waadi kərəwagenə	maaligəyə-tə	kændəwa-genə	giya
back-LOC	sit.CAUS.REFL.PP	palace-DAT	escort.REFL.PP	go-PAST

'They bathed Appuwa in fragrant water, dressed him in royal robes, sat him on the elephant's back and escorted him to the palace (for the coronation ceremony).'

mee widiə-tə	Appuwa	Etugalpur-ee	rajə	unaa	Sirimal ethana
this way-DAT	Appuwa	Etugalpura-LOC	king	become.PAST	Sirimal ethana

agə	bisəwə	unaa
top	queen	become.PAST

'This is how Appuwa was enthroned at Etugal City and Sirimal ethana became the queen consort.'

miyə giyə	Wath-himi	kumaarəya	dewi-ek	unaa.
die.PT	Wath-hime	prince	god-INDF	become.PAST

'And the Prince Wath-himi who had been killed became a god.'

Janii janayaa-ge	dukə	bala-nnə	sudu aswəy-ek	piṭə	nægə-la
many people-GEN	suffering	see-INF	white horse-INDF	back	ride-PP

Etugala	haraha	særisara-nne	ee	Galee Bandara	deiyo
Etugala	across	travel-NPT.FOC	that	Galee Bandara	god

'It is this God Galee Bandara that travels across Etugala riding a white horse to care about the sufferings of many people.'

Conversation: "Audition"

The following text was taken from a novel which was originally written as the script for a radio drama. According to the introduction written by the program director of the local FM radio, the drama was produced using data collected through a social survey and was broadcast in a morning program aimed at housewives. The situation depicted in the text is from the starting scene in which a group of young people are practicing for a music band.

kawadaawat	nætuwə	ayya	ma-ṭə	ee gollo	bæænḍ	prakṭis
ever	without	elder brother	I-DAT	those people	band	practice

kərə-nə	tænə-ṭə	kataa kəraamə	puduma-t	hituna
do-NPT	place-DAT	call.TEMP	surprise-too	feel-PAST

'I was surprised to be called by my elder brother for the first time to the place they practice for the band.'

mokədə	eyaa	kawadaawat	eyaa-ge	yaalu-wo	issərəha-ṭə	maṭə
because	he	ever	he-GEN	friend-PL	before-DAT	I-DAT

e-nnə	de-nne	næe
come-INF	give-NPT-FOC	no

'The reason is, he never allows me to join his friends.'
Lit. 'The reason is, he never allows me to go before his friends.'

ayya	maa-wə	nangi	kenek	parissaŋ kərə-nəwa-ṭa-t	wadaa
elder brother	I-ACC	younger sister	one	protect-IND-DAT-too	than

taatta kenek	daruw-ek	parissaŋ kərə-nəwa	wage	parissaŋ kəree
father one	child-INDF	protect-IND	like	protect.PAST.FOC

'He protected me in the way a father protects his child rather than the way an elder brother does his sister.'

"æi kataa kəl-ee"
why call.PAST-FOC
'Why did you call me?'

"oyaa-țə bæri-də apee loonch ekə-țə hondə ḍaansin aițəms țikak
you-DAT can't-Q our launch one-DAT good dancing items several
hadə-la de-nnə"
make-PP give-INF
'Can't you make for us some nice dances for our launching (of the band)?'

"maŋ Asha mis-gen aha-la balə-nnam"
I Asha miss-ABL ask-PP see-OPT
'I'll try and talk to Miss Asha about it.'

"gææni kæməti wei-də?"
woman like-INFER-Q
('How do you think?') Will the woman like the idea?'

"akəmæti we-nə ekak nææ"
dislike-NPT NM no
'She'll not dislike it.'

"mmh kataa kərə-la balə-nəwa-ko"
mmh talk-PP see-IND-ko
'mmh... then try and talk to her.'

"maŋ ya-nnaŋ"
I go-OPT
'OK. Let me be off.'

"mokədə hadissi țikak in-nəwa-ko wædəgat wædə-kə-țə
why hurry a little be-IND-ko important job-INDF-DAT
kataakəraamə duwa-nnə hadə-nəwa"
call.TEMP run-INF try-IND
'Why are you in such a hurry? Wait a moment. While you have been called for an important job, you're trying to run away.'

Appendix

Appendix A

Numerals

Noninal form	**Adjectival form**
1. ekə	ek/ekə
2. dekə	de
3. tunə	tun
4. hatərə	hatərə/haarə
5. paha	pas/pan
6. hayə	hayə
7. hatə	hat
8. aʈə	aʈə
9. naməyə/nawəya	namə/nawə
10. dahayə	daha/daa
11. ekolaha	ekolos
12. dolaha	dolos
13. dahatunə	dahatun
14. daahatərə	daahatərə
15. pahalohə	pahalos
16. daasəyə	daasəyə
17. daahatə	daahat
18. dahaaʈə	dahaaʈə
19. dahanawəya	dahanawə
20. wissə	wisi
30. tiha	tis
40. hatəliha	hatəlis
50. panaha	panas
60. hæTə	hætə
70. hættææwə	hættææ
80. asuuwə	asuu
90. anuuwə	anuu
100. siiyə	siyə/ekəsiyə
1000. daahə	daas/ekədaas
10000. dahadaaha	dahadaas

100000.	laksəyə	laksə
1000000.	dasəlaksəyə	dasəlaksə
10000000	kooʈiə	kooʈi

Appendix B

Interrogative words

kaudə 'who (human)'
kookədə 'which one (noun)'
kohedə 'where (non-specific)'
kotənədə 'where (specific)'
kohaaʈə 'where (direction)'
kohomədə 'how'
koi 'which (adjective)'
kochchərə 'how' (degree)'
kiiədə 'how much'
kiiyaddə 'how many'
kiiəʈədə 'when (time)' or 'at what price'
kawədadə 'when (day)'
mokaddə 'what (sg.)' (noun)
monəwadə (what (pl.)' (noun)
monə 'what' (adjective)
mokaadə 'who (animal or derogatory)'
monundə 'who (animal, pl.)'
mokədə 'what' or 'why'
æi 'why'

Appendix 285

Appendix C

Verbal Inflection Paradigm

	Indicative	Emphatic/focus	Imperative	Volitive optative	Infinitive	Gerund	Adverbal participle	Adjective-participle	Subjunctive	Others
Active non-past	kapənəwa	kapanne	kapannə kapəpan	kapannam	kapannə	kæpiimə kæpillə kæpumə	kapətə	kapənə	kapətot kapətat	kapəmu kapaawi kapai kapaddi
Active past	kæpua	kæpue					kapaa kapəla	kæpuə kapaapu	kæpuot kæpuat	kæpuaawe kæpuaamə
Causative non-past	kappənəwa kappəwə-nəwa	kappanne kappəwa-nne	kappannə kappəpan kappəwə-pan	kappannam kappəwa-nnam	kappannə kappəwa-nnə	kæppiimə kæppə-wiimə		kappənə kappəwə-nə	kappətot kappəwətot kappətat kappəwa-tat	kappəmu kappəwəmu kappəwaawi kappəwai kappəwaddi
causative past	kæppuwa kæppeuwa	kæppuwe kæppeuwe					kappəla kappəwaa kappəwə-la	kæppuu kæppəwuu kappəwə-pu	kæppuwot kæppeuwot kæppuwat kæppeuwat	kæppuwaawe kæppeuwaa-we kæppuwamə
Involitive non-past	kæpenəwa	kæpenne	kæpennə kæpiyan	kæpennam	kæpennə	kæpiimə kæpillə kæpumə		kæpenə	kæpetot kæpetat	kæpemu kæpeewi kæpei kæpeddi
Involitive past	kæpuna	kæpune					kæpii kæpila	kæpuna kæpichchə	kæpunot kæpunat	kæpunaawe kæpunaamə

References

Abhayasinghe, A.A. 1973. *A Morphological Study of Sinhalese*. Unpublished Ph.D. Dissertation. University of York.
Abhayasinghe, A.A. 1990. *Sinhala bhashawe sarala wakya wibhagaya* [Syntax of Simple Sentences in Sinhala]. Kadawata: Author Publication.
Abhayasinghe, A.A. 1992. *Sinhala bhashawe sankirna wakya wibhagaya* [Syntax of Complex Sentences in Sinhala]. Kadawata: Author Publication.
Austin, J.L. 1962. *How to Do Things with Words*. Cambridge, Mass: Harvard University Press.
Bhat, D.N.S. 1988. *Grammatical Relations in Indian Languages*. Mysore: Central Institute of Indian Languages.
Bolinger, D.L. 1977. *Meaning and Form*. London: Longman.
Bril, Isabelle. 2004. Deixis in Nêlêmwa (New Caledonia). In Gunter Senft (ed.), *Deixis and Demonstratives in Oceanic languages, Pacific Linguistics* 562, 99–128.
Brown, Penelope & Stephen Levinson. 1987. *Politeness: Some universals in Language Usage*. Cambridge: Cambridge University Press.
Bybee, Joan L., Revere D. Perkins, & William Pagliuca. 1994. *The Evolution of Grammar: Tense, Aspect and Modality in the Languages of the World*. Chicago: University of Chicago Press.
Chafe, Wallace. 1987. Cognitive constraints on information flow. In Russell Tomlin (ed.), *Coherence and Grounding in Discourse*, 21–25. Amsterdam: John Benjamins.
Chafe, Wallace. 1994. *Discourse, Consciousness and Time*. Chicago: University of Chicago Press.
Chandralal, Dileep. 1993. Correspondence between Semantic Categories and Morphosyntax: Case Marking and Clause Structure in Sinhala. *Bunkagaku Nenpo* 12: 1–48. Kobe University.
Chandralal, Dileep. 2005. *Language and Space: Cognitive Semantics of Sinhala Grammatical Categories*. Colombo: Vishva Lekha Publications.
Chatterji, Suniti Kumar. 1926. *The origin and Development of the Bengali Language*, 2 parts. Culcutta: Culcutta University Press.
Chatterji, Suniti Kumar. 1948. The Sinhala Speech. In *Ceylon Souvenir, February 4, 1948*. New Delhi: Publications Division, Ministry of Information and Broadcasting.
Coates, William A. & M.W.S. De Silva. 1960. Segmental Phonemes of Sinhalese. *University of Ceylon Review* 18:163–175.
Codrington, H.W. 1929. *A Short History of Ceylon*. London: Macmillan and Co. Ltd. [reprinted, New Delhi: Asian Educational Services, 1994].
Colombo. 2001. *Statistical Pocket Book 2001: The Democratic Socialist Republic of Sri Lanka*. Colombo: Department of Census and Statistics. (Web site: www.statistics.gov.lk)
Dantsuji, Masatake. 1987. Some Acoustic Observations on Half Nasals in Sinhalese. Paper presented at the 11th International Congress of Phonetic Sciences August 1–7, 1987, Tallinn, Estonia, USSR.
De Abrew, K.K.D. 1963. *A Syntactical Study of the Verbal Piece of Colloquial Sinhalese*. Unpublished M.A. thesis, Cornell University.
De Abrew, Kaluhath Kamal. 1981. *The Syntax and Semantics of Negation in Sinhala*. Unpublished Ph.D. Dissertation. Cornell University.
De Saram, D.D. 1964. *The Nominal in Colloquial Sinhalese*. Unpublished M.A. thesis, Cornell University.

De Silva, M.W.S. 1958. Gender in Colloquial Sinhalese. *University of Ceylon Review* 16:119–24.
De Silva, M.W.S. 1959. Syllable Structure in Spoken Sinhalese: A prosodic Statement. *University of Ceylon Review* 17:106–16.
De Silva, M.W.S. 1960. Verbal Categories in Spoken Sinhalese. *University of Ceylon Review* 18:96–112.
De Silva, M.W.S. 1967. Effects of Purism on the Evolution of the Written Language: Case History of the Sinhalese Situation. *Linguistics* 36:5–17.
De Silva, M.W.S. 1969. Sinhalese. In T. Seboek (ed.), *Current Trends in Linguistics* v. The Hague: Mouton.
De Silva, M.W.S. 1974. Convergence in Diglossia: the Sinhalese Situation. In F. Southworth & M.L. Apte, (eds.), *Contact and Convergence in South Asian Languages*: 61–96 (Special Number of IJDL 3.1).
De Silva, M.W.S. 1976a. *Diglossia and Literacy*. Mysore: Central Institute of Indian Languages.
De Silva, M.W.S. 1976b. Verbal Aspects of Politeness Expression in Sinhalese with Reference to Asking, Telling, Requesting and Ordering. *Anthropological Linguistics*, Vol. XVIII: 360–70.
De Silva, M.W.S. 1979. *Sinhalese and Other Island Languages in South Asia. Ars Linguistics* 3. Tübingen: Gunter Narr Verlag.
Dharmadasa, K.N.O. 1967. *Spoken and Written Sinhalese: A Contrastive Study*, Unpublished M. Phil. thesis, University of York.
Diessel, Holger. 1999. *Demonstratives: Form, Function and Grammaticalization*. Amsterdam: John Benjamins Publishing Company.
Disanayaka, J.B. 1974. *Say it in Sinhala*. Colombo: Lake House.
Disanayaka, J.B. 1976. *National Languages of Sri Lanka I: Sinhala*. Colombo: Department of Cultural Affairs.
Dixon, R.M.W. 1979. Eragativity. *Language* 55: 59–138.
Fairbanks, Gair & De Silva. 1968. *Colloquial Sinhalese (Sinhala)*, Part 1 & 2. Ithaca, N.Y.: South Asia Program, Cornell University.
Fernando, M.S. 1973. *The Syntax of Complex Sentences in Sinhalese*. Unpublished Ph.D. dissertation. University of London.
Fillmore, Charles J. 1968. The Case for Case. In Bach & R. Harms (eds.), *Universals in Language Theory*. Holt, Rinehart and Winston.
Fillmore, Charles J. 1975. Santa Cruz Lectures on Deixis 1971. Reproduced by the Indiana University Linguistics Club.
Fillmore, Charles J. 1982. Towards a descriptive framework for spatial deixis. In *Jarvella and Klein* 1982.
Foley, A. William & Robert D. Van Valin. 1984. *Functional Syntax and Universal Grammar*. Cambridge: Cambridge University Press.
Gair, James, W. 1968. Sinhalese Diglossia. *Anthropological Linguistics* 10,8: 1–15.
Gair, James, W. 1970. *Colloquial Sinhalese Clause Structure*. The Hague: Mouton.
Gair, James, W. 1976. Is Sinhala a Subject language? (or, How restricted is Your PNP?) In Manindra Verma (ed.), *The Notion of Subject in South Asian Languages*, 39–64. Madison: South Asia program, University of Wisconsin.
Gair, James W. 1983. Non-Configurationality, Movement, and Sinhala Focus. Paper presented at the Linguistics Association of Great Britain, Newcastle.
Gair, James W. 1986. Sinhala Diglossia Revisited, or Diglossia dies hard. In Bh. Krishanamurti, Colin P. Masica & Anjani Sinha (eds.), *South Asian Languages: Structure, Convergence and Diglossia*, 147–64. Delhi: Motilal Banarsidass.
Gair, James, W. 1991a. Discourse and Situational Deixis in Sinhala. In *Studies in Dravidian and general Linguistics. Osmania University Publications in Linguistics* 6, 448–467.
Gair, James W. 1991b. Subjects, Case and INFL in Sinhala. In Manindra K. Verma & K.P. Mohanan (eds.), *Experiencer Subjects in South Asian Languages*. SLA Stanford University Press.

Gair, James W. 1998. *Studies in South Asian Linguistics: Sinhala and Other South Asian Languages*. New York: Oxford University Press.

Gair, James W. et al. 1989. Acquisition of Null Subjects and Control in Some Sinhala Adverbial Clauses. *Paper and Reports on Child Language Development* 28:97–106.

Gair, James W. & John C. Paolillo. 1988. Sinhala Nonverbal Sentences and Argument Structures. *Cornell Working Papers in Linguistics* 8:39–78.

Gair, James W. & L. Sumangala. 1991. What to Focus in Sinhala. In *ESCOL '91: Proceedings of the Eighth Eastern States Conference on Linguistics*, 93–108.

Geiger, Wilhelm. 1912. *The Mahavamsa or The Great Chronicle of Ceylon*, translated into English by W. Geiger (Pali text Society, translation series). London: Luzas.

Geiger, Wilhelm. 1935. Sinhalese Language and Literature. In Jayatilaka et al. (eds.), *A Dictionary of the Sinhalese Language*, Installment 1.1. Colombo: Royal Asiatic Society.

Geiger, Wilhelm. 1937. The Linguistic Character of Sinhalese. *Journal, R.A.S. (Ceylon)*, Vol.xxxiv, No 90:16–43.

Geiger, Wilhelm. 1938. *A Grammar of the Sinhalese Language*. Colombo: The Royal Asiatic Society Ceylon Branch.

Gnana Prakasar, Rev. Father S. 1936. The Dravidian Element in Sinhalese. *Journal, R.A.S. (Ceylon)*, Vol. xxxiii No 89:233–253.

Genetti, Carol. 1986. The Development of Subordinators from Postpositions in Bodic Languages. *BLS* 12: 387–400.

Goffman, E. 1981. *Forms of Talk*. Philadelphia: University of Pennsylvania Press.

Greenberg, Joseph H. 1963. Some Universals of Grammar with Particular Reference to the Order of Meaningful Elements. In Greenberg (ed.), *Universals of Language*, 73–113. Cambridge, Mass: MIT Press.

Grenoble, Lenore A. 1998. *Deixis and Information Packaging in Russian Discourse*. Amsterdam/Philadelphia: John Benjamins Publishing Company.

Gunasekara, A.M. 1891. *A Comprehensive Grammar of the Sinhala Language*. Colombo: Government Press [reprinted: New Delhi: Asian Educational Services, 1986].

Gunasinghe, Hemamali. 1978. *Do and Happen: The Ergative in Colloquial Sinhala: A Semantic Analysis*. Unpublished M.A. thesis. University of Victoria.

Gunasinghe, Hemamali & Joseph F. Kess. 1985. Preliminaries to the Reanalysis of the Sinhala Passive. In Ratanakul, Thomas & Premsrirat (eds.), *Southeast Asian Linguistic Studies presented to Andre-G. Haudricourt*. Institute of Language and Culture, Mahidol University, Bangkok: 82–112.

Gunasinge, K.H.H. 1985. *Passive Voice: A New Perspective: Some Evidence for a Reanalysis from Sinhala*. Unpublished Ph.D. dissertation, University of Victoria.

Hagstrom, Paul Alan. 1998. *Decomposing Questions*. Unpublished Ph.D. dissertation. M.I.T.

Henadeerage, Deepthi Kumara. 2002. *Topics in Sinhala Syntax*. Unpublished Ph.D. thesis, The Australian National University.

Hundirapola, Ratanajoti. 1975. *The Syntactic Structure of Sinhalese and its Relation to that of the Other Indo-Aryan Dialects*. Unpublished Ph.D. dissertation, The University of Texas at Austin.

Inman, Michael. 1992. Intentionality in Sinhala. *CLS* 23: Papers from the 28th Regional Meeting of the Chicago Linguistic Society 1992, 239–250.

Inman, Michael Vincent. 1993. *Semantics and Pragmatics of Colloquial Sinhala Involitive Verbs*. Unpublished Ph.D. dissertation, Stanford University.

Iwasaki, Shoichi. 2002. *Japanese*. London Oriental and Afrcan Language Library Vol. 5, Amsterdam/Philadelpia: John Benjamin Publishing Company.

Jackendoff, Ray S. 1972. *Semantic Interpretation in Generative Grammar*. Cambridge: MIT Press.
Jarvella, Robert J. & Wolfgang Klein (eds.), 1982. *Speech, Place and Action: Studies in Deixis and related topics*. Chichester: John Wiley.
Jayasekara, Saman Buddhika. 2007. Rosa Suwanda [The Fragrance of Rose]. Alubomulla: Nadee Prakashana Publishers.
Jayewardene, R.P.T. 1971. *Case in Sinhalese*. Unpublished Ph.D. dissertation, School of Oriental and African Studies, University of London.
Kano, Mitsuru. 1994. *An Analysis of the Deictic Use in Sinhala Demonstrative Expressions in terms of Mental Domains*. ms. Nagaoka University of Technology.
Karunatillake, W.S. 1992. *An Introduction to Spoken Sinhala*. Colombo: M.D. Gunasena & Co.
Keenan, Edward L. & Barnard Comrie. 1977. Noun Phrase Accessibility and Universal Grammar. *Linguistic Inquiry* 8:1:63–99.
Keenan, Edward L. 1981. *Passive in the World's Languages*. Trier: Linguistic Agency, University of Trier.
Kekulawala, S.L. *The Phonology of the Noun in Colloquial Sinhalese*. Unpublished M.A. thesis. University of London.
Kinsui, Satoshi & Yukinori Takubo (eds.), 1992. *Shijishi* [Demonstratives]. *Nihongo kenkyuu shiryoushuu*. Tokyo: Hitsuji-shoboo.
Kiparsky, Paul & Carol Kiparsky 1971. Fact. In Danny D. Steinberg & Leon A. Jakobovits (eds.), *Semantics: an interdisciplinary reader in philosophy, linguistics, and psychology*, 345–369, New York: Cambridge University Press.
Kishimoto, Hideki. 1991. *On the Nature of Quantificational Expressions and Their Logical Form*. Unpublished Ph.D. dissertation. Kobe University.
Kishimoto, Hideki. 1992. LF Pied Piping: Evidence from Sinhala. *Gengo Kenkyuu* 102, 46–87.
Kishimoto, Hideki. 1996. Split Intransitivity in Japanese and the Unaccusative Hypothesis. *Language* 72: 248–286.
Kishimoto, Hideki. 2005. Wh-in-situ and Movement in Sinhala Questions. *Natural Language and Linguistic Theory* 23: 1–51.
Kumaratunga, Munidasa. 1983. *Wyakarana Wiwaranaya* [Grammar Analysis]. Colombo: M.D. Gunasena & Co [first edition 1937].
Kumaratunga, Munidasa. 2005. *Kriya Wiwaranaya* [Verb Analysis]. Colombo: M.D. Gunasena & Co.
Kuno, Susumu. 1973. *The Structure of the Japanese Language*. Cambridge: MIT Press.
Kuroda, S.-Y.1992. '(Ko), so, a' ni tsuite [On '(ko), so, a']. In Kinsui and Takubo 1992: 91–104.
Lambrecht, Knud. 1994. *Information Structure and Sentence Form: Topic, Focus, and the Mental Representations of Discourse Referents*. Cambridge: Cambridge University Press.
Leech, Geoffrey. 1983. *Principles of Pragmatics*. London: Longman.
Lehmann, Chritian. 1988. Towards a typology of clause linkage. In John Haimn & Sandra A.Thomson (eds.), *Clause Combining in Grammar and Discourse*, 181–225, Amsterdam/Philadelphia: John Benjamins Publishing Company.
Lehmann, Winfred P. (ed.) 1978. *Syntactic Typology: Studies in the Phenomenology of Language*. Austin: University of Texas Press.
Levinson, Stephen C. 1983. *Pragmatics*. Cambridge: Cambridge University Press.
Margetts, Anna. 2004. Spatial Deictics in Saliba. Gunter Senft (ed.), *Deixis and Demonstratives in Oceanic Languages*, 37–57. Canberra: Australian National University.
Mendis, G.C. 1932. *The Early History of Ceylon*. Colombo: Apothecaries' Co. Ltd.
Nicholas, C.W. & S. Paranavitana 1961. *A Concise History of Ceylon*, from the earliest times to the arrival of the Portuguese in 1505. Colombo: University of Ceylon Press.

Paolillo, John C. 1997. Sinhala diglosia: Discrete or Continuous Variation? *Language in Society* 26, 269–296.
Paranavitana, S.1956a. *Sigiri Graffiti, Being Sinhalese Verses of the Eighth, Ninth and Tenth Centuries*, Vol. I. London: Oxford University Press.
Paranavitana, S. 1956b. The Evolution of the Sinhala Language. In *Sri Sumangala Shabda Koshaya*, Part 2, 1: 1181–1199. Colombo: Anula Press.
Paranavitana, S. 1959. Aryan Settlements: Sinhalese. In S. Paranavitan (ed.), *University of Ceylon History of Ceylon, History of Ceylon 1*. Colombo: University of Ceylon Press.
Paranavitana, 1961. cf. Nicholas and Paranavitana 1961.
Paranavitana, S. 1970. *Inscriptions of Ceylon*, Vol.1, Early Brahmi Inscriptions. Colombo: Department of Archaeology, Ceylon.
Parawahera, Pannakitti. *Phonology and Morphology of Modern Sinhala*. Unpublished Ph.D. dissertation, University of Victoria.
Perera, H.S. & Daniel Johns. 1919. *A Colloquial Sinhalese Reader in Phonetic Transcription* (with an introduction on the phonetics of Sinhalese). Manchester: Manchester University Press.
Popper, K.R. 1972. *Objective Knowledge: an Evolutionary Approach*. Oxford: Clarendon Press.
Premaratna, Asoka Chandrasiri. 1986. *The Verb in Early Sinhalese (from the 3c. B.C. to the 10c. A.D.)*. Unpublished Ph.D. thesis, School of Oriental and African Studies, University of London.
Punchibanda, S.M. 1990. *Kataa Karana Sinhala* (Spoken Sinhala) Nagano: JICA Komagane Training Center.
Reynolds, C.H.B. 1980. *Sinhalese*. School of Oriental and African Studies, University of London.
Senft, Gunter (ed.) 2004. *Deixis and demonstratives in Oceanic languages*, Pacific Linguistics 562. Canberra: Pacific Linguistics.
Shahidullah, M. 1933. The First Aryan Colonization of Ceylon. *Indian Historical Quarterly* 9: 742–50.
Shibatani, Masayoshi. 1973. Semantics of Japanese Causativization. *Foundations of Language* 9, 327–373.
Shibatani, Masayoshi. 1976. Causativization. In M. Shibatani (ed.), *Syntax and Semantics 5, Japanese generative Grammar* 239–294, New York: Academic Press.
Shibatani, Masayoshi. 1985. Passives and related constructions: A prototype analysis. *Language* 61.4, 821–848.
Shibatani, Masayoshi. 1990. *The languages of Japan*. Cambridge: Cambridge University Press.
Siddhartha, Rev. M. 1935. The Indian Languages and their Relation with the Sinhalese Language. *Journal, R.A.S. (Ceylon)*, Vol. XXXIII, No 88, 123–150.
Silvertein, Michael. 1976. Hierarchy of features and ergativity. R.M.W. Dixon (ed.), *Grammatical Categories in Australian Languages*. Canberra: Australian Institute of Aboriginal Studies.
Sumangala, Lelwala. 1991. "Inner" and "Outer" subjects in Sinhala. *The Cornell University Working Papers in Linguistics*, No. 9, 229–57.
Sumangala, Lelwala. 1992. *Long Distance Dependencies in Sinhala: The Syntax of Focus and Wh questions*. Unpublished Ph.D. dissertation, Cornell University.
Tilakaratne, Sunanda. 1993. *A Cognitive Semantic Study of Locative Expressions in Sinhala and a Comparison with English Locative Expressions*. Unpublished Ph.D. dissertation, University of Kansas.
Traugott, Elizabeth Closs. 1989. On the Rise of Epistemic Meanings in English: An Example of Subjectification in Semantic Change. *Language* 65: 31–55.
Traugott, Elizabeth Closs & Richard B. Dasher. 2001. *Regularity in Semantic Change* (Cambridge Studies in Linguistics). Cambridge: Cambridge University Press.
Van Valin, Robert D. 1984. A typology of syntactic relations in clause linkage. *BLS* 10:542–558.

Vendler, Zeno. 1957. Verbs and times. *The Philosophical review* 66:143–160. (reprinted in *Linguistics in Philosophy*, (1976). Ed. by Zeno Vendlar. Cornell University Press, 97–121.
Wickramasinghe, Daya Menike. 1973. *A Study in the Syntax and Phonology of Modern Colloquial Sinhalese*. Unpublished Ph.D. Thesis, University of Exeter.
Wickramasuriya, B.S.S.A. 1965. *The Nominal Phrase in Sinhalese and its bearing on Sinhalese English*. Unpublished M.A. thesis, University of London.
Wijayawardhana, G.D., Daya Wickramasinghe & Theodora Bynon. 1995. Passive-related Constructions in Colloquial Sinhala. In D.C. Bennett, T. Bynon & B.G. Hewitt (eds.), *Subject, Voice and Ergativity, Selected Essays,* 105–141.
Wijeratne, P.B.F. 1945. Phonology of the Sinhalese Inscriptions up to the End of the 10th Century A.D. [Ph.D. thesis, University of London], published in instalments in BSOAS (Bulletin of the School of Oriental and African Studies) 11.3: 580–94 and so forth.
Wilkins, David. 1999. Eliciting contrastive use of demonstratives for objects within close personal space. Wilkins (ed.), *Manual for the 1999 field season. Version 1.0*. Nijmegen: Mimeo.

Sources

Gunaratna, Ananda. 1981. *Punchi Tanakaoplapetta* [little grasshopper]. Colombo: M.D. Gunasena Co. Ltd.
Jayasekara, Saman Buddhika. 2007. *Rosa Suwanda* [The Fragrance of Rose]. Alubomulla: Nadee Prakashana Publishers.
Ratnayaka, Madawala S. 1989. *Nil Mal Wila* [Blue Lily Pond]. Nugegoda: Sarasawi Bookshop and Publishers.
Sinhala school textbook series. 1987. *Book 2 and Book 3*. Colombo: Department of Educational Publications, Sri Lanka.

Index

A
ablative constituent 156
absolute honorific system 271
accidental agent 108, 122–123, 179
accusative 19, 106, 110, 122–125, 127–128, 157
  case 45, 102, 172, 178
  marker 156
acknowledging function 237, 246
atin constituent 101, 108, 158
atin construction 153, 158–160
active 53–54, 77–78, 95–99, 101, 122–123, 152–153
  (*see also* inactive)
  active-inactive dichotomy 8
  active-type constructions 98
Actor 8, 101, 108–111, 122
addressee 47, 71, 124, 210–212, 229, 233–235, 268–269, 272
adjectival predicates 102, 104, 195, 197
adjunct phrases 116, 121
  adjunct position 157
  adjunct relation 133
adnominal 189, 195
  clausal construction 205
adverbial 13, 55, 189, 197–199, 202–205, 214, 228–230
  clause 197–198
  expressions 13
adverbs 13, 43, 54–55
affective meaning 239
"affective" use 239
affixes 43, 56, 78
agent 53, 57, 78, 101, 122–126, 160–161, 165–167, 176–177
  agent/causer 161, 177
ambiguity 19, 127, 157, 216
anaphora 47, 244, 247, 249, 251
anaphoric reference 47, 244, 250
  relation 210
animacy 46, 52, 62, 95, 124, 146, 171–172
  hierarchy 126–127
animate participants 154, 171, 177, 179
animate subjects 46, 123
antecedent 202–203, 244
'antipassive' construction 155
applicative construction 176
"appositive construction" 133
argument structures 100–102, 116
aspectual expression 145
  (*see also* inceptive aspect, inchoative aspect, perfective aspect, processive aspect, progressive aspect, resultative aspect)
assertion marker 7, 12, 51, 102, 193
assimilation 35, 77–78, 92–94, 162
attributive clauses 196
auxiliaries 139, 145–146, 148, 151, 187–188
auxiliary verbs 136, 139, 149–151

B
base form 76, 78, 81, 130, 258
basic passive construction 158
  (*see also* canonical passive construction)
benefactive construction 169–176
biclausal sentences 204
'body-posture-change' verbs 138
Buddhism 4, 27
Buddhist Doctrine 4

C
canonical passive construction 152
cardinal vowels 28
case 44–45, 78–79, 81, 87–88, 119–124, 154
  changing device 167
  form 88, 90, 130
  markers 129, 181, 197, 199
  marking 121–124, 131–132, 221
  particles 55, 100
  persistence 167
  retaining principle 167
  suffixes 82, 100, 116
cataphora 247
causal relation 200–201
causative 53, 77–78, 95–98, 160–173, 176–180
  (*see also* direct causation, "double causatives", indirect causative construction, indirect causatives, lexical causatives, morphological causative, periphrastic causatives)
causative benefactive construction 170–173
change of state 139, 148, 150, 176
citation form 44, 58, 66–67, 72–73, 76, 143
Classical Sinhalese 5–6
classifiers 60–61
clause 7–9, 11–15, 63, 98, 129–134, 181–184, 189–205
  (*see also* subordinate clauses)
  chaining 205
  combination 15
  types 8, 98
clitic 183–184, 263
cognitive stative verb 167
cognitive verbs 173
collateral coordination 181, 183
collective compounds 87, 89
Colloquial variety 2, 122
comitative construction 112, 116
  comitative particle 109
comment component 209, 211–213, 217
common nouns 43–44
complement 8–9, 132, 189–192, 220
  clause 191–192

complementizer 191, 193
completive aspect 14, 147
'complex passives' 157
complex sentences 15, 181, 189
compound 14–15, 25, 78,
    86–89, 181–184
  nouns 43–44, 86
  sentences 181–187
compounding 14, 41, 44, 86,
    88–89
concessive clauses 203
  forms 75–76
conditional clauses 201–202
  forms 75
conjugation class 67, 69, 143
conjunctions 15, 190
conjunctive endings 181
  conjunctive particles 56, 181
constituent focus 223
"content" verbs 192
context 71, 140–141,
    154–155, 201, 210–212,
    227–228, 257
  context-construable
    information 217
  context-sensitive 254
contextual configurations 272
contrastive contexts 237
  contrastive focus 11, 217, 225
  contrastive particle 209
  contrastive reading 210
  contrastive stress 224
coordination 181–188

D
dative 17–18, 45, 103–106, 108,
    111, 113–114, 139–142
  constituents 132, 174–175
  objects 167, 174
  subject construction 153,
    160, 213
declarative expressions 134
declarative sentences 11, 210
definite 8, 44–45, 60–63, 79,
    209–210 (see also indefinite)
  definiteness 43–49, 58,
    78–79, 207–208, 210
defocusing 153, 156
deictic demonstratives 47–48,
    52, 228
deictic expressions 229, 232,
    238–241, 249
deictic system 227–228

deixis 227–229, 231–232,
    234–238, 242, 245–247
    (see also situataional deixis,
    social deixis, spatial deixis)
demonstrative pronouns 47–49,
    52, 239
demonstratives 47–48,
    227–228, 230, 242–243,
    250–251
demoted agent 158
deontic and epistemic
    modals 140
derivational morphology 77
  derivational suffixes 57, 77, 83
desententialization 193
desiderative modality 140–141
detached attitude 244, 265
determiners 227–229
detransitivization 97–98
diglossia 2, 160
Dipavansa 2
direct causation 172, 176
direct object 8, 16, 19, 127–128,
    131, 133, 154, 172, 221
Direct Speech 56, 193, 253
    (see also Indirect Speech)
directionality 111, 128, 148
directives 255
discourse 56, 207–210, 227–228,
    234, 237–238, 242–245,
    247–254
  deixis 245, 249
  reference 242, 248
  structures 227
  topic 243, 248, 251–253
disjunctive clauses 185
  disjunctive coordination
    184–186
ditransitive clauses 8
  ditransitive structure 113–114
"double causatives" 162
double focusing 221
Dravidian speech 4
Dravidians 4
dubitative 217
Dutch 6, 41–42
dynamic/active-type verbs 53

E
echo question 38, 230
ellipsis 17–19, 187–188, 204, 252
elocutionary force 272
elocutionary goal 257

embedded clause 178–179,
    190–192, 194–198, 205,
    220–222
empathy 238, 240, 242–243
EMPHATIC 55, 215–218,
    222–225
emphatic stress 216, 218,
    224–225
emphatic/focus clauses 11
endophoric or discourse
    deixis 249 (see also
    exophoric or
    situational deixis)
epenthetic vowel 92, 183
epistemic domain 141
  epistemic modality 141,
    254, 261
epithetic compounds 88
equational sentences 7, 51,
    102–103
ergative language 122, 158
evidentiality 262–263
existential construction 107, 208
  existential sentences 45
  existential verb 107, 119,
    208–209, 211–213
exophoric or situational
    deixis 249
Experiencer 17–18, 101, 104,
    122–123, 167
  "experiencer"-subjects 17
expression of ability/
    possibility 142
expressive function 239
external sandhi rules 93

F
"factivity" 191
feminine/masculine
    distinction 78
"fictive transfer" 115
fictive use 269
finite clause 144
focal negator 223
focus 11–13, 207, 215–226
  affix 215–216
  construction 215, 226, 252
  form 12–13, 75, 146, 215,
    217–223, 225–226
focused constituent 11–12, 209,
    216–217, 219–221, 223
focused sentence
    construction 215–216, 225

"footing" 233
form-function isomorphy 240–241
formal nouns 181, 189–191, 193

G
"gapping" strategy 131
geminate consonant 24
genitive 45, 79, 81, 103, 118, 129
glottalization 93
grammatical relations 121–122, 152, 170
grammatical subject 73–74, 79, 127, 153, 207
grammaticalization 174, 179, 189

H
habitual motion event 110
"half nasals" 33
head-final language 7, 9
honorific suffixes 269
honorifics 72, 254, 267–271
hortative forms 73, 259
  hortative verbs 125
hybrid compounds 88

I
identifiability 210, 215
identifying function 232, 237
idiomatic expressions 76, 86, 139
illocutionary force 183, 256, 258
imperative mood 71–73, 124, 126, 147, 254, 266
impersonal 78, 98, 124, 143, 157
impositive 256
inactive 8–9, 78, 98, 101–102, 122, 147, 149, 154
inalienable possessor 105, 198
inanimate 44–48, 60–62, 78–81, 126–127, 154, 171–172
  participants 146
inceptive aspect 150
inchoative aspect 148, 150
inclusive construction 112
indefinite 8, 45–46, 48, 51–52, 61–63, 79, 208–210
independent clause 187, 220
indicative form 52, 66, 76, 96, 258
  indicative mood 68, 71–73
  indicative verb 218

indirect causative construction 169, 176–179
indirect causatives 176, 178
indirect objects 54, 167, 174
Indirect Speech 193
inferential expressions 201
  inferential mood 74, 124, 169
  inferential suffixes 74, 125
infinitive form 75–76, 139–142, 150, 176, 203, 254
inflection 66, 69, 75–76, 78, 101, 107, 285
  inflectional forms 75–76, 143
  inflectional suffixes 52, 57, 75, 83
informing function 238–239
'ingestive' verbs 167
instrumental 45, 50, 78–79, 81, 117, 122–124, 131
interjections 43, 58
interlocutors 228, 230–232, 238–240, 242–243, 245
interrogative clauses 185–186
  interrogative expressions 11
  interrogative particle 56
  interrogative pronoun 48–49, 194–195, 220
  interrogative word 12, 135–136
intonation 16, 38, 210, 216, 258
  contours 224
  nucleus 213
  units 183
intransitive 8–9, 54, 67–70, 77, 97–98, 121–125, 172–174
  (see also transitive)
involitive 78, 98, 101, 108, 152–154, 156–157, 159–160, 178
  agent 101
  verbs 78, 178
involitivization 97–98, 153
involuntary participant 104–106
iterative and continuous aspect 150

K
kinship terms 64–65, 269–270

L
lack of empathy 238, 240, 242
Lala or Lada 3
layering 173

lexical causatives 160–161, 163, 166
lexical verb 138, 147, 170, 172, 176–177
lexical-semantic characteristics 100
lexico-grammatical structure 164
linearity 192
linguistic context 18–19, 227
Literary and Colloquial Sinhala 1, 21
  Literary variety 2, 22, 26
location 107, 114, 118–119, 211–213, 228–229
locative 45, 79, 81, 103, 207–213, 241, 246–247
  construction 208, 212
  marker 118, 129
  marking 207
  phrase 209–213

M
Mahavansa 2
main clause 7, 15, 181, 189–198, 220–221
matrix clause 176, 221
  matrix sentence 204–205
  matrix verb 221–222
Mediaeval Sinhalese 5–6
metaphorical use 257
"mitigator" 272
modal construction 140–141
  modal expressions 159
  modal-specific characteristics 159
modality 139–142, 254, 261
Modern Indo-Aryan languages 2
modifiers 7, 10, 129–130, 189, 197
morphological causative 163, 165–167, 169–170, 172, 176, 179
morphological process 77, 152
multi-clause sentences 221
multiple foci 222–223

N
narrated event 228, 243–245
narrative 243–244, 248–252
nasal assimilation 35
nasalization 93

negation 18–19, 142, 223, 225–226, 265–266
negative particle 12–13, 135–136, 254, 265–266
neutral sentence 215, 217–218, 224
"new information" 208
nishpanna 40
nominal clause 205
nominal phrases 129
nominalization expression 62
nominalized clauses 190
non-basic passives 157
non-finite clauses 76, 204
non-linguistic contexts 261
non-nominative subjects 121–122
non-verbal clauses 7, 191
non-verbal predicates 7
North Indian languages 5, 41
notional passives 156
noun coordinator 182
"Noun Phrase Accessibility Hierarchy" 132
noun-coordinating particle 137, 182
numeral compounds 59–60, 87
numeral phrases 44, 46, 60, 87
numeral system 58

O
object complements 191
object/patient relation 127
oblique phrase 152
oblique relations 131–132
"old information" 207
onomatopoeia 39
optative mood 73–74, 260
optative verbs 125–126

P
participant dimension 232
participant framework 249–250
passive 53–54, 77–78, 95–96, 152–160, 168–169 (see also non-basic passives, notional passives, 'semantic passive')
passive construction 152, 154, 156–158
passive morphology 157–158
patient 110, 126–127, 157
perceived factivity 261

perfective aspect 145–146
periphrastic causatives 160, 169, 176
permissive construction 259
permissive forms 72–73, 124, 258
pitch 37–38, 134
polite markers 259
politeness 71, 75, 254–256, 271–272
Portuguese 6, 26, 41–42
possessor 105–106, 118, 129, 198, 214
pragmatic aspects 207, 226
pragmatic distance 185
pragmatic force 16, 254
pragmatic inference 264
pragmatic particles 199
Prakritic dialect 4
pre-nasalized stops 21, 33, 93
presentational focus 217, 225
presentative 238–241, 247, 250
presupposition 16, 136, 191, 210, 216–218, 222, 225
processive aspect 149
progressive aspect 149–150
progressive assimilation 35, 162 (see also regressive assimilation)
pronouns 17, 43, 46–49, 126, 229–230, 233, 239, 268–270
proper nouns 43, 80
proposition 143, 191, 217, 220, 262–263
propositional negation 266
Proto-Sinhalese 5–6
prototypical causative situation 170–171
purpose clauses 203

Q
quantifiers 61–62
question particle 11–12, 135–136, 219, 221
quotative marker 190, 193–194, 201, 205
quotative particles 56

R
"reanalysis" 226
reciprocal verbs 112, 116, 136–137
reduplicated form 17, 75–76
reduplication 58, 89–90

Reference Grammar theory 122
referent tracking 243
reflexive verbs 136–139
regional dialect 229
regressive assimilation 35
relative clause 63, 121, 129, 131–134, 136, 205
resultative aspect 146
retroflex 26, 30–32
rhyme 38, 88

S
salience 210, 215
sandhi 76, 91, 93–94
script 21, 27, 281
'semantic passive' 158
semantic roles 122, 154
semi-transitive verbs 54, 174
semi-vowels 29–30
Sidat Sangarawa 6
Sigiri Graffiti 6
Sinhalese Prakrit 5
situataional deixis 249
situational context 155, 162
social deixis 229, 254, 267
sociopragmatics 254
sound symbolism 38–39
South-Indian languages 5
SOV order 8, 12
spatial context 235
spatial deictics 242, 246
spatial deixis 227–228
special honorific expressions 271
speech event 228, 233, 258
speech levels 268
Spoken Sinhala 1, 21
stative verbs 178
stative/processive verbs 53
"strong case marking" language 123
STRONG LEXICAL CASE-ASSIGNMENT HYPOTHESIS 123
subcategorize 66, 221
subject 7–9, 16–20, 101–102, 109, 121–122, 126–127
complement 191
participants 201
position 124, 142, 155–157, 161, 166, 173
role 121
subjecthood properties 121

subjectless sentences 18, 156
subjectless transitive clause 155
subordinate clauses 15, 144, 189, 191, 196–197
subordinate marker 190
subordination 181, 189–190, 194, 197
syllabic 22–24, 26, 35
syllable 28–29, 33–38, 69–70, 74–76
syntactic pivots 121
syntactic role 127
syntactic structure 217
syntactic subjecthood 121–122

T
tadbhawa 40–42
Tamil 1, 4–6, 41–42
tatsama 40–42, 87
temporal clauses 15, 198–199
temporal forms 75–76, 144, 229
temporal relation 145, 198
tense 52, 66–73, 75–76, 139, 143–146
textual content 242
textual information 248
thematic dimensions 242
thematic flow 250–252
thematic status 242–243
thematic role 122–123, 154
theme 11–12, 101, 123
tone patterns 37
topic 7, 123, 155, 157, 188–189, 207, 209–215
  position 128, 155, 157, 189, 207, 214
  topic-comment articulation 155
  topic-comment organization 207, 211, 215, 217
transient locative 213
transitive 8, 19–20, 54, 97–98, 101, 121–123, 160–162, 164–170
transitivity 50, 54, 146, 172
truth-conditional meaning 182

U
Undergoer 101, 106, 122, 127, 156–157

V
valency 8, 101, 152, 156, 161, 175–176
Vanga 2–3

verbal negator 223
verbal nouns 43, 49–50, 57
verbal phrases 136
"verbal transmission" sense 171
verbs of motion 214
vocative 58, 79, 118, 269
voice 30, 37, 152, 155, 218
volitional/involitional distinction 124
volitionality 95, 100–101, 158
volitive 78, 98, 101, 123–126, 152–153, 157

W
weather-talk 231
wh constituent 219–220
wh focus 220
wh form 219–221
wh questions 219
wh word 220
wide scope reading 220
word formation 83, 85, 89

Y
yes/no questions 218

Z
zero anaphora 251

In the *London Oriental and African Language Library* the following titles have been published thus far or are scheduled for publication:

15 **CHANDRALAL, Dileep:** Sinhala. 2010. xv, 296 pp.
14 **DUM-TRAGUT, Jasmine:** Armenian. Modern Eastern Armenian. 2009. xv, 742 pp.
13 **DHONGDE, Ramesh Vaman and Kashi WALI:** Marathi. 2009. xviii, 340 pp.
12 **KACHRU, Yamuna:** Hindi. 2006. xxii, 309 pp.
11 **EDWARDS, Malcolm:** Egyptian Colloquial Arabic. ca. 300 pp. *Forthcoming*
10 **SAEED, John:** Somali. 1999. xv, 295 pp.
9   **NGUYỄN, Đình-Hoà:** Vietnamese. 1997. x, 290 pp.
8   **NAYLOR, Paz B.:** Tagalog. *Forthcoming*
7   **JAGGAR, Philip J.:** Hausa. 2001. xxxiv, 754 pp.
6   **BENNETT, David C.:** Chinese. *Forthcoming*
5   **IWASAKI, Shoichi:** Japanese. 2002. xx, 360 pp. *A revised edition in preparation*
4   **CHANG, Suk-Jin:** Korean. 1996. xviii, 252 pp.
3   **DENWOOD, Philip:** Tibetan. 1999. xxii, 374 pp.
2   **HEWITT, George:** Georgian: A Structural Reference Grammar. 1995. xviii, 716 pp.
1   **INGHAM, Bruce:** Najdi Arabic. Central Arabian. 1994. xvi, 215 pp.